W9-ABL-575

THEOLOGY OF HOPE

THEOLOGY OF HOPE

*On the Ground and the Implications
of a Christian Eschatology*

JÜRGEN MOLTMANN

HARPER & ROW, PUBLISHERS

NEW YORK AND EVANSTON

Translated by James W. Leitch from the German
Theologie der Hoffnung
5th ed., Chr. Kaiser Verlag, Munich, 1965

LIBRARY OF CONGRESS CATALOG CARD NUMBER: 67-21550

TO MY WIFE

CONTENTS

7

Contents

* V EXODUS CHURCH

PREFACE

THE FOLLOWING efforts bear the title *Theology of Hope*, not because they set out once again to present eschatology as a separate doctrine and to compete with the well known text-books. Rather, their aim is to show how theology can set out from hope and begin to consider its theme in an eschatological light. For this reason they enquire into the ground of the hope of Christian faith and into the responsible exercise of this hope in thought and action in the world today. The various critical discussions should not be understood as rejections and condemnations. They are necessary conversations on a common subject which is so rich that it demands continual new approaches. Hence I hope they may make it clear that even critical questions can be a sign of theological partnership. I have thus to thank all who have stimulated, and all who have opposed me.

For the reading of the proofs and for many of the references I am grateful to my assistant, Mr Karl-Adolf Bauer.

JÜRGEN MOLTMANN

11

ABBREVIATIONS

AGFNRW	Veröffentlichungen der Arbeitsgemeinschaft für Forschung des Landes Nordrhein-Westfalen
ET	English translation
EvTh	*Evangelische Theologie*
ExpT	*Expository Times*
NF	Neue Folge
NTS	*New Testament Studies*
RGG	*Religion in Geschichte und Gegenwart*
TLZ	*Theologische Literaturzeitung*
TWNT	*Theologisches Wörterbuch zum Neuen Testament*
VT Suppl.	Supplements to *Vetus Testamentum*
WA	Complete Works of Luther, *Weimarer Ausgabe*
ZTK	*Zeitschrift für Theologie und Kirche*

INTRODUCTION:
MEDITATION ON HOPE

1. What is the 'Logos' of Christian Eschatology?

ESCHATOLOGY WAS long called the 'doctrine of the last things' or the 'doctrine of the end'. By these last things were meant events which will one day break upon man, history and the world at the end of time. They included the return of Christ in universal glory, the judgment of the world and the consummation of the kingdom, the general resurrection of the dead and the new creation of all things. These end events were to break into this world from somewhere beyond history, and to put an end to the history in which all things here live and move. But the relegating of these events to the 'last day' robbed them of their directive, uplifting and critical significance for all the days which are spent here, this side of the end, in history. Thus these teachings about the end led a peculiarly barren existence at the end of Christian dogmatics. They were like a loosely attached appendix that wandered off into obscure irrelevancies. They bore no relation to the doctrines of the cross and resurrection, the exaltation and sovereignty of Christ, and did not derive from these by any logical necessity. They were as far removed from them as All Souls' Day sermons are from Easter. The more Christianity became an organization for discipleship under the auspices of the Roman state religion and persistently upheld the claims of that religion, the more eschatology and its mobilizing, revolutionizing, and critical effects upon history as it has now to be lived were left to fanatical sects and revolutionary groups. Owing to the fact that Christian faith banished from its life the future hope by which it is upheld, and relegated the future to a beyond, or to eternity, whereas the biblical testimonies which it handed on are yet full to the brim with future hope of a messianic kind for the world, –

15

owing to this, hope emigrated as it were from the Church and turned in one distorted form or another against the Church.

In actual fact, however, eschatology means the doctrine of the Christian hope, which embraces both the object hoped for and also the hope inspired by it. From first to last, and not merely in the epilogue, Christianity is eschatology, is hope, forward looking and forward moving, and therefore also revolutionizing and transforming the present. The eschatological is not one element *of* Christianity, but it is the medium of Christian faith as such, the key in which everything in it is set, the glow that suffuses everything here in the dawn of an expected new day. For Christian faith lives from the raising of the crucified Christ, and strains after the promises of the universal future of Christ. Eschatology is the passionate suffering and passionate longing kindled by the Messiah. Hence eschatology cannot really be only a part of Christian doctrine. Rather, the eschatological outlook is characteristic of all Christian proclamation, of every Christian existence and of the whole Church. There is therefore only one real problem in Christian theology, which its own object forces upon it and which it in turn forces on mankind and on human thought: the problem of the future. For the element of otherness that encounters us in the hope of the Old and New Testaments – the thing we cannot already think out and picture for ourselves on the basis of the given world and of the experiences we already have of that world – is one that confronts us with a promise of something new and with the hope of a future given by God. The God spoken of here is no intra-worldly or extra-worldly God, but the 'God of hope' (Rom. 15.13), a God with 'future as his essential nature' (as E. Bloch puts it), as made known in Exodus and in Israelite prophecy, the God whom we therefore cannot really have in us or over us but always only before us, who encounters us in his promises for the future, and whom we therefore cannot 'have' either, but can only await in active hope. A proper theology would therefore have to be constructed in the light of its future goal. Eschatology should not be its end, but its beginning.

But how can anyone speak of the future, which is not yet here, and of coming events in which he has not as yet had any part? Are these not dreams, speculations, longings and fears, which must all remain vague and indefinite because no one can verify them? The term 'eschato-*logy*' is wrong. There can be no 'doctrine' of the last things, if by 'doctrine' we mean a collection of theses which can be understood on the basis of experiences that constantly recur and are open to anyone. The Greek term *logos* refers to a reality which is there, now and always, and is given true expression in the word appropriate to it. In this sense there can be no *logos* of the future, unless the future is the continuation or regular recurrence of the present. If, however, the future were to bring something startlingly new, we have nothing to say of that, and nothing meaningful can be said of it either, for it is not in what is new and accidental, but only in things of an abiding and regularly recurring character that there can be log-ical truth. Aristotle, it is true, can call hope a 'waking dream', but for the Greeks it is nevertheless an evil out of Pandora's box.

But how, then, can Christian eschatology give expression to the future? Christian eschatology does not speak of the future as such. It sets out from a definite reality in history and announces the future of that reality, its future possibilities and its power over the future. Christian eschatology speaks of Jesus Christ and *his* future. It recognizes the reality of the raising of Jesus and proclaims the future of the risen Lord. Hence the question whether all statements about the future are grounded in the person and history of Jesus Christ provides it with the touchstone by which to distinguish the spirit of eschatology from that of utopia.

If, however, the crucified Christ has a future because of his resurrection, then that means on the other hand that all statements and judgments about him must at once imply something about the future which is to be expected from him. Hence the form in which Christian theology speaks of Christ cannot be the form of the Greek *logos* or of doctrinal statements based on experience, but only the form of statements of hope and of promises for the future. All predicates of Christ not only say who he was and is, but imply statements as to who he will be and what is to be expected from him. They all say: 'He is our hope' (Col. 1.27). In thus announcing his future in the world in terms of promise, they point believers in him towards the hope of his still outstanding future. Hope's statements of promise anticipate the future. In the promises, the hidden future already announces itself and exerts its influence on the present through the hope it awakens.

The truth of doctrinal statements is found in the fact that they can be shown to agree with the existing reality which we can all experience. Hope's statements of promise, however, must stand in contradiction to the reality which can at present be experienced. They do not result from experiences, but are the condition for the possibility of new experiences. They do not seek to illuminate the reality which exists, but the reality which is coming. They do not seek to make a mental picture of existing reality, but to lead existing reality towards the promised and hoped-for transformation. They do not seek to bear the train of reality, but to carry the torch before it, In so doing they give reality a historic character. But if reality is perceived in terms of history, then we have to ask with J. G. Hamann: 'Who would form proper concepts of the present without knowing the future?'

Present and future, experience and hope, stand in contradiction to each other in Christian eschatology, with the result that man is not brought into harmony and agreement with the given situation, but is drawn into the conflict between hope and experience. 'We are saved by hope. But hope that is seen is not hope; for what a man seeth, why doth he yet hope for? But if we hope for that we see not, then do we with patience wait for it' (Rom. 8.24, 25). Everywhere in the New Testament the Christian hope is directed towards what is not yet visible; it is consequently a 'hoping against hope' and thereby brands the visible realm of present experience as a god-forsaken, transient reality that is to be left behind. The contradiction to the existing reality of himself and his world in which man is placed by hope is the very contradiction out of which this hope itself is born – it is the contradiction between the resurrection and the cross. Christian hope is resurrection hope, and it proves its truth in the contradiction of the future prospects thereby offered and guaranteed for righteousness as opposed to sin, life as opposed to death, glory as opposed to suffering, peace as opposed to dissension. Calvin perceived very plainly the discrepancy involved in the resurrection hope: 'To us is given the promise of eternal life – but to us, the dead. A blessed resurrection is proclaimed to us – meantime we are surrounded by decay. We are called righteous – and yet sin lives in us. We hear of ineffable blessedness – but meantime we are here oppressed by infinite misery. We are promised abundance of all good things – yet we are rich only in hunger and thirst. What would become of us if we did not take our stand on hope, and if our heart did not hasten beyond this world through the midst of the darkness upon the path illumined by the word and Spirit of God!' (on Heb. 11.1).

It is in this contradiction that hope must prove its power. Hence eschatology, too, is forbidden to ramble, and must formulate its statements of hope in contradiction to our present experience of suffering, evil and death. For that reason it will hardly ever be possible to develop an eschatology on its own. It is much more important to present hope as the foundation and the mainspring of theological thinking as such, and to introduce the eschatological perspective into our statements on divine revelation, on the resurrection of Christ, on the mission of faith and on history.

2. *The Believing Hope*

In the contradiction between the word of promise and the experiential reality of suffering and death, faith takes its stand on hope and 'hastens beyond this world', said Calvin. He did not mean by this that Christian faith flees the world, but he did mean that it strains after the future. To believe does in fact mean to cross and transcend bounds, to be engaged in an exodus. Yet this happens in a way that does not suppress or skip the unpleasant realities. Death is real death, and decay is putrefying decay. Guilt remains guilt and suffering remains, even for the believer, a cry to which there is no ready-made answer. Faith does not overstep these realities into a heavenly utopia, does not dream itself into a reality of a different kind. It can overstep the bounds of life, with their closed wall of suffering, guilt and death, only at the point where they have in actual fact been broken through. It is only in following the Christ who was raised from suffering, from a god-forsaken death and from the grave that it gains an open prospect in which there is nothing more to oppress us, a view of the realm of freedom and of joy. Where the bounds that mark the end of all human hopes are broken through in the raising of the crucified one, there faith can and must expand into hope. There it becomes παρρησία and μακροθυμία. There its hope becomes a 'passion for what is possible' (Kierkegaard), because it can be a passion for what has been made possible. There the *extensio animi ad magna*, as it was called in the Middle Ages, takes place in hope. Faith recognizes the dawning of this future of openness and freedom in the Christ event. The hope thereby kindled spans the horizons which then open over a closed existence. Faith binds man to Christ. Hope sets this faith open to the comprehensive future of Christ. Hope is therefore the 'inseparable companion' of faith. 'When this hope is taken away, however eloquently or elegantly we discourse concerning faith, we are convicted of having none. . . . Hope is nothing else than the expectation of those things which faith has believed to have been truly promised by God. Thus, faith believes God to be true, hope awaits the time when this truth shall be manifested; faith believes that he is our Father, hope anticipates that he will ever show himself to be a Father toward us; faith believes that eternal life has been given to us, hope anticipates that it will some time be revealed; faith is the foundation upon which hope rests, hope nourishes and sustains faith. For as no one except him who already believes His promises can look for anything from God, so again the weakness of our faith must be sustained and nourished by patient hope and expectation, lest it fail and grow faint. . . . By unremitting renewing and restoring, it [hope] invigorates faith again and again with perseverance.' Thus in the Christian life faith has the priority, but hope the primacy. Without faith's knowledge of Christ, hope becomes a utopia and remains hanging in the air. But without hope, faith falls to pieces, becomes a fainthearted and ultimately a dead faith. It is through faith that man finds the path of true life, but it is only hope that keeps him on that path. Thus it is that faith in Christ gives hope its assurance. Thus it is that hope gives faith in Christ its breadth and leads it into life.

To believe means to cross in hope and anticipation the

---

[1] Calvin, *Institutio* III.2.42. ET: *Institutes of the Christian Religion* (Library of Christian Classics vols. XX and XXI), ed. John T. McNeill, trans. Ford Lewis Battles, 1961, p. 590.

etc.: There is no promise, except what man find [illegible].
¬: There *is* a promise.

16-17]   *Introduction*   21

bounds that have been penetrated by the raising of the crucified. If we bear that in mind, then this faith can have nothing to
do with fleeing the world, with resignation and with escapism.
In this hope the soul does not soar above our vale of tears to
some imagined heavenly bliss, nor does it sever itself from the
earth. For, in the words of Ludwig Feuerbach, it puts 'in place
of the beyond that lies above our grave in heaven the beyond
that lies above our grave on earth, the historic *future*, the future
of mankind'.[1] It sees in the resurrection of Christ not the
eternity of heaven, but the future of the very earth on which his
cross stands. It sees in him the future of the very humanity for
which he died. That is why it finds the cross the hope of the
earth. This hope struggles for the obedience of the body, because it awaits the quickening of the body. It espouses in all
meekness the cause of the devastated earth and of harassed
humanity, because it is promised possession of the earth.
Ave crux – unica spes!

But on the other hand, all this must inevitably mean that the
man who thus hopes will never be able to reconcile himself
with the laws and constraints of this earth, neither with the in-
evitability of death nor with the evil that constantly bears
further evil. The raising of Christ is not merely a consolation
to him in a life that is full of distress and doomed to die, but it
is also God's contradiction of suffering and death, of humiliation and offence, and of the wickedness of evil. Hope finds in
Christ not only a consolation *in* suffering, but also the protest
of the divine promise *against* suffering. If Paul calls death the
'last enemy' (I Cor. 15.26), then the opposite is also true:
that the risen Christ, and with him the resurrection hope, must
be declared to be the enemy of death and of a world that puts
up with death. Faith takes up this contradiction and thus becomes itself a contradiction to the world of death. That is why
faith, wherever it develops into hope, causes not rest but unrest, not patience but impatience. It does not calm the unquiet
heart, but is itself this unquiet heart in man. Those who hope
in Christ can no longer put up with reality as it is, but begin to
suffer under it, to contradict it. Peace with God means conflict
with the world, for the goad of the promised future stabs in-
exorably into the flesh of every unfulfilled present. If we had

[1] *Das Wesen der Religion*, 1848.

Resignation assumes that the fut. will be essential... (ie, with respect to what really matter... like the present (and the past)).

22   *Theology of Hope*   [17-18]

before our eyes only what we see, then we should cheerfully
or reluctantly reconcile ourselves with things as they happen
to be. That we do not reconcile ourselves, that there is no
pleasant harmony between us and reality, is due to our un-
quenchable hope. This hope keeps man unreconciled, until the
great day of the fulfilment of all the promises of God. It keeps
him *in statu viatoris*, in that unresolved openness to world
questions which has its origin in the promise of God in the
resurrection of Christ and can therefore be resolved only when
the same God fulfils his promise. This hope makes the Christian
Church a constant disturbance in human society, seeking as the
latter does to stabilize itself into a 'continuing city'. It makes
the Church the source of continual new impulses towards the
realization of righteousness, freedom and humanity here in the
light of the promised future that is to come. This Church is
committed to 'answer for the hope' that is in it (I Peter 3.15). It
is called in question 'on account of the hope and resurrection
of the dead' (Acts 23.6). Wherever that happens, Christianity
embraces its true nature and becomes a witness of the future of
Christ.

3. The Sin of Despair

If faith thus depends on hope for its life, then the sin of unbelief is manifestly grounded in hopelessness. To be sure, it is
usually said that sin in its original form is man's wanting to be
as God. But that is only the one side of sin. The other side of
such pride is hopelessness, resignation, inertia and melancholy.
From this arise the *tristesse* and frustration which fill all living
things with the seeds of a sweet decay. Among the sinners whose
future is eternal death in Rev. 21.8, the 'fearful' are mentioned
before unbelievers, idolaters, murderers and the rest. For the
Epistle to the Hebrews, falling away from the living hope, in
the sense of being disobedient to the promise in time of oppression, or of being carried away from God's pilgrim people as by
a flood, is the great sin which threatens the hopeful on their way.
Temptation then consists not so much in the titanic desire to be
as God, but in weakness, timidity, weariness, not wanting to be
what God requires of us.

God has exalted man and given him the prospect of a life
that is wide and free, but man hangs back and lets himself down.

God promises a new creation of all things in righteousness and peace, but man acts as if everything were as before and remained as before. God honours him with his promises, but man does not believe himself capable of what is required of him. That is the sin which most profoundly threatens the believer. It is not the evil he does, but the good he does not do, not his misdeeds but his omissions, that accuse him. They accuse him of lack of hope. For these so-called sins of omission all have their ground in hopelessness and weakness of faith. 'It is not so much sin that plunges us into disaster, as rather despair', said Chrysostom. That is why the Middle Ages reckoned *acedia* or *tristitia* among the sins against the Holy Spirit which lead to death.

Joseph Pieper in his treatise *Über die Hoffnung* (1949) has very neatly shown how this hopelessness can assume two forms: it can be presumption, *praesumptio*, and it can be despair, *desperatio*. Both are forms of the sin against hope. Presumption is a premature, selfwilled anticipation of the fulfilment of what we hope for from God. Despair is the premature, arbitrary anticipation of the non-fulfilment of what we hope for from God. Both forms of hopelessness, by anticipating the fulfilment or by giving up hope, cancel the wayfaring character of hope. They rebel against the patience in which hope trusts in the God of the promise. They demand impatiently either fulfilment 'now already' or 'absolutely no' hope. 'In despair and presumption alike we have the rigidifying and freezing of the truly human element, which hope alone can keep flowing and free' (p. 51).

Thus despair, too, presupposes hope. 'What we do not long for, can be the object neither of our hope nor of our despair' (Augustine). The pain of despair surely lies in the fact that a hope is there, but no way opens up towards its fulfilment. Thus the kindled hope turns against the one who hopes and consumes him. 'Living means burying hopes', says Fontane in one of his novels, and it is these 'dead hopes' that he portrays in it. Our hopes are bereft of faith and confidence. Hence despair would seek to preserve the soul from disappointments. 'Hope as a rule makes many a fool.' Hence we try to remain on the solid ground of reality, 'to think clearly and not hope any more' (Camus), and yet in adopting this so-called realism dictated by the facts we fall victim to the worst of all utopias – the utopia of the *status quo*, as R. Musil has called this kind of realism.

The despairing surrender of hope does not even need to have a desperate appearance. It can also be the mere tacit absence of meaning, prospects, future and purpose. It can wear the face of smiling resignation: *bonjour tristesse!* All that remains is a certain smile on the part of those who have tried out the full range of their possibilities and found nothing in them that could give cause for hope. All that remains is a *taedium vitae*, a life that has little further interest in itself. Of all the attitudes produced by the decay of a non-eschatological, bourgeois Christianity, and then consequently found in a no longer Christian world, there is hardly any which is so general as *acedia, tristesse*, the cultivation and dandling manipulation of faded hopes. But where hope does not find its way to the source of new, unknown possibilities, there the trifling, ironical play with the existing possibilities ends in boredom, or in outbreaks of absurdity.

At the beginning of the nineteenth century the figure of presumption is found at many points in German idealism. For Goethe, Schiller, Ranke, Karl Marx and many others, Prometheus became the great saint of the modern age. Prometheus, who stole fire from the gods, stood in contrast to the figure of the obedient servant of God. It was possible to transform even Christ into a Promethean figure. Along with that there frequently went a philosophical, revolutionary millenarianism which set itself to build at last that realm of freedom and human dignity which had been hoped for in vain from the God of the divine servant.

In the middle of the twentieth century we find in the literary writings of the existentialists the other form of apostasy from hope. Thus the patron saint that was Prometheus now assumes the form of Sisyphus, who certainly knows the pilgrim way, and is fully acquainted with struggle and decision and with patient toil, yet without any prospect of fulfilment. Here the obedient servant of God can be transformed into the figure of the honest failure. There is no hope and no God any more. There is only Camus' 'thinking clearly and hoping no more', and the honest love and fellow-feeling exemplified in Jesus. As if thinking could gain clarity without hope! As if there could be love without hope for the beloved!

Neither in presumption nor in despair does there lie the power to renew life, but only in the hope that is enduring and sure. Presumption and despair live off this hope and regale themselves at its expense. 'He who does not hope for the unexpected, will not find it', runs a saying of Heraclitus. 'The uniform of the day is patience and its only decoration the pale star of hope over its heart' (I. Bachmann).

Hope alone is to be called 'realistic', because it alone takes seriously the possibilities with which all reality is fraught. It does not take things as they happen to stand or to lie, but as progressing, moving things with possibilities of change. Only as long as the world and the people in it are in a fragmented and experimental state which is not yet resolved, is there any sense in earthly hopes. The latter anticipate what is possible to reality, historic and moving as it is, and use their influence to decide the processes of history. Thus hopes and anticipations of the future are not a transfiguring glow superimposed upon a darkened existence, but are realistic ways of perceiving the scope of our real possibilities, and as such they set everything in motion and keep it in a state of change. Hope and the kind of thinking that goes with it consequently cannot submit to the reproach of being utopian, for they do not strive after things that have 'no place', but after things that have 'no place *as yet*' but can acquire one. On the other hand, the celebrated realism of the stark facts, of established objects and laws, the attitude that despairs of its possibilities and clings to reality as it is, is inevitably much more open to the charge of being utopian, for in its eyes there is 'no place' for possibilities, for future novelty, and consequently for the historic character of reality. Thus the despair which imagines it has reached the end of its tether proves to be illusory, as long as nothing has yet come to an end but everything is still full of possibilities. Thus positivistic realism also proves to be illusory, so long as the world is not a fixed body of facts but a network of paths and processes, so long as the world does not only run according to laws but these laws themselves are also flexible, so long as it is a realm in which necessity means the possible, but not the unalterable.

Statements of hope in Christian eschatology must also assert themselves against the rigidified utopia of realism, if they would keep faith alive and would guide obedience in love on to the path towards earthly, corporeal, social reality. In its eyes the world is full of all kinds of possibilities, namely all the possibilities of the God of hope. It sees reality and mankind in the hand of him whose voice calls into history from its end, saying, 'Behold, I make all things new', and from hearing this word of promise it acquires the freedom to renew life here and to change the face of the world.

4. Does Hope Cheat Man of the Happiness of the Present?

The most serious objection to a theology of hope springs not from presumption or despair, for these two basic attitudes of human existence presuppose hope, but the objection to hope arises from the religion of humble acquiescence in the present. Is it not always in the present alone that man is truly existent, real, contemporary with himself, acquiescent and certain? Memory binds him to the past that no longer is. Hope casts him upon the future that is not yet. He remembers having lived, but he does not live. He remembers having loved, but he does not love. He remembers the thoughts of others, but he does not think. It seems to be much the same with him in hope. He hopes to live, but he does not live. He expects to be happy one day, and this expectation causes him to pass over the happiness of the present. He is never, in memory and hope, wholly himself and wholly in his present. Always he either limps behind it or hastens ahead of it. Memories and hopes appear to cheat him of the happiness of being undividedly present. They rob him of his present and drag him into times that no longer exist or do not yet exist. They surrender him to the non-existent and abandon him to vanity. For these times subject him to the stream of transience – the stream that sweeps him to annihilation.

Pascal lamented this deceitful aspect of hope: 'We do not rest satisfied with the present. We anticipate the future as too slow in coming, as if in order to hasten its course; or we recall the past, to stop its too rapid flight. So imprudent are we that we wander in times which are not ours, and do not think of the only one which belongs to us; and so idle are we that we dream of those times which are no more, and thoughtlessly overlook that which alone exists. . . . We scarcely ever think of the present; and if we think of it, it is only to take light from it to arrange the future. The present is never our end. The past and the present are our means; the future alone is our end. So we never live, but we hope to live; and, as we are always preparing to be happy, it is inevitable we should never be so.'[1] Always the protest against the Christian hope and against the transcendent consciousness resulting from it has stubbornly insisted on the rights of the present, on the good that surely lies always to hand, and on the eternal truth in every moment. Is the 'present' not the only time in which man wholly exists, which belongs wholly to him and to which he wholly belongs? Is the 'present' not time and yet at once also more than time in the sense of coming and going – namely, a *nunc stans* and to that extent also a *nunc aeternum*? Only of the present can it be said that it 'is', and only present being is constantly with us. If we are wholly present – *tota simul* – then in the midst of time we are snatched from the transient and annihilating workings of time.

Thus Goethe, too, could say: 'All these passing things we put up with; if only the eternal remains present to us every moment, then we do not suffer from the transience of time.' He had found this eternally resting present in 'nature' itself, because he understood 'nature' as the *physis* that exists out of itself: 'All is always present in it. Past and future it does not know. The present is its eternity.' Should not man, too, therefore become present like nature?

> Why go chasing distant fancies?
> Lo, the good is ever near!
> Only learn to grasp your chances!
> Happiness is always here.

Thus the true present is nothing else but the eternity that is immanent in time, and what matters is to perceive in the outward form of temporality and transience the substance that is immanent and the eternal that is present – so said the early Hegel. Likewise Nietzsche endeavoured to get rid of the burden and deceit of the Christian hope by seeking 'the eternal Yea of existence' in the present and finding the love of eternity in 'loyalty to the earth'. It is always only in the present, the moment, the *kairos*, the 'now', that being itself is present in time. It is like noon, when the sun stands high and no-

[1] Blaise Pascal, *Pensées*, No. 172. ET by W. F. Trotter (Everyman ed.), 1943, pp. 49f.

thing casts a shadow any more, nor does anything stand in the shadow.

But now, it is not merely the *happiness of the present*, but it is more, it is the *God of the present*, the eternally present God, and it is not merely the present being of man, but still more the eternal presence of being, that the Christian hope appears to cheat us of. Not merely man is cheated, but still more God himself is cheated, where hope does not allow man to discover an eternal present. It is only here that the objection to our future hopes on the ground of the 'present' attains to its full magnitude. Not merely does life protest against the torture of the hope that is imposed upon it, but we are also accused of godlessness in the name of the God whose essential attribute is the *numen praesentiae*. Yet what God is this in whose name the 'present' is insisted upon as against the hope of what is not yet?

It is at bottom ever and again the god of Parmenides, of whom it is said in Fragment 8 (Diels): 'The unity that is being never was, never will be, for now it Is all at once as a whole' (νῦν ἔστιν ὁμοῦ πᾶν). This 'being' does not exist 'always', as it was still said to do in Homer and Hesiod, but it 'is', and is 'now'. It has no extension in time, its truth stands on the 'now', its eternity is present, it 'is' all at once and in one (*tota simul*). In face of the epiphany of the eternal presence of being, the times in which life rises and passes fade away to mere phenomena in which we have a mixture of being and non-being, day and night, abiding and passing away. In the contemplation of the eternal present, however, 'origin is obliterated and decay is vanished'. In the present of being, in the eternal Today, man is immortal, invulnerable and inviolable (G. Picht). If, as Plutarch reports, the divine name over the portal of the Delphic temple of Apollo was given as *EI*, then this, too, could mean 'Thou art' in the sense of the eternal present. It is in the eternal nearness and presence of the god that we come to knowledge of man's nature and to joy in it.

The god of Parmenides is 'thinkable', because he is the eternal, single fulness of being. The non-existent, the past and the future, however, are not 'thinkable'. In the contemplation of the present eternity of this god, non-existence, movement and change, history and future become unthinkable, because they

'are' not. The contemplation of this god does not make a meaningful experience of history possible, but only the meaningful
negation of history. The *logos* of this being liberates and raises
us out of the power of history into the eternal present.

In the struggle against the seeming deceit of the Christian
hope, Parmenides' concept of God has thrust its way deeply
indeed into Christian theology. When in the celebrated third
chapter of Kierkegaard's treatise on *The Concept of Dread* the
promised 'fulness of time' is taken out of the realm of expectation that attaches to promise and history, and the 'fulness of
time' is called the 'moment' in the sense of the eternal, then we
find ourselves in the field of Greek thinking rather than of the
Christian knowledge of God. It is true that Kierkegaard modi-
fied the Greek understanding of temporality in the light of the
Christian insight into our radical sinfulness, and that he intensi-
fies the Greek difference between *logos* and *doxa* into a paradox,
but does that really imply any more than a modification of the
'epiphany of the eternal present'? The present is not a concept
of time. The eternal conceived as the present is arrested temporal succession. The moment characterizes the present as a
thing that has no past and no future. The moment is an atom
of eternity. It is the first reflection of eternity in time, its first
attempt as it were to halt time.' It is understandable that then
the believer, too, must be described in parallel terms to the
Parmenidean and Platonic contemplator. The believer is the
man who is entirely present. He is in the supreme sense contemporaneous with himself and one with himself. 'And to be
with the eternal's help utterly and completely contemporaneous
with oneself today, is to gain eternity. The believer turns his
back on the eternal so to speak, precisely in order to have it by
him in the one day that is today. The Christian believes, and
thus he is quit of tomorrow.'

Much the same is to be found in Ferdinand Ebner, whose
personalist thinking and pneumatology of language has had
such an influence on modern theology: 'Eternal life is so to speak
life in the absolute present and is in actual fact the life of man
in his consciousness of the presence of God.' For it is of the
essence of God to be absolute spiritual presence. Hence man's
'present' is nothing else but the presence of God. He steps out
of time and lives in the present. Thus it is that he lives 'in

God'. Faith and love are timeless acts which remove us out of
time, because they make us wholly 'present'.

Christian faith then means tuning in to the nearness of God
in which Jesus lived and worked, for living amid the simple,
everyday things of today is of course living in the fulness of
time and living in the nearness of God. To grasp the never-
returning moment, to be wholly one with oneself, wholly self-
possessed and on the mark, is what is meant by 'God'. The
concepts of God which are constructed in remoteness from God
and in his absence fall to pieces in his nearness, so that to be
wholly present means that 'God' happens, for the 'happening'
of the uncurtailed present is the happening of God.

This mysticism of being, with its emphasis on the living of the
present moment, presupposes an immediacy to God which the
faith that believes in God on the ground of Christ cannot adopt
without putting an end to the historic mediation and reconciliation of God and man in the Christ event, and so also, as a result
of this, putting an end to the observation of history under the
category of hope. This is not the 'God of hope', for the latter is
present in promising the future – his own and man's and the
world's future – and in sending men into the history that is not
yet. The God of the exodus and of the resurrection 'is' not
eternal presence, but he promises his presence and nearness to
him who follows the path on which he is sent into the future.
YHWH, as the name of the God who first of all promises his
presence and his kingdom and makes them prospects for the
future, is a God 'with future as his essential nature', a God of
promise and of leaving the present to face the future, a God
whose freedom is the source of new things that are to come. His
name is not a cipher for the 'eternal present', nor can it be
rendered by the word *EI*, 'thou art'. His name is a wayfaring
name, a name of promise that discloses a new future, a name
whose truth is experienced in history inasmuch as his promise
discloses its future possibilities. He is therefore, as Paul says,
the God who raises the dead and calls into being the things
that are not (Rom. 4.17). This God is present where we wait
upon his promises in hope and transformation. When we have
a God who calls into being the things that are not, then the
things that are not yet, that are future, also become 'thinkable'
because they can be hoped for.

The 'now' and 'today' of the New Testament is a different
thing from the 'now' of the eternal presence of being in Parmenides, for it is a 'now' and an 'all of a sudden' in which the
newness of the promised future is lit up and seen in a flash. Only
in this sense is it to be called an 'eschatological' today. 'Parousia' for the Greeks was the epitome of the presence of God, the
epitome of the presence of being. The parousia of Christ, however, is conceived in the New Testament only in categories of
expectation, so that it means not *praesentia Christi* but *adventus
Christi*, and is not his eternal presence bringing time to a standstill, but his 'coming', as our Advent hymns say, opening the
road to life in time, for the life of time is hope. The believer is
not set at the high noon of life, but at the dawn of a new day at
the point where night and day, things passing and things to
come, grapple with each other. Hence the believer does not
simply take the day as it comes, but looks beyond the day to
the things which according to the promise of him who is the
creator ex nihilo and raiser of the dead are still to come. The
present of the coming parousia of God and of Christ in the
promises of the gospel of the crucified does not translate us out
of time, nor does it bring time to a standstill, but it opens the
way for time and sets history in motion, for it does not tone
down the pain caused us by the non-existent, but means the
adoption and acceptance of the non-existent in memory and
hope. Can there be any such thing as an 'eternal Yea of being'
without a Yea to what no longer is and to what is not yet? Can
there be such a thing as harmony and contemporaneity on
man's part in the moment of today, unless hope reconciles
him with what is non-contemporaneous and disharmonious?
Love does not snatch us from the pain of time, but takes the
pain of the temporal upon itself. Hope makes us ready to bear
the 'cross of the present'. It can hold to what is dead, and hope
for the unexpected. It can approve of movement and be glad
of history. For its God is not he who 'never was nor will be,
because he now Is all at once as a whole', but God is he 'who
maketh the dead alive and calleth into being the things that are
not'. The spell of the dogma of hopelessness – *ex nihilo nihil
fit* – is broken where he who raises the dead is recognized to be
God. Where in faith and hope we begin to live in the light of the
possibilities and promises of this God, the whole fulness of life

discloses itself as a life of history and therefore a life to be loved. Only in the perspective of this God can there possibly be a love that is more than *philia*, love to the existent and the like – namely, *agape*, love to the non-existent, love to the unlike, the unworthy, the worthless, to the lost, the transient and the dead; a love that can take upon it the annihilating effects of pain and renunciation because it receives its power from hope of a *creatio ex nihilo*. Love does not shut its eyes to the non-existent and say it is nothing, but becomes itself the magic power that brings it into being. In its hope, love surveys the open possibilities of history. In love, hope brings all things into the light of the promises of God.

Does this hope cheat man of the happiness of the present? How could it do so! For it is itself the happiness of the present. It pronounces the poor blessed, receives the weary and heavy laden, the humbled and wronged, the hungry and the dying, because it perceives the parousia of the kingdom for them. Expectation makes life good, for in expectation man can accept his whole present and find joy not only in its joy but also in its sorrow, happiness not only in its happiness but also in its pain. Thus hope goes on its way through the midst of happiness and pain, because in the promises of God it can see a future also for the transient, the dying and the dead. That is why it can be said that living without hope is like no longer living. Hell is hopelessness, and it is not for nothing that at the entrance to Dante's hell there stand the words: 'Abandon hope, all ye who enter here.'

An acceptance of the present which cannot and will not see the dying of the present is an illusion and a frivolity – and one which cannot be grounded on eternity either. The hope that is staked on the *creator ex nihilo* becomes the happiness of the present when it loyally embraces all things in love, abandoning nothing to annihilation but bringing to light how open all things are to the possibilities in which they can live and shall live. Presumption and despair have a paralysing effect on this, while the dream of the eternal present ignores it.

5. Hoping and Thinking

But now, all that we have so far said of hope might be no more than a hymn in praise of a noble quality of the heart. And

Christian eschatology could regain its leading role in theology as a whole, yet still remain a piece of sterile theologizing if we fail to attain to the new thought and action that are consequently necessary in our dealings with the things and conditions of this world. As long as hope does not embrace and transform the thought and action of men, it remains topsy-turvy and ineffective. Hence Christian eschatology must make the attempt to introduce hope into worldly thinking, and thought into the believing hope.

In the Middle Ages, Anselm of Canterbury set up what has since been the standard basic principle of theology: *fides quaerens intellectum – credo, ut intelligam.* This principle holds also for eschatology, and it could well be that it is of decisive importance for Christian theology today to follow the basic principle: *spes quaerens intellectum – spero, ut intelligam.* If it is hope that maintains and upholds faith and keeps it moving on, if it is hope that draws the believer into the life of love, then it will also be hope that is the mobilizing and driving force of faith's thinking, of its knowledge of, and reflections on, human nature, history and society. Faith hopes in order to know what it believes. Hence all its knowledge will be an anticipatory, fragmentary knowledge forming a prelude to the promised future, and as such is committed to hope. Hence also *vice versa* the hope which arises from faith in God's promise will become the ferment in our thinking, its mainspring, the source of its restlessness and torment. The hope that is continually led on further by the promise of God reveals all thinking in history to be eschatologically oriented and eschatologically stamped as provisional. If hope draws faith into the realm of thought and of life, then it can no longer consider itself to be an eschatological hope as distinct from the minor hopes that are directed towards attainable goals and visible changes in human life, neither can it as a result dissociate itself from such hopes by relegating them to a different sphere while considering its own future to be supra-worldly and purely spiritual in character. The Christian hope is directed towards a *novum ultimum*, towards a new creation of all things by the God of the resurrection of Jesus Christ. It thereby opens a future outlook that embraces all things, including also death, and into this it can and must also take the limited hopes of a renewal of life, stimulating them, relativizing

them, giving them direction. It will destroy the _presumption_
in these hopes of better human freedom, of successful life, of
justice and dignity for our fellow men, of control of the possibilities of nature, because it does not find in these movements the
salvation it awaits, because it refuses to let the entertaining and
realizing of utopian ideas of this kind reconcile it with existence.
It will thus outstrip these future visions of a better, more
humane, more peaceable world – because of its own 'better
promises' (Heb. 8.6), because it knows that nothing can be 'very
good' until 'all things are become new'. But it will not be in the
name of 'calm despair' that it seeks to destroy the presumption
in these movements of hope, for such kinds of presumption still
contain more of true hope than does sceptical realism, and more
truth as well. There is no help against presumption to be found
in the despair that says, 'It will always be the same in the end',
but only in a persevering, rectifying hope that finds articulated
expression in thought and action. Realism, still less cynicism,
was never a good ally of Christian faith. But if the Christian
hope destroys the presumption in futuristic movements, then
it does so not for its own sake, but in order to destroy in these
hopes the _seeds of resignation,_ which emerge at the latest with
the ideological reign of terror in the utopias in which the
hoped-for reconciliation with existence becomes an enforced
reconciliation. This, however, brings the movements of historic
change within the range of the _novum ultimum_ of hope. They are
taken up into the Christian hope and carried further. They become precursory, and therewith provisional, movements. Their
goals lose the utopian fixity and become provisional, penultimate, and hence flexible goals. Over against impulses of this
kind that seek to give direction to the history of mankind,
Christian hope cannot cling rigidly to the past and the given
and ally itself with the utopia of the _status quo._ Rather, it is
itself summoned and empowered to creative transformation of
reality, for it has hope for the whole of reality. Finally, the
believing hope will itself provide _inexhaustible resources_ for the
creative, inventive imagination of love. It constantly provokes
and produces thinking of an anticipatory kind in love to man
and the world, in order to give shape to the newly dawning
possibilities in the light of the promised future, in order as far
as possible to create here the best that is possible, because what

is promised is within the bounds of possibility. Thus it will
constantly arouse the 'passion for the possible', inventiveness
and elasticity in self-transformation, in breaking with the old
and coming to terms with the new. Always the Christian hope
has had a revolutionary effect in this sense on the intellectual
history of the society affected by it. Only it was often not in
church Christianity that its impulses were at work, but in the
Christianity of the fanatics. This has had a detrimental result
for both.

But how can knowledge of reality and reflection upon it be
pursued from the standpoint of eschatological hope? Luther
once had a flash of inspiration on this point, although it was not
realized either by himself or by Protestant philosophy. In 1516
he writes of the 'earnest expectation of the creature' of which
Paul speaks in Rom. 8.19: 'The apostle philosophizes and
thinks about things in a different way from the philosophers
and metaphysicians. For the philosophers fix their eyes on
the presence of things and reflect only on their qualities and
quiddities. But the apostle drags our gaze away from contemplating the present state of things, away from their essence and
attributes, and directs it towards their future. He does not speak
of the essence or the workings of the creature, of *actio, passio* or
movement, but employs a new, strange, theological term and
speaks of the expectation of the creature (*exspectatio creaturae*).'
The important thing in our present context is, that on the basis
of a theological view of the 'expectation of the creature' and its
anticipation he demands a new kind of thinking about the
world, an expectation-thinking that corresponds to the Christian hope. Hence in the light of the prospects for the whole
creation that are promised in the raising of Christ, theology will
have to attain to its own, new way of reflecting on the history of
men and things. In the field of the world, of history and of
reality as a whole, Christian eschatology cannot renounce the
intellectus fidei et spei. Creative action springing from faith is
impossible without new thinking and planning that springs
from hope.

For our knowledge and comprehension of reality, and our
reflections on it, that means at least this: that in the medium of
hope our theological concepts become not judgments which
nail reality down to what it is, but anticipations which show

reality its prospects and its future possibilities. Theological concepts do not give a fixed form to reality, but they are expanded by hope and anticipate future being. They do not limp after reality and gaze on it with the night eyes of Minerva's owl, but they illuminate reality by displaying its future. Their knowledge is grounded not in the will to dominate, but in love to the future of things. *Tantum cognoscitur, quantum diligitur* (Augustine). They are thus concepts which are engaged in a process of movement, and which call forth practical movement and change.

'*Spes quaerens intellectum*' is the first step towards eschatology, and where it is successful it becomes *docta spes*.

[handwritten notes, largely illegible]

J.M. seems, at least in part, to be arguing:
Kn. Zone regis creative acting & thinking;
these are serious, w.o. hope.
∴ We need a new theol. of hope,

Argued from faith alone were promise of showing
the textual aspect of the hope, but is, I think,
unconvincing — perhaps has, he wants to
claim too much for hope,

to what is "hope", or "the hope"?
e.g., vs. "expectation," "trust," etc.

I

ESCHATOLOGY AND REVELATION

I. THE DISCOVERY OF ESCHATOLOGY
AND ITS INEFFECTIVENESS

THE DISCOVERY of the central significance of eschatology for
the message and existence of Jesus and for early Christianity,
which had its beginnings at the end of the nineteenth century in
Johannes Weiss and Albert Schweitzer, is undoubtedly one of
the most important events in recent Protestant theology. It
had a shattering effect, and was like an earthquake shaking the
foundations not only of scientific theology, but also of the
Church, of piety and of faith as existing within the framework
of nineteenth-century Protestant culture. Long before world
wars and revolutions had awakened the Western consciousness
of crisis, theologians like Ernst Troeltsch had the as yet hardly
comprehended impression that 'everything is tottering'. The
recognition of the eschatological character of early Christianity
made it clear that the automatically accepted idea of a har-
monious synthesis between Christianity and culture was a lie
(Franz Overbeck). In this world with its assured and axiomatic
religious positions in the realm of thought and will, Jesus appeared as a stranger with an apocalyptic message that was
foreign to it. At the same time there arose a feeling of estrangement and a sense of the lost and critical state of this world.
'The floods are rising – the dams are bursting', said Martin
Kähler. It is all the more astonishing that the 'new' element
in the discovery of the eschatological dimension of the whole
Christian message was considered to represent for traditional
Christianity in its present and existing form only a 'crisis' which
had to be assimilated, mastered and overcome. None of the
discoverers took his discovery really seriously. The so-called
'consistent eschatology' was never really consistent, and has
therefore led a peculiar shadow-existence to this day. The very

37

concepts in which attempts were made to comprehend the
peculiarity of the eschatological message of Jesus manifest a
typical and almost helpless inadequacy. Johannes Weiss in his
pioneer work, *Die Predigt Jesu vom Reiche Gottes*, in 1892 formulated his insight as follows: 'The kingdom of God is in Jesus'
view an absolutely supra-worldly factor which stands in exclusive contrast to this world. . . . The ethico-religious use of
this concept in recent theology, which wholly strips it of its
original eschatological and apocalyptic sense, is unjustified. It is
only seemingly biblical, for it uses the expression in a different
sense from Jesus.'[1] As compared with the picture of Jesus advanced by his father-in-law Albrecht Ritschl, this statement
provides a sharp antithesis. But is the 'supra-worldly' already
the 'eschatological'? Jesus here no longer appears as the moral
teacher of the Sermon on the Mount, but with his eschatological
message he becomes an apocalyptic fanatic. 'He has nothing
more in common with this world, he has one foot already in the
next.'[2] Thus after his sally into the no-man's-land of eschatology
Johannes Weiss returned again at once to the liberal picture of
Jesus.

It was no different with Albert Schweitzer. The greatness of
his work lay in the fact that he took seriously the foreignness of
Jesus and his message as compared with all the liberal nineteenth-century pictures of Jesus. 'Eschatology makes it impossible to attribute modern ideas to Jesus and then by way of
"New Testament Theology" take them back from Him as a
loan, as even Ritschl not so long ago did with such *naïveté*.'[3] But
the startling thing about Schweitzer's work on the other hand
is that he had no eschatological sense at all – neither for theo-

---

[1] J. Weiss, *Die Predigt Jesu vom Reiche Gottes*, 1892, pp. 49f.

[2] *Ibid.*, 2nd ed., p. 145. On the limitations of the recognition of the eschatological
message of Jesus in Johannes Weiss, cf. F. Holmström, *Das eschatologische Denken
der Gegenwart*, 1936, pp. 61ff.: 'Weiss, it is true, seeks to root out the Ritschlian
idea of the kingdom of God from New Testament theology, yet it remains still
unbroken in systematic and practical theology' (p. 62); 'For Christianity today,
normative significance thus attaches not to the eschatological figure of Jesus, but
to the traditional liberal ideal picture of the moral teacher of wisdom' (p. 71).
'The "time-conditioned" character of Johannes Weiss' own view of the significance
of the eschatological motif can thus be seen from the fact that he regards it merely
as a time-conditioned element in Jesus' own preaching.'

[3] A. Schweitzer, *Von Reimarus zu Wrede. Eine Geschichte der Leben-Jesu-Forschung*,
1st ed. 1906, p. 322. ET by W. Montgomery: *The Quest of the Historical Jesus: a
critical study of its progress from Reimarus to Wrede*, 2nd English ed., 1911 (trans. of
1st German ed. of 1906), p. 250. (The 3rd English ed. of 1954 has a new Introduction by the author, but is otherwise the same as in 1911.)

logical nor for philosophical eschatology. The consequences
which he drew from his discovery of the apocalyptic of Jesus
were aimed at the final conquest and annihilation of what he
considered an illusionary eschatologism. His philosophy of life
and of culture is governed by the overcoming of that painful
impression which he described as follows in the first edition of
his *Quest of the Historical Jesus*: 'There is silence all around. The
Baptist appears and cries: "Repent, for the Kingdom of
Heaven is at hand." Soon after that comes Jesus, and in the
knowledge that He is the coming Son of Man lays hold of the
wheel of the world to set it moving on that last revolution which
is to bring all ordinary history to a close. It refuses to turn, and
He throws Himself upon it. Then it does turn; and crushes Him.
Instead of bringing in the eschatological conditions, He has
destroyed them. The wheel rolls onward, and the mangled body
of the one immeasurably great Man, who was strong enough to
think of Himself as the spiritual ruler of mankind and to bend
history to His purpose, is hanging upon it still. That is His
victory and His reign.'[1] The 'wheel of history', symbol of the
eternal recurrence of the same cycle, takes the place of the
eschatological arrow-flight of history. The experience of two
thousand years of delayed parousia makes eschatology impossible today.

After the first World War the founders of 'dialectical theology' took the eschatology that had thus been suppressed by
idealism and condemned to ineffectiveness, and set it in the
centre not only of exegetical but now also of dogmatic study. In
the second edition of his *Römerbrief*, Karl Barth in 1921 makes
the programmatic announcement: 'If Christianity be not altogether and unreservedly eschatology, there remains in it no
relationship whatever to Christ.'[2] Yet what is the meaning of
'eschatology' here? It is not history, moving silently and in-
terminably onwards, that brings a crisis upon men's eschatological hopes of the future, as Albert Schweitzer said, but on the
contrary it is now the *eschaton*, breaking transcendentally into
history, that brings all human history to its final crisis. This,
however, makes the *eschaton* into a transcendental eternity, the

[1] *Ibid.* 1906, p. 367, ET pp. 368f. This passage was deleted in the later (German)
editions.
[2] *Der Römerbrief*, 2nd ed. 1922, p. 298 (ET by E. C. Hoskyns: *The Epistle to the
Romans*, 1933, p. 314).

E: Weiss & Schweitzer "die," era hot. but their Isolation keeps them from handling it. "Dialectical theol." – epidetritorisch, etc. (Barth, Bult.) transcendentalizing it.

40 *Theology of Hope* [33-34]

transcendental meaning of all ages, equally near to all the ages of history and equally far from all of them. Whether eternity was understood in transcendental terms, as in Barth, who spoke of the unhistorical, supra-historical or 'proto-historical', or whether the *eschaton* was understood in existentialist terms, as in Bultmann, who spoke of the 'eschatological moment', or whether it was axiologically understood, as in Paul Althaus, who saw 'every wave of the sea of time break as it were on the strand of eternity', – everywhere in these years, even as they strove to get the better of the historic eschatology which was construed by religion in terms of saving history and by secularism in terms of belief in progress, men became the victims of a transcendental eschatology which once again obscured rather than developed the discovery of early Christian eschatology. It was precisely the transcendentalist view of eschatology that prevented the break-through of eschatological dimensions in dogmatics. Thus all that remains as the outcome of the 'eschatological struggle of today' is in the first instance the unsatisfactory result that there certainly exists a Christian eschatology which sees history in terms of saving history and regards eschatology as concerned merely with the final, closing events of history, that there certainly exists a transcendental eschatology, for which the *eschaton* as good as means the transcendental 'present of eternity', and that there exists an eschatology interpreted in existentialist terms, for which the *eschaton* is the crisis of kerygmatic involvement, but that Christian eschatology is not yet by any means in a position to break through the categories which provide the framework of these forms of thinking. This, however, is the inescapable task of theological thought, if the 'discovery' sixty years ago of the eschatological message of early Christianity is to be properly understood and is to involve consequences for theology and for the existence of the Church.

Now these forms of thinking, in which the real language of eschatology is still obscured today, are entirely the thought forms of the Greek mind, which sees in the *logos* the epiphany of the eternal present of being and finds the truth in that. Even where the modern age thinks in Kantian terms, this conception of truth is at bottom intended. The real language of Christian eschatology, however, is not the Greek *logos*, but the *promise*

3 pres. sorts of "M." eschat. – all are trapped in Greek thought the paths

there 3 eppl. of ebat.:
① P. 69ff. ② 50ff. ③ 58ff.

which has stamped the language, the hope and the experience of Israel. It was not in the *logos* of the epiphany of the eternal present, but in the hope-giving word of promise that Israel found God's truth. That is why history was here experienced in an entirely different and entirely open form. Eschatology as a science is therefore not possible in the Greek sense, nor yet in the sense of modern experimental science, but only as a know-ledge in terms of hope, and to that extent as a knowledge of history and of the historic character of truth. These differences between Greek thought and that of Israel and Christianity, between *logos* and promise, between epiphany and *apokalypsis* of the truth have today been made clear in many fields and by various methods. And yet Georg Picht is right when he says, 'The epiphany of the eternal present of being distorts to this day the eschatological revelation of God.'[1] In order to attain to a real understanding of the eschatological message, it is ac-cordingly necessary to acquire an openness and understanding *vis-à-vis* what 'promise' means in the Old and New Testaments, and how in the wider sense a form of speech and thought and hope that is determined by promise experiences God, truth, history and human nature. It is further necessary to pay atten-tion to the continual controversies in which the promise-centred faith of Israel found itself, in every field of life, en-gaged with the epiphany-based religions of the world about it, and in which its own truth came to light. The controversies continue also through the New Testament, especially where Christianity encountered the Greek mind. They are part of Christianity's task also today – and that, too, not only in what modern theology has to say for itself, but also in reflecting on the world and in the experience of history. Christian eschatology in the language of promise will then be an essential key to the unlocking of Christian truth. For the loss of eschatology – not merely as an appendix to dogmatics, but as the medium of theological thinking as such – has always been the condition that makes possible the adaptation of Christianity to its en-vironment and, as a result of this, the self-surrender of faith. Just as in theological thought the blending of Christianity with the Greek mind made it no longer clear which God was really being spoken of, so Christianity in its social form took over the

[1] G. Picht, *Die Erfahrung der Geschichte*, 1958, p. 42.

heritage of the ancient state religion. It installed itself as the 'crown of society' and its 'saving centre', and lost the disquieting, critical power of its eschatological hope. In place of what the Epistle to the Hebrews describes as an exodus from the fixed camp and the continuing city, there came the solemn entry into society of a religious transfiguration of the world. These consequences, too, have to be borne in mind if we are to attain to a liberation of eschatological hope from the forms of thought and modes of conduct belonging to the traditional syntheses of the West.

2. PROMISE AND REVELATION OF GOD

In addressing ourselves to the combined topic of 'promise' and 'revelation' the purpose is not only to enquire into the relation between the two, but also to develop a view of the 'revelation of God' which is 'eschatological' in so far as it seeks to discover the language of promise. The concepts of revelation in systematic theology have been fashioned throughout in adoption of, and controversy with, the Greek metaphysic of the proofs of God. 'Revelation theology' today consequently stands in emphatic antithesis to so-called 'natural theology'. That means, however, that these concepts of revelation are constantly preoccupied with the question of whether or not God can be proved. On this front, a theology of revelation can ally itself with a negative natural theology and be derived from the dogma of the non-provability of God. But a concept of revelation arrived at in this way is threatened with the loss of all its content. Its reduction of everything to the problem of the knowledge of God brings about the much lamented formalism of revelation theology.

But now the more recent theology of the Old Testament has indeed shown that the words and statements about the 're-vealing of God' in the Old Testament are combined throughout with statements about the 'promise of God'. God reveals himself in the form of promise and in the history that is marked by promise. This confronts systematic theology with the question whether the understanding of divine revelation by which it is governed must not be dominated by the nature and trend of the promise. The examination in the field of comparative religion

of the special peculiarity of Israelite faith is today bringing out
ever more strongly the difference between its 'religion of promise' and the epiphany religions of the revealed gods of the world
around Israel. These epiphany religions are all 'religions of
revelation' in their own way. Any place in the world can become the epiphany of the divine and the pictorial transparency
of the deity. The essential difference here is accordingly not
between the so-called nature gods and a God of revelation, but
between the God of the promise and the gods of the epiphanies.
Thus the difference does not lie already in the assertion of
divine 'revelation' as such, but in the different ways of conceiving and speaking of the revelation and self-manifestation of the
deity. The decisively important question is obviously that of the
context in which the talk of revelation arises. It is one thing to
ask: where and when does an epiphany of the divine, eternal,
immutable and primordial take place in the realm of the
human, temporal and transient? And it is another thing to ask:
when and where does the God of the promise reveal his faithfulness and in it himself and his presence? The one question
asks about the presence of the eternal, the other about the future
of what is promised. But if promise is determinative of what is
said of the revealing of God, then every theological view of
biblical revelation contains implicitly a governing view of
eschatology. Then, however, the Christian doctrine of the
revelation of God must explicitly belong neither to the doctrine
of God – as an answer to the proofs of God or to the proof of
his non-provability – nor to anthropology – as an answer to the
question of God as asked by man and given along with the
questionableness of human existence. It must be eschatologically understood, namely, in the field of the promise and expectation of the future of the truth.[1] The question of the
understanding of the world in the light of God and of man in
the light of God – this was the concern of the proofs of God –
can be answered only when it is plain which God is being spoken
of, and in what way or with what purpose and intention he reveals himself. We shall therefore have to take some of the concepts of revelation in more recent systematic theology and
examine them first in regard to the view of eschatology by

[1] So also G. Gloege, *RGG*[3] IV, col. 1611: 'The concept of revelation belongs to
eschatology.'

which they are governed and secondly in regard to their immanent links with traditional proofs of God.

The other reason for understanding revelation in the light of promise arises from the theology of the Reformers. The correlate of faith is for the Reformers not an idea of revelation, but is expressly described by them as the *promissio dei: fides et promissio sunt correlativa*. Faith is called to life by promise and is therefore essentially hope, confidence, trust in the God who will not lie but will remain faithful to his promise. For the Reformers, indeed, the gospel is identical with *promissio*. It was only in Protestant orthodoxy that under the constraint of the question of reason and revelation, nature and grace, the problem of revelation became the central theme of dogmatic prolegomena. It was only when theology began to employ a concept of reason and a concept of nature which were not derived from a view of the promise but were now taken over from Aristotle, that the problem of revelation appeared in its familiar form. There arose that dualism of reason and revelation which made theological talk of revelation increasingly irrelevant for man's knowledge of reality and his dealings with it. The result of this unhappy story is, that our task is to set the subject of divine revelation no longer in antithesis to man's momentary understanding of the world and of himself, but to take this very understanding of self and the world up into, and open its eyes for, the eschatological outlook in which revelation is seen as promise of the truth.

The formalism which is everywhere so striking in the modern concept of revelation has its ground in the approach which adopts the seemingly perfectly natural method of deriving the theological content of 'revelation' from the word 'revelation'. 'In general, we understand by revelation *the disclosure of what is veiled, the opening up of what is hidden*' (R. Bultmann).[1] 'In the New Testament, ἀποκαλύπτειν refers to the removing of a veil, φανεροῦν to the emerging of the hidden, δηλοῦν to the making known of what is otherwise unknown, and γνωρίζειν to the imparting of what is otherwise not available' (O. Weber).[2] 'A closed door is opened, a covering is taken away. In the darkness light dawns, a question finds its answer, a riddle its solution' (K. Barth).[3] This general explanation of the word then results for Bultmann

[1] *Glauben und Verstehen*, III, 1960, p. 1 (ET by Schubert M. Ogden, *Existence and Faith*, 1960, p. 59).   [2] *Grundlagen der Dogmatik*, I, 1955, p. 188.
[3] *Das christliche Verständnis der Offenbarung* (Theologische Existenz heute, NF vol. 12), 1948, p. 3 (cf. ET by R. Gregor Smith in *Against the Stream: Shorter Post-war Writings 1946-52*, 1954, p. 205, slightly altered). Cf. also p. 5 (ET p. 207): 'Revelation in the Christian sense of the term means revelation, disclosure of something which is *hidden* from man not only in fact but *in principle*.'

in what for him is the decisive question whether revelation is an importation
of knowledge or an event which transposes me into a new state of my self.[1]
As long as every man knows of his death, and his existence is placed by it in
a state of radical questionableness, he can also know in advance what revelation and life is. God's revelation proves to be an event affecting the peculiar existence of the particular individual, and therewith an answer to the
question raised by the questionableness of his being. Barth on the other hand
defined the general use of the word revelation in the Christian sense by
saying that here revelation is the self-revelation of the Creator of all that is,
of the Lord of all being, and hence transcendent self-revelation of God.
While Bultmann endeavours to bring out as against the supra-naturalistic
orthodox concept of revelation the fact that revelation has the character of
an event in history, Barth was concerned for the absolute independence,
unprovability, underivability and incomparability of the self-revelation of
God. Just as Bultmann developed his understanding of revelation within
the framework of a new proof of God from existence, so the concept of the
self-revelation of God developed by Barth corresponds with Anselm's ontological proof of God as interpreted in his book *Fides quaerens intellectum* (1930).
This book on Anselm contains highly significant prolegomena to the *Church
Dogmatics*. This means, however, that both writers are wrestling with specific
theological traditions and find in the *concept* of revelation the starting point
for a new way of speaking of the revelation of God, without first asking what
is the reference and bearing of the words for the revelation of God in the Old
and New Testaments. To set out from a general explanation of terms means
to let these expressions remain in the first instance where they originally
belong, i.e. where they stand in the epiphany religions. It then becomes all
the more difficult later on to discover specifically in the 'revelation of God'
the new content of the biblical proclamation. Too little attention is paid to
the fact that the expressions for 'revelation' in the biblical scriptures have
completely broken out of their original religious context and are employed
with a meaning of a different kind. This different kind of meaning is mainly
determined by the events of promise.

3. TRANSCENDENTAL ESCHATOLOGY

What is the underlying view of eschatology which governs
and dominates the concept of the 'self-revelation of God' as
found in Barth, and the understanding of revelation as the
'disclosure of authentic selfhood' as found in Bultmann?

We shall find that the idea of self-revelation both in its theological and in its anthropological form has been formulated
under the spell of a 'transcendental eschatology'. I choose the
expression 'transcendental eschatology', which Jakob Taubes
and Hans Urs von Balthasar have used to designate Immanuel

[1] *Glauben und Verstehen*, III, 1960, p. 2 (ET p. 59).

Kant's doctrine of the end, because it accords better than the usual designation 'presentative eschatology' with the categories of thought in which the corresponding view of revelation is here formulated.

Within the framework of a transcendental eschatology, the question of the future and the goal of revelation is answered by means of a reflection: the wherefore and the whence are the same, the goal of revelation is identical with its origin. If God reveals nothing other than 'himself', then the goal and the future of his revelation lies in himself. If revelation happens to man's self, then its goal is that man should attain to his authenticity and primordiality, that is, to himself. This means, however, that revelation and the *eschaton* coincide in either case in the point which is designated God's or man's 'self'. Revelation does not then open up a future in terms of promise, nor does it have any future that would be greater than itself, but revelation of God is then the coming of the eternal to man or the coming of man to himself. It is precisely this reflection on the transcendent 'self' that makes eschatology a transcendental eschatology. 'Revelation' consequently becomes the apocalypse of the transcendent subjectivity of God or of man.

The classical philosophical form of transcendental eschatology is found in Immanuel Kant. Its basic features recur wherever Kantian thinking is found in the revelational theology of modern times. In his short, almost forgotten treatise on *Das Ende aller Dinge* (1794), Kant addressed himself to the eschatology of the eighteenth century as expressed in terms of cosmology and saving history, and subjected it to a critique corresponding to his great critiques of theological metaphysics.[1] There can be no such thing as an intellectual knowledge of the 'last things', since these 'objects . . . lie wholly beyond our field of vision'.[2] It is therefore idle to 'brood over what they are in themselves and in essence'.[3] Taken as particular objects accessible to the intellect, they are 'wholly void'.[4] No provable and convincing knowledge of them can be attained. Yet they

---

[1] Quoted according to the edition: I. Kant, *Zur Geschichtsphilosophie* (1784–1798), ed. A. Buchenau, Berlin 1947, pp. 31ff. For an analysis and assessment, cf. Hans Urs von Balthasar, *Prometheus*, Studien zur Geschichte des deutschen Idealismus, 1947, pp. 91ff.; J. Taubes, *Abendländische Eschatologie*, 1947, pp. 139ff.; H. A. Salmony, *Kants Schrift: Das Ende aller Dinge*, 1962.
[2] *Op. cit.*, p. 40.   [3] *Ibid.*   [4] *Ibid.*

are not for that reason to be considered 'void' in every respect. For what the intellect finds itself certainly bound to dismiss as null and void, acquires through the practical reason a significance of its own that is highly existential, namely moral. The ideas of the last things have therefore to be ethically examined, and considered in the sphere of the moral reason, of the practical ability to be a self. The method will be to start as if we had 'here to do merely with ideas . . . which reason creates for itself', as if we were 'playing' with ideas which 'are given us by the legislative reason itself with a practical purpose', in order to reflect on them according to 'moral principles concerned with the ultimate goal of all things'.[1]

Now with this critical appropriation of traditional eschatological ideas Kant has not only brought about an ethical reduction of eschatology. Rather, its immediate effect is, that through excluding the eschatological categories of hope, the reality appearing to, and perceptible by, the theoretic reason can now be rationalized on the basis of eternal conditions of possible experience.[2] If the *eschata* are supra-sensible and as such beyond all possibility of knowledge, then eschatological perspectives are in turn also completely irrelevant for the knowledge of the world of experience. 'And since our intuition is always sensible, no object can ever be given to us in experience which does not conform to the condition of time.'[3] Whereas for

---

[1] *Op. cit.*, p. 44. The whole passage runs: 'Since we have here to do merely with ideas (or are *playing* with ideas) which *reason creates for itself*, the objects of which (if they have any) lie wholly beyond our field of vision, yet which, although for speculative knowledge they are extravagant, are nevertheless *not* for that reason *to be considered void in all respects*, but are given us by the legislative reason itself with a practical purpose, not in order that we should brood over what their objects are in themselves and in essence, but in order that we should ask what we have to make of them with a view to the moral principles concerned with the ultimate goal of all things (with the result that these things which *would otherwise be wholly void* acquire *objective, practical reality*) – since all this is so, we have a clear field before us to take *this product of our own reason*, the general concept of an end of all things, and to classify it and order its subordinate concepts according to the relation it bears to our perceptive faculty' (my italics).

[2] Kant: 'The abiding and unchanging "I" (of pure apperception) forms the correlate of all our representations' (*Critique of Pure Reason*, A 123, ET by N. Kemp Smith, 1929, p. 146). 'Thus the time in which all change of appearances has to be thought, remains and does not change' (*ibid.*, B 225, ET p. 213). 'Time is nothing but the form of inner sense, that is, of the intuition of ourselves and of our inner state' (*ibid.*, B 49, ET p. 77). On this, cf. G. Picht, *op. cit.*, p. 40: 'The abiding present of eternity – that is the ground of the concept of time in Kant. . . . It is the religious experience of traditional metaphysical theology, which conceived God as the Absolute, i.e. as the immutable substance of Being in its eternal presence.'

[3] *Critipue of Pure Reason*, B 52, ET p. 78.

Herder eschatology still meant the inner impetus and the orientation towards the future of a dynamically open cosmos of all living things, Kant has the sensual impression of a 'world machine' and a 'mechanism of nature'.[1] The *res gestae* of history are consequently for the intellect the same in principle as the *res extensae* of nature. Thus along with cosmological eschatology his criticism applies also to every conceivable eschatology expressed in terms of history and saving history. It is not simply that its place is taken by an ethical eschatology of moral ends. That is only one consequence. Rather, the *eschata* form themselves into eternal, transcendental conditions for the possibility of experiencing oneself in a practical way. Man, who 'as belonging to the sensuous world recognizes himself to be necessarily subject to the laws of causality', nevertheless becomes 'in practical matters, in his other aspect as a being in himself, conscious of his existence as determinable in an intelligible order of things'.[2] In moral action man gets 'beyond the mechanism of blindly working causes'[3] 'into an order of things totally other than that of a mere mechanism of nature'.[4] He attains to the non-objective, non-objectifiable realm of freedom and of ability to be a self. Thus, as Hans Urs von Balthasar aptly remarks, 'transcendental philosophy becomes the method towards inward apocalypse'.[5] In place of cosmological and historic eschatologies comes the practical realization of eschatological existence.

G. W. F. Hegel in his early treatise *Glauben und Wissen* with the sub-title *oder die Reflexionsphilosophie der Subjektivität* (1802) has impressively described his dissatisfaction with the results of this reflective philosophy:

The great form of the world spirit, however, which has discovered itself in these philosophies, is the principle of the North and, from the religious point of view, of Protestantism, the subjectivity in which beauty and truth presents itself in feelings and dispositions, in love and understanding. Religion builds its temples and altars in the heart of the individual, and sighs and prayers seek the God whose contemplation is forbidden because there is always the danger of the intellect, which would see the contemplated object as a thing, the forest as firewood. It is true that the inward must also be-

---

[1] *Critique of the Practical Reason*, A 174 (ET by L. W. Beck, Chicago 1948 and London 1949, p. 202).
[2] *Ibid.*, A 72 (ET p. 152).   [3] *Ibid.*, A 191.   [4] *Ibid.*, A 74.
[5] Hans Urs von Balthasar, *op. cit.*, p. 92.

come outward, the intention attain to reality in action, the immediate religious feeling express itself in outward movement, and the faith that flees the objectivity of knowledge take objective form in thoughts, concepts and words; but the objective is very carefully distinguished by the intellect from the subjective, and it is the element which has no value and is nothing, just as the struggle of subjective beauty must be precisely to take all due precautions against the necessity of the subjective's becoming objective. . . . It is precisely as a result of its fleeing the finite and holding fast to subjectivity that it finds the beautiful turned altogether into things, the forest into firewood, pictures into things that have eyes and do not see, ears and do not hear, while the ideals that cannot be taken in wholly intelligible reality like sticks and stones become fabrications of the imagination and every relation to them is seen as empty play, or as dependence on objects and as superstition.[1]

This critique of the reflective philosophy of Kant's transcendental subjectivity Hegel later developed further in his critique of romanticism.[2] In doing so he had in view what has been called the 'dual track in the history of modern thought' (J. Ritter) in which Descartes' methodizing approach to world experience is inevitably joined dialectically by Pascal's *logique du cœur*, the rational system of the Enlightenment by aesthetic subjectivity, historical scepticism by the non-historical mysticism of the solitary soul, the positivism of a science that is independent of values (Max Weber) by the appealing tones of the philosophy of existence (Karl Jaspers). For theology, this resulted in the dilemma that according as the story of Christ became for the intellect an 'accidental truth of history', so faith was transformed into an immediate contemplation of 'eternal truths of reason' – that according as the proclamation in history degenerated into the 'mere historical faith of the Church', so faith exalted itself into the 'pure, immediately God-given faith of reason'. Hegel here perceived that both elements in this process, objectification and subjectivity, are abstract products of reflective philosophy and therefore dialectically condition each other. Both involve a negation and a break-away from history: 'The world has congealed, as it were, it is not a sea of being, but a being that has turned into mechanical clockwork.'[3]

[1] Quoted according to the edition in the Philosophische Bibliothek 62b, ed. F. Meiner, 1962, p. 3. Note the almost verbal polemical allusion to the Kant passage quoted above, p. 47 n 1.
[2] Cf. G. Rohrmoser, *Subjektivität und Verdinglichung: Theologie und Gesellschaft im Denken des jungen Hegel*, 1961, pp. 75ff.; O. Pöggeler, *Hegels Kritik der Romantik*, Phil. Diss., Bonn 1956; J. Ritter, *Hegel und die französische Revolution* (AGFNRW 63), 1957.
[3] K. Jaspers, *Descartes und die Philosophie*, 2nd ed. 1948, p. 85.

A new concept of the cosmos in terms of natural science obscures the experience of reality as history; while on the other hand human existence pales to an ineffable, solitary subjectivity, which must flee all contact with reality and all concessions towards it in order to abide by itself. This cleavage into objectification and subjectivity is not to be escaped – nor can theology escape it in bringing the gospel to the modern world – by declaring one side of this kind of thinking to be vain, deficient, corrupt and decadent. Rather, theology will have to take the hardened antitheses and make them fluid once more, to mediate in the contradiction between them and reconcile them. That, however, is only possible when the category of history, which drops out in this dualism, is rediscovered in such a way that it does not deny the antithesis in question, but spans it and understands it as an element in an advancing process. The revelation of God can neither be presented within the framework of the reflective philosophy of transcendental subjectivity, for which history is reduced to the 'mechanism' of a closed system of causes and effects, nor can it be presented in the anachronism of a theology of saving history, for which the 'forest' has not yet become 'firewood' and 'sacred history' has not yet been subjected to critical historical thinning. Rather, the essential thing will be to make these abstract products of the modern denial of history fluid once more, and to understand them as forms assumed in history by the spirit in the course of an eschatological process which is kept in hope and in motion by the promise grounded in the cross and resurrection of Christ. The conditions of possible experience which were understood by Kant in a transcendental sense must be understood instead as historically flowing conditions. It is not that time at a standstill is the category of history, but the history which is experienced from the eschatological future of the truth is the category of time.

4. THE THEOLOGY OF THE TRANSCENDENTAL SUBJECTIVITY OF GOD

Karl Barth gave as one of the reasons for the complete recasting of his commentary on Romans in the second edition of 1921 the fact that he was indebted to his brother Heinrich Barth for 'better acquaintance with the real orientation of the

ideas of Plato and Kant'.[1] It will be owing to this influence that
the eschatology which in the first edition of 1919 was not un-
friendly towards dynamic and cosmic perspectives retreated
from now on into the background of Barth's thinking, and that
early dialectical theology set to work in terms of the dialectic
of time and eternity and came under the bane of the transcendental eschatology of Kant. Here 'end' came to be the equiva-
lent of 'origin', and the *eschaton* became the transcendental
boundary of time and eternity. 'Being the transcendent meaning
of all moments, the eternal "Moment" can be compared with
no moment in time', says Barth in comment on Rom. 13.12:
'The night is far spent, the day is at hand.'[2] 'Of the *real* end of
history it may be said at any time: The end is near!'[3] His exposition of I Cor. 15 shows a corresponding lack of interest in
an eschatology that deals with the history of the end: 'The history of the end must be for him [the radical biblical thinker]
synonymous with the pre-history, the limits of time of which he
speaks must be the limits of all and every time and thus necessarily the origin of time.'[4]

From the point of view of the history of philosophy this
transcendental eschatology was working with a combination of
Ranke's saying that 'every epoch has an immediate relation
to God' and Kierkegaard's dictum that 'where the eternal is
concerned there is only one time: the present'. 'Every moment
in time bears within it the unborn secret of revelation, and every
moment can thus be *qualified*', said Barth in 1922, and Bultmann
in 1958 in the last paragraph of *History and Eschatology* says the
same in almost the same words – though to be sure with the
addition, 'You must awaken it.'[5]

What do these eschatological statements – if we would call
them 'eschatological' – imply for the understanding of the revelation of God?

Karl Barth's doctrine of the 'self-revelation' of God was first
developed in detail in 1925 in his essay on 'The Principles of
Dogmatics according to Wilhelm Herrmann', in taking up and

[1] *Der Römerbrief*, 2nd ed. 1922, Preface VI (cf. ET p. 4).
[2] *Ibid.*, p. 484 (ET p. 498).
[3] *Die Auferstehung der Toten*, 2nd ed. 1926, p. 60 (ET by H. J. Stenning: *The
Resurrection of the Dead*, 1933, p. 112).
[4] *Ibid.*, p. 59 (ET p. 110).
[5] Cf. *Römerbrief*, 2nd ed. 1922, p. 483 (ET p. 497) and R. Bultmann, *History
und Eschatology*, 1957, p. 155.

surmounting the celebrated 'self' of Herrmann.[1] The idea of
'self-revelation' has a previous history in the nineteenth
century in the school of the Hegelian theologians. For the
twentieth century, however, and especially for Barth and
Bultmann, the emphasizing of 'self' in connection with revelation comes from Herrmann, whose pupils both of them were
in Marburg. Without entering further into Hermann's theology,[2] we can preface our enquiry here by a quotation from
his book *Gottes Offenbarung an uns* (1908), in order to indicate
the problem involved in the idea of 'self-revelation': 'We have
no other means of knowing God except that he reveals himself
to us ourselves by acting upon us.'[3]

With the actualism which in this statement links together
revelation, action, and knowledge of God, Barth and Bultmann
are in agreement. The question – not for the understanding of
the statement as Herrmann meant it, but for the point at which
Barth and Bultmann start with, and depart from, Herrmann –
is how the content is to be understood. Does the statement
mean that God himself must reveal himself to us, or that God
must reveal himself to us ourselves? Does the 'self' of the self-
revelation refer essentially to God or to man?

What Herrmann meant by this statement is plain. Revelation is not instruction, and not an emotional impulse. Revelation of God cannot be objectively explained, but it can
certainly be experienced in man's own self, namely, in the
non-objectifiable subjectivity of the dark, defenceless depths in
which we live the moment of involvement. The revealing of God
in his working upon ourselves is therefore as unfathomable, as
non-derivable, as much grounded in itself as the living of life,
which no one can explain, but everyone can experience.[4] That
is why no catchword is more characteristic of the theology of
Herrmann than the word 'self' in an anthropological sense.

[1] In *Die Theologie und die Kirche* (Ges. Vorträge II), 1928, pp. 240ff. (ET by
L. P. Smith: *Theology and Church*, 1962, pp. 238ff.).
[2] On this cf. the latest study by T. Mahlmann, 'Das Axiom des Erlebnisses bei
Wilhelm Herrmann', *Neue Zeitschrift für systematische Theologie*, 4, 1962, pp. 11ff.
[3] *Gottes Offenbarung an uns*, 1908, p. 76. (The German – *dass er sich uns selbst
offenbart* – can also mean, 'that he himself reveals himself to us'—*Translator*.)
[4] These are ideas and parallels arrived at by Herrmann in his encounter with
the rising vitalist philosophy of Bergson, Simmel and Driesch. Cf. T. Mahlmann,
op. cit., p. 29: 'Life creates its own justification by its action (*ZTK* 12, 1912, p. 75).
That life is grounded in itself, has its origin only in itself, accordingly means that
life is self-assertion, that it asserts itself continually without demonstrable ground.'

Barth, however, argues in his essay that the word 'self' in this sense cannot after all be the last word in the theology of revelation. 'Herrmann knows that one does *not* "experience" God the Father, Son and Holy Spirit, the mystery of God. "Even where he reveals himself, God continues to dwell in darkness." '[1] Precisely when it comes to the doctrine of the Trinity, he says, there appears a reservation even in Herrmann, despite all the emphasis on our own personal experience. Whether this is true of Herrmann need not concern us here. For the development of Barth's theology it is important that he starts at this point, and goes on by putting the subjectivity of God in place of the subjectivity of man which Herrmann means by 'self'. He asks whether in speaking of 'the majesty of the Triune God', we have not to think of 'the unabrogable subjectivity of God, who exclusively determines *himself*, and is knowable exclusively through *himself* in the "purest act" (*actus purissimus*) of his Triune Personality'.[2] 'The lion breaks his cage; a wholly different "Self" has stepped on to the scene with *his* own validity.' 'Man asks about his "self" only because and if God is pleased to give him knowledge of *his* "Self"', only because and if God's Word is spoken to him. Dogmatics should *begin* with "God said" (*Deus dixit*), repudiating the wholly futile attempt to recover it, if at all, only as a mere "reflection of faith" on the heights of some alleged "experience" (as if there were such a thing as an "experience" of it!).'[3] For Barth, the science of theology is accordingly grounded not in religious experience, but in the *autopistia* of Christian truth, in the fact that it is grounded in itself, and 'what is already established can well be left without proof'.[4]

Herrmann – this was his Kantian heritage – had taken it to be self-evident that revelation cannot be objectively grounded, proved to the theoretic reason. The non-objectifiability of God and the non-objectifiability of each peculiar existence or each peculiar 'self' constituted one and the same mystery for him. The ungroundable character of God and the ungroundable character and *gratuité* of life that is lived merged for him into one. That is why he held knowledge of God to be the 'defenceless

---

[1] K. Barth, *op. cit.*, p. 262 (ET p. 254).
[2] *Ibid.*, p. 264 (ET p. 256, slightly altered).
[3] *Ibid.*, pp. 266f. (ET p. 258, slightly altered).
[4] *Ibid.*, p. 267 (ET p. 258).

expression of religious experience'. He saw the 'danger' of
the intellect and of objectification precisely as Hegel had described it. 'Everything that science can grasp is – dead.'[1] 'To
know a thing is to gain control of it, to make it serviceable to us.
The living world, inaccessible as it is to science . . . is disclosed
to us through *self-reflection*, i.e. through honest reflection on
what we in actual fact experience.'[2] For that reason we cannot
say of God what he himself objectively is, but only what effect
he has on ourselves.

For Barth, however, this defenceless non-groundability of
religious experience cannot yet claim the required *autopistia*
and *autousia*, but can only be a pointer towards the ground that
is really grounded in itself, that 'is never in any sense "object",
but is always unchangeably subject'.[3] It is the sovereignty of
the self-existent God in contrast and in counter to all propositions of man's consciousness. Nor does the negative talk of the
non-provability, the non-groundability and the non-objectifiability of God yet achieve that change of thought which Barth
demands – the change to the transcendental subjectivity, expressed in trinitarian terms, of the God who reveals himself to
man in the act of the *Deus dixit*. It is a change of thought that
was foreshadowed in the ontological proof of God in Anselm
and then executed by Hegel, and was later carried further by
Barth in the idea of the self-revelation of God in his name.

In this way Herrmann's 'self' acquires in Barth a *theological*
form. Yet it should be noted that it still retains all the attributes,
all the relations and distinctions, in which it had been formulated by Herrmann.

God cannot be proved, neither from the cosmos nor from the
depths of human existence. He proves himself through himself. His revelation is the proof of God given by God himself.[4]
No one reveals God but himself alone. Who this God is, is
first learned from his revelation. He reveals not this and that,
but himself. By being the one who acts in his revelation, God is
the one who describes himself.[5] God cannot be commended

[1] *Realencyklopädie für prot. Theol. und Kirche* 16, p. 592, quoted by T. Mahlmann,
op. cit., p. 21.
[2] *ZTK* 22, 1912, p. 73, quoted by T. Mahlmann, *op. cit.*, p. 35.
[3] K. Barth, *op. cit.*, p. 269 (ET p. 260).
[4] *Das christliche Verständnis der Offenbarung* (Theologische Existenz heute, NF 12),
1948, p. 7 (ET p. 209).
[5] *Ibid.*, p. 8.

and defended in his self-revelation, but he can only be believed
– and that, too, as a result of his making himself credible.[1] His
word, in which he himself is present, cannot and need not be
proved. It vindicates itself. Where the knowledge of God stood
in Herrmann as the 'defenceless expression of religious experience', there we now have the self-revelation of God in the
proclamation of the *Deus dixit* in the same defencelessness –
namely, non-groundable and therefore indestructible, unprovable and therefore irrefutable, grounding and proving itself.

Now all these reflections on the subjectivity of God could also
be sublime speculations on God. Barth, however, when he
speaks of the self-revelation of God, would speak of nothing
else but 'that little bundle of reports' on the existence of Jesus
Christ which date from the days of the Roman Empire. But it is
just here, where this history is concerned, that there arises a
series of questions:

Does 'self-revelation of God' mean God's eternal self-
understanding? Does the doctrine of the Trinity mean the eternal trinitarian reflection of God upon himself? Does 'self-
revelation' mean the pure present of the eternal, without history
or future? The adoption of the term 'self' still retains even in
the idea of the self-revelation of God its old reflective note from
the thought of Herrmann. It contains the reflection that arises
when God can no longer be proved from the world after the
manner of the proofs of God, and it is to that extent a polemic
term encumbered by the problem complex of the provability
of God. It is therefore difficult to apply it to that bundle of
reports about Jesus of Nazareth, for these statements and com-
munications did not arise in the realm of the Greek metaphysics of the proofs of God, but in a wholly different context.

In itself it would here be a simple matter to transfer to God
the structures of personality, personal selfhood, personal self-
reflection and self-disclosure. Barth, however, did not take this
path towards theological personalism, but developed the idea
of self-revelation in the context of the doctrine of the Trinity
and linked it with the proclamation of the lordship of God. The
doctrine of the Trinity results from the developing of the self-
revelation, i.e. from the questions of the subject, predicate and
object of the event, *Deus dixit*. God himself is the revealer, the

[1] *Ibid.*, p. 13.

act of revealing, and the revealed.[1] Whereas in the first outline
of Barth's dogmatics, in his *Christliche Dogmatik* I (1927), Herrmann's idea of subjectivity is still dominant, in the *Church
Dogmatics* I/1 (1932) it recedes in favour of a detailed doctrine
of the immanent Trinity. Yet even here the immanent form of
the divine Trinity appears to give the revelation of God the
character of transcendental exclusiveness as a 'self-contained
novum'.[2] What seems in this context to be more important than
the trinitarian development of the self-revelation of God is the
connecting of it with the 'lordship of God'. That God reveals
'himself' means that he reveals himself '*as* God and Lord'. Self-
revelation accordingly does not mean for Barth personalistic
self-disclosure of God after the analogy of the I-Thou relationship between men. God reveals himself in actual fact as 'somebody' and 'something' for man, not as pure, absolute Thou.
That would in any case, like the individual, be 'ineffable'. He
reveals himself 'as' the Lord. The announcing of the *basileia* is
the concrete content of the revelation. The meaning of God's
lordship, however, is again to be learned from his concrete
action in relation to man in his revelation, so that here, too, act
and content still fall together in the first instance. What does
'self-revelation' mean in this context? It means that in his
revelation God does not disguise himself, does not appear behind a mask, does not identify himself with something other
than what he himself is – that what he reveals himself *as*, he
is 'beforehand in himself' – that consequently in the revelation
of God *as* the Lord, man has to do with God *himself*, can depend
on himself. Thus in revealing 'something' (his lordship) and
'somebody' (namely, himself in his Son), God reveals himself.

Once this connection is realized, then G. Gloege's and W. Pannenberg's
criticism[3] of Barth's theology of self-revelation, in which they suspect a
gnostic use of terms and a modern personalism, proves to be unjust. But
then W. Kreck's interpretation of self-revelation also appears questionable:
'We must therefore here abide by Barth's fundamental epistemological
proposition: God (and therefore also man as God's creature and image)
can be known only through God.'[4] Kreck sets this proposition in antithesis
to any knowledge of God by way of the *analogia entis*. This well-known pro-

[1] *Christliche Dogmatik* I, 1927, pp. 127, 140, 154ff.
[2] *Kirchliche Dogmatik* I/1, 1932, p. 323 (ET p. 352).
[3] G. Gloege, art. 'Offenbarung, dogmatisch', *RGG*, 3rd ed., col. 1611. W.
Pannenberg, *Offenbarung als Geschichte*, 1961, p. 14.
[4] In *Antwort. Festschrift für Karl Barth*, 1956, p. 285.

position, however, is not one of Christian theology, but has its source in Neoplatonic gnosticism, appears in the reflections of mediaeval mysticism, and is found also in Hegel's philosophy of religion. Taken in itself, it represents the highest stage of the self-reflection of the Absolute that was attained within the sphere of Greek philosophy of religion. On this principle the question of revelation and of knowledge of God would form a closed circle which is strictly speaking impenetrable. It is not applicable to that bundle of historic reports from which Christian faith lives, but rather to an esoteric gnosis. 'Revelation', however, must at once involve the crossing of the boundary between like and unlike, if it is to be revelation. Where there is knowledge of God on the ground of revelation, we should sooner have to assert the opposite principle: only unlikes know each other. God is known only by non-God, namely by man, as 'God' and 'Lord'. Now of course Kreck in this proposition is thinking of pneumatology: 'No man can say that Jesus is the Lord, but by the Holy Spirit' (I Cor. 12.3). But this Spirit has his place in the event of Christ and in the word, not in a divine circle *supra nos*. The immanent form of the doctrine of the Trinity is always in danger of obscuring the historical and eschatological character of the Holy Spirit, who is the Spirit of the resurrection of the dead.

Barth later himself revised the transcendental eschatology of his dialectical phase. 'It showed that although I was confident to treat the beyondness of the coming kingdom with absolute seriousness, I had no such confidence in relation to its coming as such.'[1] On the passage we quoted from the commentary on Rom. 13.12 he now says: 'It is also clear that . . . I missed the distinctive feature of the passage, the teleology which it ascribes to time as it moves towards a real end. . . . The one thing that remained as the only tangible result was precisely that one-sided supra-temporal understanding of God which I had set out to combat.'[2] That, however, surely means that in this 'supra-temporal understanding' the truth of God, in regard both to the concept of the *eschaton* and to the concept of revelation, had been taken as epiphany of the eternal present and not as apocalypse of the promised future. But now if, as we have seen, Barth's concept of the self-revelation of God was shaped precisely by this transcendental eschatology, must there not then come a corresponding revision in the understanding of revelation? Can the impression then be allowed to stand that 'self-revelation of God' means the 'pure presence of God', an 'eternal presence of God in time', a 'present without any

---

[1] *Kirchliche Dogmatik* II/1, p. 716 (ET p. 635, slightly altered), cf. also I/2, pp. 55ff. (ET pp. 50ff.).
[2] *Ibid.*, II/1, p. 716 (ET p. 635, slightly altered).

future'?[1] Can it then be said that the story of Easter 'does not speak eschatologically'? If that were so, then the event of the resurrection of Christ would in itself already be the eschatological fulfilment, and would not point beyond itself to something still outstanding that is to be hoped for and awaited. To understand the revelation in Christ as self-revelation of God, is to take the question as to the future and the goal indicated by revelation, and answer it with a reflection on the origin of revelation, on God himself. With this reflection, however, it becomes almost impossible to see the revelation of the risen Lord as the ground for still speaking of an outstanding future of Jesus Christ. If the idea of self-revelation is not to change tacitly into an expression for the God of Parmenides, then it must have an open eye for the statements of promise in the third article of the Creed. Yet this must not happen in such a way that the future redemption which is promised in the revelation of Christ would become only a supplement, only a noetic unveiling of the reconciliation effected in Christ, but in such a way that it gives promise of the real goal and true intention of that reconciliation, and therefore of its future as really outstanding, not yet attained and not yet realized. Then the word of God – *Deus dixit* – would not be the naked self-proof of the eternal present, but a promise which as such discloses and guarantees an outstanding future. Then the result of this revelation in promise would be a new perception of history's openness towards the future. Not all ages would have an equally immediate relation to God and an equal value in the light of eternity, but they would be perceived to be in a process determined by the promised *eschaton*. If the revelation of God in the resurrection of Christ contains within itself an eschatological differentiation, then it opens the way for history in the category of expectation and remembrance, of assurance and imperilment, of promise and repentance.

5. THE THEOLOGY OF THE TRANSCENDENTAL SUBJECTIVITY OF MAN

The fact that Rudolf Bultmann is by far the more faithful pupil of W. Herrmann has been noted by many, both in positive and in negative terms. Some hold that Bultmann's existential-

---

[1] *Kirchliche Dogmatik* I/2, pp. 125f. (ET pp. 114f.). Also in I/1, pp. 486f. (ET pp. 530f.), 'eschatological' can be synonymous with 'related to the eternal reality', and 'future' with 'what accrues to us from the side of God'.

istic approach merely lifts Herrmann's principles into the sphere of ontological conceptuality,[1] while others find on the contrary already in Herrmann a conquest of Kantian idealism and an anticipation of the dimensions of modern existentialistic questions and insights.[2] It is Bultmann's inheritance from Herrmann that excites also Barth's criticism.[3] And in actual fact Herrmann's passionate sense of 'self' does enter into Bultmann's emphasis on the 'self-understanding', while the problem of personal, individual appropriation of the faith, which Herrmann felt so keenly, appears again in the problem of understanding. The transition from the Kantianism of the early Herrmann to the existentialist theology of Bultmann was doubtless made possible by the influence of vitalist philosophy on the later Herrmann.

Of Herrmann's basic principles, the most outstanding in the theology of Bultmann is the exclusive relation to existence, or self, of all statements about God and his action. To be sure, in his essay of 1924 on 'Die liberale Theologie und die jüngste theologische Bewegung', in which he expresses his agreement with dialectical theology, he says: 'The object of theology is God, and the objection to liberal theology is, that it treated not of God but of man. God means the radical negation and cancellation of man.'[4] Nevertheless this very essay ends with the programmatic statement: 'The object of theology is certainly God, and theology speaks of God by speaking of man as he is confronted by God, that is, in the light of faith.'[5] Thus God can be spoken of only in connection with our own existence. If faith is a matter of comprehending our own existence, then that means at the same time comprehending God, and *vice versa*. 'If we would speak of God, then manifestly we must *speak of ourselves*.'[6]

---

[1] O. Schnübbe, *Der Existenzbegriff in der Theologie R. Bultmanns,* 1959, p. 82.
[2] E. Fuchs, *Hermeneutik,* 1954, p. 30.
[3] K. Barth, *Rudolf Bultmann: Ein Versuch, ihn zu verstehen* (Theologische Studien 34), 1952, p. 47 (cf. ET by R. H. Fuller: *Kerygma and Myth* II, 1962, pp. 122f.) 'Can one do him justice without seeing that his main characteristics, the simplification, the concentration, the ethical and anthropological form he gives to the Christian message and to Christian faith, but also his holy respect for the "profane" laws of the world and of its science, and also his horror of the good work of accepting the truth of what cannot really be accepted – are all things he could, and probably did, learn from Herrmann long before he appropriated Heidegger's methods and concepts?'
[4] *Glauben und Verstehen* I, 1933, p. 2.   [5] *Ibid.,* p. 25.   [6] *Ibid.,* p. 28.

existential verständlich! the two
of eg. theol. stmts.

The relation which all statements about God and his action bear to existence, or self, is *exclusive*. This, too, is inherited from Herrmann. It involves the rejection of all objective statements about God which are not existentially verifiable but are derived from the realms of mythology and world-picture without regard to our own existence – indeed, it is only arrived at in the light of the antithesis that has continually to be stated anew between *Weltanschauung* and self-understanding, between objectified statements and the non-objectifiability of God and of existence. Here, ever since his review of Barth's *Römerbrief* in 1922, lies the main emphasis in his criticism of Barth's theological development.[1]

Let us consider first of all Bultmann's thesis of the unobservable, hidden correlation of God and the 'self' of man. For him, as for Herrmann, God and the 'self' of man stand in unsevered relation to each other. Man by his creation is appointed to be himself. Hence questionableness is the structure of human existence. Man is by nature in quest of himself. In and with the question raised by his existence there arises the question of God. 'We cannot speak about our existence when we cannot speak about God; and we cannot speak about God when we cannot speak about our existence. We could only do the one along with the other. . . . If it is asked how it can be possible to speak of God, then the answer must be: only in speaking of us.'[2] Hence man attains to himself only in God, and only where he attains to himself does he attain to God. To both – God and the human self, or rather each peculiar existence – belongs the characteristic of non-objectifiability. The closed system of cause and effect in the discernible, explicable, objectively demonstrable world of things and of history is therefore set aside (*a*) when I speak of God's action, and (*b*) when I speak of myself. 'In faith the closed weft presented or produced by objective observation is transcended . . . when it (faith) speaks of the activity of God. In the last resort it is already transcended when I speak of myself.'[3] The statements of scripture arise out of existence and are addressed to existence. They have not to justify themselves

---

[1] In *Christliche Welt* 1922, Nos. 18–22. Now in *Anfänge dialektischer Theologie*, I (Theologische Bücherei 17, 2), 1962, pp. 119ff.

[2] *Glauben und Verstehen*, I, 1933, p. 33.

[3] *Kerygma und Mythos*, II, 1952, p. 198 (ET by R. H. Fuller: *Kerygma and Myth*, 1957, pp. 198f.).

at the forum of an objectifying science of nature and history, since the latter does not even set eyes on the non-objectifiable existence of man.[1] That determines the programme of existentialist interpretation and of demythologizing. This interpretation is governed by the question of God that is given with the questionableness of existence, and it is accordingly directed towards an understanding that has neither mythical nor scientific objectivity but is in each several instance individual appropriation in the spontaneity of that subjectivity which is non-objectifiable because transcendental.[2]

Whereas Barth broke away from Herrmann by separating, as we have seen, the non-objectifiable subjectivity of God in the act of the *Deus dixit* from the subjectivity of man, that is, God's 'self' from 'man's self', Bultmann remains under the spell of the hidden correlation of God and self. Hence for him the self-revelation of God finds its measure and development not in a doctrine of the Trinity, but in place of that we find the disclosing of the authenticity or selfhood of man. It is true that God's action, God's revelation, God's future are unprovable, yet that does not by any means imply that our statements are arbitrary, but all the statements in question find non-objectified verification, so to speak, in man's coming to himself. The place of the proofs of God from nature and from history is taken, not by an unprovability of God that opens the door to arbitrariness, but by an *existential proof of God*, by speaking and thinking of God as the factor that is enquired after in the question raised by man's existence. That is an advanced, deepened and re-shaped form of the only proof of God left over by Kant – the moral proof of God supplied by the practical reason. God is – objectively – unprovable, and so likewise is his action and revelation. But he proves himself to the believing 'self'. This is no proof of the existence of God, but a proof of God through existing authentically. It is true that in this interpretation the Christian hope leaves the future as God's future 'empty' as far as mythological, prognosticative pictures of the future are concerned, and renounces all wishful thinking. Yet there is a very precise criterion for determining what God's 'future' then is –

---

[1] *Ibid.*, p. 187.
[2] On Bultmann's equating of theological anthropology with the anthropology of transcendental subjectivity, cf. W. Anz, 'Verkündigung und theologische Reflexion', *ZTK* 58, 1961, Beiheft 2, pp. 47ff., esp. 68ff.

namely, 'the realization of human life'[1] which is the object of
the question raised by the questionableness of human existence.
'Eschatology has wholly lost its sense as goal of history, and
is in fact understood as the goal of the individual human
being.'[2] It is therefore just as impossible for Bultmann as for
Kant that eschatology should provide a doctrine of the 'last
things' in the world process, but the *logos* of the *eschaton* becomes
the power of liberation from history, the power of the desecu-
larization of existence in the sense of liberating us from understanding ourselves on the basis of the world and of works.

This proof of God from existence, in the framework of which
theological questions are here asked and theological statements
made, has a long previous history in dogmatic thought. Karl
Jaspers points out that 'existence and transcendence' is the
rendering in philosophical language of what the language of
myth calls 'soul and God', and that in both languages it is
defined as 'not world'.[3] This, like occasional quotations also
in Bultmann,[4] refers us back to Augustine. From Augustine *via*
mediaeval mysticism and the Reformation to the rationalism
of the Enlightenment, and on to Herrmann, this proof of God
has left its mark on the Western consciousness.

The identification of the hiddenness of God and of man's self, or his soul
(not as a substance in Aristotle's sense, but as subject) presupposes already
in Augustine that for himself man is immediately given and that he can
therefore be immediately certain of himself, whereas the world, the things of
nature and the events of history are accessible to him only through the
mediation of the senses. 'Of all the things that we can perceive, know and
love, none is so certain to us as that we exist. Here we are not troubled by
the deception of a mere semblance of the truth. For we grasp this truth not
as we grasp things external to us, by means of any of our bodily senses;
but without the intrusion of any illusory phantasies I am completely certain that I exist, that I know and that I love.'[5] Because of this immediacy,
this proof of God is superior to the others known to Augustine, such as the
cosmological and aesthetic: '*Noli foras ire, in te ipsum redi, in interiore homine
habitat veritas.*' This way to knowledge of God from knowledge of self found a
following in the Augustinian mysticism of the Middle Ages, especially in
Bernard of Clairvaux. It is against the background of the Augustine renaissance in the Reformers that we have to understand Calvin when he says:
'All our wisdom, so far as it really deserves to be called wisdom and is true

---

[1] 'The Christian Hope and the Problem of Demythologizing', *ExpT* 65, 1954,
p. 278.   [2] 'History and Eschatology in the New Testament', *NTS* 1, 1954, p. 13.
[3] *Philosophie* II, 1932, p. 1.
[4] E.g. *Kerygma und Mythos* II, 1952, p. 192 (ET p. 192).
[5] *De civitate Dei* XI, 26. Similarly also *De lib. arb.* II, 3 and *De trinitate* X, 10.

and dependable, ultimately embraces two things: the knowledge of God and our self-knowledge. These two, however, are interconnected in manifold ways, and therefore it is not at all such a simple matter to say which comes first and produces the other as its result.'[1] Calvin worked out a thoroughly dialectic relation between the two: without knowledge of God no self-knowledge, without self-knowledge no knowledge of God. It is likewise under the bane of the Augustinian tradition that Luther roundly asserts: *Cognitio Dei et hominis est sapientia divina et proprie theologica. Et ita cognitio Dei et hominis, ut referatur tandem ad deum justificantem et hominem peccatorem, ut proprie sit subjectum Theologiae homo reus et perditus et deus justificans vel salvator. quicquid extra istud argumentum vel subjectum quaeritur, hoc plane est error et vanitas in Theologia* ('The knowledge of God and man is wisdom that is divine and properly speaking theological. And the knowledge of God and man is such that it refers ultimately to the God who justifies and the man who is a sinner, so that the proper subject of theology is man as condemned and lost and God as Justifier or Saviour. Any question which lies outside this argument or subject is plainly idle and wrong in theology.')[2] Whereas in Augustinian mysticism, however, the correlation of knowledge of God and self-knowledge could be taken as immediate and unmediated, for the Reformers, and still for Pascal, both are mediated by the knowledge of Christ: the crucified Christ is the mirror of God and the mirror of ourself. Nevertheless in the Reformers, too, as already in Augustine, this concentration of theology upon the knowledge of God and of self leaves no room over for any consideration of God's world. On the contrary, this threatens to be banished from theology. Descartes then drops all proofs of God from the world. *Semper existimavi duas quaestiones, de Deo et de Anima, praecipuas esse ex iis quae Philosophiae potius quam Theologiae ope sunt demonstrandae* ('I have always considered two questions – that of God and that of the soul – to be chief among those that require to be proved by means of philosophy rather than theology').[3] Descartes' third Meditation on the immediate self-consciousness and the consciousness of God therein given takes up – *via* the French Augustine renaissance of the seventeenth century – the reflection of Augustine quoted above. Since, however, the proof of God is found in the immediate self-consciousness and the reflecting subject knows himself and God *'per eandem facultatem'* and *'simul'*, the field of *res extensae* is left to a calculability that is void of God and oblivious of being. Ever since the scientific and historical Enlightenment, what theology says, thinks and proclaims about the action of God has been directed ever more strongly to that subjectivity of man which was given a free rein precisely by the secularization of the world effected by the Enlightenment. Much as in the passages cited from Bultmann, we find also in G. Ebeling: 'Thus the fact of man's identity being open to question opens also the question of God.'[4] This proof of God from

[1] *Institutio* I, i, 1. [2] *WA* 40, II, 327f.
[3] Descartes, *Meditationes de prima philosophia*. For the proof of God from the immediate self-consciousness, cf. the third Meditation.
[4] *Wort und Glaube*, 1960, p. 441 (ET by J. W. Leitch: *Word and Faith*, 1963, pp. 418f.). On pp. 366f. (ET pp. 348f.) it is shown in detail how far the comprehensive analysis of reality, whose final result today is held to be the observing of the 'radical questionableness of reality', has certain things in common with the under-

existence, in the form of the question of God that arises from the questionability of human existence, involves the same presupposition as the proofs
of God from the world or from history. It presupposes an antecedently given
relation to God of the soul, the self or existence, even if this relation cannot
be objectively proved but only subjectively experienced in the experience
of certainty. In the restless heart that is due to his creation, man is engaged
in the quest for God, whether he knows it or not.

The peculiar radicality of this proof of God from existence is
due to the form now assumed by subjectivity as a product of
reflective philosophy. Inasmuch as this subjectivity understands
itself as the incomprehensible immediacy of our existing, it is
attained by distinguishing itself from the non-self, from the
world of observable, calculable and disposable things and of our
own objectifications. If he is to be able to be a person in the
proper sense, man must distinguish himself radically from his
world. All statements on the relation of the person to God become definable only by means of the opposite, relation to
the world. Man then continually distinguishes between his being
part of the world and his being his own self, and so makes the
world a secularized world and his self the pure receiving of his
person from God. This process of abstracting our own individual
subjectivity from all relationships to the world in endless reflection is a modern phenomenon. The proof of God from existence was not found in this antithesis either in Augustine or in
the Reformers. On the contrary, they knew of God's working –
albeit a hidden working – in the world, in nature and in history,
and expounded it in the doctrine of created orders. The concept of science which Herrmann and Bultmann have taken over
from Kantianism, however, no longer allows of this. For them,
scientific knowledge is thought to be of an objectifying kind and
its categories are designed for a 'closed system of cause and
effect' and a world-order regulated by set laws, both in natural
and in historical science. For the experience we have of reality
under these categories, God and his action remain hidden in
principle. Hence the result is, as for Kierkegaard, the alliance of
a theoretic atheism and a believing heart. Theological import-

taking of the so-called proofs of God. This analogy, however, is at once restricted
by Ebeling: 'The problem of true transcendence seems to us to arise at a totally
different point from where the usual so-called proofs of God placed it: not with the
question of the *primum movens* or such like, but with the problems relating to personal being, like the question of meaning, the question of guilt, the question of
communication, etc.' These questions which arise in the realm of personal being,
however, are not 'totally different' from those posed by experience of the world.

ance can therefore attach only to these scientific efforts as such –
and that, too, for the existing subject of the act of knowing. If
this scientific way of thinking about reality and of dealing with
it has its ground in man's practical turn of mind and his will to
power, in his desire to command, to survey, to calculate, to
assert himself and make himself secure, then from the theological
point of view that comes near to man's attaining to self-assurance from his works. This means that for the man who is confronted by the message of grace, the dimension 'world' is now
relevant only within the framework of the question of justification – in the question whether he seeks to understand himself
'from the world' as the disposable realm of his works, or 'from
God' the Indisposable. For the subject in search of himself,
'world' and 'God' thereby become radical alternatives. Man
comes to stand 'between God and the world' (Gogarten). There
is no need to mention that this view of 'God' and 'world' as
alternatives has a previous history in gnosticism and in mysticism. More important is the fact that this kind of theological
understanding of 'world' forces both man's scientific and his
practical dealings with reality into a legalism which does not
accord with this reality. Does the objective knowledge of the
world and of history necessarily fall, in the view of theology,
under 'the law'? Is any self-understanding of man conceivable
at all which is not determined by his relation to the world, to
history, to society? Can human life have subsistence and dura-
tion without outgoing and objectification, and without this does
it not evaporate into nothingness in endless reflection? It is the
task of theology to expound the knowledge of God in a correlation between understanding of the world and self-understanding.

The categorical framework of a transcendental subjectivity
also dominates Bultmann's understanding of revelation. The
revelation of God is accordingly a matter of man's coming to
himself, truly understanding himself. 'Revelation means *that
opening up of what is hidden which is absolutely necessary and decisive
for man if he is to achieve "salvation" or authenticity*.'[1] This presupposes for one thing that man cannot of himself attain to his
authenticity, but must seek for revelation, but secondly that he
is necessarily destined to come to his authenticity. If his authenticity is disclosed to him by revelation, then the divinity of God

[1] *Glauben und Verstehen* III, 1960, p. 2 (ET p. 59).

discloses itself to him therein. Christian proclamation and
Christian faith answer this anterior question of man about
himself – the question which in virtue of his questionable
nature he himself is – not by what they say and what they
mediate, but by what they are. 'Revelation does not mediate
any speculative knowledge, but *it addresses us*. The fact that
in it man learns to understand himself, means *that he learns to
understand each several "now" of his life, each several moment, as one
qualified by the proclamation*. For to be in the moment is his
authentic being.'[1] Revelation in this sense is the event of preaching and faith. Revelation is the coming about of the ἀκοὴ τῆς
πίστεως. 'The preaching is itself revelation and does not merely
speak about it.'[2] 'It is only *in* faith that the object of faith is disclosed; therefore, faith itself belongs to revelation.'[3] Not in
what the word of proclamation says or in what it points to, but
in the fact that it 'happens', addressing, accosting, appealing,
lies the event of revelation. '*What, then, is revealed?* Nothing at all,
so far as the quest for revelation is a quest for doctrines. . . .
But everything, so far as *man has his eyes opened regarding himself
and can understand himself again*.'[4] Thus here the event of the
proclamation that addresses us, and of the decision of faith that
understands and appropriates it, is itself revelation. Since the
governing question of revelation is constituted by the questionableness of human existence itself, the revelation discloses a
self-understanding in authenticity, certainty and identity with
oneself. The active event of revelation is itself the presence of
the *eschaton*, for 'to be in the moment' of proclamation and
faith is the 'authentic being' of man. Authentic being, however,
means the restoring of man's original being in the sense of
creatureliness and the attaining of finality in the sense of
eschatology. Both are fulfilled in the historicality determined by
word and faith. In the 'moment' of revelation, creation and
redemption coincide.[5] *What* is revealed is identical with the event,
the fact *that* revelation takes place.

---

[1] *Glauben und Verstehen* III, 1960, p. 30 (ET p. 86, slightly altered).
[2] *Ibid.*, p. 21 (ET p. 78).   [3] *Ibid.*, p. 23 (ET p. 79).
[4] *Ibid.*, p. 29 (ET p. 85, slightly altered).
[5] *Ibid.*, p. 29: 'There did not appear in Jesus a different light from the light that
always shone already in the creation. Man does not learn a different understanding
of himself in the light of the revelation of redemption from the understanding he
ought always to have of himself already in view of the revelation in creation and
law, namely, as God's creature' (cf. ET p. 86).

Here two questions arise:

1. When the questionableness of human existence is exclusively made the governing question of revelation and salvation, and this question is narrowed down to the alternative of understanding oneself either from the disposable 'world' or the indisposable 'God', then the self-evidence of the 'self-understanding' is manifestly not called in question, neither hermeneutically in relation to the received texts nor theologically. Yet why should the anterior understanding which causes man to ask for 'revelation' be only an 'unknowing knowledge' 'about himself' and 'not a knowledge of the world'?[1] Why is the word that has all along been the light of men 'naturally . . . not a cosmological or theological theory but . . . an understanding of oneself through acknowledging the Creator'?[2] Why does revelation not supply a '*Weltanschauung*', but a new 'self-understanding'? What Bultmann presupposes in this context as a 'natural' and self-evident alternative, is not in the least 'natural', but is an exact description of a definite *Weltanschauung*, a definite view of history and a definite analysis of time, according to which man has become questionable to himself in his social, corporeal and historic relations to the world and attains his selfhood by differentiation from the external world and reflection upon his objectifications. Basically, however, '*Weltanschauung*' and 'self-understanding' lie on the same plane. The one presupposes the other and is inseparably bound up with it. Only in his outgoing towards the world does man experience himself. Without objectification no experience of oneself is possible. Always man's self-understanding is socially, materially and historically mediated. An immediate self-consciousness and a non-dialectical identity with himself is not possible to man – that is shown precisely by the dialectical antithesis of world and self in Bultmann.

2. The theological question arises whether it is really true that in the event of revelation in proclamation and faith man already comes 'to himself' in that authenticity which is at once both original and final. In that case faith would itself be the practical end of history and the believer would himself already

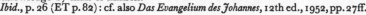

---

[1] *Ibid.*, p. 26 (ET p. 83): 'Thus there is a "natural revelation". . . . But . . . the knowledge of it is not a knowledge of the world, a theistic view of God. Rather it is a knowledge by man of himself.'

[2] *Ibid.*, p. 26 (ET p. 82): cf. also *Das Evangelium des Johannes*, 12th ed., 1952, pp. 27ff.

be perfected. There would be nothing more that still awaits him, and nothing more towards which he is on his way in the world in the body and in history. God's 'futurity' would be 'constant' and man's openness in his 'wayfaring' would likewise be 'constant' and 'never-ending'.[1] This, however, is just what would cause believing existence, understood in an 'eschatological' sense of this sort, to turn into a new form of the 'epiphany of the eternal present'.[2] If Jesus with his word has already reached his 'goal'[3] in faith itself, then it is hardly conceivable that faith is directed towards *promissio* and that faith has itself a goal (I Peter 1.9) to which it is on the way, that 'it doth not yet appear what we shall be' (I John 3.2), and that faith is thus out for something which is promised to it but which is not yet fulfilled. If it is precisely believers who wait for the redemption of the body, on the ground of the eschatologically understood 'earnest of the Spirit' who is the Spirit of the raising of the dead, then in so doing they make it known that they have not yet attained to identity with themselves, but that in hope and confidence they are living to that end and here defy the reality of death. It is precisely in the context of the eschatological distinction of 'not yet', in which faith stretches out towards the future, that it becomes possible to perceive a world that is not identical with 'world' in the antithetical sense in which the

[1] *Glauben und Verstehen* III, p. 121: '. . . his constant futurity is his beyondness'. P. 165: '. . . the God of history . . . the ever coming God'. *Das Urchristentum im Rahmen der antiken Religionen*, 2nd ed., 1954, p. 228 (ET by R. H. Fuller: *Primitive Christianity in its Contemporary Setting*, 1956, p. 208): 'The openness of Christian existence is never-ending.'

[2] J. Schniewind already saw and criticized this, *Kerygma und Mythos* I, pp. 100ff. (ET pp. 75ff.). P. 103 (ET p. 78): 'If the "eschatological attitude" means a life based on invisible, intangible realities, that is much too wide a definition. For it is then identical with religion as such.' P. 105 (ET p. 81): 'Eschatology deals with the *eis ti* and the *telos*, with the meaning and goal of the time process, but not with the eternal present.'

[3] G. Ebeling, *Das Wesen des christlichen Glaubens*, 1959, pp. 68, 72 (ET by R. Gregor Smith: *The Nature of Faith*, 1961, pp. 60, 62), *Wort und Glaube*, 1960, p. 311 (ET p. 298) and frequently. This does not prevent Ebeling from understanding faith as 'essentially a faith that relates to the future' (p. 248, ET p. 241) and saying, '. . . faith . . . *is* the future' (*Wesen des christlichen Glaubens*, p. 231, ET p. 175). This future of faith, however, appears only in reflection on the dimension of faith itself, and is understood as 'pure (that surely means unmediated) future' or 'futurity'. But that is to regard faith as being eternally hope. Future in the sense of futurity, and hope in the sense of hoping, thereby become dimensions or ecstatic extensions of the 'now of eternity'. Cf. *Theologie und Verkündigung*, 1962, pp. 89f. (ET by John Riches, *Theology and Proclamation*, 1966, pp, 89 f.), and the criticism of H. Schmidt, 'Das Verhältnis von neuzeitlichem Wirklichkeitsverständnis und christlichem Glauben in der Theologie G. Ebelings', *Kerygma und Dogma* 9, 1963, pp. 71ff.

doctrine of justification uses the term to denote the epitome of
corruption, law and death. If faith awaits the 'redemption of the
body', and a bodily resurrection from the dead, and the annihilation of death, then it begins to see itself in a profound bodily
solidarity with the 'earnest expectation of the creature' (Rom.
8.19ff.), both in its subjection to vanity and in the universal
hope. Then it does not regard the world from the standpoint of
the 'law'. It sees it not merely as 'world' in the sense of being
unable to understand itself from the world, but perceives it in
the eschatological perspective of promise. The world itself is
subjected along with it to vanity, in hope. The future which the
promise of the God of the resurrection opens to faith is given to
the creature along with it and to it along with the creature. The
creature itself is a 'wayfarer', and the *homo viator* is engaged
along with reality in a history that is open towards the future.
Thus he does not find himself 'in the air', 'between God and the
world', but he finds himself along with the world in that process
to which the way is opened by the eschatological promise of
Christ. It is not possible to speak of believing existence in hope
and in radical openness, and at the same time consider the
'world' to be a mechanism or self-contained system of cause and
effect in objective antithesis to man. Hope then fades away to
the hope of the solitary soul in the prison of a petrified world,
and becomes the expression of a gnostic longing for redemption.
Talk of the openness of man is bereft of its ground, if the world
itself is not open at all but is a closed shell. Without a cosmic
eschatology there can be no assertion of an eschatological exist-   * * *
ence of man. Christian eschatology therefore cannot reconcile
itself with the Kantian concepts of science and of reality. The
very mode of our experience of the world is not adiaphorous.
On the contrary, world-picture and faith are inseparable – precisely because faith cannot suffer the world to become a picture
of God, nor a picture of man.

6. 'PROGRESSIVE REVELATION' AND THE ESCHATOLOGY OF SALVATION HISTORY

The intention behind the old idea of understanding God's
revelation as 'progressive revelation' was to construe revelation
in historic terms and see the history of the world as revelation.
Ideas of this kind go back to late federal theology (J. Cocceius)

and the early pietistic theology of history, the so-called 'prophetic' and 'economic' theology of the seventeenth and eighteenth centuries.[1] In contrast to Orthodoxy's supranaturalistic and doctrinaire view of revelation, the Bible was here read as a history book, as the divine commentary upon the divine acts in world history. This new historic understanding of revelation had its ground in the rebirth of eschatological millenarianism in the post-reformation age. It was the start of a new, eschatological way of thinking, which called to life the feeling for history. The revelation in Christ was accordingly seen in the light of history as a transitional stage in a more far-reaching 'kingdom of God' process, and taken as an ultimate datum for the future, yet also one that points beyond itself. The revelation of God is consequently not an 'eternal moment', and the *eschaton* that comes to light in it is not a *'futurum aeternum'*, but the revelation in Christ is then the last, decisive element in the history of a kingdom whose pre-history begins in the Fall and indeed already in the Creation – whether with the proto-gospel of Gen. 3.15 or with the promise of the divine image in Gen. 1.28 – and whose final history extends historically and noetically beyond the revelation in Christ. The revelation in Christ is thus placed under the head of a history of revelation, whose progressiveness is expressed in the idea of the developing of salvation stage by stage according to a previously fixed plan of salvation. This theology of the 'plan' of saving history has many striking parallels with the scientific deism of the seventeenth and eighteenth centuries and is in every sense a religious product of the Enlightenment. For that reason it can find expression in terms both of pietism and of rationalism, both of history of salva-

---

[1] G. Schrenk, *Gottesreich und Bund im älteren Protestantismus, vornehmlich bei J. Cocceius*, 1923; G. Möller, 'Föderalismus und Geschichtsbetrachtung im 17. und 18. Jahrhundert', *Zeitschrift für Kirchengeschichte*, 3rd Series, I, vol. 50, 1931, pp. 397ff.; J. Moltmann, 'J. Brocard als Vorläufer der Reich-Gottes-Theologie', *Zeitschrift für Kirchengeschichte*, 4th Series, IX, vol. 71, 1960, pp. 110ff.; G. Weth, *Die Heilsgeschichte*, 1931; F. W. Kantzenbach, 'Vom Lebensgedanken zum Entwicklungsdenken in der Theologie der Neuzeit', *Zeitschrift für Religions- und Geistesgeschichte* 15, 1963, pp. 55ff.; E. Fülling, *Geschichte als Offenbarung*, 1956. For a critical assessment cf. K. G. Steck, *Die Idee der Heilsgeschichte. Hofmann – Schlatter – Cullman* (Theologische Studien 56), 1959. Steck's concluding recommendation that new consideration should today be given to Fichte's statement, 'It is only the metaphysical that brings blessedness, and not by any means the historical; the latter brings only prudence', certainly does not seem to me to offer any solution, in view of the context in which this statement stands in Fichte himself.

tion and of history of progress.[1] Yet its real appeal lies not so
much in the enlightened explanation of the divine saving plan
of history, but rather in taking the testimonies of scripture,
which point historically towards each other and also beyond
themselves, and using them to turn history into a 'system of
hope' (J. A. Bengel) by which to answer the question of the
future and goal which the Christian revelation contains for the
nations, for our bodily existence, for nature and for Israel. This
theology of a progressive revelation of God in the history of
salvation – conceived as esoteric knowledge on the part of those
in initiated circles – is 'economic' to the extent that it brings to
light the 'economies', or saving dispensations, of God in the
past and thus turns past history into comprehended history,
while on the other hand it draws conclusions for God's future
action from his ways in the past. It is 'prophetic' in the ultimate
sense, since it seeks to take prophecies and events in the past
which point beyond the present, and use them as a means of
discovering and portraying the future.

Its truth surely lies in the mere fact of its taking the trouble to
enquire at all into the inward tendency and eschatological outlook which the divine revelation in history has towards the
future. Its mistake, however, is to be seen in the fact that it
sought to discover the eschatological progressiveness of salvation
history not from the cross and the resurrection, but from other
'signs of the times' – from an apocalyptic view of the corruption
of the Church and the decay of the world, or from an optimistic
view of the progress of culture and knowledge – so that revelation became a predicate of history, and 'history' was turned
deistically into a substitute for God.

What made this theology of salvation history possible was that
resurgence of apocalyptic thought and hope which both in the
theological and in the secular realm accompanied the birth of
the 'modern age'. Yet it is an apocalyptic which is evolved from
the standpoint of cosmology and world history and based on a
historico-theological proof of God from history. It did not pass
through the fires of Kantian criticism, nor did it – even in its
nineteenth-century representatives – ever submit itself to that

[1] One need think only of the astonishing parallel between pietistic and enlightened millenarianism, of Bengel and Lessing, C. A. Crusius and Ötinger,
Herder and Menken, Hegel and von Hofmann, Rothe and Blumhardt. On this
point cf. F. Gerlich, *Der Kommunismus als Lehre vom tausendjährigen Reich*, 1921.

criticism, while for its own part it was hardly ever critical of that criticism either. Where it appears in the theology of salvation history in nineteenth-century romanticism, it retains this uncritical character throughout. That means, however, that it never really entered into the spirit of the modern age but assumed the remoteness of esoteric church teaching. Yet that is not to dismiss the truth contained in this kind of theological thinking. Its underlying polemic against an abstract materialism and an unhistoric historicism must be noted, even if that polemic failed on the whole to succeed.

In the pietism of Württemberg, history was understood by J. A. Bengel and F. Ötinger as a living 'organism'. Ötinger's *Theologia ex idea vitae deducta* (1765) introduced the concept of life into theology and attempted by this means to make room for thinking of a comprehensive kind.[1] This concept of life and of organism was not so much naturalistic, but rather had an eschatological orientation towards the awaited break-through of the glorious heavenly life in the resurrection. Its polemic was directed against the mechanistic world picture of the natural science of the Enlightenment, and against the idealistic subjectivism which went along with it. History, it maintained, should not be regarded as a collection of facts existing outside of man, but should be understood as a 'stream of life' which 'organically' surrounds man. Although the terms employed are derived from the life of nature and appear little suited for the comprehending of history, yet the criticism they express of Lamettrie's *L'homme machine* and of the unhistoric scientific materialism of the Enlightenment of Western Europe is noteworthy. The idea of the 'world machine' and of the 'forest' that has turned to 'firewood' is assailed by the salvation history school's theology of life. The new central concepts 'history' and 'life' thereby acquire significance for the overcoming of the modern antithesis of 'subjectivity and objectification'. They were also taken over by Hegel in this sense, presumably from the Württemberg tradition. At all events it is in harmony with the intentions of Ötinger when Karl Marx in his critique of abstract scientific materialism and of Ludwig Feuerbach says: 'As soon as we have this active life process before us, history

[1] W. A. Hauck, *Das Geheimnis des Lebens: Naturanschauung und Gottesauffassung Fr. Chr. Ötingers*, 1947.

ceases to be a collection of dead facts, as in the still abstract
thought even of the empiricists, or a series of imagined actions
on the part of imagined subjects, as with the idealists.'[1] Both
abstractions, subjectivity and objectification, acquire reality
and lose their abstract, non-historic character in the dialectical
process. The only question is, what constitutes this process,
what is the subject of it, and what is its goal.

The idea of salvation history has furthermore an emphatically
anti-historical tenor. Auberlen declared: 'The task of theology
today consists in overcoming rationalistic unhistorical historicism . . . through the knowledge of sacred history.'[2] The only
noteworthy thing about this statement is the assertion that
historicism is 'unhistorical'. The overcoming of it by means of
a manifestly non-rational knowledge of 'sacred history' remains
an illusion unless and until a new understanding of *ratio* can be
acquired. The theology of salvation history was never itself able
to bring about a critical change in the epistemological principles
of historical science, and consequently always appears in the
age of critical historical research to be an anachronistic means
of glossing over the crisis in which the theology of revelation
finds itself in the modern age. The 'disenchanting' of history
by historical science certainly cannot be undone by weaving
a romantic, metahistorical, believing spell into history again.
Only when critical historical science discovers its own historicality and learns to take it as a presupposition and a methodological principle, is there any chance of its realizing the possibility of attaining a 'historic' understanding of history and
getting beyond an 'unhistorical historicism'. The traditional
theology of salvation history bears much the same relationship

---

[1] *Frühschriften*, ed. Landshut, 1953, p. 350. Cf. also p. 330: 'Of the inborn
attributes of matter, movement is the first and foremost, not merely in the sense of
mechanical and mathematical movement, but still more as the impetus, the vital
spirit, the tension, the pain (to use Jacob Böhme's word) of matter. . . . In the
course of its further development materialism becomes one-sided. . . . Sensuality
loses its blossom and becomes the abstract sensuality of the geometrist. Physical is
sacrificed to mechanical or mathematical movement. Materialism becomes mis-
anthropic', because, as it is said elsewhere (pp. 338, 346, 354), it 'shuts itself off
from history'. This romanticist struggle on Marx's part against the sensual materialism of Feuerbach and against abstract, scientific materialism repeated itself in the
Russian revolution in practical terms in the conflict between Trotsky and Stalin.
Trotsky understood the revolutionary not as the 'mechanic of force', but as 'doctor'
to the life process of the social organism. This conflict repeated itself in theoretical
terms in the discussion between G. Lukács, K. Korsch and Lenin.

[2] Quoted by G. Weth, *op. cit.*, p. 97.

to historical criticism as does Goethe's theory of colour to
Newton's analysis of light. It has aesthetic and poetic categories
of its own, but none by which the reality of history today could
be grasped and altered.

The real concern of the theology of salvation history, however, lay not so much in the metahistorical grasp of 'sacred history', but was rather to show that revelation has a face towards
world history and eschatology. This purpose underlies the concept of 'progressive revelation'.

Within the confines of a transcendental eschatology, revelation,
as we have seen, becomes indifferent towards the ages of history.
All ages are given an equally immediate relation to eternity,
and history becomes the epitome of transience. R. Rothe rightly
observes in his celebrated essay on revelation: 'It (scripture)
shows us a revelation of a totally different kind. It describes it
above all as a series – and that, too, a constantly self-coherent
series – of wondrous *facts of history* and *dispensations in history*
which then form the starting point for instances of supernatural
prophetic illumination that have a definite pragmatical connection with them and assume manifold forms, as visions and
as inward experiences of being addressed by the Spirit of God,
not so much in order to communicate new knowledge of religious truth as to give advance intimation of future events in
history.'[1] Both forms of revelation, that of 'outward manifestation' and that of 'inward inspiration' – a distinction which is
made again and again between 'revelation in act' and 'revelation in word' – are historically conditioned, from which it
follows that the divine revelation takes place gradually through
the dialectic of word and event in a succession of happenings
which are foretold and come to pass, and that it presses towards
an end in which it is itself fulfilled 'The advancing development of the kingdom of the Redeemer is at the same time also a
continually advancing revelation of the absolute truth and perfection of the same.'[2] Thus in R. Rothe, and then with modifica-
tions also in Biedermann and E. Troeltsch God's revelation is
certainly understood as self-revelation, yet is linked with the idea
which the concept of salvation history provides of an eschatological and progressive, dialectically advancing self-realization of

[1] R. Rothe, *Zur Dogmatik*, 1863, p. 59.
[2] *Ethik*, 1867, § 570. Cf. also A. E. Biedermann, *Christliche Dogmatik*, 1884, § 987.

the Revealer. That means, however, that present history, the history of the modern age in its cultural, scientific and technical progress, must be represented as an element in the process of the self-realizing revelation of God and his kingdom. When, therefore, an outmoded and antiquated Christianity raised the apologetic question of its own present relevance, the theology of progressive revelation characteristic of cultural Protestantism had to answer by showing that the modern age which was superseding traditional Christianity was secretly Christian or had a secret part in the history of the kingdom. 'Why is the Church opposed to cultural development?' asked R. Rothe, and answered: 'Oh, I blush to set it down: because it fears for belief in Christ. That is for me not faith, but faint-heartedness. But that is precisely what comes of disbelief in the real, effective world-dominion of the Saviour.'[1] In E. Troeltsch this question takes the form: 'Are we still to be seen in continuity with Christianity, or are we growing towards a religious future which is no longer Christian?'[2] His answer was the idea of a progressive revelation which in every age anew brings the spirit of the age into synthesis with the traditional Christian message. Similar questions and answers played an active part in the circles around the Blumhardts and among the 'religious socialists'.

Although the theology of progressive revelation never succeeded, in Rosenstock-Huessy's phrase, in 'overcoming modernity', yet it does contain elements that are not to be dismissed simply by the fact that a transcendental eschatology makes all ages of history indifferent. Although the idea of salvation history is philosophically anachronistic and theologically deistic, yet it does preserve the question of the eschatological future outlook which the Christian revelation holds for a world involved in history. That is to say, all the themes of the eschatology of salvation history – such as the mission to the nations, the discussion of the future of Israel, the future of world history, of creation and of the body – are the proper themes of Christian eschatology as such, only they cannot be conceived in the traditional terms of salvation history. The decisive question is, whether 'revelation' is the illuminating interpretation of an existing, obscure life process in history, or whether revelation itself originates drives and directs the process of history; whether consequently,

---

[1] R. Rothe, *Vorträge*, 1886, p. 21.　　　[2] *Glaubenslehre*, 1925, p. 49.

as Barth has asked, revelation is a predicate of history, or
whether history has to be understood as a predicate of the
eschatological revelation and to be experienced, expected and
obediently willed as such.

(Jm)

7. 'HISTORY' AS INDIRECT SELF-REVELATION OF GOD

Another attempt to free theological consideration of the 'self-
revelation' of God from the fetters of the reflective philosophy
of transcendental subjectivity – an attempt, moreover, which
in many respects leaves the discussion still open – is found in
the programmatic volume *Offenbarung als Geschichte* (1961) by
W. Pannenberg, R. Rendtorff, U. Wilckens and T. Rendtorff.[1]
Since Kant's critique and the concept of science that was
based on it, the impression had arisen that there can be no
proof of God and of his action in history, and no objective
demonstration of revelation, and this had compelled theology
to speak of revelation only in the context and framework of
transcendental subjectivity. That, however, is not by any
means to say that theology had at last settled down to its own
business, but rather that it had entered into a negative alliance
with a particular, modern mode of experiencing the world. If
this spell is to be broken and an alternative to this kind of
theology of revelation is to be found, then that must of necessity
be bound up with an alternative to the modern, post-Kantian
concept of science, to the critical concept of reason, and to the
historicism of a critical historical treatment of reality. An alternative to faith's theology of revelation must then also bring
criticism to bear on that critique of knowledge which Kant
set up 'in order to find a place for faith'. It must raise the question of God no longer in an exclusive sense on the ground of the
questionableness of man's subjectivity, but in an inclusive sense
on the ground of the questionableness of reality as a whole, and
it is in this comprehensive context that it must speak of God's
revelation and action.

[1] Cf. further, W. Pannenberg, 'Heilsgeschehen und Geschichte', *Kerygma und
Dogma* 5, 1959, pp. 218–237, 259–288; R. Rendtorff, ' "Offenbarung" im Alten
Testament', *TLZ* 85, 1960, cols. 833–838; K. Koch, 'Spätisraelitisches Geschichts-
denken', *Historische Zeitschrift*, Aug. 1961; W. Pannenberg, 'Hermeneutik und
Universalgeschichte', *ZTK* 60, 1963, pp. 90ff.; R. Rendtorff, 'Geschichte und
Wort im Alten Testament', *EvTh* 22, 1962, pp. 621ff.

Offenbarung als Geschichte therefore sets out not from the proof of God from existence, or from showing that the question of God arises from the questionableness of existence. Rather, it starts from the proof of God from the cosmos, or by showing that the question of God arises from consideration of the question of reality as a whole. The place of the 'kerygma theology', and of the idea of an immediate self-revelation of God in the appeal of the word, is therefore taken by the recognition of an 'indirect self-revelation of God in the mirror of his action in history'.[1] 'The facts as acts of God shed a reflected light on God himself, tell us indirectly something about God himself.'[2] Since, however, each individual event, taken as an act of God, only partially illumines the nature of God, revelation in the sense of the full self-revelation of God in his glory can be possible only where the whole of history is understood as revelation. 'History as a whole is thus revelation of God. Since it is not yet finished, it is only in the light of its end that it is recognizable as revelation.'[3] Hence the full self-revelation of God takes place 'not at the beginning but at the end of the revealing history'.[4] The apocalyptic writers of late Judaism had extraordinary visions in which they foresaw such an end of history in the general resurrection of the dead. In the (risen) 'destiny' of Jesus of Nazareth the end of history has accordingly been forestalled. For in his resurrection there has already happened to him what still awaits all men.[5] If his resurrection is the 'forestalling', the anticipation, the prolepsis of the universal end, then it follows that in his destiny God himself is indirectly revealed as the God of all men.[6]

This theology of universal history obviously intends in the first instance to extend and supersede the Greek cosmic theology. The place of the cosmological proof of God, which argued from 'reality as cosmos' to the one divine *arche* and so provided proof of a cosmological monotheism, is taken by a theology of history which argues back in the same way from the unity of 'reality as history' to the one God of history.[7] The epistemological

---

[1] *Offenbarung als Geschichte*, p. 15.   [2] *Ibid.*, p. 17.
[3] R. Rendtorff, *TLZ* 85, 1960, col. 836.   [4] *Offenbarung als Geschichte*, p. 95.
[5] *Ibid.*, p. 104.   [6] *Ibid.*, pp. 98, 104ff.
[7] For the application of the retroflexive argument cf. W. Pannenberg, 'Die Aufnahme des philos. Gottesbegriffes als dogmatisches Problem', *Zeitschrift für Kirchengeschichte* 70, 1959, p. 11; 'Heilsgeschehen und Geschichte', *op. cit.*, p. 129;

method remains the same, only in place of the self-contained cosmos whose eternally recurring sameness makes it a theophany in its symmetry and harmony, we have an open-ended cosmos with a teleological trend towards the future. 'History' thus becomes the new summary term for 'reality in its totality'.[1] In place of the metaphysical point in which the unity of the cosmos culminates, we have the eschatological point in which history finds its unity and its goal. Just as in the light of that culminating metaphysical unity the cosmos could be recognized as indirect revelation of God, so now in the light of the end of history, history can be recognized as indirect revelation of God. The retention of the retroflexive argument in the knowledge of God – 'in the mirror of his acts in history' – has the result that knowledge of God becomes possible in principle only *post festum* and *a posteriori*, in looking back upon completed facts in history and on prophecies that have come true in it. That, however, would be knowing God with the eyes of 'Minerva's owl', which according to Hegel begins its flight only 'when a form of life has grown old and reached perfection'.[2] The place of the kerygma theology, which perceived God in the event of being addressed by the word, would then be taken by a theology of history, which hears God in the 'language of the facts'. Just as in Greek cosmic theology the eternal being of God is indirectly manifest in that which is, and can be inferred from it, so here God's being would be recognized in the hasbeens of history. Now of course the fact that the 'end of history' is not yet here, but has only been forestalled in the destiny of Jesus, also makes the recognition of God in history into a knowledge that is always only of proleptic, anticipatory character. Yet the basic Old Testament insight that 'history is that which happens between promise and fulfilment' – the insight from which Pannenberg and Rendtorff set out – is ultimately abandoned in favour of an eschatology which is expressed in

---

Offenbarung als Geschichte, p. 104. This retroflexive argument presupposes an unbroken link between God and history, on the ground of which we can argue back from it to him. Since this is also the basis of the cosmological proof of God, 'history' is here understood as indirect theophany, just as the cosmos then was in Greek cosmology. It is a question, however, whether this is a biblical understanding of history.

[1] 'Heilsgeschehen und Geschichte', *op. cit.*, p. 222.
[2] G. W. F. Hegel, *Grundlinien der Philosophie des Rechts*, ed. J. Hoffmeister, 4th ed., 1956, Vorrede 17.

terms of universal history and which proves itself by reference
to 'reality as a whole' in an effort to improve on Greek cosmic
theology.[1] This eschatology acquires its eschatological character
only from the fact that reality cannot yet be contemplated as a
whole because it has not yet come to an end. With this, however, the Old Testament God of promise threatens to become
a θεὸς ἐπιφανής, whose epiphany will be represented by the
totality of reality in its completed form. The world will one
day be theophany, indirect self-revelation of God *in toto*. Because it is not yet so, reality is open-ended towards the future
and all knowledge of God and the world has an eschatologically
qualified 'provisional' character. This, however, would mean
that the thought structures of Greek cosmic theology remain in
principle, and are simply given an eschatological application.
The retention of the retroflexive method thereby leads to a view
of 'historic fact' which, with its implied concept of being, of
'mirror' and 'image', appears to resist any combination with
faith and hope and even with 'history'.[2] It remains unclear
whether the place of the theophany in nature is taken merely
by a theophany in history regarded as open-ended nature, or
whether what is meant is the fundamentally different condition
on which it becomes possible to perceive reality as history,
namely, from the standpoint of promise. This theology of history as opposed to the theology of the word remains subject to
Kant's critique of theological metaphysics, as long as it itself
fails to undertake critical reflection on the conditions of the
possibility of perceiving reality as history in the eschatological
and theological sense. We are told that this 'theology of history'
differs from the traditional theology of salvation history in that it

[1] This critical observation has already been made also by James M. Robinson,
'The Historicality of Biblical Language', *The Old Testament and Christian Faith*, ed.
B. W. Anderson, 1963, pp. 128f.
[2] Here H. G. Greyer, 'Geschichte als theologisches Problem', *EvTh* 22, 1962,
p. 103, is right when he says: 'A fact is a completed event (*factum*) and as such has
had its day, and the form of consciousness appropriate to it is memory and its
methodically developed form in the knowledge of historical science; promise, however, always has its day still ahead of it.' To be sure, there is also such a thing as
hope in the *modus* of memory and as a historical event that has its future still ahead
of it. Only that would have to be formulated in a new concept of memory and
historical knowledge. Cf. J. Moltmann, 'Verkündigung als Problem der Exegese',
Monatsschrift für Pastoraltheologie 52, 1963, pp. 24ff.; K. Barth, *Römerbrief*, 2nd ed.,
1922, p. 298 (ET p. 314): 'All that is not *hope*, is wooden, dead, hampering, as
ponderous and awkward as the word reality. There there is no freedom, but only
imprisonment.' E. Bloch, *Das Prinzip Hoffnung* I, 1959, p. 242: 'A fact (*factum*) is
a lump of dead matter *alien to history*.'

seeks to be 'historically verifiable in principle'.[1] But that is just what cannot be maintained, unless and until the concept of the 'historical' is transformed and the theology of history becomes the very ground of its redefinition.

As long as this theology of history regards 'God' as the object that is in question when we enquire about the unity and whole-ness of reality, then its starting point is obviously different from that of the question about God and his faithfulness to his promises in history – a question which first arises only in the context of promise and expectation, as in the Old Testament. This is certainly not to say that Pannenberg's question as to an appropriate understanding of the world on the part of theology, or a proof of its statements about God by reference to the whole of reality, is any less relevant than the question as to an appro-priate self-understanding or the proving of our statements about God by reference to human existence in Bultmann. On the contrary, the 'theology of history' is a necessary supple-ment to the 'theology of existence'.

The conflict between a theology of revelation in terms of word and one in terms of history is irresolvable, unless and until these two end-products of abstraction from reflective philosophy are surmounted by a third view which is either comprehensive or open in character. This attempt is made in a second aspect of the development of 'revelation as history' in the concept of the *'history of tradition'*.[2] When history is regarded as the history of tradition, then we have no longer an alterna-tive to the kerygma theology, as in the expression 'language of the facts' (which was after all intended only polemically), but we have here an attempt to bring together again the separated elements, namely, 'word', word-event, interpretation, evalua-tion, etc., on the one hand, and *'factum'*, facts and coherent groups of facts on the other. The theology of history with its 'language of the facts' does not mean the *bruta facta*, which pre-sent themselves to positivistic historicism as the end-products of abstraction from tradition, but means the divine 'language of the facts in that context of tradition and expectation in which the events in question take place'.[3] In this sense 'history is

[1] W. Pannenberg, 'Heilsgeschehen und Geschichte', *op. cit.*, p. 287.
[2] This phrase is used with special emphasis in the essays by W. Pannenberg and R. Rendtorff in *Studien zur Theologie der alttestamentlichen Überlieferungen*, 1961.
[3] W. Pannenberg, *Offenbarung als Geschichte*, p. 112.

always also the history of tradition'.[1] 'History of tradition is in fact to be regarded as the profounder term for history as such.'[2] The events which reveal God must be taken in and with the context in tradition in which they took place and along with which alone they have their original significance. Thus when history is regarded as the history of tradition, the modern distinction between 'factuality' and 'significance' is set aside in a way analogous to that of G. Ebeling's 'theology of the word-event'. As in the latter case the events are asserted along with the word in which they were originally announced, so here the words and traditions are asserted along with the historic events.[3] The decisive question, however, is *how* the Cartesian and Kantian distinction between reality and the perception of it is overcome. If our intention is to see real events in that original context in experience and tradition in which they found expression at the time, then we can set out either hermeneutically from the word-event or in terms of universal history from the particular event in the totality of historic reality. In both cases, however, we must stand the test of that historical criticism to which the traditions are, and must be, subjected by the modern consciousness. The fact that the past encounters us in the 'language of tradition' and is accessible only therein has never been disputed. The only question has been, whether this 'language of the tradition' is 'correct' as far as the reality accessible to historical criticism is concerned. The historical criticism of the Christian traditions has ever since the Enlightenment presupposed with increasing radicalness a crisis in the traditions, if not indeed a revolutionary break in them.[4] Since this crisis and this criticism, 'tradition' is no longer 'taken for granted'. The relationship to history as tradition has become one of reflection and has lost its immediacy. If, therefore, we would understand 'history as tradition', then we shall have to find a new concept of 'tradition', which cancels out historical criticism and its sense of the crisis in history, yet without negating or muzzling it. This problem is not solved simply by showing that in many and devious ways modern historic thinking

---

[1] *Offenbarung als Geschichte*, p. 112.
[2] W. Pannenberg, *Studien zur Theologie der alttestamentlichen Überlieferungen*, p. 139.
[3] G. Ebeling, *Theologie und Verkündigung*, 1962, p. 55 (ET p. 57).
[4] Cf. J. Ritter's verdict in the discussion on J. Pieper, *Über den Begriff der Tradition* (AGFNRW 72), 1958, pp. 45ff.

derives by historic tradition from the historic thinking of the Bible, for of course the point is not so much the origin of the modern historical consciousness, but rather its future.

Particularly difficult from the theological standpoint is the thesis that the raising of Jesus from the dead is the historically demonstrable prolepsis, the anticipation and forestalling of the end of universal history, so that in it the totality of reality as history can be contemplated in a provisional way. The thesis that this event of the raising of Jesus must be 'historically' verifiable in principle, would require us first of all so to alter the concept of the historical that it would allow of God's raising the dead and would make it possible to see in this raising of the dead the prophesied end of history. To call the raising of Jesus historically verifiable is to presuppose a concept of history which is dominated by the expectation of a general resurrection of the dead as the end and consummation of history. Resurrection and the concept of history then contain a vicious circle for the understanding.

The important question for theology, however, is whether such an apocalyptic view of history – and, moreover, one reduced to the expectation of a general resurrection of the dead – is adequate to embrace the Easter appearance of the risen Lord in the context of tradition and expectation in which it was perceived by the disciples. If it were solely the risen 'destiny' of Jesus that constituted the forestalling of the end of all history and the anticipation of the 'destiny' still awaiting all men, then the risen Jesus himself would have no further future. Nor would it be for Jesus himself that those who know him would wait, but only for the repetition of his destiny in themselves. The Church would be waiting for that which has already happened to Jesus to be repeated for itself, but not for the future of the risen Lord. Certain as it is that the Easter appearances of Jesus were experienced and proclaimed in the apocalyptic categories of the expectation of the general resurrection of the dead and as a beginning of the end of all history, it is nevertheless equally certain that the raising of Jesus was not merely conceived solely as the first instance of the final resurrection of the dead, but as the source of the risen life of all believers. It is not merely said that Jesus is the first to arise and that believers will attain *like him* to resurrection, but it is proclaimed that he is himself the resurrection and the life and that consequently believers find their future *in* him and not merely *like* him. Hence they wait for their future by waiting for his future. The horizon of apocalyptic expectation is not by any means wide enough to embrace the post-Easter apocalyptic of the Church. The place of apocalyptic self-preservation to the end is taken by the mission of the Church. That mission can be understood only when the risen Christ himself has still a future, a universal future for the nations. Only then does the Church's approach to the nations in the apostolate have any historic meaning. The apocalyptic outlook which interprets the whole of reality in terms of universal history is secondary compared with this world-transforming outlook in terms of promise and missionary history.

Finally, from the theological standpoint it may be due to the one-track character of the apocalyptic of universal history that the theological significance of the cross of Jesus recedes in favour of his resurrection. Between the expectations of late Jewish apocalyptic and of Christian eschatology stands the cross of Jesus. Hence all Christian resurrection eschatology bears the mark of an *eschatologia crucis*. That is more than merely a break in the coherent historic tradition of apocalyptic expectations. The contradiction of the cross permeates also the whole existence, life and theological thinking of the Church in the world.

If the programme of 'Revelation as History' is concerned to construct on the basis of the resurrection hope theological concepts and approaches to reality which will put an end to the above-mentioned negative alliance with the spirit of the modern age, then it is completely in accord with the demand made by Barth and Bonhoeffer that the 'lordship of Christ' must be consistently testified and presented all the way to the very heart of secular reality. Whether the statement about 'proving the divinity of the biblical God by reference to the totality of the momentary experience of reality'[1] is appropriate to this, remains the question, for that is a task which will end not so much in confirming or superseding as in conflict and divergence. The uncritical use of such terms as 'historical', 'history', 'facts', 'tradition', 'reason', etc., in a theological sense, appears to show that the methodical, practical and speculative atheism of the

[1] *Offenbarung als Geschichte*, p. 104 n. 17, and frequently.

modern age is here circumvented rather than taken seriously.
If this very atheism – as it has been most profoundly understood by Hegel and Nietzsche – derives from the nihilistic
discovery made on the 'speculative Good Friday', that 'God is
dead',[1] then the only real way of vindicating theology in face
of this reality, in face of this reason, and in face of a society thus
constituted, will be in terms of a theology of resurrection – in
fact, in terms of an eschatology of the resurrection in the sense
of the future of the crucified Lord. Such a theology must accept
the 'cross of the present' (Hegel), its godlessness and god-
forsakenness, and there give theoretical and practical proof of
the 'spirit of the resurrection'. Then, however, revelation would
not manifest and verify itself *as* history of our present society, but
would disclose to this society and this age for the very first time
the eschatological process of history. The theologian is not concerned merely to supply a different *interpretation* of the world, of
history and of human nature, but to *transform* them in expectation of a divine transformation.

8. THE ESCHATOLOGY OF REVELATION

It is ultimately always a result of the influence of Greek
methods of thought and enquiry when the revelation of God
which is witnessed in the biblical scriptures is understood as
'epiphany of the eternal present'. That describes the God of
Parmenides rather than the God of the exodus and the resurrection. The revelation of the risen Christ is not a form of this
epiphany of the eternal present, but necessitates a view of
revelation as apocalypse of the promised future of the truth. In
the light of this future of the truth, manifest in the promise, man
experiences reality as history in all its possibilities and dangers,
and is broken of that fixed view of reality in which it becomes an
image of the deity.

Christian theology speaks of 'revelation', when on the ground
of the Easter appearances of the risen Lord it perceives and proclaims the identity of the risen one with the crucified one. Jesus
is recognized in the Easter appearances as what he really *was*.
That is the ground of faith's 'historical' remembrance of the life

[1] G. W. F. Hegel, *Glauben und Wissen*, ed. F. Meiner (Philosophische Bibliothek
62b), 1962, pp. 123f.

and work, claims and sufferings of Jesus of Nazareth. But the
messianic titles, in which this identity of Jesus in cross and
resurrection is claimed and described, all anticipate at the same
time the not yet apparent future of the risen Lord. This means
that the Easter appearances and revelations of the risen Lord
are manifestly understood as foretaste and promise of his still
future glory and lordship. Jesus is recognized in the Easter
appearances as what he really *will be*. The 'vital point' for a
Christian view of revelation accordingly lies neither in 'that
which came to expression in the man Jesus' (Ebeling) nor in
the 'destiny of Jesus' (Pannenberg) but – combining both of
these – in the fact that in all the qualitative difference of cross
and resurrection Jesus is the same. This identity in infinite
contradiction is theologically understood as an event of identification, an act of the faithfulness of God. It is this that forms
the ground of the promise of the still outstanding future of
Jesus Christ. It is this that is the ground of the hope which
carries faith through the trials of the god-forsaken world and
of death.

   'Revelation' in this event has not the character of *logos*-
determined illumination of the existing reality of man and the
world, but has here constitutively and basically the character
of promise and is therefore of an eschatological kind. 'Promise'
is a fundamentally different thing from a 'word-event' which
brings truth and harmony between man and the reality that
concerns him. 'Promise' is in the first instance also a different
thing from an eschatologically oriented view of reality as universal history. Promise announces the coming of a not yet
existing reality from the future of the truth. Its relation to the
existing and given reality is that of a specific *inadaequatio rei et
intellectus*. On the other hand, it does not merely anticipate and
clarify the realm of coming history and the realistic possibilities
it contains. Rather, 'the possible', and therewith 'the future',
arises entirely from God's word of promise and therefore goes
beyond what is possible and impossible in the realistic sense. It
does not illuminate a future which is always somehow already
inherent in reality. Rather, 'future' is that reality which fulfils
and satisfies the promise because it completely corresponds to it
and accords with it. It is only in that event which is spoken of
as 'new creation out of nothing', as 'resurrection of the dead',

as 'kingdom' and 'righteousness' of God, that the promise contained in the resurrection of Christ finds a reality which accords with it and completely corresponds to it. The revealing of
the divinity of God therefore depends entirely on the real fulfilment of the promise, as *vice versa* the fulfilment of the promise
has the ground of its possibility and of its reality in the faithfulness and the divinity of God. To that extent 'promise' does not
in the first instance have the function of illuminating the existing reality of the world or of human nature, interpreting it,
bringing out its truth and using a proper understanding of it to
secure man's agreement with it. Rather, it contradicts existing
reality and discloses its own process concerning the future of
Christ for man and the world. Revelation, recognized as promise and embraced in hope, thus sets an open stage for history,
and fills it with missionary enterprise and the responsible exercise of hope, accepting the suffering that is involved in the
contradiction of reality, and setting out towards the promised
future.

This certainly does not mean that the need to attain to an
appropriate understanding of existence and to find our bearings in universal history is rendered superfluous. Only both
of these, the illumination of the historic character of human
existence and the anticipatory illumination of contexts and
prospects in terms of universal history, will have to be co-
ordinated with the apostolic process of history which God's
revelation calls to life in promise. The God-revealing event of
promise can find articulated expression only in the midst of,
and by reference to, the questionableness of the world as a whole
and of human nature itself, but it is neither exhausted therein
nor identical therewith. It takes up both into the peculiar context of its own enquiry, in which context the knowledge of the
truth presents itself in the form of a question that is open towards the fulfilment of the promise.

If it is true that the appearances of the risen Lord are to be
taken as a foretaste of his own future, then they are to be understood in the context of the Old Testament history of promise,
and not in analogy to an epiphany of the truth in the Greek
sense. The witnesses of Easter do not recognize the risen Lord
in a blaze of heavenly, supra-worldly eternity, but in the foretaste and dawn of his eschatological future for the world. They

do not regard him as the one who has been 'immortalized', but as the one who 'is to come'. They saw him not as what he is in timeless eternity, but as what he will be in his coming lordship. We can therefore say: the risen Lord encounters us as the living Lord, inasmuch as he is in motion, on the march towards his goal.[1] 'He is still future to himself.'[2] With the resurrection, his work is 'not yet completed, not yet concluded'.[3] These statements come from Barth's later work and show plainly the direction which the revision of his eschatology of eternity must take. The appearances of the risen Lord were recognized as the promise and anticipation of a really outstanding future. Because in these appearances a process was manifestly perceptible, they provoked testimony and mission. The future of the risen Lord is accordingly here present in promise; it is accepted in a hope that is prepared to suffer, and it is grasped by the critical mind that reflects on men and things in hope.

But what does it mean to say that the risen Lord in his revelation is the promise of his own future? It would have to mean that Jesus reveals and identifies himself as the Christ both in identity with himself and in differentiation from himself. He reveals and identifies himself as the crucified one, and to that extent in identity with himself. He reveals himself as the Lord on the way to his coming lordship, and to that extent in differentiation from what he will be. The revelation of his future in his appearances is therefore a 'hidden' one. He is the hidden Lord and the hidden Saviour. Through hope the life of believers is hidden with him in God – yet in a hiddenness that is made for future unveiling, and aims at it, and presses towards it. The future of Jesus Christ is in this context the revelation and manifestation of him who has come. Faith is directed in hope and expectation towards the revelation of what it has

---

[1] K. Barth, *Kirchliche Dogmatik* IV/3, p. 377 (ET pp. 326f.): 'He Himself encounters us here as the *living One* also in the concrete sense that . . . precisely here He obviously finds Himself in *motion* or on His *way* as divine-human Mediator, *striding* from His commencement to the goal already included and indicated in it. . . . As the Revealer of His work He has not yet reached His goal. He is still moving towards it. He is marching from its beginning in the revelation of *His* life to the end of His not yet accomplished revelation of the life of *all* men and *all* creation as enclosed in His life, of their life as new creation on a new earth and under a new heaven.' Whereas in Barth's doctrine of revelation the resurrection event stands under the head of the 'pure presence of God', in his doctrine of reconciliation it comes to stand under the head of 'anticipation' of the universal redemption and consummation.

[2] *Ibid.*, p. 378 (ET p. 327, slightly altered).   [3] *Ibid.*, p. 385 (ET p. 334).

already found hidden in Christ. And yet the future of the risen
Lord, that which in his resurrection is promised, intended and
held in prospect, involves not merely a noetic expectation. His
future is not merely the unveiling of something that was hidden,
but also the fulfilment of something that was promised. The
revelation in the appearances of the risen Christ has therefore to
be described not only as 'hidden', but also as 'unfinished', and
has to be related to a reality which is not yet here. It is still
outstanding, has not yet come about, has not yet appeared, but
it is promised and guaranteed in his resurrection, and indeed
is given along with his resurrection as a necessary consequence:
the end of death, and a new creation in which amid the life
and righteousness of all things God is all in all. Thus the future
of the risen Lord involves also the expectation of a creative
act. The word in which this comes to expression is therefore
gospel and promise in one. If 'revelation' in the context of the
Easter appearances does not refer to a completed, self-contained
process or to the presence of eternity, then it must be understood as an open-ended revelation that points forwards and
leads forwards. This, its eschatological openness, will certainly
not be filled up, carried on and completed by the subsequent
Church and its history. If it is towards *his own* future and promise that the revelation of the risen Lord is open, then its openness to the future surpasses all subsequent Church history and
is absolutely superior to it. The remembrance of the promise
that has been given – of the promise in its givenness (*Er-
gangenheit*), not in its pastness (*Ver-gangenheit*) – bores like a
thorn in the flesh of every present and opens it for the future. In
this sense the revelation of the risen Lord does not become
'historic' as a result of the fact that history continues willy-
nilly, but it stands as a sort of *primum movens* at the head of the
process of history. It is in virtue of this revelation that the reality
of man and his world becomes 'historic', and it is the hope set
'upon this revelation that makes all reality inadequate and as
such transient and surpassable. It is the *promissio inquieta* that is
the true source of Augustine's *cor inquietum*. It is the *promissio
inquieta* that will not suffer man's experience of the world to
become a self-contained cosmic image of the deity, but keeps
our experience of the world open to history.

If revelation is promise in this sense, then it has to be related

to the process which is brought about by missionary enterprise.
The process of witness to the eschatological hope by those who
in each succeeding present have to answer for their hope, the
apostolate which involves the world of the nations in this
process, and the exodus from the present of a self-contained
existence into the promised future – these are the things that
constitute the history which 'corresponds' to this kind of revelation, because it is called to life by this revelation. Awareness of
history is awareness of mission, and the knowledge of history
is a transformatory knowledge.

Now this revelation of God in the event of promise can always
be expressed only in relation to, and critical comparison with,
man's experience of the world and of existence at any given
moment. Here lies the justification for the views of revelation we
have discussed, which see it in the context of the proof of God
from existence or of the proof of God from the totality of reality.
If God is not spoken of in relation to man's experience of himself and his world, then theology withdraws into a ghetto and
the reality with which man has to do is abandoned to godlessness. Since the days of the early Christian apologists, the
promissio Dei of which the biblical scriptures speak has always
been considered in the form of the Greek *logos*. Yet it should be
noted that between the two extreme possibilities of ghetto and
assimilation, the *promissio Dei* has always worked as a ferment of
destruction of the Greek *logos* – namely, in such a way that the
illuminating truth of the Greek *logos* has been given eschatological, and therewith historic, character.

In this process, theology can give polemical and liberating
proof of its truth even today. Yet it is just when we perceive the
revelation of God in the promise and are thereby led to ask
what light this sheds on the humanity of man and the reality
of the world, that we then find ourselves in the neighbourhood
of the proofs of God and of 'natural theology'.

Following an ancient definition, 'natural theology' is understood as a
'*theologia naturalis, generalis et immediata*', i.e. a knowledge of God which is not
mediated but given along with reality, universally accessible and immediate. To this there belonged the knowledge that the world is God's world,
or that to ask about the origin or the totality of reality is to ask about God,
and secondly, the knowledge of man's peculiar standing in the cosmos, a
general idea that to be man is to be subject to the claims of God's law – in

other words, the knowledge that the question raised in the questionableness of human existence is the question of God. Whatever the way in which these proofs of God, or indications of the question of God, were presented by Christian theology as universally accessible, they were always so presented as to provide pointers to, and suitable agreements with, the 'supernatural, special and historically mediated' knowledge of God. Whatever Western theology may have taken up and represented in this way as 'natural theology', it was never 'natural' and was neither 'universally human' nor 'immediate'. On closer inspection, 'natural theology' always contained knowledge historically mediated from particular intellectual traditions – from the Stoa, from Plato and Aristotle, etc. The common sense which was appealed to always proves to be a common sense that has developed in history and bears a Western stamp. The 'natural' element in 'natural theology' was thus not at all something that comes 'by nature', but always came from history and was an adoption of what society regarded as natural, i.e. as axiomatic. The Aristotle who was held to be the father of natural theology is no longer by any means identical with the historical Aristotle, but was an Aristotelian heritage worked over by Christian theology. What was called 'nature' and 'universal consciousness of God' in a Christian sense had always already been determined by the content for which it was supposed to provide a general framework. Thus it is true that 'natural theology' is a presupposition of the theology of revelation – in the sense that revelation first posits, creates and fashions it in its specific form. That is not by any means to put an end to the business of natural theology. On the contrary, it is a necessary part of reflection upon nature and human existence in the light of revelation. It therefore continues to be a necessary part of theology as such, if the latter would give expression to the universal sweep of the revelation of God. But as a pre-sup-*position* of theology – a position already predetermined by theology – it belongs to the presentation of revelation's universal, eschatological outlook of expectation. In this sense H. J. Iwand's thesis is correct: 'Natural theology is not that from which we come, but the light to which we are going. The *lumen naturae* is the reflection of the *lumen gloriae*. . . . The reform that is required of theology today consists in assigning revelation to this age, but natural theology to the age to come.'[1] In this sense 'natural theology' – theology of existence and theology of history – is a halo, a reflection of the future light of God upon the inadequate material of present reality, a foretaste and advance intimation of the promised universal glory of God, who will prove himself to all and in all to be the Lord. What is called 'natural theology' is in actual truth *theologia viatorum*, an anticipation of the promised future in history as a result of obedient thinking. Hence it always remains historic, provisional, variable and open. If it means perceiving and reflecting upon the reality in which every man stands, but doing so on the basis of faith and hope, then for that reason it does not have the appeal that its statements are 'self-evident', but it is essentially polemical or, as E. Brunner says, 'eristical'. We shall have to turn the proofs of God the other way about and not demonstrate God from the world but the world from God, not God from existence but existence from God – and that, too, in

[1] H. J. Iwand, *Nachgelassene Werke I, Glauben und Wissen*, 1962, pp. 290f.

constant critical debate with other ways of asserting truth and showing the meaning of things. In this sense the work of 'natural theology' belongs not to the *praeambula fidei*, but to *fides quaerens intellectum*.

The man who is the recipient of this revelation of God in promise is identified, as what he is – and at the same time differentiated, as what he will be. He comes 'to himself' – but in hope, for he is not yet freed from contradiction and death. He finds the way of life – but hidden in the promised future of Christ that has not yet appeared. Thus the believer becomes essentially one who hopes. He is still future to 'himself' and is promised to himself. His future depends utterly and entirely on the outcome of the risen Lord's course, for he has staked his future on the future of Christ. Thus he comes into harmony with himself *in spe*, but into disharmony with himself *in re*. The man who trusts himself to the promise is of all people one who finds himself a riddle and an open question, one who becomes in his own eyes a *homo absconditus*. In pursuit of the promise, he finds he is in search of himself and comes to regard himself as an open question addressed to the future of God. Hence the man who hopes is of all people the one who does not stand harmoniously and concentrically in himself, but stands ex-centrically to himself in the *facultas standi extra se coram Deo*, as Luther called it. He is ahead of himself in hope in God's promise. The event of promise does not yet bring him to the haven of identity, but involves him in the tensions and differentiations of hope, of mission and of self-emptying. If revelation encounters him as promise, then it does not identify him by disregarding what is negative, but opens him to pain, patience and the 'dreadful power of the negative', as Hegel has said. It makes him ready to take the pain of love and of self-emptying upon himself in the Spirit of him who raised Jesus from the dead and who quickens the dead. 'Yet it is not the life which abhors death and keeps itself pure of corruption, but the life which endures it and maintains itself in the midst of it, that is the life of the spirit.' 'The power of the spirit is only so great as its outgoing, its depth only so deep as the extent to which in its expending it ventures to spread itself and to lose itself.'[1] Thus the promised identity of man leads into the differentiation of self-emptying.

[1] G. W. F. Hegel, *Phänomenologie des Geistes*, ed. J. Hoffmeister (Philosophische Bibliothek 114), 1949, pp. 29 and 15 (cf. ET by J. B. Baillie, *The Phenomenology of Miad*, 2nd ed., 1931, pp. 93 and 74).

He gains himself by abandoning himself. He finds life by taking death upon him. He attains to freedom by accepting the form of a servant. That is how the truth that points forward to the resurrection of the dead comes to him.

But if the event of promise in the resurrection identifies man by leading him to the emptying of himself, this experience of self is immediately bound up with a corresponding experience of the world. Man does not gain himself by distinguishing himself from 'the world', but by emptying himself into it. But in what way must the 'world' then be experienced? It cannot be taken as a rigid cosmos of established facts and eternal laws. For where there is no longer any possibility of anything new happening, there hope also comes to an end and loses all prospect of the realizing of what it hopes for. Only when the world itself is 'full of all kinds of possibilities' can hope become effective in love. 'To hope there belongs the knowledge that in the outside world life is as unfinished as in the Ego that works in that outside world.'[1] Thus hope has the chance of a meaningful existence only when reality itself is in a state of historic flux and when historic reality has room for open possibilities ahead. Christian hope is meaningful only when the world can be changed by him in whom this hope hopes, and is thus open to that for which this hope hopes; when it is full of all kinds of possibilities (possible for God) and open to the resurrection of the dead. If the world were a self-contained system of cause and effect, then hope could either regard this world as itself the fulfilment, or else in gnostic fashion transcend and reflect itself into the supra-worldly realm. That, however, would be to abandon itself.

On the ground of the promised future of the truth the world can be experienced as history. The eschatological sense of the event of promise in the resurrection of Christ awakes in remembrance and expectation our sense for history. Hence every view which sees the world as a self-contained cosmos, or history as a universal whole that contains and manifests the divine truth, is broken down and transposed into the eschatological key of 'not yet'. Our knowledge, as a knowledge of hope, has a transcendent and provisional character marked by promise and expectation, in virtue of which it recognizes the open horizon of the future of reality and thus preserves the finitude of human experience.

[1] E. Bloch, *Das Prinzip Hoffnung* I, 1959, p. 285.

To think God and history together on the ground of the event
of promise in the resurrection of Christ, does not mean to prove
God from the world or from history, but *vice versa* to show the
world to be history that is open to God and to the future. Christian theology will thus not be able to come to terms with, but
will have to free itself from, the cosmologico-mechanistic way
of thinking such as is found in the positivistic sciences – whether
in the positivism of the scientific disenchanting of the world,
by which the world not only becomes 'godless', as Max Weber
has said, but also becomes a world without alternatives, without possibilities and without any future, or in the factualized and
institutionalized relationships of the scientific civilization of
modern society, which in the same way is threatened with the
loss not only of its future but of its own historic character as
well. Theology will be able to free itself, however, only by breaking up this kind of thinking and these relationships and striving
to set them in the eschatological movement of history. It will
not be able to free itself from them by falling back upon a
romanticist glorification of reality. The 'firewood' does not
again become a 'forest', nor the 'tale of events' again become
'sacred history', and the traditions of the West do not again
become unequivocal links in the chain of historic tradition. The
experience of the world as history can hardly take the form of
again considering the experience of history either in terms of
fate, in that passivity in which we suffer birth and death, or in
terms of chance. 'The universal endeavour of human reason is
directed towards the abolition of chance', as W. Humboldt
already aptly remarked. The scientific and technical efforts of
the modern age have at least since the French revolution been
aimed at bringing about the end of this kind of history, the end
of the history of chance, of contingency, of surprise, crisis and
catastrophe. To demonstrate to this increasingly rounded
scientific and technical cosmos its own historic character does
not mean revealing to it the critical nature of its own self,
but exhibiting to it and to the men in it that history which is
experienced in the light of the promised future of the truth.
Both intellectual forms – the objectification of the world and the
subjectivity of existence – stand in contrast to *the* history which
is experienced in the light of the future of the truth. Hence for
Christian theology 'history' cannot mean that it has again to

proclaim the truth of God in combination with the old experiences of fate and chance, but that it has to give this world itself a place in the process that begins with the promise and is kept going by hope. The problem of history in the 'modern age' is presented not so much in terms of the difference between Greek glorification of the cosmos and the biblical hope in history, but rather in terms of the difference between a scientific and technical millenarianism, which seeks the end of history in history, on the one hand, and, on the other an eschatology of history, which arises from the event of promise in the resurrection, and for which the 'end of history' in the 'modern age' can no more be the promised and expected end than the 'modern age' (*Neuzeit*) itself can be the 'new age' (*neue Zeit*) in the apocalyptic sense – as this expression (*Neuzeit*) was surely meant to be. Positivism, which was originally intended by Auguste Comte to have a thoroughly millenarian sense, can therefore be given historic character only by being transcended and superseded by the new expectations of an eschatological outlook. This will reveal its historic form and significance and the finitude of its epistemological horizon.

Christian theology has one way in which it can prove its truth by reference to the reality of man and the reality of the world that concerns man – namely, by accepting the questionableness of human existence and the questionableness of reality as a whole and taking them up into that eschatological questionableness of human nature and the world which is disclosed by the event of promise. 'Threatened by death' and 'subjected to vanity' – that is the expression of our universal experience of existence and the world. 'In hope' – that is manifestly the way in which Christian theology takes up these questions and directs them to the promised future of God.

II

PROMISE AND HISTORY

IF WE WOULD trace out the Old Testament's peculiarly am-
biguous, unemphatic and yet widely broadcast observations on
'revelation' and turn them to good account for dogmatics, then
it is not advisable to set out from the assumption that every
man's existence, threatened as it is by chaos and transience,
leads him to ask after 'revelation', nor yet to start with the
question how the hidden God, the Origin and the Absolute,
becomes manifest to men estranged from him. Rather, it is
essential to let the Old Testament itself not only provide the
answers, but also pose the problem of revelation, before we draw
systematic conclusions. If this is to be attempted in the following
pages, it is of course impossible to enter into questions of a
detailed exegesis. But it will have to be a case of clarifying and
defining the concepts employed in exegesis. In so doing we shall
often come upon religious-historical ideas, and shall also have
to employ such ideas. That, however, is not intended to imply
any general religious-historical presuppositions. Our task is not
to take the various religious ideas and forms of belief and sub-
sume them under a general concept of religion. But the contours of what is meant by promise and hope stand out most
clearly in face of other religions and forms of belief which are
grappled with and contested, and for that reason they can best
be illumined in comparison and contrast.

I. EPIPHANY RELIGIONS AND FAITH IN TERMS
OF PROMISE

If we ask for a summary statement of the conclusions emerging from the study of the history of religion in Israel and the
surrounding oriental world, then the Old Testament materials

appear from this standpoint to be 'syncretistic documents'.
'Israel achieved a syncretism between the religion of the nomad
and of the Canaanite peasant. It is through this syncretism that
it became what it was in classical times.'[1] The term 'syncretism'
here calls for further clarification. It certainly cannot mean an
easy blend of disparate elements nor yet, of course, an alliance
between hostile brethren against a third, common enemy, as was
originally the case with the Cretans. It cannot even mean mere
intermixture, but is intended to express the process of struggle
between two mutually incompatible forms of faith. It is a
struggle which is kindled in various historic situations by various
matters about which conflict arises and, precisely from the
various tensions, we are enabled to recognize the peculiarity of
the contending parties. The exact nature of the two opposing
sides cannot at any point be defined in spatial or temporal, and
indeed hardly even in clearcut ideological terms. And yet the
process of struggle is apparent at every point, both in Israel's
conflict with its neighbours and also within the empirical Israel
itself. It can be seen specially clearly in specific historic situations. It can also be latent for centuries and obscured to the
point of being unrecognizable. While the 'peculiar religious
position' of Israel can consequently hardly be stated in terms
of a unique 'religion of Israel', it certainly does emerge in the
fact that such a process of tense struggle pervades its whole
history.

The definition of these tendencies of tension in general terms
of the history of culture and of religion has to my mind been
most clearly stated by Victor Maag, following Martin Buber
and others. He sees the tension in the fact that in the Israel of
Palestine the vectoral and kinetic elements of the old nomad
religion and the static elements of the peasant religion of
Canaan meet each other. 'Nomadic religion is a religion of
promise. The nomad does not live within the cycle of seed-
time and harvest, but in the world of migration.'[2] 'This in-
spiring, guiding, protecting God of the nomads differs quite
fundamentally in various respects from the gods of the agrarian
peoples. The gods of the nations are locally bound. The transmigration God of the nomads, however, is not bound terri-

---

[1] V. Maag, 'Malkût Jhwh', *VT Suppl.* VII (Congress Volume: Oxford 1959),
1960, p. 137.   [2] *Ibid.*, p. 140.

torially and locally. He journeys along with them, is himself on
the move.'[1] The result of this is a different understanding of
existence: 'Here existence is felt as history. This God leads men
to a future which is not mere repetition and confirmation of the
present, but is the goal of the events that are now taking place.
The goal gives meaning to the journey and its distresses; and
today's decision to trust in the call of God is a decision pregnant with future. This is the essence of promise in the light of
transmigration.'[2]

No doubt Maag's view of the nomad religion of promise in
contrast to the mythical and magical religion of peasant culture
contains typical ideal elements, but it does make intelligible
the tension in which Israel found itself, and – what is still more
important – it gives significance to the question how and by
what means it came about that when Israel passed from the
nomadic and semi-nomadic life to the settled life of Canaan it
did not, like all peoples and tribes on crossing this first cultural
frontier of human life, abandon the nomad religion and the God
of promise in favour of the epiphany gods that sanctify land,
life and culture, but was able to take the occupation of the land
and the fact of building and dwelling in the land and incorporate them in the original religion of promise as a new experience of history. The peculiar thing about the Israel of
history appears to lie neither in its nomadic origin, which it
had in common with others, nor in the occupation of the land
and the transition to agricultural and municipal life, which it
likewise had in common with others, but in the fact which
causes this process of conflict and is manifested in various
situations – the fact that the Israelite tribes took the wilderness
God of promise with them from the wilderness along with the
corresponding understanding of existence and the world, retained them in the land amid the totally new experiences of
agrarian life, and endeavoured to undergo and to master
the new experiences in the land in the light of the God of
promise.

The process of conflict which this entailed is seen very clearly
in the relationship to God, and here in turn in the ideas of the
appearing and revealing of God. The oldest usage, and one
presumably common to the whole orient, is found where the

[1] *Ibid.*, pp. 139f.   [2] *Ibid.*, p. 140.

deity 'discloses himself'.[1] The Niphal of *ra'ah* is a *terminus techni-cus* for such hierophanies. These are originally bound to a spe-cific place, which is then honoured in the cultus as a place of the divine epiphany. In Exodus 3.2 we find an expression of this kind: 'And the *mal'ak Jahwe* appeared unto him in a flame of fire out of the midst of the bush.' The land of oriental culture is full to the brim of such appearances through which places are sanctified to become places of the cultus. Stones, waters, trees, groves, mountains, etc., can become the bearers of hierophanies. There arise cult legends which provide the aetiology of such sacred places and rituals which bestow divine hallowing on the land round about and on those who dwell on it and cultivate it. Such places of the cultus are gateways, as it were, through which the gods come to hallow the land, and the men who dwell upon it experience the sanctifying of their cultivation of the land. Men thus 'live as close as possible to the gods' (M. Eliade).[2] In the cultus at the place of the hierophany their culture is secured against chaos by being anchored in the original sacred event of the cosmogony, or by being connected with the sacred centre of the world. Constructive enterprise and residential life is sanctified and protected by means of mythical, magical and ritual relationships of correspondence with the eternal, the original, the holy, and the cosmic order.

In corresponding ways time, whose passage discloses the horrors of chaos, is ordered and sanctified by means of sacred festivals which celebrate the epiphany, the arrival of the gods, and so make men 'contemporaries of the gods'. Time the de-stroyer is regenerated by means of periodic return to the time of the first beginning. To the sanctification conferred at the places of epiphany upon the area in which man lives and builds, menaced as it is by chaos, there corresponds the sanctification of time in the cyclic recurrence of the epiphany of the gods in times of festival.

[1] R. Rendtorff, 'Die Offenbarungsvorstellungen im Alten Israel', in *Offenbarung als Geschichte*, 1961, pp. 23f.

[2] M. Eliade, *The Sacred and the Profane: the Nature of Religion*, ET by W. R. Trask, 1961, pp. 24ff., 91ff.

[3] W. F. Otto, *Die Gestalt und das Sein*, 1955, p. 255: 'The festival always means the return of a world hour at which the most ancient, most venerable and most glorious state is here again; a return of the golden age in which our ancestors had such close intercourse with the gods and the spirits. This is the point of festive exaltation which, wherever there are real festivals, is different from all other gravity and all other joy.'

Whether men polytheistically worship a number of local
deities, or pantheistically find all times and places full of the
divine (Thales: πάντα πλήρη θεῶν),[1] whether the invisible,
the original divine world, becomes epiphanous through a series
of intermediate authorities, whether princes set up as θεὸς
ἐπιφανής or teachers and miracle-workers as θεῖος ἀνήρ, or
whether this divine, absolute eternal Origin is conceived as
becoming epiphanous through itself – all this makes no essential
difference here, but is a continuation and sublimation of this
epiphany religion which revolves around the θεὸς ἐπιφανής.
This epiphany religion forms the presupposition and the abiding foundation of the natural theology of Greek philosophy of
religion, and of oriental philosophies of religion. It gives rise
to what is here the decisive question of the 'self-disclosing',
'appearing', 'revealing' of the divine. It is here important to
see that these epiphanies have their point in themselves, in their
coming about. For where they come about, there comes the
hallowing of place, of time and of men in that act in which
man's ever-threatened culture is granted correspondence with,
and participation in, the eternal divine cosmos. The threat to
human existence from the forces of chaos and of annihilation is
overcome through the epiphany of the eternal present. Man's
being comes into congruence with eternal being, understands
itself in correspondence and participation as protected by the
presence of the eternal.

Now the striking thing is, that Israel was but little concerned
to understand the essential meaning of the 'appearances' of
Yahweh in terms of such hallowing of places and times, but for
Israel the 'appearing' of God is immediately linked up with the
uttering of a word of divine promise.[2] Where Yahweh 'appears', it is manifestly not in the first instance a question of

---

[1] On the fundamental significance of this statement for the religion and philosophy of ancient Greece, cf. W. Jaeger, *Die Theologie der frühen griechischen Denker*,
1953, pp. 31ff.
[2] R. Rendtorff, *op. cit.*, p. 24. Likewise also W. Zimmerli, ' "Offenbarung" im
Alten Testament', *EvTh* 22, 1962, p. 16: 'The sacredness of a place is supposed to
be legitimized through the account of the appearing of the deity at this place. Then,
however, we find in the Old Testament a development in which it is increasingly
only the mainstay of the ἱερὸς λόγος that remains – less and less weight attaches to
the sensually perceptible appearing of Yahweh, but instead the divine word of
promise is brought out ever more fully as the real content of the scenes of revelation. The emphasis is shifted away from the sensually perceptible appearance, the
manifestation of Yahweh, on to the announcement of his action.'

cultivating the place and time of his appearance. The point of
the appearances to particular men in particular situations lies
in the promise. The promise, however, points away from the
appearances in which it is uttered, into the as yet unrealized
future which it announces. The point of the appearance then
lies not in itself, but in the promise which becomes audible in
it, and in the future to which it points. In the various strata of
the tradition of such appearances of promise, the concomitant
circumstances of epiphany then actually take second place in
Israel's faith to the call and the pointer to the future. With that,
the concept of revelation found in the epiphany religions is
transformed. It is subordinated to the event of promise. Revelation is understood from the standpoint of the promise contained
in the revelation. Here Yahweh's revelation manifestly does
not serve to bring the ever-threatened present into congruence
with his eternity. On the contrary, its effect is that the hearers
of the promise become incongruous with the reality around
them, as they strike out in hope towards the promised new
future. The result is not the religious sanctioning of the present,
but a break-away from the present towards the future. If the
mythical and magical cults of the epiphany religions have the
purpose of annihilating the terrors of history by anchoring life
in the original sacred event, and if in tendency they are 'anti-
historical' (M. Eliade),[1] then the God who gives his promises
in the event of promise is one who makes possible for the very
first time the feeling for history in the category of the future, and
consequently has a 'historicizing' effect.[2] This tendency to run
counter to the mythical world by understanding epiphany and
revelation from the standpoint of the event of promise is
manifestly the reason why the words for 'revelation' are employed in the Old Testament so ambiguously and unsystem-
atically. Yahweh is not in this sense an 'apparitional God'.
The sense and purpose of his 'appearances' lies not in themselves, but in the promise and its future.

The effects of the struggle in the history of Israel between
faith in terms of promise and religion in terms of epiphany have
been brought out by Old Testament research at many points.

[1] M. Eliade, *The Myth of the Eternal Return*, ET by W. R. Trask, 1955, p. 152.
[2] G. von Rad, *Theologie des Alten Testamentes* II, 1960, p. 117 (ET by D. M. G.
Stalker: *Old Testament Theology*, 1965, p. 104).

Where the bands of Israel enter the land, they receive the land and the new experiences of settled life as 'fulfilment of the promise', as realization of the pledge given in the wilderness by the God of promise who had caused their fathers to journey into it. Life amid the fulness and increase of their own people is like-wise understood in the light of the promise. Thus the assurance of their own existence is attained through historic remembrance of the previous promise of the God who guided their nomad fathers, and the gift of land and people is seen as the visibly maintained faithfulness of Yahweh. This is an essentially different assurance of existence from what Israel found in the land and fertility cults of Palestine. Land and life are not brought into congruence with the gods by means of an epi-phany religion, but are understood as a piece of history in the vast course of the history of promise.[1]

The cyclic annual festivals of nature religion which Israel found waiting for it and duly took over, are subjected to an important 'historicizing'. They are interpreted in terms of the historic data of the history of promise.[2]

The mythical and magical rituals which establish the above-mentioned relationship of correspondence between threatened human existence and the protecting divine being are 'futurized', i.e. they are interpreted in terms of the future of the divine promise. V. Maag has pointed this out in the case of the rituals of the kingdom cult of Jerusalem.[3] What by their origin were magical formulae are integrated into the divine promise for the future. The expression 'eschatology' which is employed at this point for the new sense in which the mythical and magical formulae are re-interpreted, is rightly a disputed term, since it normally means the 'last' things and not merely 'future' things.

---

[1] W. Zimmerli, 'Verheissung und Erfüllung', *EvTh* 12, 1952, pp. 39ff.

[2] G. von Rad, *op. cit.*, pp. 117ff. (ET pp. 104ff.).

[3] V. Maag, *op. cit.*, p. 150: 'When the ritual of Jerusalem spoke of the king who would bring world peace, then the heart of the former nomad still heard this in the categories of expectation and understood it in the same way as the ancestral pro-mises. Thus what was by origin a magical formula became a divine promise for the future.' His observation on p. 114 is also interesting: 'What order is in this world, was settled by the cosmogonic gods once for all at the start. The myth and ritual of the New Year festival provide the most forceful sanction conceivable for what has positive existence and validity in state and society. This static positivism knows no new horizons towards which a people could be led, no God who is on the way to letting men see what they have never yet seen. . . . To a positivism of this kind, however, Yahweh never really submitted, even though court and temple circles naturally also tried to impose it on him.'

For that reason it will be better to refer to the basic character
of a religion of promise. In this we could find the continuing
source and driving force of such re-interpretations in these
stages of the history of Israel. As it is impossible to find the
source of 'eschatology' in the empty heart that has experienced
disappointment with cult and ritual, so it is equally impossible
to speak of eschatology of the nomads. But it might well be
that the faith which lives in terms of promise could prove to
be the *primum movens* which enabled Israel, or at least specific
circles in the empirical Israel, to master the situations of the
land settlement and later to master the situations of world
history. The whole force of promise, and of faith in terms of
promise, is essentially to keep men on the move in a tense
inadaequatio rei et intellectus as long as the *promissio* which governs
the *intellectus* has not yet found its answer in reality. It is in
promise, which keeps the hoping mind in a 'not yet' which
transcends all experience and history, that we find the ground
for the breakdown of the mythical and magical relations of
correspondence, for the 'historicizing' of the nature festivals in
terms of the data of the history of promise, and for the futuriz-
ing of their content in terms of the future of the promise. It is
from promise that there arises that element of unrest which allows of no coming to terms with a present that is unfulfilled.
Under the guiding star of promise this reality is not experienced
as a divinely stabilized cosmos, but as history in terms of moving
on, leaving things behind and striking out towards new horizons as yet unseen. The real question now is whether and how
experiences of a new kind in the occupation of the land and
later in the conflicts of world history are mastered by faith in
the promise, how they are incorporated into the promise that
transcends every present, and how the promise is expounded
and unravelled in these experiences.

2. THE WORD OF PROMISE

If in the word promise we have before us a key-word of
Israel's 'religion of expectation', then it must now be explained
what we have to understand by 'promise' and more specifically
by the 'promise of (the guide-)God'.[1]

[1] For the expression 'guide-God' cf. M. Buber, *Königtum Gottes*, 2nd ed., 1936,
p. xi; *The Prophetic Faith*, ET by C. Witton Davies, 1949, p. 10.

(*a*) A promise is a declaration which announces the coming of a reality that does not yet exist. Thus promise sets man's heart on a future history in which the fulfilling of the promise is to be expected. If it is a case of a divine promise, then that indicates that the expected future does not have to develop within the framework of the possibilities inherent in the present, but arises from that which is possible to the God of the promise. This can also be something which by the standard of present experience appears impossible.[1]

(*b*) The promise binds man to the future and gives him a sense for history. It does not give him a sense for world history in general, nor yet for the historic character of human existence as such, but it binds him to its own peculiar history. Its future is not the vague goal of possible change, nor the hope aroused by the idea of possible change; it is not openness towards coming events as such. The future which it discloses is made possible and determined by the promised fulfilment. It is in the first instance always a question here of Buber's 'hopes of history'. The promise takes man up into its own history in hope and obedience, and in so doing stamps his existence with a historic character of a specific kind.

(*c*) The history which is initiated and determined by promise does not consist in cyclic recurrence, but has a definite trend towards the promised and outstanding fulfilment. This irreversible direction is not determined by the urge of vague forces or by the emergence of laws of its own, but by the word of direction that points us to the free power and the faithfulness of God. It is not evolution, progress and advance that separate time into yesterday and tomorrow, but the word of promise cuts into events and divides reality into one reality which is passing and can be left behind, and another which must be expected and sought. The meaning of past and the meaning of future comes to light in the word of promise.

(*d*) If the word is a word of promise, then that means that this word has not yet found a reality congruous with it, but that on the contrary it stands in contradiction to the reality open to experience now and heretofore. It is only for that reason that the word of promise can give rise to the doubt that

[1] For what follows cf. the definitions of promise by W. Zimmerli, 'Verheissung und Erfüllung', *EvTh* 12, 1952, pp. 38ff.

measures the word by the standard of given reality. And it is only for that reason that this word can give rise to the faith that measures present reality by the standard of the word. 'Future' is here a designation of that reality in which the word of promise finds its counterpart, its answer and its fulfilment, in which it discovers or creates a reality which accords with it and in which it comes to rest.

(*e*) The word of promise therefore always creates an interval of tension between the uttering and the redeeming of the promise. In so doing it provides man with a peculiar area of freedom to obey or disobey, to be hopeful or resigned. The promise institutes this period and obviously stands in correspondence with what happens in it. This, as W. Zimmerli has illuminatingly pointed out, distinguishes the promise from the prophecies of a Cassandra and differentiates the resulting expectation of history from belief in fate.[1]

(*f*) If the promise is not regarded abstractly apart from the God who promises, but its fulfilment is entrusted directly to God in his freedom and faithfulness, then there can be no burning interest in constructing a hard and fast juridical system of historic necessities according to a schema of promise and fulfilment – neither by demonstrating the functioning of such a schema in the past nor by making calculations for the future. Rather, the fulfilments can very well contain an element of newness and surprise over against the promise as it was received. That is why the promise also does not fall to pieces along with the historical circumstances or the historical thought forms in which it was received, but can transform itself – by interpretation – without losing its character of certainty, of expectation and of movement. If they are *God's* promises, then God must also be regarded as the subject of their fulfilment.

(*g*) The peculiar character of the Old Testament promises can be seen in the fact that the promises were not liquidated by the history of Israel – neither by disappointment nor by fulfilment – but that on the contrary Israel's experience of history gave them a constantly new and wider interpretation. This aspect comes to light when we ask how it came about that the tribes of Israel did not proceed to change their gods on the occupation

[1] W. Zimmerli, *op. cit.*, p. 44.

of the promised land, but the wilderness God of promise remained their God in Canaan. Actually, the ancestral promises
are fulfilled in the occupation of the land and the multiplication
of the people, and the wilderness God of promise makes himself superfluous to the extent that his promises pass into fulfilment. The settled life to which they have attained in the land
has little more to do with the God of promise on the journey
through the wilderness. For the mastering of the agrarian
culture the local gods are to hand. It could of course be said
that the ancestral promises regarding the land have now been
fulfilled and liquidated but that, for example, the promises of
guidance and protection for the hosts of Israel in the holy wars
continue and are still live issues. But it could also be said that
the God who is recognized in his promises remains superior to
any fulfilment that can be experienced, because in every fulfilment the promise, and what is still contained in it, does not yet
become wholly congruent with reality and thus there always
remains an <u>overspill</u>. The fulfilments in the occupation of the
land do not fulfil the promise in the sense that they liquidate it
like a cheque that is cashed and lock it away among the documents of a glorious past. The 'fulfilments' are taken as expositions, confirmations and expansions of the promise. The greater
the fulfilments become, the greater the promise obviously also
becomes in the memory of the expositor at the various levels of
the tradition in which it is handed down. There is no trace
here of what could be called the 'melancholy of fulfilment'.
This peculiar fact of the promise that goes on beyond experiences of fulfilment could also be illustrated by the traces the
promise leaves in the hopes and desires of men. It is ultimately
not the delays in the fulfilment and in the parousia that bring
men disappointment. 'Disappointing experiences' of this kind
are superficial and trite and come of regarding the promise in
legalistic abstraction apart from the God who promises. On the
contrary, it is every experience of fulfilment which, to the extent
that we reflect on it as an experience behind us, ultimately contains a disappointment. Man's hopes and longings and desires,
once awakened by specific promises, stretch further than any
fulfilment that can be conceived or experienced. However
limited the promises may be, once we have caught in them a
whiff of the future, we remain restless and urgent, seeking and

searching beyond all experiences of fulfilment, and the latter leave us an aftertaste of sadness. The 'not yet' of expectation surpasses every fulfilment that is already taking place now. Hence every reality in which a fulfilment is already taking place now, becomes the confirmation, exposition and liberation of a greater hope. If we would use this as a help towards understanding the 'expanding and broadening history of promise',[1] if we ask the reason for the abiding overplus of promise as compared with history, then we must again abandon every abstract schema of promise and fulfilment. We must then have recourse to the theological interpretation of this process: the reason for the overplus of promise and for the fact that it constantly overspills history lies in the inexhaustibility of the God of promise, who never exhausts himself in any historic reality but comes 'to rest' only in a reality that wholly corresponds to him.[2]

3. THE EXPERIENCE OF HISTORY

Beneath the star of the promise of God it becomes possible to experience reality as 'history'. The stage for what can be experienced, remembered and expected as 'history' is set and filled, revealed and fashioned, by promise.

The promises of God disclose the horizons of history – whereby 'horizon', as it is aptly put by H. G. Gadamer, is not to be understood as 'a rigid boundary', but as 'a thing towards which we are moving, and which moves along with us'.[3] Israel lived within these moving horizons of promise and experienced reality within the fields of tension they involve. Even when the period of nomadic wanderings ended in Palestine, this mode of experiencing, remembering and expecting reality as history still remained and characterized this people's wholly peculiar relation to time. The realm of Palestinian culture did not turn time for them into a figure of cyclic recurrence, but on the contrary, a historic experience of time repeatedly asserted

[1] G. von Rad, 'Typologische Auslegung des Alten Testamentes', *EvTh* 12, 1952, pp. 25f.
[2] G. von Rad, 'Es ist noch eine Ruhe vorhanden dem Volke Gottes' (1933) in *Ges. Studien zum Alten Testament* (Theologische Bücherei 8), pp. 101ff. (ET: 'There Remains Still a Rest for the People of God', *The Problem of the Hexateuch and Other Essays*, 1966, pp. 94ff.).
[3] H. G. Gadamer, *Wahrheit und Methode*, 1960, pp. 231f., 286ff.

itself prevailingly over an unhistoric experience of space and turned the occupied areas (*bewohnte Räume*) of the land into temporal periods (*Zeiträume*) of an all-embracing history.

What could here be experienced as 'history' in the potential changes of reality always reached as far as the promises of God stretched men's memories and expectations. 'Israel's history existed only in so far as God accompanied her, and it is only this time-span which can properly be described as her history.'[1] This fact of God's accompanying his people, however, was always seen within the area of tension between a manifest promise on the one hand and the expected redeeming of this promise on the other. It was within the span of this tension that history became of interest to Israel. 'Only where Yahweh had revealed himself in his word and acts did history exist for Israel.'[2] This means, however, that the experience of reality as history was made possible for Israel by the fact that God was revealed to Israel in his promises and that Israel saw the revealing of God again and again in the uttering of his promises.

Now, if events are thus experienced within the horizon of remembered and expected promises, then they are experienced as truly 'historic' events. They do not then have only the accidental, individual and relative character which we normally ascribed to historic events, but then they have always at the same time also an unfinished and provisional character that points forwards. Not only words of promise, but also the events themselves, in so far as they are experienced as 'historic' events within the horizon of promise and hope, bear the mask of something that is still outstanding, not yet finalized, not yet realized. 'Here everything is in motion, the accounts never balance, and fulfilment unexpectedly gives rise in turn to another promise of something greater still. Here nothing has its ultimate meaning in itself, but is always an earnest of something still greater.'[3] The overspill of promise means that the facts of history can never be regarded as processes complete in themselves which have had their day and can manifest their

---

[1] G. von Rad, *Theologie des Alten Testamentes* II, 1960, p. 120 (ET p. 106).
[2] G. von Rad, 'Offene Fragen im Umkreis einer Theologie des Alten Testamentes', *TLZ* 88, 1963, col. 409.
[3] G. von Rad, 'Typologische Auslegung', *op. cit.*, p. 29, cf. also p. 30: 'Thus in the presentation of a fact there is very often something that transcends what actually happened.'

mmg. of his events were 'complete' but inexhaustible; ——— - why - until this

own truth by themselves. They must be understood as stages on a road that goes further and elements in a process that continues. Hence the events that are 'historically' remembered in this way do not yet have their ultimate truth in themselves, but receive it only from the goal that has been promised by God and is to be expected from him. Then, however, the events that are thus experienced as 'historic' events give a foretaste of the promised future. The overspill of promise means that they have always a provisional character. They contain the note of '*provisio*', i.e. they intimate and point forward to something which does not yet exist in its fulness in themselves. Hence the history that is thus experienced and transmitted forces every new present to analysis and to interpretation. Events that have been experienced in this way 'must' be passed on, because in them something is seen which is determinative also for future generations. They cast their shadow, or shed their light, on the way ahead. On the other hand they may also be freely interpreted and actualized by each new present, since they are never so firmly established that we could restrict ourselves merely to ascertaining what they once were.[1]

The ancient historic traditions give expression to experiences which Israel had of its God and his promises. But if these promises reach out into that future which is still ahead of the present, then the historic narratives concerned cannot merely narrate experiences of the past. Rather, the whole narrative and representation of this past will lead us to open ourselves and our present to that same future. The reality of history (*Wirklichkeit der Geschichte*) is narrated within the horizon of the history of the working (*Wirkungsgeschichte*) of God's promises. The stories of Israelite history – the histories of the patriarchs, of the wilderness, of David – are treated as themes pregnant with future. Even where the historic tradition passes over into legendary tradition, the peculiarly Israelite tradition is still dominated by the hopes and expectations kindled by Yahweh's promises. Since the history that was once experienced contains an element that transcends history in its pastness and is pregnant with future, and to the extent that this is so, two things

[1] On this point cf. H. W. Wolff, 'Das Geschichtsverständnis der alttestamentlichen Prophetie', *EvTh* 20, 1960, pp. 218ff., and G. von Rad's comment in 'Offene Fragen', *op. cit.*, pp. 413f.

follow: first, this history must again and again be recalled and brought to mind in the present, and secondly, it must be so expounded to the present that the latter can derive from history an understanding of itself and its future path and can also find its own place in the history of the working of God's promises.

The peculiarity of Israelite accounts of history as 'historiography conditioned by faith in the promise'[1] is particularly outstanding in comparison with the accounts of history in other peoples and other religions. 'In the Greek and Roman mythologies, the past is re-presented as an everlasting foundation. In the Hebrew and Christian view of history the past is a promise to the future; consequently, the interpretation of the past becomes a prophecy in reverse.'[2]

The history of Israel shows again and again that the promises to which Israel owes its existence prove amid all the upheavals of history to be a *continuum* in which Israel was able to recognize the faithfulness of its God.[3] It could perhaps be said that the promises enter into fulfilment in events, yet are not completely resolved in any event, but there remains an overspill that points to the future. That is why reality, as it comes and is awaited and as it passes and is left behind, is experienced as history, and not as a cosmic and ever-recurring constant. It is experienced not in the epiphany of the eternal present, but in expectation of the manifestation and fulfilment of a promised future. That is why the present itself, too, is not the present of the Absolute – a present with which and in which we could abide – but is, so to speak, the advancing front line of time as directed purposefully towards its goal in the moving horizon of promise. If the promise of God is the condition on which it becomes possible to have historic experience of reality, then the language of historic facts is the language of promise – otherwise events can be called neither 'historic' nor 'eloquent'. The promises of God initiate history for Israel and retain the control in all historic experiences.

Where we abstract from the process of promise, historic events are robbed of the outlook that makes them 'historic'. Where the promises lose their power and significance as initiators

---

[1] W. Zimmerli, 'Verheissung und Erfüllung', *op. cit.*, p. 50.
[2] K. Löwith, *Meaning in History*, 1949, p. 6.
[3] H. W. Wolff, 'Das Kerygma des Jahwisten', *EvTh* 24, 1964, p. 97.

of history, there the events of history are rounded off, as it
were, to become facts of the past, processes complete in themselves. They are then treated and presented in the light of other
outlooks. Where God's revelation is no longer seen in promise
and mission, we can, for example, reflect upon the eternal, immortal and absolute being of the Deity. Then historic events
belong within the sphere of transience. They are then no longer
provisional events that point to the future of promise, but
transient and relative events that reflect the eternal intransience
of the Deity. Then there can in principle be 'nothing new under
the sun'. A history of such facts can then be contemplated as a
succession of completed processes, a series of images of eternal
ideas. In what they have been, we then seek to discover eternal
Being. In their coherent working we then seek to discover eternal laws. We have then, however, to look around for other conditions for the possibility of perceiving reality as history. Yet
here the question constantly arises, whether this other picture of
history and the designations derived from it are really adequate
to the understanding of history in a historic sense and can stand
theological and philosophical comparison with Israel's experience of history, conditioned as it was by faith in the promise
and determined by hope.

The very use of the term 'fact', 'divine fact of history', is
incapable of expressing what Israel experienced in history. For
this term implies a concept of being, of absoluteness, of immutability and finality, which refuses to be combined with
promise, hope and future, and therefore also with 'history'.[1]

Now it has also been observed that very many of the prophets' words about the future, especially their political predictions, did not come to pass in the way they were originally
meant, and that history has thus outrun, and thereby anti-

---

[1] The use of the expression 'divine fact of history' in G. von Rad's *Theologie des
Alten Testamentes* is at many points unclear and allows manifold interpretations. If
according to vol. I, p. 112 (ET p. 106) the 'faith of Israel is fundamentally grounded
in a theological view of history', i.e. 'it knows itself founded on facts of history and
knows itself fashioned and refashioned by facts in which it saw the hand of Jahweh
at work', then it is surely, as von Rad himself goes on to emphasize, the 'faith of
Israel' for which these 'facts' are pregnant with future because of the divine promises in which they are interwoven – it is not such an understanding of the facts
as results from critical historical examination. If according to vol. II, p. 117 (ET
p. 104) the 'historic acts by which Jahweh founded the community are absolute',
then this surely means that because they have the character of promise they over-
reach their temporal transience and move into the future – it does not mean absoluteness in the sense of intransience.

quated, many words of promise. And this has been made a reason for no longer understanding history from the standpoint of promise but seeing in history a reality which overreaches these words of promise. 'History has outrun the words.'[1] Is it possible where the Old Testament is concerned to speak in principle of 'history's remaining short of the promise',[2] and thus of expectations which again and again transcend the new situations of history and make them 'historic', or does 'history outrun the promises' and does the consciousness of Israel already show some indication of a view of history that no longer has promise, hope and mission for the future as the condition that makes it possible?

Now it is certain that apart from the promises that fell by the way in the course of history, there are also and above all others to which Israel owed its existence as 'Israel' in a theological and a historic sense, in the constant recalling of which and the ever new embracing and interpretation of which Israel consequently found its identity and continuity. These include not only the 'basic promises' of Exodus and the Sinaitic covenant – 'I am the Lord thy God'[3] – but for example also the promises to Abraham.[4] It cannot be said that mummified formulae of promise were capable of mastering new experiences of history, neither can it be said that some kind of numinous history as it ran mysteriously on rendered the promises obsolete. The process of word and history surely went on in such a way that men were neither concerned to discover from history the formal confirmation of the ancient promises, nor yet to take the promises merely as interpretations of history. Rather, the really new experiences, such as the occupation of Canaan and then later on the collapse of the kingdom, could be taken as explications of the traditional promises by means of new acts of Yahweh, and the new events could be understood in the light of the attested promise of Yahweh's faithfulness. Thus we find promise and history in a process of transformation, in which the traditional accounts of the promises took their place in the mastering of the new experiences of history, while the new experiences of history were understood as transformations and expositions of the promises. The result of these processes of

---

[1] W. Pannenberg, *Offenbarung als Geschichte*, postscript to the 2nd ed., p. 132.
[2] W. Zimmerli, ' "Offenbarung" im Alten Testament', *EvTh* 22, 1962, p. 31.
[3] Thus F. Baumgärtel, *Verheissung*, 1952, p. 133.
[4] H. W. Wolff, 'Das Kerygma des Jahwisten', *op. cit.*, pp. 95ff.

transformation, however, was never the emergence of views of history that were no longer based on promises and no longer bound to them. Never did men reflect on the overwhelming power of history and the powerlessness of the out-dated promises, and abandon the rest of the future to other powers than the God of promise. The tension of promise and fulfilment was not left behind by the simple progress of Israel's history, but was much more strongly creative of Israel's historic progress. As a result of those experiences of history for which the old election traditions were no match, the tension was actually heightened in the prophets. Only, this tension which has its origin in promise and its goal in fulfilment must not be represented in too schematic a form. Between promise and fulfilment there is a whole variety of intermediate links and processes, such as exposition, development, validation, assertion, renewal, etc. Between promise and fulfilment stretches the process of the history of the working of the word – an event of tradition, in which the promise is transmitted to coming generations in interpreted and actualized form, and every new present is exposed to the promised future in hope and obedience. This event of tradition, which creates continuity amid the changes of history, cannot already be taken in itself as a profounder concept of history. The process of tradition, in which we recall history and undergo new historic experiences, is understandable only in the light of the *tradendum* or object to be transmitted – viz., the promise and the future prospect it implies for events.

4. REVELATION AND KNOWLEDGE OF GOD

How does God become knowable, if his revelations are essentially promises which open up new, historic and eschatological horizons for the future? How have we to understand the revelation of God, if election, covenant, promise and mission belong not merely accidentally but essentially to the event of revelation?

For W. Zimmerli,[1] revelation means 'self-presentation', 'self-representation' and 'self-disclosure' of God. This, he finds, is indicated by the recurring

[1] Cf. W. Zimmerli, *Gottes Offenbarung. Gesammelte Aufsätze* (Theologische Bücherei 19), 1963, and his essay ' "Offenbarung" im Alten Testament' in *EvTh* 22, 1962, pp. 15–31.

formula, 'And they shall know that I am Yahweh.'[1] In the strangely awkward formulation of this statement about the knowledge of God, the place of the object is taken by a noun clause in which Yahweh's 'I' appears as subject. This means that knowledge of God is related not to a predicable object (he – Yahweh), but manifestly to an event of revelation in which Yahweh remains the subject even of the process of knowing. Zimmerli accordingly calls the stereotype phrase *'ani Yahweh'* a 'formula of self-presentation' and finds in it the standard view of revelation in the Old Testament.

But (1) how does he understand and interpret the exegetical findings in regard to this constantly recurring formula? This self-disclosure of Yahweh is a 'word of revelation in which the "I" discloses itself in its "I"-character'.[2] 'Self-presentation' means 'emergence in the unmistakably unique "I"-mystery expressed in the proper name.'[3] 'A hitherto unnamed person emerges from his unknownness by making it possible to know and name him by his own name. The emphasis lies on the naming of Yahweh's proper name, which contains within it the whole fulness and glory of him who here names himself.'[4] In the proper name declared by his own self lies the guarantee that the 'I' is this unmistakably individual person.[5] The declaring of the name is – as also in profane analogies: 'I am Joseph', 'I am David' – not a predicative statement but an act of self-disclosure, 'a thoroughly personal event'.[6] It is 'God proclaiming himself' in his name as subject.[7]

(2) With this personalistic understanding of the self-revelation of God, what is the meaning of 'history'? History is then a 'creaturely tool in the free hand of God',[8] the 'place of the knowledge of God',[9] the 'place where the truth of his word of revelation becomes knowable in its execution'.[10] Events, where Yahweh appoints speakers to proclaim the name of Yahweh over them, can become 'address in bodily form' to man. Then they become events which seek to be heard in our own day as a summons in the name of Yahweh and to be answered in obedience.[11] History is then 'a penultimate thing' and has only a 'subservient function' as compared with the personal self-demonstration of Yahweh.[12]

(3) What is then the goal of the promises of God? If his self-revelation is understood in such personal terms, then the things announced in the promises obviously lose their importance. 'Rather, this formula (*viz.*, the formula of self-presentation) brings out how completely the material content is swallowed up by the sole emergence of the "I".'[13] 'Yahweh himself is the future of which the prophets speak.'[14] 'Everything that Yahweh has to tell his people and to announce to them appears as a development of the basic declaration: I am Yahweh.'[15] The history of the promise then serves towards ever profounder knowledge of God on man's part.

[1] *Gottes Offenbarung*, p. 16.   [2] ' "Offenbarung" im AT', *op. cit.*, p. 22.
[3] *Ibid.*, p. 21.   [4] *Gottes Offenbarung*, p. 11.
[5] ' "Offenbarung" im AT', *op. cit.*, p. 21.   [6] *Gottes Offenbarung*, p. 124.
[7] *Ibid.*, p. 126.   [8] ' "Offenbarung" im AT', *op. cit.*, p. 28.
[9] *Ibid.*, p. 29.   [10] *Gottes Offenbarung*, p. 22.
[11] ' "Offenbarung" im AT', *op. cit.*, pp. 28f.
[12] *Ibid.*, p. 29.   [13] *Ibid.*, p. 21.
[14] 'Verheissung und Erfüllung', *EvTh* 12, 1952, p. 44.
[15] *Gottes Offenbarung*, p. 20.

Here several questions arise. With these personalistic descriptions of the revelation of God, which doubtless bring out the indisputable lordship of God even in the process of knowing, is it possible to avoid a transcendental misunderstanding of the self-revelation of God?

If the words of promise are the real content of the Old Testament scenes of revelation, can we then turn things the other way round and make the personal epiphany of Yahweh as Subject the real content of the scenes that constitute the history of the promise? If the revelation of God is understood in such a personal way, why *must* the self-presentation of Yahweh find its explication in the word of promise? But if promise is constitutive for the revealing of Yahweh, does the formula of self-presentation not then contain more than merely a self-disclosing of the mystery of a person – namely, a pledge of faithfulness which points to events to come?[1] Then, however, the history instituted by the promise of Yahweh and by his oath of faithfulness would not be in itself indifferent – the mere place and material for the knowledge of God. Then the name of Yahweh would not merely disclose the secret of his person, but would at the same time also be a name of pilgrimage and a name of promise, which shows what can be relied upon in the darkness of the future. All this Zimmerli says as well,[2] but the personalistic descriptions of the self-revelation of God seem to stand in a certain tension with the recognized theological significance of the promise. Revelation of Yahweh surely stands not only at the beginning of the history of promise, with the result that the promises and commandments are given in his 'name', but there is revelation also in that future to which the promises point and towards which the commandments set us on the way. There, however, it is not only the personal name of Yahweh that will be revealed, but his divinity and glory will be revealed in all lands, so that the ancient promise 'I am Yahweh' will be fulfilled in the '*kabod Yahweh*', the glory of God, that fulfils all things. But then the things announced in the promises become identical with the fact that the one and only divinity of God is glorified in all things. That 'Yahweh himself' is the future of which the prophets speak, would then have to mean that the whole creation is made good and comes to its own in his all-embracing lordship, his peace and his righteousness as an event that is really to be expected. This, however, can hardly be stated in terms of a personalistic, or indeed transcendental, concept of revelation.

In objection to Zimmerli's view of revelation R. Rendtorff has pointed out that Zimmerli himself says of Exodus 3: 'By pointing back to things already known, or to earlier events, God presents himself as the one who is known.'[3] It is not an unknown God who emerges from his unknownness in

---

[1] *Gottes Offenbarung*, p. 21, cf. also pp. 100f.

[2] ' "Offenbarung" im AT', *op. cit.*, p. 19: 'God thereby enters into, and speaks from within, this history whose further future is made visible in the promises that then follow.' *Gottes Offenbarung*, pp. 100f.: 'Rather, the announcing of the name leads on immediately to Yahweh's promise that it is his will to have historic dealings with Israel. Consequently if we would know Yahweh in his name, then it is not a matter of hearing secret things from the dark background of this name, but of paying attention to the historic acts towards Israel (Yahweh, "your God") of the one who thus reveals himself in his name.'   [3] *Offenbarung als Geschichte*, p. 33.

naming his name, but 'the same' who was with the fathers. Hence for Rendtorff the real God-revealing factor lies in the reference back to previous and already known history. 'The God who here speaks is he who has hitherto already given repeated proof of his power.[1] 'Thus men's eyes are directed towards coming events; but by being combined with the reference back to the previous action of the God of their fathers, the event which is expected in the future is given its place in the whole history of this God hitherto.'[2] Thus for Rendtorff it is from the complex of the history wrought by him that God becomes manifest, knowable and predicable. Through his historic acts he is known to anyone who looks at events themselves with open eyes. The 'events themselves' can and should produce knowledge of Yahweh in those who see them. Hence the formula 'I am Yahweh' especially when attention is paid to the active verbs which are always combined with is in the subordinate clauses, cannot be taken merely as a formula of personal self-presentation, but is rather a pregnant expression for Yahweh's claim to power as manifested in events. 'Yahweh' would accordingly be not a proper name that reveals the mystery of his 'I', but a divine predicate that is arrived at from the experience of history and is synonymous with 'the mighty one'. It is not the name that is the object of knowledge, but the claim to power contained in it. Yahweh is revealed through his acts in history. 'The aim of this whole history is thus to bring about knowledge of Yahweh, knowledge of the fact that he alone is God and has power.'[3] Our question as to the full self-revelation of God is answered in the Old Testament by the expression '*kabod Yahweh*'. The glory of Yahweh is revealed in historic acts to which Israel looks back. The prophets expect it to be ushered in by a future event. Then all peoples will themselves know the glory of Yahweh.

Here history has not merely the function of serving the personal encounter with God, but history 'itself' is revealing. Yahweh is recognizable as 'the mighty one' in the mirror of his historic acts. The historic connection between God's new action and his action hitherto makes God's divinity recognizable. If, however, history itself is understood in this way as indirect self-revelation of God, then the place of the cosmos as a theophany is obviously taken by history as a theophany.[4] This leads perforce to the idea that the one God can be indirectly known in the unity of universal history as seen from its end. But now, in the Old Testament practice of referring back new revelations of God to things already known, it is not a case of arguing back from effect to cause or from the act to the doer, but it is a question of recognizing again that God is the same God all the way from promise to fulfilment: 'Ye shall know that I, Yahweh, have spoken it, and performed it' (Ezek. 37.14). The promise that was given is remembered where the faithfulness of Yahweh is revealed in the event. So also the future *kabod Yahweh*, which will reveal the divinity of God to all peoples, is no event without a witness, but Israel is appointed 'for a witness to the peoples' (Isa. 55.4). It is not that consummated history reveals God, but God's universal revelation in the coming of the fulness of his glory brings history to its consummation. Despite these objections, however, we must hold fast to Rendtorff's extension of Zimmerli's concept of revelation: 'God himself' cannot

[1] *Ibid.*   [2] *Ibid.*, pp. 33 f.   [3] *Ibid.*, p. 36.   [4] Cf. pp. 77f. above.

merely mean God in person, God in the mystery of his 'I', but must always
also mean God as God and Lord, God in the mystery of his lordship.
Where God himself is revealed, there his lordship and his power are revealed, and his lordship and power are revealed where his promises of
blessing, peace and righteousness are fulfilled by him himself. To know
'I am Yahweh' and to know his glory which comes to pass, are one and the
same thing.

If we are prepared to understand divine revelation and the
knowledge of God within the horizon of history as the sphere
of promise, then we shall be able to reach the following
conclusions:

(1.) God reveals himself as 'God' where he shows himself as
the same and is thus known as the same. He becomes identi-
fiable where he identifies himself with himself in the historic
act of his faithfulness. The presupposition for the knowledge of
God is the revealing of God by God. To that extent God remains Subject and Lord even of the process of man's knowing.
Man's knowing is responsible knowing. But if the revelations
of God are promises, then God 'himself' is revealed where he
'keeps covenant and faithfulness for ever' (Ps. 146.6). Where
God, in his faithfulness to a promise he has given, stands to that
which he has promised to be, he becomes manifest and knowable as the selfsame Self. 'God himself' cannot then be understood as reflection on his transcendent 'I-ness', but must be
understood as his selfsame-ness in historic faithfulness to his
promises. If God confesses to his covenant and promises in
adopting, confirming, renewing, continuing and fulfilling
them, then God confesses to God, then he confesses to himself.
In proving his faithfulness in history, he reveals himself. For
the essence and the identity of the God of promise lies not in
his absoluteness over and beyond history, but in the constancy of
his freely chosen relation to his creatures, in the constancy of
his electing mercy and faithfulness. Hence knowledge of God
comes about not in view of a transcendent Super-Ego, nor yet
in view of the course of an obscure history, but in view of the
historic action of God within the horizon of the promises of
God. God reveals himself in his name, which discloses the
mystery of his Person to the extent that it discloses the mystery
of his faithfulness. The name of God is a name of promise,
which promises his presence on the road on which we are set by

promise and calling. The name of God and the promises contained in the name of God are therefore not only formulae of self-presentation, but they also tell us something 'about' God, for in them he gives surety for his future. They tell us who he will be. They tell us that he will be found on the road his promises point to the future, and where he will be found on that road. That is why the revelation of God and the corresponding knowledge of God are always bound up with the recounting and recalling of history and with prophetic expectation. These two things are not merely developments of his self-revelation, but are obviously a constitutive part of the revelation of his faithfulness and sameness and uniqueness.

Martin Buber has declared: 'It may be claimed to be a fundamental principle of the history of religion that experience of God begins with the experience of a single phenomenon, but knowledge of God begins with the identification of two, i.e. cognition begins with re-cognition.'[1] This is to my mind a specifically Old Testament thought. To know God means to re-cognize him. But to re-cognize him is to know him in his historic faithfulness to his promises, to know him therein as the selfsame Self and therefore to know himself. The identifying of two experiences is possible only where there is self-identification, or the revelation of historic faithfulness, because this God guarantees his promises by his name.

(2.) If knowledge of God is a re-cognizing of God, because revelation of God means that God confesses to God in historic faithfulness to his promises, then it can hardly be said that the historic complex of particular historic events 'itself' reveals God. But the history of promise, i.e. the history initiated by promise and covenant and expected as a result of them, does reveal the faithfulness of God to the extent that in it he keeps faith with his promises and thereby remains true to himself. It would again be taking over the Greek concept of knowledge, if we were to say that knowledge of God would always be possible only *a posteriori* on the ground of fulfilled promises if it is in the historic issue that the God of promise proves himself to be the God who gives a successful issue to his prophets. God is not first known at the end of history, but in the midst of history while it is in the making, remains open and depends on the play

[1] M. Buber, *Königtum Gottes*, 2nd ed. 1936, p. xliii.

of the promises. That is why this knowledge must constantly
remain mindful of the promises that have been issued and of
the past exercise of God's faithfulness, and at the same time be
a peculiarly hopeful knowledge. It must be a knowledge that
does not merely reflect past history – as a mental picture of
completed facts of history – but it must be an interested knowledge, a practical knowledge, a knowledge that is upheld by
confidence in the promised faithfulness of God. To know God
is to suffer God, says an old adage. But to suffer means to be
changed and transformed. Knowledge of God is then an anticipatory knowledge of the future of God, a knowledge of the
faithfulness of God which is upheld by the hopes that are called
to life by his promises. Knowledge of God is then a knowledge
that draws us onwards – not upwards – into situations that are
not yet finalized but still outstanding. It is a knowledge not of
the looks of past history, but of the outlooks involved in the
past promises and past faithfulness of God. Knowledge of God
will then anticipate the promised future of God in constant
remembrance of the past emergence of God's election, his
covenant, his promises and his faithfulness. It is a knowledge
that oversteps our bounds and moves within the horizon of
remembrance and expectation opened up by the promise, for
to know about God is always at the same time to know ourselves called in history by God.

Just as the promises are not descriptive words for existing
reality, but dynamic words about acts of faithfulness to be
awaited from God, so knowledge of God cannot consist in a
résumé of the language of completed facts. The truth of the
promise lies not in any demonstrable correspondence with the
reality which was or which is. It lies not in the *adaequatio rei et
intellectus*. The promise here proves its truth, on the contrary,
in the specific *inadaequatio intellectus et rei* in which it places the
hearer. It stands in a demonstrable contradiction to the historic
reality.[1] It has not yet found its answer, and therefore draws
the mind to the future, to obedient and creative expectation,
and brings it into opposition to the existing reality which has not
the truth in it. It thus provokes a peculiar incongruence with

[1] Over against Deut. 18.21f. and Jer. 28.9, which see the criterion of true
prophecy in the 'coming to pass of the word', do we not find a different criterion
in Jer. 23.22 and 29: 'Is not my word like as a fire? saith the Lord; and like a
hammer that breaketh the rock in pieces?'?

being, in the consciousness of hoping and trusting. It does not glorify reality in the spirit, but is out for its transformation. Hence it does not give rise to powers of accommodation, but sets loose powers that are critical of being. It transcends reality not by rising to an unreal realm of dreams, but by pressing forwards to the future of a new reality.

(3.) The guarantee of the promise's congruity with reality lies in the credibility and faithfulness of him who gives it. Yet this argument would remain abstract, and would fail to do justice to the character of the promise as the word in which God promises himself and confronts man as 'I Yahweh', if it disregarded the fact that promises effectually strain towards a real, future event of fulfilment. This future to which the promise points can be expressed by a theological personalism only as the personal future of God 'himself'. Our hope in the promises of God, however, is not hope in God himself or in God as such, but it hopes that his future faithfulness will bring it also the fulness of what has been promised. To be sure, it can be said that our hope is hope in the coming of the faithfulness of God, that it expects the promised future from the coming of God himself and not apart from him. Yet it would surely be an abstraction which would not do justice to the Old Testament hope, if we were to describe this hope as *spes purissima in Deum purissimum*.[1] Hope, where it holds to the promises, hopes that the coming of God will bring it also 'this and that' – namely, his redeeming and restoring lordship in all things. It does not merely hope personally 'in him', but has also substantial hopes of his lordship, his peace and his righteousness on earth. Otherwise hope itself could unobtrusively change into a kind of fulfilment and there would be nothing more in which our hopes could be fulfilled.

An understanding of the promise must combine both the personalistic and the historic and substantial concepts of truth. Hope's assurance springs from the credibility and faithfulness of the God of promise. Hope's knowledge recalls the faithfulness

---

[1] Luther, *WA* 5, p. 166: *Adeo scil. omnia a nobis aufferenda sunt, ut nec optima dei dona, idest ipsa merita, reliqua sint, in quibus fidamus, ut sit spes purissima in purissimum deum: tunc demum homo vere purus et sanctus est* ('For so completely have we to renounce all things that not even the best gifts of God, i.e. not even his merits, remain to be objects of our faith, that our hope be purely hope purely in God: only then is a man truly pure and holy').

of this God in history and anticipates the real fulfilment in a multitude of pre-conceptions, not to say realistic utopias – yet all this without prejudice to the freedom of the God who promises. An assurance of hope without such knowledge would be vague adventuring. A knowledge without such assurance would be historical speculation.

The God who is present in his promises is for the human spirit an ob-ject (*Gegen-stand*) in the sense that he stands opposed to (*entgegen-steht*)[1] the human spirit until a reality is created and becomes knowable which wholly accords with his promises and can be called 'very good'. Hence it is not our experiences which make faith and hope, but it is faith and hope that make experiences and bring the human spirit to an ever new and restless transcending of itself.

5. PROMISE AND LAW

If the promises of God create an interval of tension between their being issued and their coming to pass, and thereby institute freedom for obedience, then importance attaches to the question of directions for the filling out of this interval and of the existence thus constituted in it. This is understandable, since a promise does not announce an inescapable fate, but sets men on a road that leads to another land and another reality. If we again take our cue from the theme of nomadic life, then we can say that originally promise is combined with obedience, and obedience with a change of place and a change of existence. It is necessary to arise and go to the place to which the promise points, if one would have part in its fulfilment. Promise and command, the pointing of the goal and the pointing of the way, therefore belong immediately together.

In this context the judicial character of promise will also have to be taken into account. Promise is the one side of the covenant in which God's association with the people of his choice is grounded. To this extent promise founds upon election, and election always means being called into the history of promise. Whoever receives the promises, God enters into cove-

---

[1] The play here on the German words *Gegenstand* and *entgegenstehen* is to some extent contained also in the English word 'object', which by derivation means 'lying before' or 'lying opposite'. – *Translator*.

nant with him and he with God. In the covenant, God in his
freedom binds himself to be faithful to the promise he has given;
and if this covenant extends to a future in which fulfilments are
to ensue, then it cannot be regarded as a historical fact, but is
to be understood as a historic event which points beyond itself
to the future that is announced. The covenant will have to be
understood as a history-making event which opens up specific
possibilities of history. The covenant must be understood as a
'historic process' or, as Jacques Ellul calls it on the basis of
parallels in law, a 'contract requiring adherence' which is not
exhausted in a single transaction, but whose effects continue
until the promised fulfilment.[1] To this extent the promise of the
covenant and the injunctions of the covenant have an abiding
and guiding significance until the fulfilment.

The obedience which the injunctions demand springs of
firm confidence, and is a natural consequence of the promises.
To 'keep' the covenant which God has founded means both to
'keep' the words of the promise and 'to keep his commandments'. We 'keep' the commandments by obedience. We
'keep' the promises when 'with all our heart and all our strength'
we trust and hope in them and do not doubt. All the commandments are explications of the one commandment, to love
God and to cleave to him (Deut. 6.5), and this one commandment is but the reverse side of the promise. It commands
(*gebietet*) what the promise offers (*bietet*). Hence not only disobedience is punished by not experiencing the fulfilment, but
so also is resignation, weariness, departure from the living
hope. Despondency and despair are sin – indeed they are the
origin of all sins.[2] Hence *vice versa* the commandments are 'easy'
to fulfil in the power that comes of hoping in God and waiting
upon him. The commandments of the covenant, which point
our hopes in the promise to the path of physical obedience, are
nothing else but the ethical reverse of the promise itself. The
promised life here appears as the life that is commanded. Hence
the demands for obedience and the demands for hope are
alike related to that horizon which opens up before the present

[1] J. Ellul, *The Theological Foundation of Law*, ET by M. Weiser, 1961, p. 50.
[2] Despair and despondency are merely the reverse side of that *superbia* in which
Luther saw the origin of all sins. On this point cf. the fine treatise by J. Pieper,
Über die Hoffnung, 1949, pp. 51ff. and K. Barth, *Church Dogmatics* IV/2, § 65: 'The
Sloth and Misery of Man'.

"law" as the ethical ... of the ...;
commands, ... promises, ... themselves
their tradition

?
(Luther.)
('J.P.S.')

loopint
alternat
to std
von ...

122 · Theology of Hope [110]

in the light of the historic datum of the covenant, and which makes the present the front-line for the onset of the promised new life. In this conjunction with the promises of the covenant, the commandments all have a paracletic and parenetic significance, but they are not legal conditions or what theologians commonly call 'law'. If the commandments are the ethical side of the promise and obedience is the fruit of hope, then the commandments are just as little rigid norms as the promises are, but they go along with the promise, producing history and transforming themselves on the path through the ages towards the fulfilment. They are not abstract norms of ideal orders that always exist and reflect their images in time, but they are a real foreshadowing of the historic prospects extended to specific men by the historic datum of the covenant. The commandments have accordingly just as much a future tenor as the promises. Their goal is the reality of that human dignity which is vouchsafed to men through fellowship with the God of promise.

It is therefore plain that theological reflection on the law can begin at the point where the promise itself is rendered questionable by non-realization or by delay in its fulfilment. The theological reflection which separates the law from its future can arise in the vacuum created by the postponement of the promise, and on the basis of historic experiences which contradict the promised future. The non-realization of promises upon which we had depended, the distress that arises when the protection and guidance of the God of promise fail to come, makes the following theological reflections possible:

(a) God lies. They were his promise and his covenant, but he has not kept them. 'Wilt thou indeed be unto me as a deceitful brook, as waters that fail?' (Jer. 15.18, RV).

(b) God is faithful. He does not deny himself. What he says comes to pass. Therefore if it does not come to pass, it was not the promise of God, but the lie of false prophets. History itself proves them to be false prophets. Reflections of this kind were manifestly often brought forward even against the charismatic leaders of Israel.

(c) The reflection turns against the sorely tried, or even al-

[1] On this paragraph cf. G. von Rad, *Theologie des Alten Testamentes* II, pp. 402ff.: 'Das Gesetz' (ET pp. 388ff.: 'The Law').

ready disappointed man himself. The reason for the with-
holding of the fulfilment, for the distance and absence of God
and for his judgment, lies in man, whether because he has departed from the hope in the God of the promise and fallen into
idolatry (the golden calf) or the worship of other gods, or
because of his disobedience to the injunctions of the commandments. Then the hidden uncleanness and sin must be searched
out and purification and atonement sought, in order to establish the promise once more.

This last reflection, however, turns the promise into an object
and regards it in abstraction from the God who promises. It
becomes an object whose power can be manipulated by means
of repentance and the rites of the cultus. Whereas in essence a
divine promise itself contains the power of its fulfilment in the
faithfulness and might of the God who promises, in reflection
in the vacuum caused by its delay there arises a peculiar con-
ditionalizing of the promise. Its fulfilment is made to depend
on obedience, and obedience is understood as a *conditio sine qua
non* and as a return achievement on man's part. Perfect obedience to the promise and its injunctions must bring its fulfilment, while every imperfection gives further cause for delay.
Here we have a reversal of subjects which is often subtle and
from the historical standpoint calls for very careful differentiation: if obedience is a consequence of the promise that incites
us to arise and set off towards a definite goal and entrusts the
fulfilment to the power of the God who promises, so now *vice
versa* the fulfilment can be regarded as the consequence of
human obedience. Here the obedience of man need not as yet
be understood as the efficient cause of the fulfilment, but can
also be taken merely as the occasion for the fulfilment by God
himself. But this means that the power of the promise to attain
to fulfilment lies no longer in the faithfulness of God himself,
but in the obedience of man.

In the Old Testament, too, such reflections are not unknown.
It is plain that they already arise very early. They arise at every
point where in the absence of the promised salvation, in mis-
fortune and god-forsakenness, the people begin to raise the
questions of why and wherefore and how long. These questions
become acute in popular complaint, and the attempted answers are given on the basis of the covenant and of divine

justice. Is it conceivable that this last reflection dominates the rabbinical teaching of late Judaism? Could it possibly be that the Torah theology of late Judaism has a formative influence in what New Testament scholars often describe as 'delay of the parousia'? In modern Jewish theology the reversing of the subjects is plainly the ground of its remarkable proximity to German idealism, to activistic messianism and to the Russian 'husbandmen of God'. Then 'the redemption of the world is left to the power of our conversion. God has no wish for any other means of perfecting his creation than by our help. He will not reveal his kingdom until we have laid its foundations.'[1]

One could call this 'the promise in the form of the law'. Then it would have to be pointed out in this context that while Paul's controversy with the Judaism of the Torah and with Jewish Christians is certainly on the question of the law, yet its concern is surely the promise (Gal. 3.15ff.). Promise in the form of gospel, or promise in the form of law – that is the question. And it could well be that 'promise in the form of gospel' brings to light once more the original meaning of the law as being the injunctions that are bound up with the promise.

6. PROMISE IN THE ESCHATOLOGY OF THE PROPHETS[2]

Since the rediscovery of the eschatological character of the words of the Bible witnesses, the concept 'eschatology' has become hazy. Whereas in orthodox dogmatics it referred to the last, often unrelated and supplementary, article '*de novissimis*',

---

[1] M. Buber, *Gog und Magog*, 1949, p. 297. H.-J. Kraus, 'Gespräch mit M. Buber', *EvTh* 12, 1952, pp. 76ff. Combined with this is also another thought – that Yahweh mysteriously requires the action of Israel as his son. Cf. L. Baeck, *Das Wesen des Judentums*, 2nd ed. 1959, pp. 132ff.; C. Cohen, *Religion der Vernunft aus den Quellen des Judentums*, 2nd ed. 1929, pp. 140, 172, 233, 431.

[2] For what follows cf. M. Buber, *The Prophetic Faith*, ET 1949; T. C. Vriezen, 'Prophecy and Eschatology', *VT Suppl.* I (Congress Volume: Copenhagen 1953), 1953, pp. 199–229; H. W. Wolff, 'Das Geschichtsverständnis der alttestamentlichen Prophetie', *EvTh* 20, 1960, pp. 218–235; G. von Rad, *Theologie des Alten Testamentes* II, pp. 125ff.: 'Die Eschatologisierung des Geschichtsdenkens durch die Propheten' (ET pp. 112ff.: 'History related to Eschatology: Israel's Ideas about Time and History, and the Prophetic Eschatology'); O. Plöger, *Theokratie und Eschatologie*, 1959; D. Rössler, *Gesetz und Geschichte*, 1960; K. Koch, 'Spätisraelitisches Geschichtsdenken am Beispiel des Buches Daniel', *Historische Zeitschrift*, 1961, vol. 193, pp. 1–32.

in dogmatics and exegesis today it has acquired various senses
and means, according to the particular material to which it is
applied, simply 'future', or 'extending beyond the present', or
'last age', or 'transcendent', or 'directed towards a final goal',
or 'finally valid'. Among Old Testament scholars the termino-
logical dispute narrows down to the question whether hopes
within history can already be called eschatological, or whether
the term should be reserved for prophecies which speak of the
end of history as such, and thus of events which lie outside
the realm of history.[1] Can a distinction be made between historic eschatologies and cosmic eschatologies, between eschatologies within history and transcendental eschatologies? Does
the *eschaton* mean merely 'future', or is it applied to the absolute future as opposed to history?

It is hardly possible to expound specific complexes of ideas as
'eschatological schemata'. It is also scarcely possible to establish the points at which we can say, 'Here prophetic promise
ends, and there eschatology begins.' But it can be said in the
first instance that those promises and expectations are eschatological which are directed towards a historic future in the sense
of the ultimate horizon. Now, the concept 'horizon', as meaning a boundary of expectation which moves along with us and
invites us to press further ahead, already fits in with the general
concept of promise. 'Israel's faith in God has a future content.'[2]
And it is quite true that picturing the future in terms of the
threat of judgment and the promise of salvation is not a specific
characteristic of the prophets of classical times, but that it could
rather be said, on the contrary, that classical prophecy is a
specific characteristic of Israelite belief in the promise.[3] 'This
faith that looks to the future took over various themes in order
to make plain what the future of God meant in various particular circumstances.'[4] That presupposes faith in the God
of promise, who is the God who will be, and cannot be

---

[1] G. von Rad, *op. cit.*, p. 128 (ET p. 114) in the form of a question to G. Hölscher,
S. Mowinckel and G. Fohrer.

[2] Cf. also O. Procksch, *Theologie des Alten Testamentes*, 1950, p. 582. Cf. also M.
Buber, *op. cit.*, p. 8.

[3] Cf. here the new questions in the study of the prophets: R. Bach, *Die Aufforder-
ung zur Flucht und zum Kampf im alttestamentlichen Prophetenspruch*, 1962; R. Rendtorff, 'Erwägungen zur Frühgeschichte des Prophetentums in Israel', *ZTK* 59,
1962, pp. 145ff.

[4] Jepsen, Art. 'Eschatologie' in *RGG*[3] II, col. 661.

psychologically explained on the basis of disappointment with the cultic θεὸς ἐπιφανής who is subsequently 'eschatologized.'[1]

This would mean, however, that the eschatology of the prophets grew up on the soil of Israel's faith in the promise, and that in prophetic eschatology faith in the promise is wrestling with new experiences of God, of judgment and of history and thereby undergoing new, profound changes. In the prophets, despite all the newness of their message, the God who confronts Israel with his claims is no other than the *Deus spei*, the God of hope.

What part of the promised future is the ultimate future, what part of the historic *novum* is the *novum ultimum*, is determined by the perspective in which the viewer sees the time that is now void but will then be filled. The ideas of time are first determined by the expectations. Here it is quite possible for the eschatological perspectives to expand, and for that which appeared to one generation as 'ultimate' to be seen by a later generation as within history and surpassable. The ideas of 'end' and 'goal' all depend on what a thing is supposed to be the end of and for what it is supposed to be the goal. What is here regarded as 'time' is then concrete time as seen in the processes of historic and expected changes. To that extent the sense of time and the ideas of time also change along with the expectations. The abstract scientific concept of time, which has categorically determined modern thinking since Kant, must not be applied here until we have tested its eschatological scope – which in Kant's case means its transcendental scope.[2]

But when and how do hopes for history become hopes that are to be called 'eschatological'? When does a promise become an eschatological promise? Is it demonstrable and conceivable that the historic, moving horizon of promise can reach ultimate bounds?

The concept 'eschatology' is here intended to mark the peculiarity of the prophets as distinct from those who had earlier spoken for the religion of Yahweh and also as distinct from later apocalyptic writers.

[1] Thus e.g. M. Buber, *Königtum Gottes*, 2nd ed. 1936, p. x, and S. Mowinckel, *Psalmenstudien* II, p. 324. On this, G. von Rad, *op. cit.*, p. 130 (ET p. 116): 'If we hold by what the prophets say, it will not do to put the "experience of disillusionment" at the head as the evocative factor proper.'

[2] Cf. pp. 45ff. above.

From the standpoint of the history of religion, the 'mastering' of agrarian culture in Israel's occupation of Canaan has been described as the first decisive frontier crossed by the tribes of Israel. In this 'opening up of the realm of sedentary experience by Yahwism',[1] the latter itself underwent considerable expansion.[2] The 'mastering' of those great experiences in the world history of the seventh and sixth centuries, in which Israel perished as a nation and yet survived itself in the religious sphere,[2] could be called the second major frontier. On this frontier, too, faith in the promise undergoes tremendous expansion: in the message of the classical prophets, which is closely bound up with these experiences of history and of judgment, it develops into the prophetic eschatology.

The message of these prophets arises in the shadow of the increasing menace from Assyria, Babylon and Persia, the gathering storm of destruction that broods over the national, political and Palestinian life of Israel in both kingdoms. The prophets see before them the annihilation of Israel's existence and of the whole history of promise and fulfilment thus far vouchsafed to Israel by its God. They interpret this history of collapse as Yahweh's judgment on his apostate people. This means that the new historic action of Yahweh in the history of the nations, which for Israel becomes the history of its destruction, is seen by them as being on the same level as, and even competing with, the historic acts of Yahweh in their own past as remembered in the cultus and the festivals. This new, and as yet dark and unfathomable action of Yahweh will even go the length of outreaching and replacing his past action upon his people. In the historic judgment on Israel, Yahweh not only annuls the debts of Israel, but he annuls also the institutions of his own covenant in his unfathomable freedom to adopt new ways.

'The message of the prophets has to be termed eschatological wherever it regards the old historic bases of salvation as null and void,' says G. von Rad in his new view of the matter, 'but we ought then to go on and limit the term. It should not be applied to cases where Israel gave a general expression of her faith in her future, or, as does happen, in the future of her

[1] V. Maag, *op. cit.*, p. 153 n. 1.
[2] A. Alt, 'Die Deutung der Weltgeschichte im Alten Testament', *ZTK* 56, 1959 p. 129.

sacred institutions. The prophetic teaching is only eschatological when the prophets expelled Israel from the safety of the
old saving actions and suddenly shifted the basis of salvation
to a future action of God.'[1] This allows no recognition to the
psychological explanation of 'eschatology' as given by Mowinckel and Buber following the example of Albert Schweitzer.
It was not that the 'disappointments of history' in regard to
promises in which they had believed, and which depended on
the land, the cultus and the temple, caused men to give eschatological form to their hopes for history. What did cause them to
do this was experiences which were understood as judgments of
Yahweh, and indeed not merely as judgment upon what by the
standard of the ancient covenant ordinances was a disobedient
people, but also as judgment on the history of Yahweh's relationship with this people hitherto. How far, amid the breakdown of what has hitherto been and the breaking in of new,
hitherto unknown action on God's part, does the message of
the prophets become 'eschatological'? This surely cannot lie
merely in the break-away from the 'future of the Yahweh who
has come', which up to that point had also been known, to the
'future of the Yahweh who is to come', which up to that point
had not been known.

   The threat that the history of the attacking peoples will bring
Yahweh's judgment upon Israel marks a quite decisive universalizing of the divine action. The experience of being crushed
between the great world powers is understood as a judgment of
Yahweh. Yet even as early as Amos this threat of judgment is
universal: God judges all wrong, including that among the
peoples who do not know his law. Consequently the God who
uses the nations to judge his apostate people is also their Lord
and will also be their Judge. For if he appoints the nations to
execute judgment on Israel, then he is obviously their God and
Lord. If he uses these nations to judge Israel according to his
law, then he will also judge these nations according to his law,
given though it is in the first instance only to Israel. As a result
of their onslaught upon Israel, and because according to the
message of the prophets Israel must take this onslaught as a
judgment of its God, the nations are involved in the fate of
Israel and come within the range of Yahweh's working in judg-

---

[1] G. von Rad, *op. cit.*, pp. 131f. (ET p. 118).

ment and in blessing. On its political deathbed Israel brings
the nations, as it were, into the hands of its God and into his
future. By this very means Yahweh's threats and promises for
the future are set free from their restriction to the one specific
people and its particular future in history, and become eschatological. The moving horizon of the assurances for the future
given by the God of promise, once it is extended to embrace
'all peoples', then reaches the utmost bounds of human reality
as such, and becomes universal and so also eschatological. The
horizon of the coming God thereby attains a *non plus ultra*.

However widely it extends to embrace all peoples, and however deeply it goes to the roots of earthly existence, the prophets' message of judgment nevertheless points once more to a
different future, to a day of Yahweh, which will arise out of the
night of judgment. This judgment certainly means the annihilation of the people and of the history to which this people
owes its existence, but it does not mean the annihilation of
Yahweh's faithfulness to himself. It can therefore be conceived
as a judgment that paves the way for something finally new, and
as annihilation for the sake of greater perfection. Thus there
arise visions of the end, of the unheard-of new salvation that is
on the way, of the new covenant, of the coming glory of Yahweh in his sovereignty over all the earth – and all this, too, not
only for Israel, but so to speak for all the peoples that have
participated in the judgment upon Israel and have thus been
involved in the history of Yahweh's relationship with Israel.
It is only through the above-mentioned universalizing of the
judgment that the coming salvation of Yahweh first becomes
eschatological in its breadth and unrestrictedness.

How is this conceived? To begin with, 'the new thing' whose
coming is foretold is conceived in analogy to the previous
saving acts of God in the history of the fulfilling of his promises
in his people's past – as the occupation of a new land, as the
setting up of a new David and a new Zion, as a new exodus,
as a new covenant. That is to say, it is conceived as a 'renewal'
and return of what is past and lost, so that beginning and end
correspond to each other.[1] But these are analogies which seek to
interpret the wholly non-analogous. It cannot be a question
merely of the restitution of the good old days, for new and

[1] G. von Rad, *op. cit.* II, p. 131 (ET p. 117); H. W. Wolff, *op. cit.*, pp. 224f.

unheard-of things have already been done by Yahweh. The judgment has become universal, and therefore the nations – in the
first instance those participating in the judgment, then, *pars
pro toto*, through them 'all peoples' – are taken up into the new,
coming acts of God. Already in the judgment Yahweh glori-
fies himself upon them. How much more will he glorify himself upon them when his new saving acts in Israel come to light.
'Salvation has become universal, even if it is Israelite and even
if it is received *via* Israel.'[1] To be sure these visions of salvation,
which are to be called 'eschatological' in virtue of the fact that
in their unrestrictedness they break through all spatial and
racial limitations and extend to the utmost bounds of human
reality in 'all peoples', are *Israelo-centric eschatologies.* This is
already implied in the fact that they are expressed in the form
of analogy to the past saving history of Yahweh's relationship
with his people and on the ground of the basic experience of
judgment in the history that is concentrated upon Israel. Yet
the extension to all peoples of the threat of judgment and of
the promise of salvation in itself already involves what T. C.
Vriezen calls the 'missionary task of Israel' – the task of being a
light to the Gentiles and a witness for Yahweh in his controversy with the gods of the nations. But the more the new saving
action of God that is to come outstrips all analogies from the
history of Israel's dealings with its God in past experience and
tradition, and the more the judgment that begins with Israel
moves on through the history of the nations, the more clearly
there appear the first signs of a *universal eschatology of mankind.*
Here, however, we have presumably already the beginning of
what must be called apocalyptic.

Thus we can speak of a real 'eschatology' only at the points
where, in the limitations and perspectives of history, the horizon
of the promised future embraces in the *eschaton* the *proton* of the
whole creation, where the horizon of the God who announces
himself and is on his way extends to all peoples, for there is
nothing that can be conceived as wider in extent than that.

Along with this universalizing, however, there goes also an intensification of the promise up to the limits of existence as such.
What the ancient faith in the promise expected from the nearness and then from the presence of the God of promise was

[1] T. C. Vriezen, *An Outline of Old Testament Theology*, ET, 1958, p. 360.

Promise and History

guidance, preservation, protection, blessing, fulness of life, etc., and these expectations were given content from the concrete experience of deprivations, of being abandoned to hunger, thirst, wretchedness and the oppression and menace of their enemies. That is, the expectations receive their content in the mind's eye from the contrary experiences that were endured under the absence and hiddenness of the God of promise. The positive content of the ideas is all supplied by negation of the negative. In the same way the visionary ideas of the prophetic promises receive their content from the negative experiences of Yahweh's judgment. This means, however, that the visions of the promised glorifying of Yahweh develop in the light of the new experiences of judgment. Yahweh's coming glory shows itself in overcoming the experienced judgment and turning it to blessing. If this were to be expressed in theological terms, we should have to say: it shows itself in the overcoming of God by God – of the judging, annihilating God by the saving, life-giving God, of the wrath of God by his goodness. If we would illustrate it by the people concerned, then the coming new action of Yahweh must be exemplifiable in the overcoming of the experiences of judgment, in the overcoming of hunger and poverty, of humiliation and offence, of international wars and polytheism, and finally of a god-forsaken death. These conquests of the experienced negative aspects of existence that are understood as judgments of Yahweh are all summed up in the content of the expectation that is bound up with the coming fulness of the glory of Yahweh. The content of the expectation in the 'predictions' is thus supplied on the one hand by recollections and analogies from the history of the fulfilment of Yahweh's promises in the good old days of his people's past whose return is hoped for – while on the other hand it is provided by negation of the negative elements in the new experiences of judgment. To this end, ideas of international peace, etc., can then also be taken over from other peoples, so far as they can be given eschatological form.

But in the message of the prophets there still remains at first one boundary – *death*. As long as death is felt to be the natural boundary of life, God remains a God of the living. But if death – or at least early death – is experienced as exclusion from the promise of fulness and consummation of life, and thus as an effect of judgment, then the hope of the overcoming of God's judgment by his life-creating glory must be exemplified also in relation to this boundary. Hence on the periphery of the prophetic message death appears as a suffering of divine judgment, and the messianic salvation in which the judgment is annulled is exemplified in a conquest of dying and of death. Yahweh remains a God of the living. The suffering endured at the ultimate boundary of life does not lead to the adoption of Egyptian ideas of a Beyond. But if the death-boundary is understood as a judgment of Yahweh, then his power extends also beyond death. The dead, too, can be recognized as included within the realm of his promise and glory, and even death itself is seen as a transformable possibility in his hand and no longer as a fixed reality that sets a limit to his working. Thus the term 'eschatological' would now have to be used for a promise whose horizon of expectation surmounts and overcomes all experiences of the total judgment of God in life and death. Only when the horizon of expectation extends beyond what is felt to be the final boundary of existence, i.e. beyond the bounds of death, does it reach an *eschaton*, a *non plus ultra*, a *novum ultimum*.

The universalizing of the promise finds its eschaton *in the promise of Yahweh's lordship over all peoples.*

The intensification of the promise finds its approach to the eschatological in the negation of death.

Now of course it must be noted that these limits of the eschatological, as they have here been terminologically defined, are nowhere so plain and clear-cut in the classical prophets. The latter stand in the midst of the history of their people and in the transition from the breakdown of the old to the breaking in of the new. History for them does not stand still as in the apocalyptic visions of the end. They do not, like the apocalyptic sects, stand in unworldly detachment over against the 'world', the nations and the people of Israel, so that they could give themselves over to contemplating the worldliness of the world and its future fate. On the contrary, here everything is still in flux and the history whose future they announce is still mobile. They know that they themselves and their message are a factor in the movement of the history of God. Thus they certainly speak of 'history' as the 'work of Yahweh' or the 'plan of Yahweh' (Isa. 28.29), and also of the 'whole work of Yahweh'

(Isa. 10.12). Yet that is not a history surveyed apocalyptically from the standpoint of the end at which all things stand still, but it is a future announced from the <u>midst of the process of</u> history. When they speak of <u>Yahweh's plan</u>, they are not thinking of insight into the divine determination of the world, but mean <u>the constancy of his historic faithfulness</u>. They see judgment and history in the light of the freedom of Yahweh, not as immutable fate. Hence the plans of Yahweh can be 'repented of' by Yahweh, and the proclamation of them leads the present into decisions which have an influence on the future of the divine action also. As distinct from any fatalistic apocalyptic view of history, the mobility of history as the prophets see it, and as they stand in it with their own witness, can therefore be called 'a purposeful conversation of the Lord of the future with Israel'.[1] It could thus be said that while the prophetic message in its breadth and in its existential depth does reach the utmost bounds of reality and thereby become eschatological, yet these bounds are not predetermined but are themselves flexible.

7. THE HISTORIFYING OF THE COSMOS IN APOCALYPTIC ESCHATOLOGY

It is difficult to explain the phenomenon of late Jewish apocalyptic and its contents.[2] Have we here to do with a legitimate continuation of the prophetic message, or with a falling away from the prophetic faith in the promise? Is it a case of the intrusion of the dualistic world-picture of Iranianism or, if this is so, had an inward openness for it already been prepared by the message of the prophets?

It can be said in the first instance that the futuristic and eschatological outlook is common to both the prophets and the apocalyptists. Then, however, distinctions will at once have to be made.

(a) Apocalyptic cherishes a religious, <u>deterministic</u> view of history. The temporal sequence of the aeons is settled from the start and history gradually unfolds a plan of Yahweh's. In the

---

[1] H. W. Wolff, *op. cit.*, p. 231.
[2] Cf. the completely divergent verdicts of G. von Rad, *op. cit.* II, pp. 314ff. (ET pp. 301ff.) on the one hand, and on the other hand of K. Koch, *op. cit.*, and W. Pannenberg, *Offenbarung als Geschichte*, 1961, pp. 103ff.

prophets, however, there is no trace of the idea that the *eschata* have been firmly determined since the beginning of time.

(b) In apocalyptic the factor standing over against the God who acts in history is the 'world' that lies under the power of evil. In the prophets, however, we have 'Israel and the nations'.

(c) The apocalyptic expectation is no longer directed towards a consummation of the creation through the overcoming of evil by good, but towards the separation of good and evil and hence the replacement of the 'world that lies under the power of evil' by the coming 'world of righteousness'. This shows a fatalistic dualism which is not yet so found in the prophets.

(d) The judgment is not seen as something which in the freedom of God can be recalled and which can be averted, if it may be, by repentance, but as an immutable fate that is assuredly coming, as a *fatum irreparabile*.

(e) The prophets stood in the midst of the people of Israel and thus also in the midst of its history. The apocalyptists stand in the post-exilic congregation of the righteous of Yahweh.[1]

(f) The prophets in their predictions quite openly took their stand in their own historic present. From that standpoint they unfold their historic perspectives. The apocalyptist, however, veils his own place in history.

In short, the question arises whether apocalyptic thinking does not ultimately show signs of non-historic thinking. Does the apocalyptic division of world history into periods according to the plan of Yahweh not merely interpret in terms of universal history earlier, foreign schemata of a cosmological kind? Apocalyptic as the 'science of the highest' has such an encyclopaedic character, just like the esoteric apocalyptic of the pietistic theology of saving history in the seventeenth and eighteenth Christian centuries.

On the other hand, it has been pointed out with good reason how firmly the apocalyptic picture of history is rooted in the historic thinking of Israel and bound up with the prophetic eschatology. In this context Daniel becomes the executor of the testament of the prophets with his first 'sketch of world history in terms of universal history'.[2]

[1] O. Plöger, *op. cit.*, pp. 63ff.   [2] K. Koch, *op. cit.*, p. 31.

This contradictory impression arises from the fact that in the eschatology of the prophets the horizon of the promise, both in its breadth and in its depth, reaches the limits of what can be described as cosmic finitude. When, however, the moving historic horizon of the historic hopes reaches these *eschata*, then there arises the possibility of abandoning the point of perspective in history and reading the course of world history backwards from the end now contemplated, as if universal history were a *universum*, a predetermined cosmos of history. Numerical speculations from ancient cosmology are introduced in order to provide an order for the periods of world history corresponding to the spatial order. The world empires are fixed. The *eschaton* becomes a *fatum*. Then the place of election, which determines the ground of obedience and hope, is taken by providence which determines events. The place of the promise which is trusted in hope contrary to all apparent hope is taken by the end drama. The place of the *eschaton* which is brought about by God in his freedom is taken by a historic finale that comes about in the course of time. The place of the faithfulness of God to which, in his freedom, the fulfilment of the promised future is entrusted is taken by the plan of God which is firmly established from the beginning of time and gradually disclosed by history. In place of a historic theology we have a theology of history and in place of a historic eschatology comes an eschatological contemplation of history. Like the eighteenth-century theology of saving history, apocalyptic contains perceptible traces of the distant God of deism. On the other hand it must not be overlooked that in the speculative apocalypses there is also always a note of exhortation to be found. It is the exhortation to persevere in the faith of the righteous: he who endures to the end will be saved. It follows that faith and unbelief, good and evil, election and reprobation, righteous and unrighteous are firmly established, and what matters is to abide by what we are. This again is wholly in harmony with the place of apocalyptic in the life of those who form a community apart.

What is the result of thus comparing the eschatology of the prophets with the historic hopes of early Israel on the one hand and with cosmological apocalyptic on the other? In asking this, we are now asking about the systematic consequences for the outline of eschatology as such.

In the first instance we find an extreme contradiction in the theological evaluation of apocalyptic. G. von Rad holds that the characteristic apocalyptic division of world history into periods from the standpoint of the world consummation is 'simply the interpretation and actualization of earlier cosmological schemata found in myth'. K. Koch and W. Pannenberg see it as the first attempt to provide a sketch of world history on the basis of the prophetic eschatology. Both verdicts have their ground in the recognition of the fact that apocalyptic applies cosmological patterns to history, with the result that either 'history' comes to a standstill or else 'history' becomes intelligible as a summary representation of reality in its totality.

But now, when we consider the relation between eschatology and cosmology in apocalyptic, there arises still a third possible interpretation and a third possible theological evaluation. The application of cosmological patterns to history as determined by the *eschaton* naturally does have the effects noted by von Rad and Koch. Yet the peculiarity and the theological significance of apocalyptic could lie contrariwise in the fact that what we have here is not by any means a cosmological interpretation of eschatological history, but an eschatological and historic interpretation of the cosmos. It might well be that the existing cosmic bounds of reality, which the moving historic horizon of the promise reaches in eschatology, are not regarded as fixed and predetermined things, but are themselves found to be in motion. It might well be that once the promise becomes eschatological it breaks the bounds even of that which aetiology had hitherto considered to be creation and cosmos, with the result that the *eschaton* would not be a repetition of the beginning, nor a return from the condition of estrangement and the world of sin to the state of original purity, but is ultimately wider than the beginning ever was. Then it would not be the case that eschatology becomes cosmological in apocalyptic, and is thereby stabilized, but *vice versa* cosmology would become eschatological and the cosmos would be taken up in terms of history into the process of the *eschaton*. This would then be the other side of the struggle in apocalyptic between eschatology and cosmology – a side which has hitherto remained unnoticed, because theology was interested only in eschatology but not in

[1] G. von Rad, *op. cit.* II, p. 321 (ET p. 308).

cosmology. If, as we might say, in the message of the prophets
the Israelite 'hope for history' was struggling with the experiences of world history, and if in this struggle world history
was understood as a function of the eschatological future of
Yahweh, so it is also in apocalyptic: historic eschatology is
here struggling with cosmology and in this struggle makes the
cosmos understandable as a historic process of aeons in apocalyptic perspective. Then it would not by any means be the
case that in the apocalyptic outlook the history that is motivated
by our hopes for history is brought to a standstill, but on the
contrary, the now universal hope for history would here be
setting the cosmos in motion. In a struggle of this kind eschatology naturally suffers serious losses. Yet we must not look
only at these, but must also see what is gained in them. The
'universe' is no longer, as in pagan cosmology, a thing to be
interpreted in astro-mythical or pantheistic or mechanistic
terms as the sum total of the world and of our satisfaction with
it. Instead, it splits into aeons in the apocalyptic process – into
a world that is coming and one that is passing away. The *totum*
of apocalyptic means a different thing from the universe of
cosmology. The whole world is now involved in God's eschatological process of history, not only the world of men and nations.
The conversion of man in the prophetic message then finds its
correlate in the conversion of the whole cosmos, of which apocalyptic speaks. The prophetic revolution among the nations ex-
pands to become the cosmic revolution of all things. Not only
the martyrs are included in the eschatological suffering of the
Servant of God, but the whole creation is included in the suffering of the last days. The suffering becomes universal and destroys the all-sufficiency of the cosmos, just as the eschatological
joy will then resound in a 'new heaven and a new earth'. In
other words, while apocalyptic does conceive its eschatology in
cosmological terms, yet that is not the end of eschatology, but
the beginning of an eschatological cosmology or an eschatological ontology for which being becomes historic and the cosmos
opens itself to the apocalyptic process. This historifying of the
world in the category of the universal eschatological future is
of tremendous importance for theology, for indeed it makes
eschatology the universal horizon of all theology as such. Without apocalyptic a theological eschatology remains bogged down

in the ethnic history of men or the existential history of the
individual. The New Testament did not close the window
which apocalyptic had opened for it towards the wide vistas
of the cosmos and beyond the limitations of the given cosmic
reality.

III

THE RESURRECTION AND THE FUTURE OF JESUS CHRIST

1. GOSPEL AND PROMISE

WHEN WE come to the question of the view of the revelation of God in the New Testament, then we discover the fact, already familiar from the Old Testament, that there is no unequivocal *concept* of revelation. What the New Testament understands by revelation is thus again not to be learned from the original content of the words employed, but only from the event to which they are here applied. The event to which the New Testament applies the expressions for revelation imparts to them a peculiar dynamic which is messianic in kind and implies a history of promise. The general impression could be described in the first instance by saying that with the cross and resurrection of Christ the one revelation of God, the glory of his lordship which embraces righteousness, life and freedom, has begun to move towards man.[1] In the gospel of the event of Christ this future is already present in the promises of Christ. It proclaims the present breaking in of this future, and thus *vice versa* this future announces itself in the promises of the gospel. The proclamation of Christ thus places men in the midst of an event of revelation which embraces the nearness of the coming Lord. It thereby makes the reality of man 'historic' and stakes it on history.

The eschatological tendency of the revelation in Christ is manifested by the fact that the revealing word is εὐαγγέλιον and ἐπαγγελία in one. J. Schniewind has rightly described ἐπαγγελία in Pauline theology as the 'complement' of εὐαγγέλιον.[2] The gospel of the revelation of God in Christ is thus in danger of

[1] H. Schulte, *Der Begriff der Offenbarung im Neuen Testament* (Beiträge zur Evangelischen Theologie 13), 1949, p. 23.
[2] *TWNT* II, p. 575, art. 'ἐπαγγελία' by J. Schniewind and G. Friedrich.

being incomplete and of collapsing altogether, if we fail to
notice the dimension of promise in it. Christology likewise
deteriorates if the dimension of the 'future of Christ' is not
regarded as a constitutive element in it.

But how is 'promise' proclaimed in the New Testament as
compared with the Old Testament history of promise? How is
the future horizon of promise asserted in the New Testament as
against the views of the Hellenistic mystery religions?

The approach to Christology has been sought in Christian
dogmatics along different lines. We here select two basic types
as illustrations of the problem.

Since the shaping of Christian dogmatics by Greek thought,
it has been the general custom to approach the mystery of
Jesus from the general idea of God in Greek metaphysics: the
one God, for whom all men are seeking on the ground of their
experience of reality, has appeared in Jesus of Nazareth – be it
that the highest eternal idea of goodness and truth has found
its most perfect teacher in him, or be it that in him eternal
Being, the Source of all things, has become flesh and appeared
in the multifarious world of transience and mortality. The
mystery of Jesus is then the incarnation of the one, eternal,
original, true and immutable divine Being. This line of approach was adopted in the Christology of the ancient Church
in manifold forms. Its problems accordingly resulted from the
fact that the Father of Jesus Christ was identified with the one
God of Greek metaphysics and had the attributes of this God
ascribed to him. If, however, the divinity of God is seen in his
unchangeableness, immutability, impassibility and unity, then
the historic working of this God in the Christ event of the cross
and resurrection becomes as impossible to assert as does his
eschatological promise for the future.

In modern times the approach to the mystery of Jesus has
often been from a general view of the being of man in history.
History has always existed, ever since man existed. But the
actual experiencing and conceiving of the existence of man as
historic, the radical disclosure of the historic character of
human existence, came into the world with Jesus. The word
and work of Jesus brought the decisive change in man's understanding of himself and the world, for by him man's self-
understanding in history was given its true expression as an

understanding of the historic character of human existence. Instead of a general question of God and a general idea of God, which finds its true expression in Jesus and is thus verified by him, what is here presupposed is a general concept of the being of man, a general questionableness of human existence, which finds its true expression in Jesus and is thus verified by him.

Both approaches to the mystery of Jesus set out from the universal, in order to find its true expression in the concrete instance of his person and his history. Neither of these approaches to Christology, to be sure, *need* bypass the Old Testament, but their way does not necessarily lie through it. The approach of Jesus to all men, however, has the Old Testament with its law and its promise as a necessary presupposition. It is therefore a real question whether we do not have to take seriously the importance for theology of the following two propositions:

1. It was *Yahweh*, the God of Abraham, of Isaac and of Jacob, the God of the promise, who raised Jesus from the dead. Who the God is who is revealed in and by Jesus, emerges only in his difference from, and identity with, the God of the Old Testament.

2. *Jesus was a Jew*. Who Jesus is, and what the human nature is which is revealed by him, emerges from his conflict with the law and the promise of the Old Testament.

If we take these starting points seriously, then the path of theological knowledge leads irreversibly from the particular to the general, from the historic to the eschatological and universal.

The first proposition would mean, that the God who reveals himself in Jesus must be thought of as the God of the Old Testament, as the God of the exodus and the promise, as the God with 'future as his essential nature', and therefore must not be identified with the Greek view of God, with Parmenides' 'eternal present' of Being, with Plato's highest Idea and with the Unmoved Mover of Aristotle, not even in his attributes. Who he is, is not declared by the world as a whole, but is declared by Israel's history of promise. His attributes cannot be expressed by negation of the sphere of the earthly, human, mortal and transient, but only in recalling and recounting the history of his promise. In Jesus Christ, however, the God of Israel has revealed himself as the God of all mankind. Thus the path leads

from the *concretum* to the *concretum universale*, not the other way
round. Christian theology has to think along *this* line. It is not
that a general truth became concrete in Jesus, but the concrete,
unique, historic event of the crucifying and raising of Jesus by
Yahweh, the God of promise who creates being out of nothing,
becomes general through the universal eschatological horizon
it anticipates.[1] Through the raising of Jesus from the dead the
God of the promises of Israel becomes the God of all men. The
Christian proclamation of this God will accordingly always
move within a horizon of general truth which it projects ahead
of it and towards which it tends, and will claim in advance to
be general in character and generally binding, even if its own
universality is of an eschatological kind and does not come of
abstract argument from the particular to the general.

If on the other hand theology takes seriously the fact that
Jesus was a Jew, then this means that he is not to be understood
as a particular case of human being in general, but only in connection with the Old Testament history of promise and in conflict with it. It is through the event of the cross and resurrection,
which is understandable only in the context of the conflict between law and promise, that he becomes the salvation of all
men, both Jews and Gentiles. It is the Christ event that first
gives birth to what can be theologically described as 'man',
'true man', 'humanity' – 'neither Jew nor Greek, neither bond
nor free, neither male nor female' (Gal. 3.28). Only when the
real, historic and religious differences between peoples, groups
and classes are broken down in the Christ event in which the
sinner is justified, does there come a prospect of what true
humanity can be and will be. The path leads here from the
historic and unique to the universal, because it leads from the
concrete event to the general in the sense of eschatological
direction. Christian proclamation will consequently here again
move within the horizon of general truth and make the claim
to be universally binding. It will have to expound this claim in
contra-distinction to other kinds of general anthropological
concepts of *humanitas*, precisely because its own general concept

---

[1] The trend is expressed in the New Testament in the ἐφάπαξ, in which the
thoughts of being once for all in history and of being universally eschatologically
binding intermerge. Cf. E. Käsemann, 'Das Problem des historischen Jesus', in
Exegetische Versuche und Besinnungen I, 1960, pp. 200f. (ET by W. J. Montague:
Essays on New Testament Themes [Studies in Biblical Theology 41], 1964, pp. 30f.).

of humanity has an eschatological content. It will not be able, for example, to set out from the fact that man is the being which possesses reason and language, and then go on to verify this aspect of his being by means of the event of justification, but it will set out on the contrary from the event of justification and calling, and then go on in face of other assertions as to the nature of man to uphold this event which makes man, theologically speaking, true man.

2. THE GOD OF THE PROMISE

When we take this approach to Christology into consideration, then it is peculiarly significant that in the New Testament God is known and described as the 'God of promise'. He is the θεὸς ἐπαγγειλάμενος (Heb. 10.23; 11.11, and frequently elsewhere). The essential predicate of God accordingly lies in the statement: Πιστὸς ὁ ἐπαγγειλάμενος, 'faithful is he that promised'. His essence is not his absoluteness as such, but the faithfulness with which he reveals and identifies himself in the history of his promise as 'the same'. His divinity consists in the constancy of his faithfulness, which becomes credible in the contradiction of judgment and grace. The word which reveals God has thus fundamentally the character of promise and is therefore eschatological in kind. It is grounded upon the event of God's faithfulness and open towards it. It sets us on a path whose goal it shows and guarantees in terms of promise. It places the one who receives it in a position of insurmountable antithesis and hostility to the existing reality of this world. It gives ground for hope and criticism, and expects us to endure in hope.

The result of this is a knowledge of God fundamentally different from the knowledge of the θεὸς ἐπιφανής in the surrounding world of the epiphany religions, of the Hellenistic mystery religions and finally of Greek metaphysics, even if in actual fact signs of syncretism are to be seen everywhere in the New Testament. The life, work, death and resurrection of Jesus are therefore not described after the pattern of the appearance of epiphany gods, but in the categories of expectation that are appropriate to the God of promise. Jesus is no θεῖος ἀνήρ, no divine man, although ideas of this kind are employed at many levels in the tradition. The gospels are not cult legends, but offer historical recollections under the auspices of eschatological hope, although traits of the cult legend are also to be found. The language of Christian mission is not the language of gnostic revelation,[1] although this type of language, too, is used on occasion. 'Thus although Christianity stands in the midst of the religious life of its time, epiphany faith can influence it in the first instance only as a formal element in its presentation. For it stands under the protection of the Old Testament thought of God, which expects God to act uniquely and comprehensively upon the world.'[2]

The word ἐπαγγελία has its roots in Hellenistic usage.[3] There it is generally used of promises, vows and pledges which men make to their gods. That God is the 'God who promises' is here obviously unknown. Linguistically speaking it appears to have no previous history in the Old Testament, although it is actually only in the Old Testament traditions that a previous history exists. 'It was through Judaism that ἐπαγγελία received its peculiar character as revealing word of God in the history of salvation.'[4] Here a theology of the promises of God was developed – and that, too, both in the rabbinical Torah theology and in the apocalyptic traditions. While in the former case promise means the promised reward of the righteous and is bound up with righteousness in the sense of the Torah, in the latter case it is used in the context of election and law to describe the 'future world' as opposed to this world, which is not able to bear what is promised to the righteous. In both traditions God is recognized as the God who promises, and whose faithfulness guarantees the fulfilment.

Just as for rabbinism and apocalyptic the figure of Abraham as the example of righteousness becomes the focal point of the

[1] Cf. G. Bornkamm, *Studien zu Antike und Urchristentum*, 1959, pp. 128ff. The Pauline proclamation is to be distinguished from the revelatory speeches of θεῖοι ἄνθρωποι, who present themselves as the commissioners or representatives of some deity, bring news from heaven, summon to repentance and promise salvation. Their characteristic mark is the 'hierophantic style' of their message. The style of Pauline preaching, on the contrary, is more like the style of the Cynic and Stoic diatribe, although he obviously understood himself and his preaching not as delivering Stoic wisdom, but spoke in apocalyptic expectation as a 'precursor of the end of the world' (cf. E. Käsemann, *ZTK* 60, 1963, p. 80).

[2] H. Schulte, *op. cit.*, p. 66. A similar conclusion is arrived at by Elpidius Pax, *Epiphaneia. Ein religionsgeschichtlicher Beitrag zur biblischen Theologie* (Münchener Theologische Studien), 1955.

[3] I am here following the article 'ἐπαγγελία' in *TWNT*.

[4] *TWNT* II, p. 578.

interest in the promise, law and righteousness of God, so also
Paul sets this figure in the centre of his exposition of gospel and
promise.[1] Yet his reason for going back to Abraham as the
'father of the promise' in contrast to Moses and the law lies in
the fact that for Paul the Christ event is not a renewal of the
people of God, but brings to life a 'new people of God' made
up of Jews and Gentiles. His quarrel with the Jewish Christians
is concerned, to be sure, with law and gospel, but it is really
centred on the promise. If for him Christ is the 'end of the law'
(Rom. 10.4), yet he does not see him as the end of the promise,
but on the contrary as its rebirth, its liberation and validation.

Paul links the traditional Abrahamitic promises with the
promise of life and obviously understands 'life' no longer in the
context of possessing the land, being fruitful and multiplying,
but as 'quickening of the dead' (Rom. 4.15, 17) As in Judaism
so also he, too, is certain that God keeps his promises. Yet the
ground of this assurance is new: because God has the power to
quicken the dead and call into being things that are not, therefore the fulfilment of his promise is possible, and because he
has raised Christ from the dead, therefore the fulfilment of his
promise is certain. Lack of assurance in, or doubt of, God's will
to fulfil it is therefore robbing God of his glory. Unbelief is
doubt of God's truthfulness, of his omnipotence and his faithfulness (Rom. 4.20). Unbelief does not let God be God, for it
doubts the dependability of God which guarantees his promises.
Paul manifestly sees the concrete form of such unbelief in the
theology of Torah, righteousness, in which the power of the
promise towards its fulfilment is bound to the fulfilling of
the law. If, however, the promise of God is bound to the law,
then the promise is invalidated: it then depends no longer on
the power of the God who has promised, but on the power of
the man who obeys. But the wrath of God will be revealed
upon all who leave the law unfulfilled or transgress it. Hence
law and promise are mutually exclusive, just as glorying in the
works of the law and glorying in the God who justifies sinners

[1] Cf. C. Dietzfelbinger, *Paulus und das Alte Testament* (Theologische Existenz
heute, NF 95), 1961; E. Schlink, 'Gesetz und Paraklese', in *Antwort: Festschrift für
K. Barth*, 1956, pp. 323ff.; U. Wilckens, 'Die Rechtfertigung Abrahams nach
Röm. 4', in *Studien zur alttestamentlichen Überlieferung*, 1961, pp. 111ff.; G. Klein,
'Röm. 4 und die Idee der Heilsgeschichte', *EvTh* 23, 1963, pp. 424ff.; E. Jüngel,
'Das Gesetz zwischen Adam und Christus', *ZTK* 60, 1963, pp. 42ff.

and quickens the dead are mutually exclusive. The law does
not have within it the power of the promised life and of the
resurrection, but exposes life to death and leads it to death. The
law does not have within it the power of justification, but the
power to expose sins and to make them exceeding sinful. For
the promise has in the form of the law been made of no effect.
Just as for Paul the justification of the godless and the life that
comes of the raising of the dead belong together, so also for him
the righteousness of faith and the validation of the promise in
the raising of Christ belong together. 'If they which are of the
law be heirs, faith is made void, and the promise made of none
effect' (Rom. 4.14). But if, on the contrary, the promise is set
in force by God, then it confers righteousness by faith. 'Therefore it is "of faith", that it might be by grace; to the end the
promise might be sure (βεβαίαν) to all the seed; not to that
only which is of the law, but to that also which is of the faith
of Abraham; who is the father of us all' (Rom. 4.16). Promise
would no longer be the promise of God, who quickens the dead
and calls into being what is not, if it had anything to do with the
law. 'If the inheritance be of the law, it is no more of promise'
(Gal. 3.18). If we sought to attain the inheritance of the promise through fulfilling the law, then we should lose this inheritance, for by the promise God showed himself to Abraham
as gracious (Gal. 3.18). The true heirs of the promise and children of Abraham are therefore those who are partakers of the
promise in faith in Christ (Gal. 3.29). For by the gospel the
Gentiles become partakers of the promise in Christ (Eph. 3.6).

It is plainly recognizable how the gospel in its antithesis to
the law is here related to the promise. Paul does not use Abraham, as an example by which to illustrate his new understanding of righteousness by faith, but the struggle for the inheritance of Abraham as between the gospel of the raising of
the crucified Christ and the Torah is concerned with the 'power
of the promise'. If Christ is the 'end of the Torah' (Rom. 10.4),
yet he is there for Israel 'for the sake of the truth of God, to
confirm the promises made unto the fathers' (Rom. 15.8). If
the true heirs of Abraham, the father of the promise, are those
in whom the Abrahamitic promise gives proof of itself in the
Christ event in the power of the God who justifies men and
creates life out of death, then that is the end of the Jew's

precedence over the Gentile in the history of salvation. What was promised to Israel is now valid for all believers, both Jews and Gentiles. The promise is no longer exclusive, but becomes inclusive. It becomes universal. This universalizing of the promise comes of its being liberated from the confining grip of the law and the election of Israel. If in the power of God, as seen in the raising of the Crucified and, as a result of that, in the justification and calling of the godless, the promise has become unconditional – of grace and not of the law – then it has also become unrestricted and is therefore valid 'without distinction'. If the Christ event thus contains the validation (βεβαίωσις) of the promise, then this means no less than that through the faithfulness and truth of God the promise is made true in Christ – and made true wholly, unbreakably, for ever and for all. Nothing more stands in the way of its fulfilment, for sins are forgiven in him (Heb. 9.15). Between this once-for-all validation of the promise and its fulfilment in the glory of God there stands only the dependability of God himself. Hence the promise now determines the existence of the recipient and all he does and suffers. It is not that *vice versa* the fulfilling of the promise is determined by the existence and behaviour of the recipient.

The gospel has its inabrogable presupposition in the Old Testament history of promise. In the gospel the Old Testament history of promise finds more than a fulfilment which does away with it; it finds its future. 'All the promises of God in him are yea, and in him Amen' (II Cor. 1.20). They have become an eschatological certainty in Christ, by being liberated and validated, made unconditional and universal. The history of promise which the gospel presupposes is not annulled. The Israel which comes into view with the presupposed promise is not paganized,[1] but on the contrary it has disclosed to it in the gospel the future and the certainty of its own promises. The Christ event can be understood as a reversal of the history of promise: the first will be last. It is not that the Gentiles will come and worship when Zion is at the last redeemed from its shame, but Israel will come when the fulness of the Gentiles have become partakers of the promise in Christ (Rom. 9–11). Thus the gospel is not to be understood as antiquating the promises of Israel or even putting an end to them. In the

---

[1] Against G. Klein, *op. cit.*, p. 436.

ultimate, eschatological sense of these promises it is in fact identical with them.

On the other hand, the gospel itself becomes unintelligible,
if the contours of the promise are not recognized in it itself.
It would lose its power to give eschatological direction, and
would become either gnostic talk of revelation or else preaching
of morals, if it were not made clear that the gospel constitutes
on earth and in time the promise of the future of Christ. The
gospel is promise and as promise it is an earnest of the promised
future. 'The divine word in Christ is new solely because its
fulfilment can no longer be endangered or abolished, as was
once the case, but has become incontestable; and it is unique,
despite all its varied earthly movement and manifold testimony
and despite its prolepsis in the Old Testament, because in
Christ it not only reveals anew the one eschatological salvation,
but in addition also conclusively guarantees the realizing of
that salvation. As such it is already present and apprehensible
in history, yet solely in the form of promise, i.e. as pointing and
directing us towards a still outstanding future.'[1]

3. PAUL AND ABRAHAM

How are we to regard the connection between gospel and
promise, and thus in a wider sense also the relation between the
New and the Old Testaments? Two radically opposed conceptions suggest themselves: the continuity can be understood in
terms of a view of history as history of salvation,[2] or the discontinuity can be understood in terms of an existentialist interpretation of the gospel.[3] Both methods employ concepts of
history with which it is barely possible to comprehend the manifold perspectives in which Paul expounds the gospel's relation
to law and promise.

A view of the *continuity* in terms of the history of election or of
salvation, whatever its precise form, understands the gospel as
the fulfilment of the history that has preceded it. The event of
Christ accordingly cannot be taken by itself as an isolated fact.

[1] E. Käsemann, *Das wandernde Gottesvolk*, 4th ed. 1961, pp. 12f.
[2] This is best shown by U. Wilckens' essay, 'Die Rechtfertigung Abrahams nach
Röm. 4', *op. cit.*
[3] This emerges most clearly in G. Klein's reply to Wilckens, 'Röm. 4 und die
Idee der Heilsgeschichte', *op. cit.*

It always requires the witness of the history which it fulfils, if its significance as an event of universal eschatological salvation is to be intelligible. It is only by the witness of the Old Testament 'scripture' that the gospel shows the Christ event to be the fulfilment of the history of God's election. This is done not only by taking the saving events of the New Testament as the clue to the exposition of the Old Testament, but also *vice versa* by taking the saving events of the Old Testament as the clue to the understanding of the event of Christ. It is true of course that Paul set the Old Testament promise to Abraham in a universal eschatological context: the 'land' has become the world, and his 'seed' has become all nations.[1] But this reinterpretation must prove itself to be a true interpretation of what was to be interpreted. The Christian interpretation of Abraham must make the claim that 'this beginning of the history of election in the promise of God and the faith of Abraham' points '*in essence* to its end as its fulfilment'.[2] The result of this is on the one hand a view of the fulfilment in the Christ event in terms of 'history of election', and secondly, an 'essential' view of the meaning of this history, i.e. a view which is arrived at in the light of its end and which 'in truth' underlies the story of Abraham. The Christ event thus has its place in a definite history: it is the fulfilment of that history and as such reveals its essence and truth. Christian faith is grounded in history, itself stands in history, and trusts in history. Faith and history belong together. Faith is not a possibility which is severally, and to that extent generally, open to individuals, but is due to a definite history of election and is concrete trust in future divine action.

What is here asserted as a continuity in the history of election and salvation from Abraham to Christ is no doubt noetically accessible only from the standpoint of the Christ event. The exposition and appropriation of the promise to Abraham in Christian faith cannot, however, present itself as insight into an 'essentially' coherent chain from Abraham to Christ. Christian faith is not a view of the essence of history underlying

---

[1] Whereas U. Wilckens speaks of an extension of the promise to Abraham in Pauline exegesis (*op. cit.*, p. 124), the tendency elsewhere is apparently to speak of a 'Pauline reduction' of the Abrahamitic promises to the fact of the promise having been given to Abraham, with little regard to its content. Cf. C. Dietzfelbinger, *op. cit.*, pp. 7ff.

[2] U. Wilckens, *op. cit.*, p. 125.

the temporal and concrete statements of the Old Testament tradition. The 'newness' of the New Testament is not to be seen merely in the disclosing of the essence and truth of the Old Testament. The continuity cannot be defined merely in terms of an essence of history which becomes apparent in the light of its end.

An existentialist interpretation of the *discontinuity*, on the other hand, takes 'history' out of the light of the promise and sets it in the light of the law. History here becomes the epitome of existence under the law – of the fact that man must understand himself from his works and, in analogy thereto, from established, demonstrable complexes of history. 'History' is here understood as a genealogical force. It becomes the epitome of transience and degeneration. It becomes the realm of the things that are ready to man's hand, calculable, objectively demonstrable, at his disposal. All views of history which provide surveyable complexes thus belong in principle to the realm of deficient, objectifying thought. Understanding oneself from history is therefore synonymous with man's understanding of himself from the world. If history is understood in this way in the light of the law, then faith and history never belong together; on the contrary, faith lies 'athwart' history and destroys every kind of historic continuity, including that which is understood in terms of the history of election and salvation. Faith brings liberation from history and is itself the eschatological crisis of history in the individual. The element of continuity between Abraham and the believer is accordingly not to be regarded as a 'product of historic development', but can only be understood as 'a retrospective projection of faith',[1] which is not demonstrable by historical science and must therefore itself again be an object of faith.

But now, in this antithesis of history and faith, faith is dialectically anchored to a negative concept of history from which it must repeatedly distinguish itself. On the other hand, history is dialectically anchored to a subjectivistic concept of faith, as a result of which it must repeatedly be seen in terms of the above-mentioned identification of legalistic and objectifying thought. It is easy to see how strongly the modern positivistic concept of history prevails in this identification of legalistic

[1] Cf. G. Klein, *op. cit.*, p. 440.

and objectifying thought. The result of this concept is that the searching, knowing and objectifying subject frees itself from the power of history, of genealogy and of tradition by means of this reflection, and withdraws into the objectively incomprehensible background of a transcendental subjectivity and spontaneity. What a thus subjectified faith sees in history, must then become an 'expression' of faith itself. What a faith understood in such terms has to say of Abraham, becomes a 'projection' of faith – a projection which, because it is unprovable, faith believes. This, however, makes it unintelligible why Paul does not use the figure of Abraham merely to illustrate his own view of righteousness by faith, but enters into a dispute with Jews and Jewish Christians over the inheritance of Abraham. In this antithesis to 'history' as such, which then includes automatically also the Old Testament history of promise, it becomes as impossible to say what is 'new' in the New Testament as to say what is 'new' in gnosticism. But when the 'old' is thus defined in the light of our antithesis to a history that is seen as the realm of the objective, demonstrable and disposable, then the 'new' becomes nothing else but faith in the form of immediate subjectivity, of pure, subjective conception from the realm of the indisposable. When we see it in this light, the 'new' is not very new – not at least as compared with the ecstatic gnostic passion for newness. The Old Testament is not then regarded as being historic testimony to the promise and as such having present relevance along with its fulfilment in the New Testament, but it can be presented by a transcendentally understood faith in Christ only in terms of antithesis, as a thing we have always left beneath us.

Now it is no doubt true that Paul rejects the idea of the Jews' genealogical connection with Abraham being in itself soteriological. Yet what he puts in its place is hardly a picture of Abraham as projected by Christian faith, but he manifestly regards Abraham and his promise as forming both theologically and materially a necessary bone of contention with Torah Judaism. Projections of faith which are undemonstrable and have to be believed are not things one can contend about. A view of the essence of history, too, is really only a thing one either can or cannot see. Paul, however, deals 'objectively' with Abraham and his promise, in the sense that he understands them

as an object of contention in necessary proceedings against the
Jews. Thus it is really a question of the correct exposition of
the Abrahamitic promise as between the claims of the Torah
and the claims of the gospel. The continuity with the Abrahamitic promise can therefore be taken neither as a product of
historic development nor as a retrospective projection of faith.
The continuity of the promise to Abraham exists according
to Paul where the promise is eschatologically validated. If Paul
is concerned in this sense with the 'object' of the promise
to Abraham, then his exposition and appropriation of it is
neither a dictate of the historic development nor a creation of
his believing phantasy. His gospel does not derive by necessity
from the essence of the history of election, but neither does the
promise to Abraham appear in his gospel by chance. Because
his gospel proclaims the promise as validated in the event of
Christ, it starts the traditional promise to Abraham off on a
new history. The promise finds in the gospel its eschatological
future, while the law finds its end. The 'newness' of the gospel is
thus not 'totally new'. It proves its newness by asserting itself
against the old, against human nature in the context of law,
sin and death, and thereby bringing about the 'oldness' of the
old. It proves its eschatological newness, however, by using the
previously proclaimed promise of God as the means of its
explication. Paul rediscovers the promise to Abraham in the
gospel of Christ and therfore recalls along with the gospel of
Christ the promise to Abraham as well. The history of law and
gospel takes its bearings from the theological problem of the
past. The history of promise and gospel, however, takes its
bearings from the eschatological problem of the future. Without
the relating of the gospel to what was promised in advance, it
loses its own bearing on the eschatological future and threatens
to transform itself into gnostic talk of revelation. Without relation to the promise in the gospel, faith loses the driving-power
of hope and becomes credulity.

Because the gospel presents itself as validation of the promise
of the God of Abraham by the same God, it must enter into a
judicial process with Judaism concerning the future of the
promise, while on the other hand it must bring Gentiles to
hope in the God of promise. It has then the Old Testament at
its side neither as a historic documentation of its fulfilment nor

as a history of examples of human failure in the things of God. Just as the promise is validated in the gospel, so also the Old Testament, inasmuch as it is witness to the history of the promise, is validated and renewed in the New Testament.

Formally speaking, between the promise to Abraham that is witnessed at many levels of the Old Testament and the gospel of Christ that is witnessed in the New Testament, there takes place a 'word-history',[1] a history of tradition or the history of the working of the traditional hope. This history of word and tradition is materially determined by that future which is announced and promised in the transmission and constantly new reception of the promise. That is why Paul apparently sees the continuity as being given in the 'scripture', whose meaning and goal he finds in the present hope (Rom. 15.4). What the scripture that was 'written before our time' offers must therefore contain possibilities and a future to which present hope can be directed. The exposition and presentation of what was written 'aforetime' must accordingly pay attention to that in it which is promised, open, unsettled and points to the future. Because the gospel directs men to the future of eschatological salvation, it has its presupposition in the promises that were issued and written aforetime, and along with the future of Christ it presents also the future of what was aforetime promised (Rom. 1.2).[2] It links on to promises that have been issued but not yet fulfilled and takes them up into itself. This is a process belonging to the sphere of the history of the promise. The promise which was promised aforetime is not interpreted in terms of the history of salvation, nor is it taken as an opportune occasion for a new projection of faith, but it is validated. Something thereby happens to it – something the New Testament understands as eschatologically 'new' – but this new thing

---

[1] So E. Jüngel, *ZTK* 60, 1963, p. 46.

[2] E. Jüngel, *op. cit.*, p. 45: 'To the past there belongs, as compared with the gospel, on the one hand the promise and on the other hand the law. The promise belongs to the past as the historic presupposition of the gospel – and that, too, in the sense that the gospel makes the promise the presupposition of *itself* (cf. Rom. 1.2). Since the promise has its future in the gospel and has its own time because of this future, I call the mode in which the promise belongs to the past as compared with the gospel *the anticipation* of the gospel (*das Zuvor des Evangeliums*). Because the law has its end in the gospel and is made past because of this end, I call the mode in which the law belongs to the past as compared with the gospel *the antecedent* of the gospel (*das Vorher des Evangeliums*).'

does happen to it. Remembering the promise issued aforetime means asking about the future in the past. It is dominated by that expectation which is made possible by the eschatological validation and liberation of the promise. The promise to Abraham is called to mind in order to proclaim the gospel of Christ to Jews and Gentiles and to call them into the new people of God. The calling to mind is thus a necessary part of the proclamation of the gospel. In this way of calling to mind past promises and in this hope in the form of remembrance we are no longer presented with the alternative between a complex of saving history which is a product of history, and unprovable retrospective projections of faith which are products of subjective faith. We take the past promises up into our own eschatological future as disclosed by the gospel and give them breadth. We do not interpret past history. We do not emancipate ourselves from history altogether, but we enter into the history that is determined by the promised and guaranteed *eschaton*, and we expect from it not only the future of the present but also the future of the past.

4. FULFILMENT ECSTASY IN PRIMITIVE CHRISTIANITY AND THE *eschatologia crucis*

The promissory character of the gospel can be seen not only from the language used especially by Paul and in Hebrews. It shows itself still more plainly in the conflicts in which Paul was involved with various tendencies in primitive Christianity. As long as Christianity remained within the sphere of Judaism with its apocalyptic outlook and its expectation of the Messiah, it was only natural that it should take an eschatological view of the Christ event and of the gospel. Only, here the Christians also remained within the bounds of the Jewish expectations and understood themselves as the 'renewed people of God' and maintained the gospel as the 'renewed covenant' of Israel. It was only the move into the Gentile world that compelled them to a new understanding of the gospel. The gospel shows itself effective by justifying the godless and calling the Gentiles to the God of hope. The Church which thereby arises and consists of both Jews and Gentiles, can therefore no longer be understood as the 'renewed people of God' but now only as the 'new people of God'. This crossing of the frontiers of Israel on to Hellenistic soil, however, brought with it problems of considerable magnitude. If it was here no longer possible to understand the Church as a Christian synagogue, then it was a short step on the other hand to the misunderstanding of the Church as a Christian mystery religion. The question arises, what it was that prevented Christianity from presenting itself to the Hellenistic world as a Christian mystery religion. What was it in its inheritance that proved resistent to an assimilation of this kind?

The view of the Christian faith as a mystery religion takes palpable form for us in that ecstatic Hellenistic fervour with which Paul finds himself embroiled in Corinth.[1] Yet the various hymns and fragments of confessions in the Pauline and deutero-Pauline epistles also show that similar ideas presumably lay at the root of the whole Christian outlook where it came within the influence of the Hellenistic mystery religions. It is generally a question here of the influence exerted upon Christianity by the epiphany religion of the time, of which it can be said: 'Since the man of myth lives only for the present, epiphany is for him already fulfilment. Eschatological thinking is foreign to him.'[2] The influence of this kind of piety shows itself not only as a formal element in the self-presentation of Christianity on Hellenistic soil, but quite certainly extends also to the understanding of the event of Christ. The Christ event can here be understood in a wholly non-eschatological way as epiphany of the eternal present in the form of the dying and rising Kyrios of the cultus. Then, however, the place of the scriptural authentication κατὰ τὰς γραφάς is taken by the cultic epiphany as proof of its own self in a timeless sense. Baptism into the death and resurrection of Christ then means that the goal of redemption is already attained, for in this baptism eternity is sacramentally present. The believing participant is transposed from the realm of death, of constraining forces and of the old aeon of transience into the eternally present realm of freedom, of heavenly life and of resurrection. All that now remains for him on earth is to exhibit his new, heavenly nature in freedom. In the sacramental and spiritual presence of Christ, resurrection from the dead is already imparted to the receivers

---

[1] I am here following E. Käsemann's studies in exegetical theology.
[2] Elpidius Pax, *op. cit.*, p. 266.

and is eternally present to them. The earthly body and the things of the world fade away to become for them an unreal semblance, in the disregarding of which they must give proof of their heavenly freedom.¹ 'Among these Gentile Christians, as I Corinthians amply shows, there is a total view of the tradition at work within a framework of ideas which is not – as with Paul himself – that of the primitive Christian eschatology of the early Jewish tradition, but manifestly that of Hellenistic ideas of epiphany. As a result of this, all religious thought and experience is so strongly oriented towards the ever present event of the coming of the Spirit as the epiphanous presentation of the exalted Kyrios, that the content of the eschatologically oriented tradition is included within this total view.'²

What is the relation between this Christian mystery religion, which we have here only roughly outlined, and the primitive Christian apocalyptic expectations that were kindled by the riddle and the open question of the Easter appearance of Jesus? Did the original apocalyptic already contain the conditions of its possible transformation into terms of the epiphany piety of Hellenistic mystery religion? Did Hellenistic mystery religion in its Christian form still remain what it originally was?

It is plain that the ecstasy of Christian mystery religion has its presupposition in an apocalyptic ecstasy which was a feature of primitive Christianity, and which thought to perceive in the experience of the Spirit the fulfilment of long awaited promises. This non-Hellenistic, apocalyptic ecstasy, which arose from the consciousness of living in the age of the fulfilment of the divine promises, was then certainly able later on to identify this fulfilment with the timeless epiphany of the eternal presence of God. It was theologically able to take the original, temporal and teleological statements about the fulfilment of promises and translate them into timeless types of the presence of the eternal. It was therefore also able *vice versa*, in face of the Greek search for the eternal present in the mystery cults, to offer the cult of

¹ Schniewind, 'Die Leugner der Auferstehung in Korinth', in *Nachgelassene Reden und Aufsätze*, 1952, pp. 110ff.; E. Käsemann, 'Zum Thema der urchristlichen Apokalyptik', *ZTK* 59, 1962, p. 277.
² U. Wilckens, 'Der Ursprung der Überlieferung der Erscheinung des Auferstandenen', in *Dogma und Denkstruktur*, 1963, p. 61.

Christ as the true presence of the eternal. Thus it is a reciprocal process, whose result could be a 'presentative eschatology' on the one hand, but also on the other hand a 'presence of eternity'. The ecstatic eschatology of fulfilment could present itself in Greek terms, and the Greek idea of the presence of eternity could offer itself as a fulfilment of eschatological expectations. Thus even the Christian mystery religion still retained the appeal of finality and uniqueness, even when the explicit connection with the old eschatological hopes for the future was lost. Yet the temporally final (*das Endzeitliche*) now became the conclusively final (*das Endgültige*), and the conclusively final became the eternal.[1] In the light of this process of transformation it is possible to understand the early Church's passion for absoluteness; for with the departure from the eschatological categories of expectation the Church did not by any means turn itself into a relative body among the existing religions and cults, but took its confession of the one God, which could then be formulated in the terms of Greek metaphysics, and combined it quite definitely with a passionate assertion of the final and unique revelation of the one and only God in Christ. This process of transformation, which has often been described, took place not so much on the ground of an eschatology that had been abandoned because of the delayed parousia of Christ and the disappointed hopes of his nearness, as rather on the ground of an ecstasy of fulfilment which took the *eschaton* that was to be expected and transformed it into the presence of eternity as experienced in cultus and in spirit. It was not so much disappointed hopes but rather the supposed fulfilment of all hopes that led the acute Hellenization of Christianity but also to the acute Christianizing of Hellenism. 'Expectation of the nearness of Christ and his parousia has now become meaning-

[1] This transformation has been very acutely perceived by H. von Soden. Cf. *Urchristentum und Geschichte* I, 1951, p. 29: 'Christianity was of course originally a message of the end of the world, of the new, heavenly aeon, and to that extent was critical of all culture. Yet it was just the strictly transcendental view of the new aeon, as a renewal that was to be miraculously brought about by God, that caused the critical attitude towards the old, existing aeon to be in practice extremely conservative. The existing order of things, as being the *temporally* final order, was felt to be historically speaking the *conclusively* final order. . . . It is extremely important to be clear about this most peculiar view in early Christianity of the temporally final as the conclusively final, in other words the transformation of the temporally final into the conclusively final, of the transient into the immutable; and thus to be clear that the eschatological revolution necessarily worked out as a most conservative force. . . .'

less, because all that apocalyptic still hoped for appears to be already realized.'¹

· What are the consequences of this view of presentative eschatology as the presence of eternity? The event of promise, which is what the life and teaching, dying and raising of Jesus were held to be, now becomes an event of redemption, which can be subsequently repeated in the cultus in the form of a mystery drama. The sacramental event bestows participation in the dying and rising of the God. The solemn representation regarded the raising of Jesus as his enthronement as exalted Kyrios and took it to be already completed and therefore now awaiting only representation. 'In place of the hidden Lord of the world, who in truth is as yet only designated as such and whose return in glory to assume earthly power is still awaited by the Church, we have the Lord who now already reigns over all forces and powers and thus over the world hitherto dominated by them.² With this change from the apocalyptic of the promised and still outstanding lordship of Christ to the cultic presence of his eternal, heavenly lordship there goes at the same time also a waning of theological interest in the cross. The resurrection of Jesus is regarded as his exaltation and enthronement and is related to his incarnation. To be sure, his humiliation even to the cross can be understood as the perfecting of his incarnation, by means of which he draws all things into the sphere of his lordship, yet the cross is in this way made only a transitional stage on his way to heavenly lordship. The cross does not remain until the fulfilment of the *eschaton* the abiding key-signature of his lordship in the world. If his resurrection is understood in this sense as his heavenly enthronement, then the sacramental event which represents him in the cultus becomes a parallel to his incarnation and is taken as an earthly adumbration and accomplishment of his heavenly lordship, his heavenly life in the realm of the things that are earthly, transient and split up into a multitude of forces.

History thus loses its eschatological direction. It is not the realm in which men suffer and hope, groaning and travailing in expectation of Christ's future for the world, but it becomes the

¹ E. Käsemann, *ZTK* 59, 1962, p. 278.
² *Ibid.*, p. 274.

field in which the heavenly lordship of Christ is disclosed in Church and sacrament. In place of the eschatological 'not yet' (*noch nicht*) we have a cultic 'now only' (*nur noch*), and this becomes the key-signature of history *post Christum*. It is understandable that this disclosure of the eternal, heavenly lordship of Christ can then be regarded as a continuation of his incarnation. Here the transient continues in the light of the intransient things of heaven, the mortal continues in the light of the immortal things of heaven, and what is split up into multiplicity is transfigured in the lordship of the divinely one. A future expectation which is expressed sacramentally and in terms of salvation history takes the place of that of earthly eschatology: the Church gradually permeates the world with heavenly truth, with powers of heavenly life and with heavenly salvation. The world is led by the one Church to the Christ who is one with the one God, and is thus brought to unity and salvation. The eschatological expectation of what has 'not yet' happened becomes a noetic expectation of the universal disclosure and glorification of what has already happened in heaven. The old apocalyptic dualism which distinguished the passing aeon from the coming aeon is transformed into a metaphysical dualism which understands the coming as the eternal and the passing as transience. Instead of citizens of the coming kingdom we have a people redeemed from heaven. Instead of the citizens of the passing aeon we have those that are earthly and of the world. And finally, the cross becomes a timeless sacrament of martyrdom which perfects the martyr and unites him with the heavenly Christ.

With these few examples we can let the matter rest. The trend towards early Catholicism and the life and thought of the ancient Church is plain. The ecstasy of eschatological fulfilment in the Christ event is the presupposition for this process of the transformation of Christianity into an ecstatic form of Hellenistic mystery religion and into an ecumenical world Church. This form of 'presentative eschatology', this religion of the presence of the eternal whose eschatological determination is now only subliminal, can be called an *eschatologia gloriae,* if it is still possible to comprehend it in eschatological categories at all.

In this context Paul's passionate polemic against Hellenistic ecstasy in Corinth acquires an abiding significance, as do also his correctives to that Hellenistic type of Christian theology which afterwards became standard. His criticism clearly has two focal points. For one thing, there is an 'eschatological proviso'[1] which he maintains against this fulfilment ecstasy. It consists of the so-called 'relics of apocalyptic theology' which assert themselves in his view of the resurrection of Christ, of the sacrament, of the presence of the Spirit, of the earthly obedience of the believer, and of course in his future expectations. And secondly, there is his theology of the cross, in which he opposes the ecstasy that abandons the earth on which that cross stands. There is a profound material connection between these two starting points of his criticism. We shall therefore call the basis of his criticism the *eschatologia crucis*, meaning by this both objections in one.

When Bultmann interprets Paul by seeing the heart of Pauline theology in Paul's anthropological and existentialist interpretation of the peculiarity of presentative eschatology, then he has undoubtedly discovered an important modification of the theology of the eternal present, but not really a fundamental alternative to it. Presentative eschatology can appear equally well both in mythological dress and in existentialist interpretation. The 'presence of eternity' can be expressed both in the language of world-picture and myth, and can also be stated in paradoxical terms as a *nunc aeternum* in the history of existence. If Pauline criticism consisted merely in this transposition, then it would certainly contain an important modification of the theology of the Hellenistic church, but not a truly transforming corrective. But now, the polemic in which Paul attacks Hellenism is marked both by a new recognition of the significance of the cross of Christ and also by a new recognition of a truly futurist eschatology, and thus becomes a criticism of presentative eschatology as such.[2] 'The apostle's anti-ecstatic struggle, however, is in the last and deepest analysis fought out in the name of apocalyptic.'[3] This does not refer to mere repetitions or tiresome relics of late Jewish apocalyptic in Paul, but means his own apocalyptic, which is kindled by an eschatology

---

[1] E. Käsemann, *ZTK* 59, 1962, p. 279.
[2] E. Käsemann, *ZTK* 54, 1957, p. 14.
[3] E. Käsemann, *ZTK* 59, 1962, p. 279.

of the cross and is therefore hostile to every eschatological ecstasy of fulfilment.

Against the uniting of the believer with the dying and rising Lord of the cultus after the fashion of the mysteries Paul asserts an eschatological distinction: baptism is the means of participation in the Christ event of the crucifixion and death of Christ. Fellowship with Christ is fellowship in suffering with the crucified Christ. The baptized are dead with Christ, if they are baptized into his death. But they are not already risen with him and translated into heaven in the perfect tense of the cultus. They attain participation in the resurrection of Christ by new obedience, which unfolds itself in the realm of the hope of resurrection. In the power of the Spirit who raised Christ from the dead, they can obediently take upon them the sufferings of discipleship and in these very sufferings await the future glory. 'Participation in the resurrection is spoken of not in the perfect, but in the future tense.'[1] Christ is risen and beyond the reach of death, yet his followers are not yet beyond the reach of death, but it is only through their hope that they here attain to participation in the life of the resurrection. Thus resurrection is present to them in hope and as promise. This is an eschatological presentness of the future, not a cultic presence of the eternal. The believer does not already in the cultus and in spirit find full participation in the lordship of Christ, but he is led by hope into the tensions and antitheses of obedience and suffering in the world. The life of everyday accordingly becomes the sphere of the true service of God (Rom. 12.1ff.). Inasmuch as call and promise point the believer on the way of obedience in the body and on earth, earth and the body are set within the horizon of the expectation of the coming lordship of Christ. 'The reality of the new life stands or falls with the promise that God remains faithful and does not abandon his work.'[2] Hence the trials of the body and the opposition of the world are not understood as signs of a paradoxical presence of the eternal but are accepted in terms of seeking after, and calling for, the coming freedom in the kingdom of Christ. This is not 'now only' the sphere of transience, in which the believer has to demonstrate his heavenly freedom, but it is the reality in which the

---

[1] *Ibid.*
[2] E. Käsemann, 'Paulus und der Frühkatholizismus', *ZTK* 60, 1963, p. 83.

Paul: ethic → the coming Kingdom

Church along with the whole creation groans for its redemption from the powers of annihilation in the future of Christ and earnestly awaits it (Rom. 8.18ff.). The imperative of the Pauline call to new obedience is accordingly not to be understood merely as a summons to demonstrate the indicative of the new being in Christ, but it has also its eschatological presupposition in the future that has been promised and is to be expected – the coming of the Lord to judge and to reign. Hence it ought not to be rendered merely by saying: 'Become what you are!', but emphatically also by saying: 'Become what you will be!'

✱ The believer is given not the eternal Spirit of heaven, but the eschatological 'earnest of the Spirit' – of the Spirit, moreover, who *has* raised Christ from the dead and *will* quicken our mortal bodies (Rom. 8.11). For the word which leads the believer into the truth is promise of eternal life, but not yet that life itself. The observance of this eschatological distinction manifests itself also in the apostle's Christology. If in I Cor. 15.3–5 he takes over a primitive Christian tradition of the resurrection kerygma, yet his expositions of it in the verses that follow are nevertheless original. He extends the picture into the future and shows what is to be expected because with the resurrection of Christ it is held in prospect and has been made a certainty (I Cor. 15.25): 'He *must* reign, till he hath put all enemies under his feet.' This shows that in the future possibilities there is an element of necessity in the sense that they can be relied on and are to be expected. The tendencies and

---

[1] Paul's eschatological thinking always combines the perfect tense of the raising of Jesus with the future tense of the eschatological future. Both are seen in a context in which each is the ground of the other. The primitive Christian confession, 'that Jesus died and is risen', is thus expounded in a way totally different from the mystery cult of the dying and rising God. The Christ event is presented within the framework of an eschatological expectation of what is to come, and the future expectation is grounded in the Christ event. I Thess. 4.14 ('if we believe *that* Jesus *died* and *rose* again, even so them also which sleep in Jesus *will* God bring with him') is as typical of this as is the exposition of the confession of I Cor. 15.3–5 in I Cor. 15.20ff. In all this, the connection between the resurrection of Jesus and the future which is expected is neither uniformly apocalyptic nor uniformly christological, but mutually complementary: If there is no resurrection of the dead, then neither is Christ risen. If Christ is risen, then the dead will rise and Christ 'must' reign over all his enemies, including also death. It is not a δεῖ ('must') in terms of salvation history, but one that discloses the future necessity and future tendency inherent in the event of the resurrection of Jesus. That is why it is linked not to the expectation of a fate, as in apocalyptic, but to the Kyrios title of Jesus. Cf. U. Wilckens, 'Der Ursprung der Überlieferung . . .', in *Dogma und Denkstruktur* 1963, pp. 55ff.

latent implications in the resurrection event are drawn out into the future opened up by it. With the raising of Jesus all has not yet been done. The end of death's domination is still outstanding. The overcoming of all opposition to God is still outstanding in that future reality of which Paul says that 'God will be all in all' (I Cor. 15.28). Finally, even the coming world lordship of Christ over all his enemies can once again be eschatologically surpassed, in that not even his lordship is in itself the eternal presence of God, but has an eschatologically provisional character in which it serves the sole and all-embracing lordship of God.

When these perspectives are borne in mind, then it becomes clear that the Easter appearances of the risen Christ are not covered by the theological answer that he is the presence of the eternal, but require the development of a new eschatology. The resurrection has set in motion an eschatologically determined process of history, whose goal is the annihilation of death in the victory of the life of the resurrection, and which ends in that righteousness in which God receives in all things his due and the creature thereby finds its salvation. It is only from the standpoint of a presentative eschatology or a theology of the eternal present that the eschatological and anticipatory thinking displayed by Paul in I Cor. 15 can be regarded as a relapse into outmoded apocalyptic mythology. Yet it is not by an existentialist interpretation of the religion of the eternal present that the mythology of that religion is overcome, but only an eschatology of promise can overcome its mythical and illusionary view of the world and of human existence, because it alone takes the trials, the contradictions and the godlessness of this world seriously in a meaningful way, because it makes faith and obedience possible in the world not by regarding the contradictions as of no account, but by enabling us to believe and obey on the ground of our hope in the overcoming of these contradictions by God. Faith does not come to its own in becoming radically unworldly, but by hopeful outgoing into the world it becomes a benefit to the world. By accepting the cross, the suffering and the death of Christ, by taking upon it the trials and struggles of obedience in the body and surrendering itself to the pain of love, it proclaims in the everyday world the future of the resurrection, of life and the righteousness of God.

The future of the resurrection comes to it as it takes upon itself the cross. Thus the eschatology of the future and the theology of the cross are interwoven. It is neither that futuristic eschatology is isolated, as in late Jewish apocalyptic, nor does the cross become the mark of the paradoxical presence of eternity in every moment, as in Kierkegaard. The eschatological expectation of the all-embracing lordship of Christ for the corporeal, earthly world brings the clear perception and acceptance of the distinction of the cross and the resurrection.

Finally, it should be noticed that Paul is not so much concerned with a compromise between presentative and futuristic eschatology, that is, with a compromise between apocalyptic and Hellenism. Rather, the content of the Hellenistic idea of the presence of the eternal is futurized by him and applied to the still outstanding *eschaton*. That all-embracing truth in which the creature comes into saving harmony with God, that all-embracing righteousness in which God receives his due in all things and all becomes well, that glory of God in whose reflected light all things are transfigured and the hidden face of man disclosed – all this is set by Paul within the realm of hope in that future to which faith looks forward on the ground of the raising of the crucified Lord. The fulness of all things from God, in God and to God lies for him in the still outstanding fulfilment of the promises guaranteed in Christ. 'Eternal presence' is therefore the eschatological, future goal of history, not its inmost essence. Creation is therefore not the things that are given and lie to hand, but the future of these things, the resurrection and the new being.

God is not somewhere in the Beyond, but he is coming and as the coming One he is present. He promises a new world of all-embracing life, of righteousness and truth, and with this promise he constantly calls this world in question – not because to the eye of hope it is as nothing, but because to the eye of hope it is not yet what it has the prospect of being. When the world and the human nature bound up with it are called in question in this way, then they become 'historic', for they are staked upon, and submitted to the crisis of, the promised future. Where the new begins, the old becomes manifest. Where the new is promised, the old becomes transient and surpassable. Where the new is hoped for and expected, the old can be left behind. Thus 'history' arises in the light of its end, in the things which happen because of, and become perceptible through, the promise that lights up the way ahead. Eschatology does not disappear in the quicksands of history, but it keeps history moving by its criticism and hope; it is itself something like a sort of quicksand of history from afar. The impression of general transience that comes of looking back sorrowfully upon the things that cannot endure, has in actual fact as such nothing to do with history. Rather, that transience is historic which comes of hope, of exodus, of setting out towards the promised, not yet visible future. The reason why the Church of Christ has here no 'continuing city' is, that it seeks the 'city to come' and therefore goes forth without the camp to bear the reproach of Christ. The reason for its here having no continuing city is not that in history there is nothing that continues at all. In the eyes of Christian hope the epithet 'transient' belongs not only to the things which we generally feel are destined to pass away, but it sees as transient those very things which are generally felt to be always there and to cause the transience of all life, namely, evil and death. Death becomes transient in the promised resurrection. Sin becomes transient in the justification of the sinner and the righteousness for which we have to hope.

It is neither that history swallows up eschatology (Albert Schweitzer) nor does eschatology swallow up history (Rudolf Bultmann). The *logos* of the *eschaton* is promise of that which is not yet, and for that reason it *makes* history. The promise which announces the *eschaton*, and in which the *eschaton* announces itself, is the motive power, the mainspring, the driving force and the torture of history.

5. THE 'DEATH OF GOD' AND THE RESURRECTION OF CHRIST

Christianity stands or falls with the reality of the raising of Jesus from the dead by God. In the New Testament there is no faith that does not start *a priori* with the resurrection of Jesus. Paul is clearly taking over a basic form of the primitive Christian confession when he says in Rom. 10.9: 'If thou shalt confess with thy mouth the Lord Jesus, and shalt believe in thine heart that God hath raised him from the dead, thou shalt be saved.' The confession to the person of Jesus as the Lord and the confession to the work of God who raised him from the dead belong inseparably together, although the two formulae do not coincide but mutually expound each other. A Christian faith that is not resurrection faith can therefore be called neither Christian nor faith. It is the knowledge of the risen Lord and the confession to him who raised him that form the basis on which the memory of the life, work, sufferings and death of Jesus is kept alive and presented in the gospels. It is the recognition of the risen Christ that gives rise to the Church's recognition of its own commission in the mission to the nations. It is the remembrance of his resurrection that is the ground of the inclusive hope in the universal future of Christ. The central statements of the primitive Christian missionary proclamation are therefore: 1. 'God has raised the crucified Jesus from the dead' (Acts 2.24; 3.15; 5.31; I Cor. 15.4; and frequently elsewhere) 2. 'Of this we are witnesses.' 3. In him is grounded the future of righteousness for sinners and the future of life for those subject to death. The fact, the witness and the eschatological hope belong together in the Easter kerygma. It is true that in the different angles of approach adopted in more detailed study of the circumstances, ideas and expectations they can be distinguished, but they cannot be separated from each other. The question, 'What can I know of the historical facts?' cannot here be separated from the ethical and existential question, 'What am I to do?' and from the eschatological question, 'What may I hope for?' – just as the other questions in turn cannot be isolated. Only when concerted attention is given to these three questions does the reality of the resurrection disclose itself.

When the question of the reality of the resurrection is raised today, then it mostly takes the form: *Is* he risen? In what modus of *esse* is the reality of the resurrection to be understood? *Is* he risen in the sense of a reality accessible to 'historical science'? *Is* he risen in the sense of a reality belonging to the history of ideas and traditions? *Is* he risen in the sense of a reality that affects our own existence? *Is* he risen in the sense of a wishful reality of human longings and hopes?

The question of the reality of the resurrection of Christ can thus be asked in the light of a number of very different views of reality that are possible today. Hence it is not only the nature of the reality of the resurrection that stands in question, but also the reality on the basis of which the question of the reality of the resurrection is shaped, motivated and formulated.

We shall therefore have to try first of all to discover the point of approach at which the answer to the question of the reality of the resurrection of Christ can become plain. This approach cannot be by any single question within the context of those that can be asked on the basis of reality today, but it can only be a question which embraces the whole modern experience of the world, of self and of the future – a question which we ourselves constitute with our whole reality. If the question of the reality of the resurrection is tied down, say, to the question of the relevance and significance of this piece of church teaching, or to the question of the historical probability of the fact of Jesus' resurrection, or to the question of its real meaning for heart and conscience, or to the question of the hopes it may possibly contain, then the situation out of which the question arises and towards which it is directed is tacitly left as it was and simply taken for granted. It might well be, however, that the recognition of the reality of the resurrection calls this very situation in question.

Now of course it is difficult to find a single designation for the situation out of which the question of the reality of the resurrection of Christ can arise one way or another today. Yet it is no accident when this situation is interpreted by expounding the statement of Hegel and Nietzsche:

'God is dead.'

For that is not merely a statement of philosophical metaphysics or of theology, but is one which also seems to lie at the foundations of modern experience of self and the world and to provide the ground for the atheism that characterizes the methods of science. All possible questions as to the reality of the resurrection which are asked in such a way as to define this reality in 'historical' or 'existentialist' or 'utopian' terms, have their ground in the a-theistic form of the historian's view of history, of man's view of himself, and of his utopian view of the future. <u>In none of these ways of dealing with reality does the idea of God thrust itself upon us as necessary.</u> It has become partly superfluous, partly optional – at all events in its traditional theological and metaphysical form. Hence the proclamation of the raising of Jesus from the dead by God has also become partly superfluous, partly optional, as long as 'God' is understood as something that is known to us from history, from the world or from human existence. Only when along with the knowledge of the resurrection of Jesus the 'God of the resurrection' can be shown to be 'God' in terms of the 'death of God' that has become familiar to us from history, from the world and from our own existence – only then is the proclamation of the resurrection, and only then are faith and hope in the God of promise, something that is necessary, that is new, that is possible in an objectively real sense.

The origin of the impression that 'God is dead' gives some indication of this. The early romantic poet Jean Paul in his nightmare vision, 'Die Rede des toten Christus vom Weltgebäude herab, dass kein Gott sei' ('Address by the Dead Christ from the Heights of the Cosmic System to the Effect that there is no God'), placed this statement appropriately on the lips of the risen and returning Christ.[1] He himself wished only to give an idea of how it would feel if atheism were true – yet he had a greater effect than any other upon the romanticist nihilism of modern times. His marks are found in Stifter, Keller, Dostoievsky and Nietzsche. Heine's *Mönche des Atheismus*, the martyrs in F. Schlegel's *Diktatur des Nichts*, and also Dostoievski's *The Possessed*, were all influenced by him.[2] The setting of Jean Paul's piece is the hour of the Last Judgment. The Christ who is awaited by the dead comes and proclaims: 'There is no God. I was mistaken. Everywhere is only stark, staring nothing, the death rigour of infinity. Eternity lies in chaos, gnaws at it and turns self-ruminant.' This vision is like a commentary on I Cor. 15.13ff. Hence it is significant that the message, 'There is no God', is proclaimed in terms of despair of the hope of resurrection. It is plain that for Jean Paul the reality of God and the hope of resurrection depend on each other both for faith and for unbelief.

Hegel in 1802 described the 'death of God' as the basic feeling of the religion of modern times and saw in it a new interpretation of Good Friday: 'The pure notion, however, or infinity as the abyss which engulfs all being, must take the infinite pain – which till now was historic only in culture and in the form of the feeling upon which the religion of modern times rests, the feeling that God himself is dead (that feeling which was merely empirically expressed, so to speak, in Pascal's words: 'la nature est telle qu'elle *marque partout un Dieu perdu* et dans l'homme et hors de l'homme') – and designate it purely as an element, but also no more than an element, of the highest

---

[1] Cf. the text in G. Bornkamm, *Studien zu Antike und Urchristentum*, 1959, pp. 245ff.
[2] W. Rehm, *Experimentum medietatis, Studien zur Geistes- und Literaturgeschichte des 19. Jahrhunderts*, 1947, now partly reprinted in *Jean Paul – Dostojewski. Zur dichterischen Gestaltung des Unglaubens*, 1962.

idea, and so give a philosophical existence to that which, as could also happen, was either a moral demand for sacrifice of empirical being or else the concept of formal abstraction, and thereby restore to philosophy the idea of absolute freedom, thus taking absolute suffering, or the speculative Good Friday which was otherwise historical, and restoring it in nothing less than the full truth and stringency of its godlessness, out of which stringency alone – because the cheerful, more unfathomable and more individual aspects of the dogmatic philosophies and of the nature religions must disappear – the highest totality can and must rise again in all its seriousness and from its deepest foundation, as also all-embracingly, and in the most cheerful freedom of form' (*Glauben und Wissen*, in *op. cit.*, pp. 123f.). Hegel meant by this that modern atheism and nihilism, which causes the disappearance of all dogmatic philosophies and all nature religions, can be understood as a universalizing of the historic Good Friday of the god-forsakenness of Jesus, so that it becomes a speculative Good Friday of the forsakenness of all that is. Only then does resurrection, as a resurrection of the totality of being out of nothing, and only then does the birth of freedom and cheerfulness out of infinite pain, become a prospect necessary to all that is. If the modern a-theistic world thus comes to stand in the shadow of Good Friday, and Good Friday is conceived by it as the abyss of nothingness that engulfs all being, then there arises on the other hand the possibility of conceiving this foundering world in theological terms as an element in the process of the now all-embracing and universal revelation of God in the cross and resurrection of reality. Then the stringency of the world's god-forsakenness is not in itself enough to ruin it, but its ruination comes only when it abstracts the element of the expending and death of God from the dialectical process of God and fastens on that. The romanticist nihilism of the 'death of God', like the methodical atheism of science (*etsi Deus non daretur*), is an element that has been isolated from the dialectical process and is therefore no longer engaged in the movement of the process to which it belongs. From the theological standpoint one thing at least is unforgettably plain in Hegel – that the resurrection and the future of God must manifest themselves not only in the case of the god-forsakenness of the crucified Jesus, but also in that of the god-forsakenness of the world.[1]

This speculative dialectic even in the very matter of God or the highest idea had already eluded the grasp of Kierkegaard. Kierkegaard returned to the dualism of Kant and radicalized it. The age of infinite reflection no longer allows of any objective certainty in regard to the being or the self-motion of objects. Doubt and criticism do away with all mediation of the absolute in the objective. Thus all that remains is, in irreconcilable dialectic, the paradoxical antithesis of a theoretical atheism and an existential inner life, of objective godlessness and subjective piety. The inner life of the immediate and unmediated relationship of existence and transcendence goes hand in hand with contempt for outward things as absurd, meaningless and godless. Kierkegaard's 'individual' falls out of the dialectic of mediation

S. K.

---

[1] For an exposition cf. G. Rohrmoser, *Subjektivität und Verdinglichung*, 1961, pp. 83ff.; K. Löwith, 'Hegels Aufhebung der christlichen Religion', in *Einsichten: Festschrift für G. Krüger*, 1962, pp. 156ff.

and reconciliation and falls back upon pure immediacy. His 'inner life' is, even to the extent of verbal parallels, the 'unhappy consciousness' of Hegel's *Phenomenology of Mind*, only isolated from Hegel's dialectic and abstracted from its movement. When the unhappy consciousness of the 'beautiful soul' fastens upon itself and seeks in its own inward immediacy all that is glorious along with all that is transcendent, then at the same time it fastens down the world of objects to rigid immutability and sanctions its inhuman and godless conditions. Since no reconciliation between the inward and the outward can be hoped for, it is also pointless to expend oneself on the pain of the negative, to take upon oneself the cross of reality. The god-forsakenness and absurdity of a world that has become a calculable world of wares and techniques can now serve only as a negative urge towards the attaining of pure inwardness. This dialectic that has frozen into an eternal paradox is the mark of romanticism and of all romanticist theology.

A different exposition of the statement, 'God is dead', appears in Nietzsche and Feuerbach. 'God is dead! God stays dead! And it is we who have killed him! . . . Is not the greatness of this deed too great for us? Must we not ourselves become gods, if we are to appear worthy of it? There was never a greater deed – and whosoever is born after us belongs because of this deed to a history higher than any history was till now!' [F. Nietzsche, *Die fröhliche Wissenschaft*, No. 125.] Here the death of God is ascribed to man, who has killed him, not to God's expending of his own self. God's death is the exaltation of man above himself. History, which man takes into his own hands, is built upon the corpse of God. The cross becomes the symbol of the victory of man over God and himself. 'Dead are all gods: let us now see the superman live.' When the feeling of the modern age that God is dead is thus based on saying that we have killed him, then this is in very close proximity to Feuerbach's abolition of God through which man is said to come to himself. Only, Nietzsche is thinking of an event and of a new destiny given to our being, and not merely of a re-subjectifying of religious objectifications. The result is not man's coming to himself in his sensual presence and immediacy, but man's self-transcendence and his rising beyond himself. Yet even here in Nietzsche the place which for metaphysical thinking would belong to God, as being the place of effective cause, is now no longer experienced in the passivity of the human subject, but in his activity (M. Heidegger, *Holzwege*, 1957, pp. 236ff.). The 'world' is the projection and object of our subjectivity. It is consequently 'disenchanted' to become the material for possible changes. It is no longer able to reconcile our subjectivity with itself. The all-powerful self becomes abstract identity. This new self-transcendence in the experience of being able to dominate the world is, to be sure, the end of all cosmological metaphysics and theology, but not by any means the end of metaphysics as such, for it contains a metaphysic of subjectivity. Its 'atheism' is merely theoretic atheism in regard to the world of objects. The subject, on the other hand – that *fundamentum inconcussum* which is so certain of itself in all human activity – arrogates to itself all the traditional divine predicates of metaphysics and theology (*causa sui* in Feuerbach and Marx, transcendence in Nietzsche). If Christian faith is given its theological home in this subjectivity, then it inevitably becomes a *creatrix divinitatis*, a god-creating and god-venturing force. This faith – mysticism becomes the necessary complement of the mathematics which man uses to prescribe to the world its laws. This means, however, that here, too, we have an exposition of the statement, 'God is dead', which returns in the end to those antitheses in the modern consciousness which Hegel's dialectic was meant to reconcile. Hegel had addressed himself both to the banishing of God from the world on the part of mathematics and to the corresponding rise of man to the throne of immediate subjectivity, and had sought to understand and accept both of these as elements in the process of the self-movement of absolute Spirit. The following sentences, in which Feuerbach characterizes Hegel's solution and seeks to reduce it *ad absurdum*, give much food for theological thought: 'Hegel's philosophy was the last great attempt to restore a lost and ruined Christianity by means of philosophy – whereby, as is general in recent times, the *negation* of Christianity *is identified with Christianity itself.* This contradiction is obscured and hidden from sight in Hegel only by turning the negation of God, or atheism, into an objective determination of God – God is defined as a process, and atheism as an element in this process. But just as the faith that is reconstructed on the basis of unbelief is no true faith, because it is constantly entrammelled with its opposite, so the God who reconstructs himself on the basis of his own negation is no true God, but on the contrary a self-contradictory, atheistic God' (*Grundsätze der Philosophie der Zukunft*, 1843, § 21).

Here it becomes plain that Feuerbach knows only the God of dogmatic philosophy and nature religion, for it is only this God who in his abstract identity can be reduced to man. Christian faith, however, constantly rises on the ground of the conquest of unbelief and has the latter always at its side to vex it. The risen Christ is and remains the crucified Christ. The God who in the event of the cross and resurrection reveals himself as 'the same' is the God who reveals himself in his own contradiction. Out of the night of the 'death of God' on the cross, out of the pain of the negation of himself, he is experienced in the resurrection of the crucified one, in the negation of the negation, as the God of promise, as the coming God. If 'atheism' finds its radical form in the recognition of the universal significance of Good Friday, then it is a fact that the God of the resurrection is in some sort an 'a-theistic' God. This is presumably also what Dietrich Bonhoeffer means – in Hegel's sense, and not in Feuerbach's – when he writes: 'And we cannot be honest unless we recognize that we have to live in the world *"etsi deus non daretur"*. And this is just what we do recognize – before God! . . . God would have us know that we must live as men who manage our lives without him. The God who is with us is the God who forsakes us. . . . Before God and with God we live without God. God lets himself be pushed out of the world on to the cross. He is weak and powerless in the world, and that is precisely the way, the only way, in which he is with us and helps us.'[1] Only, the god-forsakenness of the cross cannot, as in Hegel, be made into an element belonging to the divine process and thus immanent in God. A theology of the dialectical self-movement of absolute Spirit would then be only a

---

[1] *Widerstand und Ergebung*, 1951, pp. 241f.; ET by R. H. Fuller: *Letters and Papers from Prison* (1953), 3rd ed. revised by F. Clarke, 1967, p. 196.

modification of the dialectical epiphany of the eternal as subject. Hegel attempted to reconcile faith and knowledge – but at the price of doing away with the historicity of the event of revelation and understanding it as an eternal event. 'For concept cancels time.' But the cross – the hiddenness of God and the independence of man – is not at once 'done away with' in the *logos* of reflection and of consciousness, but is taken up for the time being into the promise and hope of a still outstanding, real *eschaton*, which is a stimulus to the consciousness but is not resolved into the believing consciousness. The cross is the mark of an eschatological openness which is not yet closed by the resurrection of Christ and the spirit of the Church, but remains open beyond both of these until the future of God and the annihilation of death. When it is precisely Nietzsche's 'frantic man' who cries incessantly, 'I seek God', then that surely points in this direction. It is one thing whether the 'death of God' leads to the enthronement of deified man, and quite another thing whether the 'death of God' causes us, on the ground of our preview of resurrection in the raising of Christ, to ask, seek and hope for resurrection, life, kingdom and righteousness and thus, through this asking, seeking and hoping and the criticism, opposition and suffering that result from them, gives the world that has established itself upon the corpse of God its proper setting in the historic process of the future of the truth. The world is then not engulfed in the abyss of nothingness, but its negative aspects are taken up into the 'not yet' of hope. The world is not stabilized in eternal being, but is 'held' in the 'not yet being' of a history open towards the future.

6. THE HISTORICAL QUESTION OF THE RESURRECTION OF CHRIST AND THE QUESTIONABLENESS OF THE HISTORICAL APPROACH TO HISTORY

The first question regarding the reality of the resurrection of Christ will always be concerned with the fact which is reported and proclaimed by the Easter witnesses. Since this fact is reported as an event – namely, as the 'raising of Jesus from the dead by God' – the question as to the reality of this event will in the first instance take the form of a historical question. Even if the witnesses did not attempt after the fashion of ancient chroniclers or modern historians only to report what happened, yet they did speak of a fact and an event whose reality lay for them outside their own consciousness and their own faith, whose reality was indeed the origin of their consciousness in remembrance and hope. They did not merely wish to tell of their own new self-understanding in the Easter faith, but in that faith and as a result of it they reported something also about the way of Jesus and about the event of the raising of Jesus. Their statements contain not only existential certainty in the sense of saying, 'I am certain,' but also and together with this objective certainty in the sense of saying, 'It is certain.' They did not merely proclaim that they believe, and what they believe, but therewith and therein also the fact they have recognized. They are 'selfless witnesses', so to speak.[1] Hence it is not by any means self-evident that the point of their statements is the new self-understanding of faith.[2] Rather, the Easter narratives themselves compel us to ask about the reality of the event of which they tell. It is not their own faith, nor the demand for faith or offer of faith bound up with their proclamation, that constitutes the reality underlying their statements, but it is solely the reality of the fact declared and proclaimed that must correspond with their declarations and their proclamation. It would be foreign to the intention of the Easter texts themselves, if the 'point' of their statements were to be sought solely in the birth of faith. There can thus be no forbidding the attempt to go behind their kerygma and ask about the reality which underlies their statements and makes them dependable and credible.[3]

Now these questions as to the certainty of the reality which underlies the proclamation of the resurrection and makes it legitimate and credible have all, ever since the collapse of the orthodox way of asserting the truth, taken the form of historical examination. This is in harmony with the texts, in so far as they themselves speak of an event which can be dated. But it is alien to the texts if, and in so far as, the historical form of the question implies a definite anterior understanding of what is historically possible, and one which since the birth of the modern age does not coincide with the understanding which these texts themselves have of the historically possible as being

---

[1] For this expression cf. H. G. Gadamer, 'Zur Problematik des Selbstverständnisses', in *Einsichten. Festschrift für G. Krüger*, 1962, p. 84.

[2] Cf. R. Bultmann, *Das Verhältnis der urchristlichen Christusbotschaft zum historischen Jesus*, 1960, p. 27 (ET: 'The Primitive Christian Kerygma and the Historical Jesus' in *The Historical Jesus and the Kerygmatic Christ*, ed. and trans. C. E. Braaten and R. A. Harrisville, 1964, p. 39); H. Conzelmann, 'Jesus von Nazareth und der Glaube an den Auferstandenen', in *Der historische Jesus und der kerygmatische Christus*, 1961, p. 191: 'The appearances of the risen Lord are of course understood as taking place in space and time, that is, in the world. But the question is, what is the *point* of the appearances and consequently of recounting them. . . . The point of the statement is simply to affirm the salvation of God as the end of worldly being.'

[3] This has rightly been emphasized by von Campenhausen, Grass, Pannenberg, Wilckens and others.

the divinely possible. The concept of the historical, of the historically possible and the historically probable, has been developed in the modern age on the basis of experiences of history other than the experience of the raising of Jesus from the dead – namely, since the Enlightenment, on the basis of the experience of man's ability to calculate history and to make it. The controversy between the disciples and the Jews was concerned with the question: has God raised him from the dead according to his promises, or can God according to his promises not have raised him? The modern controversy on the resurrection, however, is concerned with the question whether resurrection is historically possible. If, as has frequently been pointed out,[1] it is true that the experiences of history on the basis of which the concepts of the historical have been constructed have nowadays an anthropocentric character, that 'history' is here man's history and man is the real subject of history in the sense of its metaphysical *hypokeimenon*, then it is plain that on this presupposition the assertion of the raising of Jesus by God is a 'historically' impossible and therefore a 'historically' meaningless statement. Yet even on this presupposition there is point in asking 'how far and with what degree of probability the actual facts and the actual course of events can still be ascertained',[2] even if that brings us to the limits of the historical as these are prescribed by the presupposed view of historic fact as such. Enquiries conducted in the light of the modern concept of the historical lead neither to the fundamental provability of the resurrection nor to fundamental historical scepticism. But they prevent theology from postulating 'historical' facts on dogmatic grounds, and they prevent theology from abandoning the ground of history altogether in despair. Neither the historian nor the theologian can allow methods based on the principle that what must not be cannot be.

But now, the historian who enquires into the reality of the resurrection of Jesus is confronted in the biblical texts not only by realities of history, but also with a different outlook on the experience and significance of history, which sets the event here recounted in a different light. The experience of history

[1] K. Löwith, *Meaning in History*, 1949.
[2] Hans von Campenhausen, *Der Ablauf der Osterereignisse und das leere Grab*, 1952, p. 7.

which is expressed in the historical approach is here confronted not merely by events which are more or less well testified, more or less imaginatively embellished, but this experience of history is confronted also by a different experience of history. Hence the historical question as to the reality of the resurrection of Jesus also recoils upon the historical enquirer and calls in question the basic experience of history which is the ground of his historical enquiry. The historical question as to the historicity of the resurrection of Christ is thereby expanded to include the questionability of the historical approach to history as such. For in the historical question of the resurrection, the texts which tell of the resurrection of Jesus have always a historical view of the world also brought to bear on them. This latter must be subjected to questioning in the process of understanding, as surely as the proclaimed resurrection of Jesus is subjected to historical questioning. Let us therefore now consider the way the historical question as to the resurrection of Jesus recoils upon the questioner.

It is generally acknowledged that historical understanding nowadays is always analogical understanding and must therefore always remain within the realm of what is understandable in terms of analogy. This method of analogy in historical understanding had been ontologically grounded by E. Troeltsch in the 'correlation which exists between all historical processes'. 'For the means by which criticism becomes possible at all is the application of *analogy*. The analogy of that which happens before our eyes . . . is the key to criticism. The illusions, . . . the formation of myths, the deceptions, the party spirit, which we see before our eyes, are the means of recognizing such things also in the tradition. Agreement with normal, usual, or at least variously attested, happenings . . . as we know them, is the mark of probability for happenings which the critic can recognize as really having happened or can leave aside. The observation of analogies between past events of the same kind makes it possible to ascribe probability to them and to interpret the unknown aspects of the one on the basis of the known aspects of the other. The omnipotence thus attaching to analogy implies, however, the basic similarity of all historical events, which is not, of course, identity . . . but presupposes that there is always a common core of similarity, on the basis of which the

differences can be sensed and perceived.'¹ If historical understanding and historical criticism thus depend on the postulate
and presupposition of a fundamental similarity underlying all
events, then historical understanding and historical criticism
manifestly depend on a specific view of the world. In this view
of the world, much as in Greek cosmology, it is presupposed
that a 'common core of similarity' underlies all the changes and
chances of history and that 'all things are eternally related at
heart'. In terms of this core of similarity, however, the historic
now becomes only accidental. Historic *events* become understandable when they are conceived as *'manifestations'* of this
common core of similarity. This, however, is to put an end to
their nature as events and to abandon the historic character of
history in favour of a metaphysic which sees all historical things
in terms of substance. In L. von Ranke and the great historians
of romanticism this core was felt to be pantheistic: all ages and
all events follow each other in meaningful succession 'in order
that what is not possible to any of them individually may happen
in *all*, in order that the whole fulness of the spiritual life breathed
into the human race by the deity should come to light in the
course of the centuries'.² For H. von Sybel the similarity
acquired a mechanistic appearance: 'The presupposition by
which the certainty of knowledge stands or falls is the regulation
of all development by absolute laws, the common unity in the
constitution of all earthly things.'³ So, too, in W. Dilthey's
philosophical hermeneutic of the history of the expressions of
human life, historical understanding rests on the presupposed
similarity of the underlying, unfathomable life. To be sure,
there is no hard and fast nature of man which exists as a self-
identical factor anterior to history and independent of it. 'The
human type melts in the process of history.'⁴ But the fact that
human existence in itself has a hermeneutic structure proves to
be the abiding core that motivates the history of man's expressions of his life and expositions of his self. From the depths of
his creative unfathomableness man must ever again seek and

¹ E. Troeltsch, 'Ueber historische und dogmatische Methode' (1898), *Gesammelte Schriften* II, pp. 729ff. (esp. p. 731).
² Quoted according to C. Hinrichs, *Ranke und die Geschichtstheologie der Goethezeit*,
1954, p. 168.
³ *Über die Gesetze historischen Wissens*, 1864, p. 16.
⁴ *Werke* VIII, p. 6, cf. also VII, p. 278 and O. F. Bollnow's comment, *Die
Lebensphilosophie*, 1958, p. 41.

find himself, ever again form and determine himself, and it is this that constitutes that common core of similarity which makes historical understanding possible and also necessary.

In face of this basing of historical understanding on a metaphysical definition of the core, the substance or the subject of history, Christian theology finds itself in grave difficulties as it seeks to reflect upon the proclamation of the resurrection. In face of the pantheistic definition of the nature of history, according to which the eternal idea does not delight to present itself wholly in an individual, it becomes impossible to regard a person and an event in history as absolute.[1] In face of the positivistic and mechanistic definition of the nature of history as a self-contained system of cause and effect, the assertion of a raising of Jesus by God appears as a myth concerning a supernatural incursion which is contradicted by all our experience of the world. And finally, in face of the philosophy of life with its definition of the creative ground of life that manifests and objectifies itself in history, the Easter texts can be taken only as expressions of the life acts of a faith which is in itself unfathomable.

A theology of the resurrection can try several ways of solving the problem of history thus presented to it. If, as is plain from the above few references, the risen Lord does not fit in with our concept of the historical,[2] it is possible to grant that the report of the raising of Jesus by God is 'unhistorical' and to look around for other ways for modern, historically determined man to approach to and appropriate the reality of the resurrection.[3] Yet in so doing, the whole realm of our knowledge of history and our dealings with it is abandoned to historical expositions of the world. If the reality of the resurrection cannot be comprehended by the historical means of the modern age, neither is the modern intellectual way of dealing with history theologically comprehensible for faith. The *fides quaerens intellectum* must then give up all claim to an *intellectus fidei* in the realm of history. This is primarily done by theology's leaving aside the historical question as to the reality of the resurrection and concentrating on the second question – the question of the character of witness and of claim that attaches to the proclamation of the Easter

[1] D. F. Strauss, *Das Leben Jesu* II, 1835, p. 734.
[2] Cf. O. Weber, *Grundlagen der Dogmatik* II, 1962, p. 83.
[3] Cf. my essay, 'Exegese und Eschatologie der Geschichte', *EvTh* 22, 1962, pp. 40f.

faith. It then leaves the knowledge of history to all possible kinds of pantheistic or atheistic principles and concentrates on the personal encounter, the non-objectifiable experience or the existential decision, to which the Easter kerygma leads. 'Thus we are simply asked whether we believe that in such things (visionary Easter experiences) God acts in the way they themselves believe and in the way the proclamation asserts.'[1] The word 'simply' here plainly recommends the leap from mediating, objectifying, historical knowledge to personal decision. The resurrection of Christ is then to be grasped neither mythically nor historically but 'only in the category of revelation'.[2] But then the message of the resurrection is left hanging in the air, and so also is the existence affected by it, without it being possible to understand the need for the proclamation and the necessity for decision in face of it at all.

Another possibility is, that we no longer regard the historical method and its view of history as being final and inescapable in its substantio-metaphysical form, and thus veer off into the subjective decision of faith, but that we seek new ways of further developing the historical methods themselves in such a way 'that they become adequate to grasp the *whole* of history in all its variety'.[3] Such an extension of the historical approach to history and the historical mediation of it can have an eye to the other side of the analogical process in historical understanding. For indeed the cognitive power of a comparative understanding need not lie merely in recognizing only the similar and common elements amid the dissimilarities in historical events and expressions of life, but can also be directed towards observing what is dissimilar and individual, accidental and suddenly new, in the similar and the like.[4] A one-sided interest in the similar, ever-recurring, typical and regular, would level down the really historic element, which lies in the contingent and new, and would thus end up by losing the feeling for history altogether. The method of understanding by comparison can thus be expanded in the direction of bringing

[1] R. Bultmann, *TLZ* 65, 1940, col. 246.
[2] K. Barth, *Die Auferstehung der Toten*, 1924, pp. 79f., ET by H. J. Stenning: *The Resurrection of the Dead*, 1933, pp. 145f.
[3] R. Rendtorff, 'Geschichte und Ueberlieferung', in *Studien zur Theologie der alttestamentlichen Überlieferungen*, 1961, p. 94, n. 39.
[4] W. Pannenberg, 'Heilsgeschehen und Geschichte', *Kerygma und Dogma* 5, 1959, p. 266.

to light the incomparable, hitherto non-existent and new. To be sure, it comes to light only in the comparison. But if we are to set eyes on it in this comparison, then we must divest ourselves of all hard and fast presuppositions about the core or the substance of history and must regard these ideas themselves as provisional and alterable. But if, as compared with the historical methods that are interested in the regular and the similar, Christian theology were to manifest merely a supplementary interest in the individual, contingent and new, then that would be only an interesting variant in the historical picture of history as a whole, yet one that would be possible and conceivable also without a theology of the resurrection. The rediscovery of the category of the contingent does not in itself necessarily involve the discovery of a theological category.[1] For the raising of Christ involves not the category of the accidentally new, but the expectational category of the eschatologically new. The eschatologically new event of the resurrection of Christ, however, proves to be a *novum ultimum* both as against the similarity in ever-recurring reality and also as against the comparative dissimilarity of new possibilities emerging in history. To expand the historical approach to the extent of taking account of the contingent does not as yet bring the reality of the resurrection itself into view. It is quite possible to overcome the anthropocentric form of historical analogy, but this does not necessarily give the latter a theological character. Only if the whole historical picture, contingency and continuity and all, could be shown to be in itself not necessary but contingent, should we come within sight of that which can be called the eschatologically new fact of the resurrection of Christ. The resurrection of Christ does not mean a possibility within the world and its history, but a new possibility altogether for the world, for existence and for history. Only when the world can be understood as contingent creation out of the freedom of God and *ex nihilo* – only on the basis of this *contingentia mundi* – does the raising of Christ become intelligible as *nova creatio*. In view of what is meant and what is promised when we speak of the raising of Christ, it is therefore necessary to expose the profound irrationality of the rational cosmos of the modern, technico-scientific world. By the raising of Christ we do not mean a possible process in world

[1] *Ibid.*, p. 277; cf. H. G. Geyer's criticism in *EvTh* 22, 1962, p. 97.

history, but the eschatological process to which world history is subjected.

·Finally, theology has the possibility of constructing its own concept of history and its own view of the tale of history on the basis of a theological and eschatological understanding of the reality of the resurrection.[1] Then the theology of the resurrection would no longer be fitted in with an existing concept of history, but an attempt would have to be made, in comparison with and contradistinction to the existing views of history, to arrive at a new understanding of history with the ultimate possibilities and hopes that attach to it on the presupposition of the raising of Christ from the dead. In conflict with other concepts of history, an *intellectus fidei resurrectionis* must then be developed which makes it possible to speak 'Christianly' of God, history and nature. The resurrection of Christ is without parallel in the history known to us. But it can for that very reason be regarded as a 'history-making event' in the light of which all other history is illumined, called in question and transformed.[2] The mode of proclaiming and hopefully remembering this event must then be presented as a mode of historical remembrance which is wholly governed by this event both in content and in procedure. It is not that from the hopeful remembrance of this event we then derive general laws of world history, but in remembering this one, unique event, we remember the hope for the future of all world history. Then the resurrection of Christ does not offer itself as an analogy to that which can be experienced any time and anywhere, but as an analogy to what is to come to all. The expectation of what is to come on the ground of the resurrection of Christ, must then turn all reality that can be experienced and all real experience into an experience that is provisional and a reality that does not yet contain within it what is held in prospect for it. It must therefore contradict all rigid substantio-metaphysical definitions of the common core of similarity in world events, and therefore also the corresponding historical understanding that works with analogy. It must develop a historical understanding which works with eschatological analogy as a foreshadowing

[1] R. R. Niebuhr, *Resurrection and Historical Reason*, 1957. Cf. L. Landgrebe's comment in 'Philosophie und Theologie', *Neue Zeitschrift für systematische Theologie* 23, 1963, pp. 3ff.
[2] L. Landgrebe, *op. cit.*, pp. 1of.

and anticipation of the future. The raising of Christ is then to be called 'historic', not because it took place *in* the history to which other categories of some sort provide a key, but it is to be called historic because, by pointing the way for future events, it *makes* history in which we can and must live. It is historic, because it discloses an eschatological future. This assertion must then give proof of itself in conflict with other concepts of history, all of which are ultimately based on other 'history-making' events, shocks or revolutions in history.

Here of course there arises an objection in the form of the question whether such theological statements are universally binding. If the modern, historical approach to history is taken as the only one that is possible, honest and binding today, then the view of reality and history which is presupposed by it has to be accepted as inevitable also for theological thought. This view of reality is then 'imposed upon us by our place in history'.[1] In the society in which Christians and non-Christians live together, it is the axiom within the framework of which alone we are able and willing to 'understand'. If according to this now universally binding and universally recognized view of reality, scientifically and historically speaking, the gods are silent – or hearing them is optional and left to the individual's discretion – then a theology of the resurrection can be developed only at a point which is not affected by this view of reality and comes under the aegis of the individual's subjectivity – which, however, means only in that realm of human subjectivity and inwardness which is set free by the rationalizing of the world and the historicizing of history. A theology of the resurrection can then no longer speak of facts of the resurrection, in terms of a metaphysic of history, but in terms of a metaphysic of subjectivity it can certainly still speak of an Easter faith for which 'resurrection of Jesus' is merely an expression of faith, and one that can be left behind in the course of history. In this form the resurrection faith that makes no assertions of the resurrection fits in exactly with the modern world's view of reality and is in a sense the ultimate religion of our society. If theology on the other hand strives to attain a theological view of history and a revolution in the historical way of thinking, then there is justification for the objection that theology is thereby driven

[1] This is F. Mildenberger's objection, *EvTh* 23, 1963, pp. 5, 274.

into the ghetto of an esoteric church ideology and can no longer make itself intelligible to anyone else.[1]

But the Church – including theology – is neither the religion of this or that society, nor yet is it a sect. It can neither be required to adapt itself to the view of reality which is generally binding in society at the moment, nor may it be expected to present itself as the arbitrary jargon of an exclusive group and to exist only for believers. As the church is engaged with its surrounding society in a struggle for the truth, so theology, too, has a part in the mission of the church. It must engage with views of history and historical world-views in a struggle for the future of the truth and therefore also in a battle for the reality of the resurrection of Jesus. If in contesting and exploding the modern historical concepts of reality we are wrestling for the mysterious reality of the resurrection of Jesus, then that is no mere wrangle about a detail of the distant past, but this reality becomes the ground for questioning also the historical means of attaining certainty about history. It is a struggle for the future of history and for the right way of recognizing, hoping and working for that future. It is a battle for the recognition of the mission of the present, and for the place and the task of human nature in it.

The point of the historical debate on the resurrection of Christ was never merely historical. Thus the specialist's question as to the historical reality of the resurrection – 'what can I know?' – points him on to the neighbouring questions, 'what am I to do?' and 'what may I hope for? What future horizon of possibilities and dangers is opened up by past history?' To put the question of the resurrection in exclusively historical terms is to alienate the texts of the Easter narrative, as we have seen. These, however, as we have seen, alienate the historian from that context of experience of the world in which he seeks to read the texts. All real understanding begins with such alienations.

7. THE APPROACH OF FORM-CRITICISM TO THE
EASTER NARRATIVES AND THE QUESTIONABLENESS
OF ITS EXISTENTIALIST INTERPRETATION

The critical examination of the resurrection narratives in regard to their historical correctness, which has been usual

[1] F. Mildenberger, *EvTh* 23, 1963, p. 275.

since the Enlightenment, has been transformed, and largely
also supplanted in scholarly interest, by form-critical examination of the narratives.[1] The form-critical approach no longer
asks about the historically accessible events which the accounts
relate and which possibly made the accounts necessary, but it
enquires into the kerygmatic motives which shaped the accounts, and examines their place in the life and conduct of
specific societies. It argues from the forms to the life of the
society, and from the life of the society to the forms. The real
subject of the accounts is then not the matter to be recounted
but the social life which finds its expression in them. The form-
critical method is originally a sociological method. From its
standpoint the Easter texts present themselves primarily as
kerygma, as proclamation by the Church in faith and to faith.
The texts are found to exist in a specific tradition of proclamation in which, according to the circumstances, the addressees
and the opponents, they could be very freely varied in the various stages of the tradition and could to a certain extent be
theologically enriched and transformed according to the new
situations. The discovery of such kerygmatic transformations in
particular elements of the tradition and in the history of the
forms in which they are stated in worship, instruction, exhortation, polemic, etc., brought out an abundance of new insights.
The question of the underlying events in which they have their
ground was not thereby discarded, yet there was a decisive
shift in the centre of the researcher's interest. It was no longer
a question of the historicity of the statements in the old sense of
historical criticism, but it was now a historical question of
the motives and forms of the statements themselves, and
of the changes undergone by these motives and forms. Yet
the insight into the fact that in these texts we have to do not
with historical reports but with testimonies of faith on the
part of the primitive Christian Church, is also a historical
insight.

The important question for theology arises only when the
results of the form-critical analyses of the primitive Christian
message are removed from their own historic ground and theologically grounded in a different reality from that of which they
speak, when the enquirer has no desire at all to know how things

[1] Cf. E. Fascher, *Die formgeschichtliche Methode*, 1924.

really were, but only how the believers saw them and how they represented them in terms of their faith, when the texts are no longer taken as statements about a reality, but are understood only as expressions of the Church's faith. Do these pieces of witness and of proclamation have their ground in a new self-understanding of the existence of the witnesses and proclaimers? Is the kerygmatic character of these statements grounded in a revelational commission which can no longer be grasped historically? The form-critical approach clearly provided the possibility of conceiving these statements as grounded elsewhere than in the reality of the events to be proclaimed – the possibility of understanding them no longer as 'statements about' something, but as 'expressions of' personal or corporate faith. This change of subject has come about through the alliance between form-critical research and dialectical theology, especially in existentialist interpretation since the twenties.

If the reality of the resurrection is not to be conceived as a historically accessible reality, then it can of course still become real for man in another sense of the word 'reality'. It can be reality for man in the sense in which he is real to himself. It is not from a historical detachment that he becomes aware of his own existential reality, but only in the immediate experience of himself as a reality that has constantly to come about anew. Similarly, the resurrection of Christ then no longer confronts him in the doubtful image of historical tradition and historical reconstructions, but then, in the Easter faith of the disciples and in the proclamation, the resurrection of Christ becomes for him a reality which affects him in the questionableness of his own existence and faces him with a decision. Doubtful as the resurrection may appear from the objectifying standpoint of historical science, it is yet in all closeness and immediacy that the Easter faith of the disciples encounters man in the claim of the proclamation and in the decisive question of faith. The Easter faith of the disciples presents itself as a possibility of existence which we can repeat and re-echo in the questionableness of our own existence. Only in being thus immediately involved by the preaching of faith today, only in beholding the Lord today, only in today obeying his absolute claim, in which salvation is disclosed for today, do we then discover the reality of the resurrection.[1] The 'reality' of the resurrection encounters us as word of God, as kerygma, to which we can no longer put the question of its historical legitimacy, but which asks us whether or not we are willing to believe.[2] The message which proclaims Jesus as the risen Lord must convince 'our heart and conscience'. It must speak of his resurrection in such a way that the latter no longer appears as a historical or mythical event, but as 'a reality that concerns our own existence'.[3]

Here the question of the 'reality' of the resurrection is raised in a way different from that of the historian. The questioner is not concerned to arrive at a historically assured picture of that event, but the question which he puts to the Easter narratives is the questionableness of his own historic existence. He does not stand outside history, in order to survey its correlations, but he stands with his own existence and decisions in the midst of history. His interest in history is therefore identical with his interest in his own historic existence. Hence in this encounter with the Easter texts he will seek an existentialist exegesis in which the exposition of history and the exposition of himself correspond. If, however, the radical questionableness of his own historic existence provides the angle from which he approaches the kerygma of the resurrection, then his question is no longer as to whether the resurrection once took place in terms of possible analogies in world history, but is directed towards the understanding of human existence which comes to expression in these narratives.[4] The place of the substantio-metaphysically conceived common core of similarity in all events, which makes analogical understanding possible, is taken by a similarity in the historic character of human existence, which is conceived in terms of fundamental ontology and makes understanding possible between one existence and another in encounter. That the resurrection actually took place is not thereby denied, but does not lie within the field of interest. That God is not perceptible apart from faith, certainly need not mean that he does

---

[1] Cf. H. Conzelmann, *op. cit.*, p. 196.

[2] R. Bultmann, *Kerygma und Mythos* I, 3rd ed. 1954, p. 46 (ET p. 41).

[3] R. Bultmann, *TLZ* 65, 1940, col. 245. Cf. H. Grass' comment in *Ostergeschehen und Osterberichte*, 2nd ed. 1962, pp. 268ff.

[4] Cf. here the hermeneutic principles developed by R. Bultmann in *Glauben und Verstehen* II, p. 232 (ET by J. C. G. Grieg, *Essays Philosophical and Theological*, 1955, pp. 258f.).

not exist apart from faith, nor yet that 'God' is merely an 'expression' for believing existence, but this question of whether God and his action exist *extra nos* does not lie within the field of our interest. Of vital interest to our existence, on the other hand, is the Easter faith of the witnesses, and the understanding of existence which emerged in primitive Christianity as a new possibility for human existence. This view of 'reality' as an event which concerns existence, or an event that happens 'to heart and conscience', can then also lead to a new mode of historical understanding. 'The Easter event of the resurrection of Christ is not a historical event; the only thing that can be grasped as a historical event is *the Easter faith of the first disciples.*' This historical statement is wholly in accord with the theological statement that the Easter faith has no interest in the historical question. 'For the historical event of the rise of the Easter faith means for us what it meant for the first disciples, namely, the self-manifestation of the risen Lord, the act of God in which the redemption event of the cross is completed.'[1] This, however, is to shift the 'reality' of the resurrection from something that happens to the crucified Jesus to something that happens to the existence of the disciples. The act of God is then the rise of the Easter faith, in so far as this Easter faith understands itself as brought about by the self-manifestation of the risen Lord. The 'reality' of the resurrection is then no longer a reality about Jesus, but is identical with the reality of kerygma and faith in a 'today' which cannot be historically authenticated but is ever and again without past or future.

It is an undeniably true insight that the Easter narratives are not meant to be 'narratives', but to be proclamation directed to faith, and that the reality of the resurrection of Jesus is inseparably bound up with the witness of universal missionary proclamation; but it is an insight that can lead in the way just indicated to no longer enquiring into the historical legitimacy of this proclamation, but putting in place of that an existential verification of it to heart and conscience or to a historic self-understanding in terms of a general historic questionableness of human existence. The transition from form-critical research to existentialist interpretation often proceeds by the following stages:

[1] R. Bultmann, *Kerygma und Mythos* I, p. 47 (ET p. 42).

1. The place of the question, 'What do the accounts in substance say?', is taken by the question, 'Who speaks in these accounts?'

2. Once it has been established that the Church in these accounts and in the forms assumed by them is expressing its relation to Jesus, there follows the further question, 'How does the Church understand its relation to Jesus?'

3. Once the Church's christological conceptions of Jesus have been established, the next question is, 'How does the Church understand itself?' Then its understanding of Christ is grounded in its understanding of faith, and its understanding of faith is grounded in its self-understanding and is understood as an expression of the self-understanding that is sought by all men. Christology is then the variable, anthropology the constant.

Just as the historical question presupposes a historical approach which sets the proclamation of the resurrection in the alien light of a mere report about the events, so too the question as to the self-understanding announced and expressed in it presupposes an approach from the angle of the general questionableness of human existence, which also sets these texts in an alien light. This whole approach in terms of 'reality' as a reality which concerns existence leaves out of account the fact that these texts speak of God and his action on Jesus, and purposely so speak – that they speak of the world and the future and certainly do not mean all this merely as an 'expression' of a new self-understanding. The existentialist interpretation examines the texts in order to find the 'meaning' of what they say, and takes it for granted from the start that this meaning is existential truth and not factual truth. This is today no doubt a 'meaningful' way of appropriating what was then proclaimed, but is not at all in harmony with its own original intention. On the other hand it is not by any means self-evident that 'understanding' today must take place only in the context of 'self-understanding' of our own particular existence. This is as far from being self-evident as is the modern custom of defining the reality of the world in terms of a hard and fast 'world picture' and projecting our age's concept of a world picture back into ages which had a completely different relation to the world.

The Easter reports in the New Testament proclaim in the
form of narrative, and narrate history in the form of proclamation. The modern alternative, reading them either as historical
sources or as kerygmatic calls to decision, is foreign to them, as
the modern distinction between factual truth and existential
truth is also foreign to them. The question therefore arises
whether the insights of form-criticism into the fact that, briefly
speaking, it was not archivists but missionaries who shaped this
tradition, would not have to be combined again in a new way
with the intention of the historical question which enquires
about the events which this proclamation brings to expression.
If the reality of the resurrection of Jesus is transmitted and
mediated to us only in the form of missionary proclamation,
and this form of transmission and mediation manifestly belongs
to the reality of the resurrection itself, then it must be asked
whether the inner compulsion to this kind of statement and
communication is not grounded in the peculiarity of the event
itself. For it cannot really be accounted for as supplement or
accident. The reality which stands behind the proclamatory
reports must plainly be of such a kind that it *compelled* proclamation to all peoples and the continual formation of new christological conceptions. The commission and authorization to this
universal mission must then be a constitutive part of the very
event of which this mission tells. If we no longer ask merely
how the Church preached and to what changes the form of its
proclamation was subjected, but *why* it spoke as it did and what
provoked its proclamation, then we are on the road to raising
the historical question in a new way and seeing the existential
truth of faith as grounded in the factual truth of what is to be
believed. The question is then no longer whether this proclamation is correct in the 'historical' sense, but whether and how the
proclamation is legitimated and necessarily called to life by
the event of which it speaks. We cannot then merely embark
on a historical examination of the past that once was, nor yet
merely provide an existentialist interpretation of present claims,
but we must enquire into what is open, unfinished, unsettled
and outstanding, and consequently into the future announced
by this event. If in this event there lies something which has not
yet been realized and strains after a particular future, then it is
understandable that this event cannot be spoken of in historical

detachment in the form of a report on a process complete in itself, but it can be spoken of only in the form of remembrance and hope. If this event of the raising of Jesus can be rightly understood only in conjunction with his universal eschatological future, then the only mode of communication appropriate to this event must be missionary proclamation to all peoples without distinction – a mission which knows itself in the service of the promised future of this event. Only missionary proclamation does justice to the historical and eschatological character of this event. It is, in the light of this event, the only appropriate way of experiencing history, historic existence and historic expectation.

What unites our present age with past ages in history is, to the extent that we have here a 'historic' relationship, not a common core of similarity nor a general historic character attaching to human existence as such, but the problem of the future. The meaning of each several present becomes clear only in the light of hopes for the future. Hence a 'historic' relationship to history will not seek merely to illumine the factual sequences of events and their laws, nor merely to explore past possibilities of existence in order possibly to repeat them, but will search the reality of the past for the possibilities that lie within it. Unborn future lies in the past. Fulfilled past can be expected from the future. Positivistic historicism reduces history to realities that can be dated and localized, without noticing the realm of future possibilities that surrounds these realities so long as they are 'historic' realities. We have here a process of exclusion and abstraction which the historian can and must employ in order to reach plain conclusions, but he must also always be clear that his picture is painted in perspective. The existentialist interpretation on the other hand seeks the existential possibilities attaching to past existence in order to repeat and re-echo them, yet without noticing that they are made possible by events which institute history and provide the gateway to the historic character of existence. This, too, is a process of exclusion and abstraction which the interpreter must employ in order to reach conclusions, but he, too, must always be clear that his picture is painted in perspective. Beyond both historicism and existentialism stands the attempt to find the ground of historic phenomena neither in a positivistic system of laws nor in the historic character of human existence, but to see them in their significance for the future.[1] This does not mean that the future, and indeed eschatological, significance of historic phenomena is confined within the framework of a teleology of universal history. Nor does it mean that the future of historic phenomena is exhausted in a present summoned to responsibility by the future. 'Meaning' (*Bedeuten*) is something which strains and stretches towards that which it seeks to indicate (*be-deuten*), to announce and to pre-figure, and which is not yet present in all its fulness. We know historic phenomena in their own peculiar historic character only when we perceive their meaning for 'their' future. Only in that light do we then also attain to a perception of their meaning for our future and to the perception of our meaning for their future.

In this sense the event of the raising of Christ from the dead is an event which is understood only in the *modus* of promise. It has its time still ahead of it, is grasped as a 'historic phenomenon' only in its relation to *its* future, and mediates to those who know it a future towards which they have to move in history. Hence the reports of the resurrection will always have to be read also eschatologically in the light of the question, 'What may I hope for?' It is only with this third question that our remembrance and the corresponding historical knowledge are set within a horizon appropriate to the thing to be remembered. It is only in the light of this question that the historic character of existence and the corresponding self-understanding are set within a horizon appropriate to the history which provides the ground of, and the gateway to, the historic character of existence.

8. THE ESCHATOLOGICAL QUESTION AS TO THE
FUTURE HORIZON OF THE PROCLAMATION OF
THE RISEN LORD

Experience and judgment are always bound up with a *horizon* of openness towards reality, in which a thing comes to view and can be experienced and in which judgments become

---

[1] This third possibility is indicated by R. Bultmann himself in *Glauben und Verstehen* III, 1960, pp. 113ff., 148f.

meaningful. A horizon of this kind contains a certain anterior knowledge of that which we learn. It is not a closed system, but includes also open questions and anticipations and is therefore open towards the new and the unknown.[1] Horizons of this kind can come from our traditions, and they can also arise from the context of our own experience and our familiarity with the world. They can arise out of the incalculable significance attaching to specific experiences we have undergone, and they can also have their source in ideas of our own which we use for the purpose of attaining to knowledge of history. Without a horizon of this kind, and in abstraction from it, no event can be experienced and stated.

In the resurrection narratives experience and judgment manifestly take place within a decidedly *eschatological horizon* of expectations, hopes and questions about the promised future. The very designations 'raising', 'resurrection', etc., contain a whole world of memories and hopes. Thus the resurrection narratives do not stand directly within a cosmological horizon of questions as to the origin, meaning and nature of the world. Nor do they stand directly within an existentialist horizon of questions as to the origin, meaning and nature of human existence. Nor, finally, do they stand directly within a general theological horizon of questions as to the nature and appearance of the deity. They stand directly within the special horizon of prophetic and apocalyptic expectations, hopes and questions about that which according to the promises of this God is to come. What is spotlighted in the resurrection appearances is therefore expounded in terms of the earlier promises, and this exposition in turn takes place in the form of prophetic proclamation of, and eschatological outlook towards, the future of Christ which was spotlighted in these appearances. Christian eschatology arose from the Easter experience, and Christian prophecy determined the Easter faith. But Christian eschatology expounded and expressed the Easter experiences in recalling and taking up the earlier promises and – in regard to Jesus himself – in recalling and taking up what had earlier been promised and proclaimed. The Easter appearances are bound

[1] We are here adopting the concept of 'horizon' as developed in the phenomenology of Edmund Husserl. Cf. E. Husserl, *Erfahrung und Urteil*, 1939, pp. 26ff.; L. Landgrebe, *Der Weg der Phänomenologie*, 1963, pp. 181ff.; H. G. Gadamer, *Wahrheit und Methode*, 1960, pp. 286ff., 356ff.

up with this eschatological horizon, both in that which they presuppose and call to mind and also in that which they themselves prefigure and provoke. The question of the divinity of God, the question of the worldliness of the world and the question of the human nature of man are not thereby rendered irrelevant, but in the light of the Easter appearances they are set within a peculiar horizon, both in regard to the way they are asked and also in regard to the point at which the answer is sought. To the extent that the earlier promises become general and universal in the resurrection event, these questions concerning the universal become relevant. But to the extent that this universality and generality appears in the Easter event in eschatological form, i.e. in hope and in looking forward, the questions are asked in a different way, and they are no longer answered on the basis of experience of the world, of man's experience of himself, or of the concept of God, but on the basis of the event of the resurrection and within the eschatological horizon of this event.

Christian eschatology differs from Old Testament faith in the promise, as also from prophetic and apocalyptic eschatology, by being Christian eschatology and speaking of 'Christ and his future'.[1] It is related in content to the person of Jesus of Nazareth and the event of his raising, and speaks of the future for which the ground is laid in this person and this event. Christian eschatology does not examine the general future possibilities of history. Nor does it unfold the general possibilities of human nature in its dependence on the future. It is therefore right to emphasize that Christian eschatology is at heart Christology in an eschatological perspective.[2]

While it is true that in the Easter experiences the modes of experiencing the 'revelation of Jesus Christ', and the forms of communicating it, incorporate apocalyptic ideas and hopes from the tradition of late Judaism, yet it is equally true that the content of this revelation breaks the bounds of late Jewish apocalyptic. For what God made manifest, according to the statements of the Easter narratives, was not the course of history, not the secrets of the higher world of heaven, not the out-

---

[1] Cf. E. Thurneysen's happy phrase, 'Christ and his future' – 'Christus und seine Zukunft', *Zwischen den Zeiten* 9, 1931, pp. 187ff.

[2] W. Kreck, *Die Zukunft des Gekommenen. Grundprobleme der Eschatologie*, 1961, pp. 120ff.

come of the future world judgment, but the future of the crucified Christ for the world.[1] Christian eschatology or eschatological Christology is therefore not to be understood as a special
case of general apocalyptic. Christian eschatology is not Chris-
tianized apocalyptic. The adoption of apocalyptic ideas and
apocalyptic hopes in the Easter narratives and in the Easter
theology of the primitive Church is plainly eclectic. Specific
memories are aroused by this event and are recalled along with
the Easter proclamation, while others are dropped. Particular
ideas of God's revelation of the end are used, yet the *Weltanschauung* of late Jewish apocalyptic and its attitude to life
are not restored as a whole. 'Resurrection from the dead' does,
to be sure, also belong to the apocalyptic expectations of God's
revelation of the end, but certainly not in every case and not even
centrally. When, however, Jesus is described as 'the firstfruits
of them that slept', then that goes beyond the bounds of
apocalyptic inasmuch as it means that the raising of the dead
has already taken place in this one case for all, and that the
raising was performed not on one faithful to the law but on one
who was crucified, and consequently future resurrection is to
be expected not from obedience to the law but from the
justification of sinners and from faith in Christ. The central
place of the Torah in late Jewish apocalyptic is thus taken by
the person and the cross of Christ. The place of life in the law
is taken by fellowship with Christ in the following of the crucified one. The place of the self-preservation of the righteous from
the world is taken by the mission of the believer to the world.
The place of the Torah shining in the light of the fulness of
divine glory is taken by the ἀποκάλυψις κυρίου, the judgment
seat of Jesus Christ before whom all things will be revealed. It
is not that the secrets of what awaits world history and the
cosmos at the end of time are disclosed in advance according to
a heavenly plan – 'what shall befall thy people in the latter
days' (Dan. 10.14) – but the universal future of the lordship
of the crucified Christ over all is spotlighted in the Easter
appearances. Yet the Old Testament, prophetic and apocalyptic expectation of a universal revelation and glorification of
God in all things is still maintained. Thus the adoption and

recalling of apocalyptic ideas and apocalyptic expectations does not by any means lead to levelling down the uniqueness of the Christ event, but it becomes possible to state the eschatological 'once for all' by means of recalling the earlier promises.

The Christian hope for the future comes of observing a specific, unique event – that of the resurrection and appearing of Jesus Christ. The hopeful theological mind, however, can observe this event only in seeking to span the future horizon projected by this event. Hence to recognize the resurrection of Christ means to recognize in this event the future of God for the world and the future which man finds in this God and his acts. Wherever this recognition takes place, there comes also a recalling of the Old Testament history of promise now seen in a critical and transforming light. Christian eschatology, which seeks to span the inexhaustible future of Christ, does not set the event of the resurrection within a framework of apocalyptic and world history. Rather, it examines the inner *tendency* of the resurrection event, asking what rightly can and must be expected from the risen and exalted Lord. It enquires about the mission of Christ and the *intention* of God in raising him from the dead. It recognizes as the inner tendency of this event his future lordship over every enemy, including death. 'For he *must* reign . . .' (I Cor. 15.25). It recognizes as the outer tendency, or as the consequence of this tendency, its own mission: 'The gospel *must* be published among all nations' (Mark 13.10).[1] Christian eschatology speaks of the future of Christ which brings man and the world to light. It does not, on the contrary, speak of a world history and a time which brings Christ to light, nor yet of man whose good will Christ brings to light. It is therefore out of the question to classify the resurrection event among the events of world history and apocalyptic and to give a date for his future or his coming again. It is not that 'time' brings his day and it is not that history proves him right, but he guides time to his day. The return of Christ does not come 'of itself', like the year 1965, but comes from himself, when and as God will according to his promise. It is

---

[1] Cf. also the corresponding, eschatologically determined ἀνάγκη or compulsion to preach in Paul, I Cor. 9.16, and E. Käsemann's comment *ZTK* 56, 1959, pp. 138–154, esp. 152f.

(handwritten marginalia at top)

therefore also out of the question to eternalize the openness of
the Christian hope towards the future. There is an end to the
openness of Christian existence, for it is not openness for a
future that remains empty, but it presupposes the future of
Christ and finds in that future its fulfilment.

One could say that Christian eschatology is the study of the
tendency of the resurrection and future of Christ and therefore
leads immediately to the practical knowledge of mission. In
that case it is false to lay down the alternative: either apocalyptic calculation of the times and apocalyptic belief in a final
destiny, or else the ethic of hope. (The speculative interpretation
of history on the part of cosmic apocalyptic is not simply replaced by a moral eschatology) To be sure, alternatives of this
kind do appear in many sayings: Ye know not when the end
cometh, therefore watch and pray. Nevertheless, experiences
of history are important for Christian eschatology. These are
the experiences involved in relation to Jesus and his mission –
namely, persecution, accusation, suffering and martyrdom.
The Revelation of John and also the Little Apocalypse of Mark
13 show that what we have here is not merely apocalyptic
speculations or moral appeals, but an eschatological grasp of
that history which is to be expected, and is experienced, in
martyrdom in the mission of Christ. Thus the experiential content of Christian eschatology is not that 'world history' which is
arrived at by exploring and comparing great events of world
history and stringing them together in a temporal succession
to form an apocalyptic system of universal history; rather, it
comprises the experiences which are undergone in the course
of the mission undertaken in world history 'to all peoples'.
The Christian consciousness of history is not a consciousness of
the millennia of all history, in some mysterious knowledge of a
divine plan for history, but it is a missionary consciousness in
the knowledge of a divine commission, and is therefore a
consciousness of the contradiction inherent in this unredeemed
world, and of the sign of the cross under which the Christian
mission and the Christian hope stand.

The Easter appearances of Christ are manifestly phenomena
of vocation. That is why the knowledge of Jesus Christ and
the knowledge of his mission and future coincide in them. That,
too, is why self-knowledge and the knowledge of being called

and sent into his future also coincide. The horizon within which the resurrection of Christ becomes knowable as 'resurrection', is the horizon of promise and mission, beckoning us on to his future and the future of his lordship. It is only in this context, on this basis and for this reason, that these other questions arise concerning the future of world history. Hence they arise in the form of the question as to the destiny of 'Israel and the nations', and are answered at that cardinal point in history constituted by the crucifixion of Christ by Jews and Gentiles and his resurrection for Jews and Gentiles. They are answered within the horizon of the mission of Christ and the mission of the Jewish and Gentile church.

It is only in this context, too, that the question of 'true human nature' arises – the question of what makes man to be true man – and is answered by the disclosure of a way, a promise and a future in which 'the truth' comes to man and he himself is brought into the truth. Communion with Christ, the new being in Christ, proves to be the way for man to become man. In it true human nature emerges, and the still hidden and unfulfilled future of human nature can be sought in it. This is an openness of human existence towards the world and towards the future – an openness grounded, manifested and kept alive by that openness of the revelation of God which is announced in the event of the resurrection of Christ and in which this event points beyond itself to an *eschaton* of the fulness of all things. The openness of Christian existence is not a special case of general human openness. It is not a special form of the *cor inquietum*, the restless heart that is part of man's created make-up. Rather, the historic and history-making *cor inquietum* of man arises from the *promissio inquieta*, and clings to it and is dependent on it. The resurrection of Christ goes on being a *promissio inquieta* until it finds rest in the resurrection of the dead and a totality of new being. Through the knowledge of the resurrection of the crucified the contradiction that is always and everywhere perceptible in an unredeemed world, and the sorrow and suffering caused by that world, are taken up into the confidence of hope, while on the other hand hope's confidence becomes earthly and universal. Any kind of docetic hope which leaves earthly conditions or corporeal existence to the mercy of their own contradictoriness and restricts itself to the Church, to the cultus or to believing inwardness, is therefore a denial of the cross. The hope that is born of the cross and the resurrection transforms the negative, contradictory and torturing aspects of the world into terms of 'not yet', and does not suffer them to end in 'nothing'.

9. THE IDENTITY OF THE LORD WHO APPEARS AS RISEN WITH THE CRUCIFIED CHRIST

How are the cross and resurrection of Jesus, that is to say, the historical and eschatological notes, combined with each other in the Easter proclamation?

None of the Easter narratives goes back any further than to the appearance of the risen Lord. Nowhere is the actual process of the raising of Jesus described in a historicizing or mythological way. What actually happened between the experience of his crucifixion and burial and his Easter appearances, is left in the darkness of the still unknown and still hidden God. Yet this event that took place between the two experiences of the cross of Jesus and his living appearance was already very early described as 'raising from the dead'. It is covered by a term for which there is no basis in experience hitherto and elsewhere. That is to say, it is described as something for which there are no analogies in the history we know, but only apocalyptic promises and hopes that where death is concerned God will give proof of his divinity at the last. 'Raising of the dead' is an expression which looks expectantly towards the future proof of God's creative power over the non-existent. What 'resurrection of the dead' really is, and what 'actually happened' in the raising of Jesus, is thus a thing which not even the New Testament Easter narratives profess to know. From the two mutually radically contradictory experiences of the cross and the appearances of Jesus, they argue to the event in between as an eschatological event for which the verifying analogy is as yet only in prospect and is still to come. That is, they use the term 'raising' to express not only a judgment about something that happened to Jesus, but at the same time also an eschatological expectation. This expectation is fulfilled in Jesus' own case in the experiences of the cross and of the appearances, and yet it still remains an expectation and a hope that precedes our own experience of being raised.

Now there is more to be said about the process of the raising of the crucified than merely that it is an eschatological mystery and that the assertions of the disciples have to be believed. The disciples' proclamation that he was raised from the dead does not arise from peculiar powers of imagination or from a unique kind of inspiration, but it arises from, and is made necessary by, the comparing of the two contradictory experiences which they have of Christ. The experience of the cross of Jesus means for them the experience of the god-forsakenness of God's ambassador – that is, an absolute *nihil* embracing also God. The experience of the appearance of the crucified one as the living Lord therefore means for them the experience of the nearness of God in the god-forsaken one, of the divineness of God in the crucified and dead Christ – that is, a new totality which annihilates the total *nihil*. The two experiences stand in a radical contradiction to each other, like death and life, nothing and everything, godlessness and the divinity of God. But how can it be possible to identify both experiences in one and the same person without resolving either the one experience or the other and making it of no account?

If this process of identification is to be made intelligible, then we must surely start from the fact that in the Easter appearances we have not merely dumb visions, but at the same time, and at bottom no doubt first and foremost, so-called auditions as well. This is indicated by the fact that these visions were entirely a matter of vocatory visions. Without the speaking and hearing of words it would have been unlikely – indeed impossible – to identify the one who appeared with the crucified Jesus. Without words spoken and heard the Easter appearances would have remained ghostly things. The appearances – for such things also exist elsewhere in the history of religion – would have been taken as hierophanies of a strange, new heavenly Being, if they had not been coupled with the speaking of the one who appeared here. The phenomenon of primitive Christian ecstasy shows that this possibility of understanding the Easter appearances as hierophanies of a new, divine spiritual Being was one that lay very close to hand. Moreover, it is surely a fact that the appearances themselves hardly provided

the possibility of identifying the one who appeared with the
one who was crucified. This possibility will therefore have to
be looked for in what is said by the one who appeared. What
he said must have contained something in the nature of a self-
identification ('It is I'). In that case the self-identification of
the one who appears in the glory of the promised divine life
with the one who was crucified can be regarded as an act of the
self-revelation of Jesus. The fundamental event in the Easter
appearances then manifestly lies in the revelation of the identity
and continuity of Jesus in the total contradiction of cross and
resurrection, of god-forsakenness and the nearness of God. That
is why the whole New Testament can assert that the disciples
at Easter did not see a new heavenly Being of some kind, but
Jesus himself. The Lord who is believed and proclaimed at
Easter therefore stands in continuity with the earthly Jesus who
had come and been crucified – a continuity which must repeatedly be sought and formulated anew and can never be
surrendered. The sole bridge of continuity between the primitive Christian proclamation and the history and proclamation of Jesus himself is *via* the raising of the one who was
crucified. This is a continuity in radical discontinuity, or an
identity in total contradiction. The enigma of this mysterious
identity between the crucified and the risen Christ is manifestly
the driving force in the christological controversies of primitive
Christianity. In all its repeatedly obvious questionableness it is
really the constant factor in the christological controversies.
The following possibilities arising here are erroneous:

1. The earthly, crucified Jesus is completely swallowed up
in the heavenly being of the risen and exalted Lord. The
memory of his words and his death is so overrun and choked
out by visions of his present heavenly being, that the harshness
of the godlessness of Good Friday is no longer noticed. This
tendency led to Docetism.

2. The Easter appearances are taken merely as divine confirmation of the claims of the dead prophet, so that while his
words certainly go on working, yet he himself does not. Then
the 'resurrection' is merely the legitimation and interpretation
of the historical. The line of continuity runs from the words of
the dead Master to the proclamation of the Church which
carries on what he said. His death is so to speak cancelled out

by the divine confirmation in the Easter appearances. The abiding continuity is then of a direct and repetitive kind and bypasses the cross and resurrection in favour of Jesus' understanding of himself or of existence. Then the Easter appearances are not signs of something new that happens to Jesus, but mean the birth of faith in Jesus' message. This tendency led to Ebionitism.

3. Jesus Christ, crucified yesterday, risen today, is in both modes of his appearing the 'same'. Then cross and resurrection are merely two modes of being, which belong to his one, eternal, and in itself unchangeable person. His earthly death and his risen life then become relative to the one substance of his person, which in itself would stand beyond death and life. This view, as suggested above all by the Christology of the ancient Church, perceives neither the deadliness of his death nor the startling newness of his resurrection. This tendency led to Modalism.

With an eye on these ideas we shall have to say that the identity of Jesus can be understood only as an identity *in*, but not above and beyond, cross and resurrection – that is, that it must remain bound up with the dialectic of cross and resurrection. In that case the contradictions between the cross and the resurrection are an inherent part of his identity. Then the resurrection can neither be reduced to the cross, as showing its meaning, nor can the cross be reduced to the resurrection, as its preliminary. It is formally a question of a dialectical identity which exists only through the contradiction, and of a dialectic which exists in the identity.

The apocalyptic expression 'raising from the dead by God' introduces a verb form into the adjectival qualifications of the person as 'crucified' and 'risen'. In the act of raising by God, Jesus is identified as the crucified one who is raised. In that case the point of identification lies not in the person of Jesus, but *extra se* in the God who creates life and new being out of nothing. He is then wholly dead and wholly raised. For this kind of thinking the self-revelation of Jesus in his appearances includes the revelation of the divinity and faithfulness of God. In that case we must say that in this event which is experienced in the crucifixion and the Easter appearances, God confesses to God and reveals his faithfulness. Then, however, this event

which is revealed in the cross and the Easter experiences points
back to the promises of God and forwards to an *eschaton* in which
his divinity is revealed in all. It must then be understood as the
eschatological coming to pass of the faithfulness of God, and at
the same time as the eschatological authentication of his promise and as the dawning of its fulfilment. It is a logical consequence of this, that then the future of Christ is not only awaited
in his universal glorification, but that his lordship is subordinated to the eschatological revelation of the divinity of God
in all that is and in all that is not, as Paul suggests in I Cor.
15.28. What happened between the cross and the Easter appearances is then an eschatological event which has its goal in
future revelation and universal fulfilment. It points beyond
itself, and even beyond Jesus, to the coming revelation of the
glory of God. Then Jesus identifies himself in the Easter appearances as the coming one, and his identity in cross and
resurrection points the direction for coming events and makes
a path for them. The Lord who appears as risen is not then
recognized as one who is eternalized or clothed in heavenly
glory, but he appears in the foreglow of the coming, promised
glory of God. What happened to him is understood as the dawn
and assured promise of the coming glory of God over all, as
the victory of life from God over death. Cross and resurrection
are then not merely *modi* in the person of Christ. Rather, their
dialectic is an open dialectic, which will find its resolving
synthesis only in the *eschaton* of all things. If, on the other hand,
cross and resurrection are seen as distinctions in the eternal
person of Jesus, then what happened between the cross and
Easter is not understood as a revelation of the divinity of God
in face of death, and is no longer taken as a creative act of God,
but is understood as the αὐτοβασιλεία of Jesus: the crucified
has arisen. Moreover, he has arisen without any special inter-
ference on God's part, because he is himself God. This view,
however, turns Easter into the birth of a new cultic Kyrios,
and can assert itself only with the greatest difficulty over against
the real experience of the existing lordship of death and the
powers of annihilation over men.

The fact that the one who appears is heard to speak contains, if we would sum up the Easter narratives, not only the
element of self-identification, but also a constant note of

mission and promise. The appearances of the risen Lord were experienced by those involved as a commission to service and mission in the world, but not as blissful experiences of union with the divine Being appearing here. The commission to apostolic service in the world was held to be *the* word of the risen Lord. His appearances were vocatory appearances by which the men involved were set to follow the footsteps of the mission of Jesus. By the revelation of the risen Lord the men involved were identified with the mission of Jesus and thus placed in the midst of a history which is instituted and determined by the mission of Jesus and by his future as revealed and made an object of hope in the fore-glow of Easter. The perceiving of the event of resurrection which took place in him thus led by logical necessity to a perception of their own mission and their own future. This is really intelligible only when the mystery of the person of Jesus and of his history in the cross and resurrection is grasped from the standpoint of his mission and in the light of God's future for the world, which his mission serves. Only when his history is thus seen as determined by the *eschaton*, and only when our own consciousness of history takes the form of a consciousness of mission, can the raising of Jesus from the dead be called 'historic'. His enigmatic identity in the contradiction of cross and resurrection has therefore to be understood as an eschatological identity. The titles of Christ which are used to express it anticipate his future. They are therefore not hard and fast titles which define who he was and is, but open and flexible titles, so to speak, which announce in terms of promise what he will be. They are therefore at the same time also dynamic titles. They are stirred and stirring ideas of mission, which seek to point men to their work in the world and their hope in the future of Christ.

10. THE FUTURE OF JESUS CHRIST

If we now ask what the future of the risen Christ contains by way of promise and expectation, then we discover promises whose content is already lit up in certain outline by the prophetic expectations of the Old Testament, but whose form is determined by the words, the suffering and the death of Christ. The future of Christ which is to be expected can be stated only in promises which bring out and make clear in the form of foreshadowing and prefigurement what is hidden and prepared in him and his history. In this case, too, promise stands between knowing and not knowing, between necessity and possibility, between that which is not yet and that which already is. The knowledge of the future which is kindled by promise is therefore a knowledge in hope, is therefore prospective and anticipatory, but is therefore also provisional, fragmentary, open, straining beyond itself. It knows the future in striving to bring out the tendencies and latencies of the Christ event of the crucifixion and resurrection, and in seeking to estimate the possibilities opened up by this event. Here the Easter appearances of the crucified Christ are a constant incitement to the consciousness that hopes and anticipates, but on the other hand also suffers and is critical of existence. For these 'appearances' make visible something of the eschatological future of the Christ event, and therefore cause us to seek and search for the future revelation of this event. Thus knowledge of Christ becomes anticipatory, provisional and fragmentary knowledge of his future, namely, of what he will be. All the titles of Christ point messianically forward in this sense. On the other hand, knowledge of the future has its stimulus nowhere else than in the riddle of Jesus of Nazareth. It will thus be knowledge of Christ in the urge to know who he is and what is hidden and prepared in him.

If, however, we take the *absconditum sub cruce* as *latency* and the *revelatum in resurrectione* as *tendency*, if we enquire about the *intention* of God in the mission of Jesus, then we light upon what was promised beforehand. The *missio* of Jesus becomes intelligible only by the *promissio*. His future, in the light of which he can be recognized as what he is, is illuminated in advance by

the promise of the righteousness of God,

the promise of life as a reult of resurrection from the dead,

and *the promise of the kingdom of God* in a new totality of being.

II. THE FUTURE OF RIGHTEOUSNESS

Righteousness means 'being in order', standing in the right relationship; it means correspondence and harmony and is to

that extent akin to 'truth'. But righteousness also means 'being
able to stand', having subsistence, finding a basis on which to
exist, and is to that extent akin to existence as such. Righteousness in the Old Testament does not mean agreement with an
ideal norm or with the *logos* of eternal being, but describes a
historic communal relationship which is founded on promise
and faithfulness. When Israel praises the righteousness of God,
then it thankfully remembers his faithfulness to his covenant
promises as it has taken practical shape in the history of Israel.
Yahweh's righteousness is his faithfulness to the covenant. That
is why his righteousness 'happens', and why one can 'tell' it
and trust in it for the future and expect 'salvation' from this
righteousness. In trusting in God's faithfulness to this covenant,
and in living in accordance with his covenant in promise and
statute, men do right by God and are set right. They are set
right not only in relation to God, but also in their mutual relationships and in relation to things.[1] This history of the divine
righteousness is manifestly recognized not only in Israel's own
history and not only in human history, but in the history and
the destiny of the whole of God's creation. By the righteousness
of God is meant the way in which in freedom he remains true
to his statutes, his word and his works and gives them subsistence. The righteousness of God requires everything that
owes its existence to the action of God, that is, the whole
creation. The righteousness of God is the essence of its stability
and the ground of its subsistence. Without his justice and faithfulness nothing can exist, but everything is swallowed up in
nothingness. Hence God's righteousness is universal. It is concerned with the justification of life and with the ground of the
existence of all things. If we expect the righteousness of God to
set man right with himself, with his fellows and with the whole
of creation, then it can become the summary expression for a
universal, all-inclusive eschatology which expects from the
future of righteousness a new being for all things. The righteousness of God then refers not merely to a new order for the existing world, but provides creation as a whole with a new ground
of existence and a new right to life. Hence with the coming

---

[1] G. von Rad has shown how the righteousness of God became for Israel the
summary expression of the right relationship between God and man, man and
fellow man, man and world. Cf. *Theologie des Alten Testamentes* I, 1958, pp. 368ff.
(ET 1962, pp. 370ff.).

of the righteousness of God we can expect also a new
creation.

In the New Testament the divine righteousness is accordingly   *NT*
understood by Paul as God's faithfulness in communal relationships, as an event brought about by God, and as an event from
which there arises a new creation and new life. Paul sees this
divine righteousness as revealed in the gospel (Rom. 1.17) and
grasped in faith. It is the christological gospel of the cross and
of the raising of Christ by God. In this event divine righteousness is revealed for the unrighteous and justification of life
(Rom. 5.18) for those who, both in a juridical and in an ontological sense, cannot stand before the wrath of God. It is the
eschatological gospel, which imputes this divine righteousness
'that must be hoped for' (Gal. 5.5) as now already present and
as savingly at work in the wrath of God that is now being revealed. It is, finally, the universal gospel, which is oriented
towards the new creation that fulfils all things, sets them right
with God and so gives them status and being.

Divine righteousness 'happens' here, and the gospel reveals
it by proclaiming the event of the obedience of Jesus even to
the death of the cross, by proclaiming the event of his surrender
to this death, and by proclaiming his resurrection and his life
as the coming of the divine righteousness to the unjust. The
realization and revelation of a new divine righteousness for
sinners thus becomes the mystery of Jesus Christ which is disclosed in the promise of the gospel: 'delivered for our offences,
and raised again for our justification' (Rom. 4.25). 'He hath
made him to be sin for us, who knew no sin; that we might be
made the righteousness of God in him' (II Cor. 5.21). Thus
there takes place in him reconciliation of the unreconciled
by God. It is important here to see that this divine righteousness
has its ground both in the event of the cross and in that of the
resurrection, that is, both in his death and in his life. A one-
sided theology of the cross would attain only to the gospel of the
remissio peccatorum, but not to the *promissio* of the new righteousness whose life is grounded in his life and whose future consists
in the future of his lordship. 'In that he died, he died unto sin
once (ἐφάπαξ): but in that he liveth, he liveth unto God. Likewise reckon ye also yourselves to be dead indeed unto sin, but
alive unto God through Jesus Christ our Lord' (Rom. 6.10–11).

The divine righteousness which is here revealed finds its measure not in the sin it forgives, but in that new life in the glory of the risen and exalted Christ which it promises and to which it points. Along with this goes the fact that since the gospel of divine righteousness has its ground in the dying and living of Jesus, sin and death are seen together. 'The wages of sin is death; but the gift of God is eternal life through Jesus Christ our Lord' (Rom. 6.23, cf. I Cor. 15.55ff.). Sin is therefore to be understood as unrighteousness, as having no ground and no rights, as being unable to stand. This includes both being lost in revolt against God and in falsehood, and also dying and being swallowed up in nothingness. The divine righteousness which is revealed in the cross and resurrection of Jesus accordingly embraces both reconciliation with God and justification of life. It embraces forgiveness of guilt and annihilation of the destiny of death. It embraces reconciliation and redemption of the mortal body. It takes place in the pledge of reconciliation and the promise of quickening. Since Jesus' resurrection and his exaltation to be Lord is not yet the consummation of his lordship, but the ground and guarantee of his liberating and remedial lordship over all, so the divine righteousness is present in faith and in baptism, yet in such a way that it is engaged in a process which will be completed only at the parousia of Christ. In this process we have the divine righteousness here always as a gift that is pledged, disputed and subject to testing, that is, we have it in terms of promise and expectancy.[1] Then, however, the promised divine righteousness sets us on a path whose tension and whose goal it announces. It is this eschatological differentiation in the revelation of Christ in gospel and promise that forms the ground of the historic and ethical statements in which Paul speaks of 'grace reigning through righteousness' (Rom. 5.21), of the 'ministration of righteousness' (II Cor. 3.9, cf. Rom. 6.13), and of 'submission unto righteousness' (Rom. 10.3). Divine righteousness is not merely a gift that has been made manifest, but means also the power of the Giver which is at work in the life of the believer. That is why the man who is justified begins to suffer under the contradiction of this world with which he has a bodily solidarity, for he must in obedience seek the divine righteousness in his body, on earth, and in all creatures.

[1] Cf. E. Käsemann, 'Gottesgerechtigkeit bei Paulus', *ZTK* 58, 1961, p. 368.

If the divine righteousness of God means that in communal relationships he is faithful to his promise and to the work of his hands, then justification has finally not only the sense that the unjust is given a right to stand before God and to endure in his judgment, but it has contrariwise also a theological sense – namely, that in this event God attains his rights over against his creation. Luther, in his Lectures on Romans in 1516, had sought to interpret this as a reciprocal event of *justificatio Dei activa et passiva*: justification means that God justifies man by grace and that man acknowledges God's justice in confessing his sins, so that in this reciprocal event not only the sinner but God, too, is given his rights.[1] If this insight of Luther's is detached from the framework of the *humilitas* Christology in which he formulated it, then it can be said that because the divine righteousness is gift and power and the communion of faith with Christ is both a dying with Christ to sin and also a living under his lordship with an outlook towards his future, therefore the event of justification is the earnest and promise of an all-inclusive setting to rights on God's part. If in the justification of the sinner God attains to his rights, then this justification is the beginning and foreshadowing of his sole lordship. The divine righteousness which is latent in the event of Christ has an inner trend towards a totality of new being. The man who is justified follows this trend in bodily obedience. His struggle for obedience and his suffering under the godlessness of the world have their goal in the future of the righteousness of the whole. Thus this struggle is a fragment of, and a prelude to, the coming divine righteousness, for it already gives God his due, and in it already God attains to his rights over his world.

Thus in the New Testament, too, we shall have to understand divine righteousness as promise. In this promise the |

---

[1] M. Luther, *Vorlesung über den Römerbrief 1515/16*, ed. J. Ficker, 1908, II, p. 65. Cf. H. J. Iwand's comment on this in *Glaubensgerechtigkeit nach Luthers Lehre*, 4th ed. 1964, pp. 11ff. This new insight on Luther's part in seeing in the event of justification not only the forgiveness of sins and the right of the godless to life before God, but *vice versa* also the judicial realization of God's right to lordship, has been regained for New Testament theology today by E. Käsemann. Cf. 'Neutestamentliche Fragen heute', *ZTK* 54, 1957, pp. 13f.; 'Gottesgerechtigkeit bei Paulus', *ZTK* 58, 1961, pp. 367ff. Only with this new insight is it possible to do away with the individualization of the event of justification in the revelation of the divinity of God, and only where that happens does the *justificatio impii* come to stand within the eschatological horizon of the *resurrectio mortuorum* and the *creatio ex nihil*.

Cit.: this is a real & anti. prob.

promised object is offered in the present, and yet it is grasped in
the believing hope which makes man ready to serve the future
of the divine righteousness in all things.

12. THE FUTURE OF LIFE

Expectation of life and recognition of death are immediately
bound up together in love. It is only in the things a man loves
that he can be hurt, and it is only in love that man suffers and
recognizes the deadliness of death. What sort of expectation of
life and what sort of experience of death were quickened by the
promises of Israel?

It is a widely established and surprising fact that 'Yahwism
turned with a special intolerance against all forms of the cult
of death'.[1] 'It is surprising that for long the Jews had no
thoughts or dreams about the last agony. They were as much
a this-worldly people as the Greeks, and yet their life was in-
comparably more vigorously determined by future goals.'[2] In
this enigmatic fact that Israel's religion of promise clings with
obstinate exclusiveness to the historic and this-worldly fulfilment of the promises, we have the presupposition for understanding the resurrection of Christ as the resurrection of the
crucified one and not as a symbol for the hope of immortality
and for the resigned attitude to life that goes along with it.

All dead things represent for Israel the acme of uncleanness.
All pollutions of this kind involve exclusion from the service
of God. It is true that the temptation to necromancy did exist
in Canaan. Yet the very rejection of it by Israel shows plainly
that the religion of promise must abjure all sacral communication with the dead. The dead are cut off from God and from
living communion with him. Because God and his promise are
life, the real bitterness of death lies not merely in the loss of life,
but also in the loss of God, in god-forsakenness.[3] For life
means giving thanks and praise in the presence of God. But in
death there can be no giving of praise, and therefore no thanks-
giving either and no harmony with God. Being able to praise
God and being no longer able to praise him are here synonyms

---

[1] G. von Rad, *Theologie des Alten Testamentes* I, p. 275 (ET p. 276).
[2] E. Bloch, *Das Prinzip Hoffnung* II, 1959, p. 1323.
[3] G. von Rad, *op. cit.* I, p. 386 (ET pp. 388f.).

for the antithesis of life and death.[1] Death cuts man off from God
by separating him from his promises and his praise. Not only
our physical end, but also sickness, exile and oppression can cut
us off from the life of praise and from the promised life and thus
be understood as death. We have our life in praising God,
hoping in him and giving thanks to him. Death therefore means
that we are far from God and he from us.

On this ground it becomes understandable that the Greek
doctrine of universal transience in the outward world and of the
essential immortality of the true being of the soul hardly gained
any admittance in Israel, but that the hopes of resurrection on
the other hand certainly did find a place on the periphery of the
Old Testament and in the apocalyptic of late Judaism. This
expectation of the resurrection of the dead is found in its
Israelite form neither in an anthropological context – as a hope
for man beyond death – nor in a cosmological context – in
recognition of immortal substances in which man participates –
but in a theological context – in expounding the power of the
God of promise, whom even death cannot rob of his due but
who must attain his due beyond death. Thus according to
Ezek. 37.11 the people of the promise can now recognize itself
only in the picture of dead bones, i.e. of hope that has come to
nothing, and is then given to hear the prophetic message of a
new promise of life by Yahweh: 'Behold, I will cause breath to
enter into you, and ye shall live' (Ezek. 37.5). This is a new promise of life, for it is no longer attached to the condition of
a possible repentance, but promises a creative act of Yahweh
upon his people beyond the bounds of the temporal and the
possible. It therefore acquires the form of a promise that has no
conditions and no presuppositions, a promise of life from the
dead on the ground of a creative act of Yahweh *ex nihilo*. Thus
in Israel the idea of 'raising of the dead' is formulated in the
first instance within the framework of the religion of promise:
it is not a case of natural reanimation, but of the fulfilling of
Yahweh's promises of life in the dead bearer of the promise. It
is not until the apocalyptic writers that 'raising of the dead'
is understood in universal terms, in the sense that even beyond

[1] *Ibid.* I, p. 367 (ET p. 370): 'Praising and not praising stand over against one
another like life and death: praise becomes the most elementary "mark of being
alive".'

death this God will achieve his judgment and his due in both righteous and unrighteous. This is entirely in harmony with the development of the Israelite confession to God the Creator and to his faithfulness as Creator. The late Israelite ideas of *creatio ex nihilo* and *resurrectio mortuorum* mark the eschatological extremities of the religion of promise.[1]

It has rightly been said: 'Should we not see this theological vacuum, which Israel zealously kept free from any sacral concepts, as one of the greatest theological enigmas in the Old Testament? The prediction that God will prepare a resurrection from the dead for his own people is found only peripherally.'[2] This 'vacuum' caused by the absence of religious ideas and hopes against death makes it possible on the one hand to experience in all its undisguised harshness the deadliness of death as compared with the promised life received from the promise of God. It can be filled on the other hand only by a hope which makes possible a whole-hearted, unrestricted and unreserved assent to life, to the body and to the world, and which yet extends beyond death. The hope of resurrection does not overcome the deadliness of death by regarding living and dying as mere summary expressions for the transience of all things and as such unimportant, but by proclaiming the victory of praise and therewith of life over death and over the curse of godforsakenness, by announcing the victory of God over the absence of God.

What is the significance of the death and resurrection of Jesus Christ in the context of these expectations?

In the context of these expectations of life, his death on the cross implies not only the end of the life which he had, but also the end of the life which he loves and in which he hopes. The death of Jesus was experienced as the death of him who had been sent as the Messiah of God, and therefore implies also the 'death of God'. Thus his death is experienced and proclaimed as god-

---

[1] W. Zimmerli, '"Leben" und "Tod" im Buch des Propheten Ezechiel', in *Gottes Offenbarung*, 1963, p. 191. Zimmerli points out how closely Ezek. 37 approaches the priestly narrative of the creation and how the prophet's conditional promises of life – 'return, and ye shall live' – are anchored in God's promise of life which unconditionally embraces the beginning (creation) and end (resurrection of the dead) of the history of the people of God. Cf. also Christoph Barth, *Die Errettung vom Tode in den individuellen Klage- und Dankliedern des Alten Testamentes*, 1947; Robert Martin-Achard, *De la mort à la resurrection d'après l'Ancien Testament*, 1956, and K. Koch's review in *Verkündigung und Forschung*, 1960/2, 1/2, pp. 57–60.

[2] G. von Rad, *op. cit.* II, p. 362 (ET p. 350).

forsakenness, as judgment, as curse, as exclusion from the promised life, as reprobation and damnation.

In the context of these expectations of life, his resurrection must then be understood not as a mere return to life as such, but as a conquest of the deadliness of death – as a conquest of god-forsakenness, as a conquest of judgment and of the curse, as a beginning of the fulfilment of the promised life, and thus as a conquest of all that is dead in death, as a negation of the negative (Hegel), as a negation of the negation of God.

It is then understandable, further, that Jesus' resurrection was not seen as a private Easter for his private Good Friday, but as the beginning and source of the abolition of the universal Good Friday, of that god-forsakenness of the world which comes to light in the deadliness of the death of the cross. Hence the resurrection of Christ was not understood merely as the first instance of a general resurrection of the dead and as a beginning of the revelation of the divinity of God in the non-existent, but also as the source of the risen life of all believers and as a confirmation of the promise which will be fulfilled in all and will show itself in the very deadliness of death to be irresistible.

To recognize the event of the resurrection of Christ is therefore to have a hopeful and expectant knowledge of this event. It means recognizing in this event the latency of that eternal life which in the praise of God arises from the negation of the negative, from the raising of the one who was crucified and the exaltation of the one who was forsaken. It means assenting to the tendency towards resurrection of the dead in this event of the raising of the one. It means following the intention of God by entering into the dialectic of suffering and dying in expectation of eternal life and of resurrection. This is described as the working of the Holy Spirit. The 'Spirit' is according to Paul the 'life-giving Spirit', the Spirit who '*raised up* Christ from the dead' and '*dwells* in' those who recognize Christ and his future, and '*shall* quicken their mortal bodies' (Rom. 8.11).

The 'Spirit' in question here does not fall from heaven and does not soar ecstatically into heaven, but arises from the event of the resurrection of Christ and is an earnest and pledge of his future, of the future of universal resurrection and of life. 'And as the power of the "flesh" is manifested in the fact that it binds man to the transitory, to that which in reality is always already past, to death, so the power of the Spirit is manifested in the fact that it gives the believer freedom, opens the way to the future, to the eternal, to life. For freedom is nothing else than being open for the genuine future, letting oneself be determined by the future. So Spirit may be called the power of futurity.'[1] Yet the difference between past and future emerges for the Spirit of faith not in the *punctum mathematicum* of the present, and not in an airy *nunc aeternum*, but in that historic event of the raising of the crucified Christ in which the power of transience and the deadliness of death are conquered and the future of life is opened once and for all. Christ did not rise into the Spirit or into the kerygma, but into that as yet undetermined future realm ahead of us which is pointed to by the tendencies of the Spirit and the proclamations of the kerygma. This realm of the future which lies before us cannot be turned into mere 'futurity' by reflecting solely on its relation to existence, but it is the future of Jesus Christ and can therefore be inferred only from the knowledge and recognition of that historic event of the resurrection of Christ which is the making of history and the key to it. The 'Spirit' who 'mortifies the things of the flesh' and gives freedom for the future is not an eternal event, but arises from a historic event and discloses eschatological possibilities and dangers. As a reminder of Christ he is also the promise of his future, and *vice versa*. Hence he leads us into the 'fellowship of the sufferings of Christ', into conformity to his death, into the love which exposes itself to death because it is upheld by hope. Hence, too, he leads into the future of that glorification of Jesus Christ on which depends the future and glorification of humanity and of all things. 'As he was crucified through weakness, yet liveth by the power of God, so we also are weak in him, but we shall live with him by the power of God' (II Cor. 13.4). Thus the Spirit is the power to suffer in participation in the mission and the love of Jesus Christ, and is in this suffering the passion for what is possible, for what is coming and promised in the future of life, of freedom and of resurrection. The Spirit subjects man to the tendency of the things which are latent in the resurrection of Jesus and which are the intended goal of the future of the risen Lord. Resurrection and eternal

[1] R. Bultmann, *Theologie des Neuen Testamentes*, 1953, p. 331 (ET pp. 334f.).

life are the future that is promised, and thereby make obedience possible in the body. In all our acts we are sowing in hope. So, too, in love and obedience we are sowing for the future of the resurrection of the body. In obedience, those who have been quickened by the Spirit are on the way towards the quickening of the mortal body.

Just as the urge of promise is towards fulfilment, as the urge of faith is towards obedience and sight, and as the urge of hope is towards the life that is promised and finally attained, so the urge of the raising of Christ is towards life in the Spirit and towards the eternal life that is the consummation of all things. This eternal life here lies hidden beneath its opposite, under trial, suffering, death and sorrow. Yet this its hiddenness is not an eternal paradox, but a latency within the tendency that presses forwards and outwards into that open realm of possibilities that lies ahead and is so full of promise. In the darkness of the pain of love, the man of hope discovers the dissension between the self and the body.[1] In the struggle for obedience

[1] The interpretation of σῶμα and corporeality in R. Bultmann (*Theologie des Neuen Testamentes*, pp. 191ff., ET pp. 195ff.) seems to be too one-sidedly personalistic. For him, σῶμα means man, 'the person as a whole'. 'He is called σῶμα in so far as he can make himself the object of his own actions, or experiences himself as the subject of something that happens or that he suffers. Thus he can be called σῶμα in so far as he has a relation to himself' (p. 192, cf. ET pp. 195f.). 'Man does not *have* a σῶμα, but he *is* σῶμα' (p. 191, ET p. 194). The former thesis no doubt aptly represents what modern philosophic anthropology calls the 'ex-centric position' of man. The second thesis, however, cancels out the dialectic of the ex-centric position of human nature. 'He neither *is* only body, nor *has* he only a body. Every claim upon his physical existence demands a balance between being and having, without and within' (H. Plessner, *Lachen und Weinen*, 3rd ed. 1961, p. 48). Bultmann sees the fact of man's 'having a relation to himself' as providing the possibility of 'being one with himself or being estranged from himself, at odds with himself' (p. 192, ET p. 196). The σῶμα πνευματικόν can therefore be understood as a reconciliation of the dualism in man between self and self (p. 195, ET p. 199). In harmony with this view of corporeality as the relation of man to himself, G. Ebeling finds that in faith man comes 'to himself' and attains to agreement with himself (*Theologie und Verkündigung*, pp. 84ff.; ET, pp. 83f.). But now, man's relation to himself is not identical with his relation to his body. His corporeal, physical and social existence is not identical with 'existence' in the sense of the relation to himself. The two belong together in such a way that according as man acquires in reflection a consciousness of his self and his subjectivity, so he attains to an objective consciousness of the world and assumes a detached attitude to the corporeal, social and cosmic 'world around him' as belonging to the world of objects. 'To become man is to be raised to openness towards the world through the spirit' (M. Scheler, *Die Stellung des Menschen im Kosmos*, 2nd ed. 1949, p. 41). The thing man becomes conscious of as his corporeality is not his 'self', but is rather the very thing from which he succeeds in differentiating himself. The fact that through the spirit, through consciousness and through reflection man can differentiate himself from himself, that he is able to objectify himself, constitutes the ambiguity of his existence: he can neither be himself without having himself, nor have himself without being himself, he achieves

and for what is due to God in the body he discovers the contradiction of the flesh and his subjection to the hostile powers of annihilation and death. In beginning to hope for the triumph of life and to wait for resurrection, he perceives the deadliness of death and can no longer put up with it. The corporeality which thus comes to the fore in hope is plainly the starting point for the solidarity of the believer with the whole of creation which, like him, is subjected to vanity – in hope. This corporeality, for the redemption of which the man of hope waits because it has not yet taken place, is the existential starting point for the universality that marks the Christian hope and for the as yet undetermined character of what is hoped for. The hope of the redemption of the body and the hope of the redemption of all creation from vanity are one. Hence it is on this hope of the redemption of the body that the universality which belongs to the Christian hope depends. On the other hand, in the contradictions of the body, in the painful difference between what he hopes and what he experiences, the man of hope perceives that his hoped-for future is still outstanding. Hence it is on the difference between hope and bodily reality that the wide open, future character of the Christian hope depends. The cosmic ideas of Christian eschatology are there-

---

neither complete distinction and objectivity in regard to himself, nor complete identity. If the promise of justification gives him a prospect of reconciliation and identity, then it cannot mean only the reconciliation of man with himself, but must also mean the redemption of his corporeality and of the world that has become to him a world of objects. Hence through the promise and the Holy Spirit he perceives not only his own reconciliation, but along with it at the same time also the unreconciled and unredeemed character of the body that is subject to death and of the world that is subject to the powers of godlessness. His reconciliation in the Spirit does not yet reconcile him with his body and his world in such a way that he would see these as the 'world around him', in such a way that like the animals (or the angels) he could attain to harmony with his environment amid existing things. E. Käsemann is therefore right when he asserts against Bultmann that 'body' for Paul is not in fact the relation of man to himself, but is that piece of world which we ourselves are and for which, as a gift of the Creator, we are responsible. 'For the apostle it means man in his worldliness, that is, in his ability to communicate' (*ZTK* 59, 1962, p. 282). If the perceiving of his corporeality is grounded for man in his being raised to openness towards the world through the spirit, if his corporeality is not his 'self' but that from which he can differentiate himself, then the perceiving of corporeality, of socialness and of worldliness becomes one. Then the perceiving of man's unredeemed corporeality is the starting point for the perceiving of man's solidarity with the whole unredeemed creation. And in this context there also finally comes to light the existential character of all man's objective statements. Objective statements are not by any means statements that are oblivious of self and of existence, but are grounded in the existential raising of man to openness towards the world through the spirit. This calls for a re-check on demythologizing and existentialist interpretation.

fore not by any means mythological, but reach forward into the open realm of possibilities ahead of all reality, give expression to the 'expectation of the creature' for a *nova creatio*, and provide a prelude for eternal life, peace and the haven of the reconciliation of all things. They bring to light not only what future means in man's 'openness towards the world', but also what future means in the world's 'openness towards man' (cf. the relation of correspondence between the 'expectation of the creature' and the 'liberty of the children of God' in Rom. 8.20ff.).

In the light of the differences which the hope of resurrection and of reconciled, perfect life finds in the existing reality of man and the world as at present experienced, and which it reveals in all their negativity, the positive side of the future for which it hopes for man and the world, for spirit and body, for Israel and the nations, can be expressed in the first instance as negation of the negative. The 'new heaven and new earth, wherein dwelleth righteousness' (II Peter 3.13), the promise that 'God shall wipe away all tears from their eyes; and there shall be no more death, neither sorrow, nor crying, neither shall there be any more pain' (Rev. 21.4), the face unveiled in the glory of God (II Cor. 2.18) and the body glorified by the Spirit of the resurrection (I Cor. 15.35ff.) – these are representations and pictures of this kind, in which the future is re-'pre'-sented and 'pro'-mised[1] in contrast to the experiences of a negative present. These ideas and pictures are fragments from a life that has been unmasked in all its flaws by hope and is therefore one of suffering. The book of Revelation is the book of the martyrs. These ideas and pictures may well be conditioned by their time – they are, and must be, if they would be critical of their time – yet they are used with the intention of expressing something which goes completely beyond the *status quo* and sets things on the move.

As long as 'every thing' is not 'very good', the difference between hope and reality remains, and faith remains irreconciled and must press towards the future in hope and suffering.

---

[1] [The somewhat curious orthography is an attempt to convey something of the author's intention in hyphenating *vor-stellen* ('represent') and using the antiquated form *vorheissen* for *verheissen* ('promise'). The stress laid on the syllables *pre* and *pro* (in German *vor*) is meant to suggest that representation and promise have literally to do with *advance* conceptions about things to come. – *Translator.*]

Thus the promise of life through the resurrection of Christ
also brings us within the tendency of the Spirit who quickens
men in suffering and whose goal is the praise of the new creation. This is something like 'progressive revelation' or 'self-
realizing eschatology', only it is a case of the *progressus gratiae*
itself. It is not objective time that brings the progress. It is not
human activity that makes the future. It is the inner necessity
of the Christ event itself, the tendency of which is finally to
bring out in all things the eternal life latent in him and the
justice of God latent in him.

13. THE FUTURE OF THE KINGDOM OF GOD AND OF
THE FREEDOM OF MAN

The real heart of eschatology, and the basic concept which
it constantly employs with varying content, is doubtless to be
found in the promise and expectation of what is known as the
'kingdom of God' and the 'lordship of God'. It is plain that
even in the early days of Israel, the hope which has its ground
in the promise is directed towards the lordship of Yahweh. It
is in his real, historic lordship that his glory manifests itself. It
is in the faithful and powerful fulfilment of his promises that he
manifests himself as himself, as God and Lord. Bound up with
the expectation of the lordship of God is the expectation that his
people, mankind, and all that he has made will attain to salvation, peace, happiness, life – in a word, to what it was truly
meant to be. Faith in his lordship finds its expression in the confession that Yahweh is king (Judg. 8.23). If we go back to the
nomadic period of the Israelite tribes, then we find the idea
that Yahweh is the Leader who goes before his people, that he
rules them by leading them as a shepherd, issuing commands,
giving counsel and announcing his will for the future.[1] Thus his
lordship does not mean in the first instance a worldly kingship
over the natural world around man, but leadership towards
the lands of promise, and thus a historic lordship which shows
itself in unique, unrepeatable, startlingly new, purposeful
events.

God's lordship originally means lordship in promise, faithfulness and fulfilment. Life under his lordship then accordingly

[1] Cf. M. Buber, *Königtum Gottes*, 2nd ed. 1936.

means the historic life of the nomad in breaking new ground and in obedient readiness to face the future – a life that is received in promise and is open to promise. It is only in controversy with the nature religions and theophanous ideas of the world in Palestine, and in the context of the development of belief in creation and of the prophetic eschatology, that the idea of God's lordship becomes universal, and that this universality of the lordship of the one God is at the same time understood eschatologically. The praises of God's royal lordship over all things, the ideas of his coming, his justice and judgment upon earth, are all related to the God who is on the march with Israel, the God of the promise and the exodus. Thus the ideas of universal theophany can be supplemented by ideas from the nature religions, and yet these latter can at once be set in an eschatological framework on the ground of the historic religion of promise.

In the idea of the lordship of God two elements are combined: remembrance of his historic lordship and confidence in it, and expectation of his universal lordship in which the world and all nations and things become his universe, his kingdom and his praise.

It is not possible to distinguish the two by making the first a matter of narrow nationalism and the second one of universal cosmic faith. Rather, the universal expectation has its ground in remembering the particular historic reality of his sovereign action in Israel. After the breakdown of Israel's historic independence, the expectation of the divine lordship was represented in rabbinic theology in the obedience of the legally righteous, while in apocalyptic theology it was futurized by means of speculations about world history, and his coming was delegated to events in the course of world history. This shows the impossibility of conceiving the promise of divine lordship in both historic and eschatological terms without its being given new content from experience.

In the New Testament the βασιλεία is obviously a central concept – especially in the synoptic tradition, and here indeed at all levels of the tradition. In particular, the message and acts, miracles and parables of Jesus before Easter are described as 'the kingdom of God'. Jesus proclaims the messianic

kingdom of God. The peculiar feature of his proclamation of
the kingdom lies in the fact that nearness to, entry into, and
inheritance of, the kingdom are bound by him to the decision
of the hearers and their attitude to his own person. The future
of the divine lordship is immediately bound up with the mystery of his own presence.

This can be understood in the sense that as the last prophet
of the coming kingdom he gives men's decision in face of his
message the character of the final, and in this sense eschatological, decision.

It can also be understood as a transformation of the kingdom
of God tradition. Then Jesus has surmounted the apocalyptic
question as to the appointed times and historic circumstances
of the arrival of the kingdom 'by concentrating on what the
announcement of the kingdom means for existence'.[1] By
proclaiming his hour as the last hour of decision, Jesus himself
demythologizes the apocalyptic pictures of the kingdom for the
sake of existential actualization. 'The eschatological proclamation and the ethical demand both point man to the fact that he
is brought before God and that God is at hand; both point him
to his Now as the hour of decision for God.'[2] In that case, however, the peculiar feature of Jesus' message of the kingdom
would lie in an existential ethicizing of it, in favour of which all
ideas of cosmological apocalyptic fade out of the picture.
But this alone gives the primitive Christian Church no reason,
and hardly even a right, to continue his proclamation. The
reason and the right of the Christian Church to carry on his
proclamation, and for its part even to transform it, surely lies
in the event which gave it cause to remember Jesus' words and
actions at all and to proclaim him as Lord of all the world –
namely, in the Easter appearances of the risen Lord. The Easter
appearances, however, were recognized and proclaimed within a horizon of apocalyptic expectation: resurrection as an
eschatological event – Jesus as the firstfruits of the resurrection.
The understanding of Jesus which results from the event of the
raising of the crucified one by God was necessarily connected
in the Church's mind with its remembrance of the understanding of God and his kingdom which results from the words and

---

[1] H. Conzelmann, Art. 'Reich Gottes', in *RGG*[3] vol. V, col. 915.
[2] R. Bultmann, *Theologie des Neuen Testamentes*, p. 20 (ET p. 21).

acts of Jesus.[1] The note of eschatological decision in his proclamation of the imminent lordship of God was therefore
necessarily transferred to the note of eschatological decision in
the message of the crucified and risen Lord. With this, however,
the proclamation of the divine lordship acquired a new apocalyptic character and could be bound up with the messianic
titles of Christ, such as Son of Man, which are found in apocalyptic. This constitutes a discontinuity between Jesus' message
of the kingdom and the Church's christological message of the
kingdom, as it is aptly expressed in the remark of Albert
Schweitzer: Jesus proclaimed the kingdom, and the Church
proclaimed – him. Yet this discontinuity exists rightly. The
Church has not to carry on Jesus' self-consciousness or self-
understanding, but to proclaim who he *is*. This, however, can
be seen only in the light of the end, i.e. of the cross and of the
Easter appearances as the foreshadowing of his eschatologically
still outstanding goal and end. The Church's statements are
based not on Jesus' self-understanding, but on that which happened to him in the cross and the resurrection. His death and
resurrection mark the discontinuity between the historical
Jesus and primitive Christian Christology. His identity, however, which lies in the fact that he who here appears as risen is
the one who was crucified and no other, forms at the same time
the bridge to the historical Jesus and provides the ground and
occasion for the historical remembrance of Jesus' message and
acts. This remembrance may be clouded in the gospel tradition
of primitive Christianity by many an enthusiastic concern for
resurrection and the Spirit, yet the Easter Christophanies are
the only adequate ground for remembering and calling to mind
his proclamation, just as his cross is the only adequate ground
for not forgetting his promise of the kingdom in face of the so-
called delay of the parousia of the kingdom. There is no need
here to subject the gospel narratives to the verdict of being

[1] For what follows cf. the discussion on kingdom of God and Son of Man: P.
Vielhauer, 'Gottesreich und Menschensohn in der Verkündigung Jesu', *Festschr. f.
G. Dehn*, 1957, pp. 51ff.; H. E. Tödt, *Der Menschensohn in der synoptischen Uberlieferung*,
1959 (ET by D. M. Barton: *The Son of Man in the Synoptic Tradition*, 1965); E.
Schweizer, 'Der Menschensohn', *Zeitschrift für NT Wissenschaft* 50, 1959, pp. 185ff.;
P. Vielhauer, 'Jesus und der Menschensohn', *ZTK* 60, 1963, pp. 133ff. (now also in
Aufsätze zum Neuen Testament [Theol. Bücherei 31], 1965, pp. 135ff.). The latter's
systematic observations on the problem how far it is true that Jesus did not under-
stand himself as the expected Son of Man, but that the Church rightly did so
(*ZTK* 60, pp. 173f.), provide our starting point here.

imaginative backward projections of the resurrection faith.
They remember Jesus on the ground of the expectations for his
future which are aroused by the resurrection appearances, and
present the earthly Jesus of the past in the light of the hopes
for his future which become possible with Easter. These hopes
are no doubt a strong motive for historical remembrance and
also for historical discoveries. The key to what he 'in fact' was
and is, is provided not by his self-understanding, whatever that
may have been, but by the understanding of his future which
Easter makes credible and enables us to hope for. It is not the
remembrance of the dead Master in the light of his death, but
the experience of Easter, that makes it necessary to identify
Jesus. It is only the enigmatic, dialectical identity of the risen
Lord with the crucified Christ that compels the acceptance of a
continuity between the primitive Christian Christology and the
message of Jesus himself. The 'self-consciousness' of Jesus does
not compel men to remain conscious of him, but their consciousness of Jesus – as fashioned by the resurrection appearances – is
certainly compelled to raise the question of its own continuity
with Jesus' consciousness.

But if the raising of Jesus from the dead is thus a constitutive
part of the Christian message of the kingdom, then it is hardly
possible any longer for the latter to be concentrated on its
'meaning for existence' and existentially ethicized, but then
it is essential to take the universal horizon of hope and promise
embracing all things and develop it just as widely as apocalyptic had done – not in the same way, but in the same cosmic
breadth. Hence we ought not to speak only of divine *lordship*,
meaning by this the eschatological subjection of man's existence
to the absolute demand, but we should also speak again of the
kingdom of God, and so bring out the all-embracing eschatological breadth of his future, into which the mission and the
love of Christ lead the man of hope.

If the Easter appearances of Jesus as perceived within the
eschatological horizon of expectation are the occasion for remembering and taking over Jesus' message of the kingdom, yet
they are at the same time also the occasion for the transforming
of this message of the kingdom. The future which remained
open in Jesus' message of the kingdom is confirmed by his
resurrection appearances, assured in anticipation as the dawn of

his parousia, and can now be called *his* future. At the later
levels of the synoptic tradition a christological understanding
of the kingdom of God asserts itself, inasmuch as the idea of the
kingdom of Christ, or of the Son of Man, is developed on the
lines of the Jewish idea of the messianic kingdom. This, however, brings with it a change in the idea of the kingdom of God
itself. To be sure, it still retains its bearing on the present decision for new obedience, but this call which summons men
to new life in obedience finds support and prospect in the re-
surrecting act of God. The sole Lord of the kingdom is the God
'who has raised Jesus from the dead' and therein shows himself
to be the *creator ex nihilo*. His kingdom can then no longer be
seen in a historic transformation of the godless state of man and
the world. His future does not result from the trends of world
history. His rule is his raising of the dead and consists in calling
into being the things that are not, and choosing things which are
not, to bring to nothing things which are (I Cor. 1.28). This
makes it impossible to conceive the kingdom of God in deistic
terms of salvation history, as a result of world history or of a
divine plan for the world. It also makes it impossible to conceive the kingdom of God 'without God' and to resolve 'God'
himself as the 'highest Good' into the ideal of the kingdom.

Finally, the enigma of the Easter appearances – understood
in the Hellenistic church as 'exaltation' – also led to regarding
Jesus as the exalted cultic Kyrios and extolling his kingdom as
his hidden heavenly lordship. Thus whatever the horizon within
which the ideas were formed, it was always the interpretation
of the resurrection of the crucified one which became determinative for the understanding of the promise of the kingdom
of God.

In the very different views which thus arose, we note the
following characteristics:

1. The experiences of the cross and of the resurrection
appearances of Jesus give a new stamp to the message of the
kingdom of God. His cross and resurrection in a certain sense
'distort' his own open picture of the future and the coming of
the kingdom of God. But at the same time, and for this reason,
the lordship of God assumes the concrete form of this event of
the raising of the crucified one. In this event the kingdom of God
is not only christologically 'distorted' (*verstellt*), but concretely

represented (*vorgestellt*). If Jesus has been raised from the dead, then the kingdom of God can be nothing less than a *nova creatio*. If the risen Lord is the crucified Christ, then the kingdom is *tectum sub cruce*. The coming lordship of God takes shape here in the suffering of the Christians, who because of their hope cannot be conformed to the world, but are drawn by the mission and love of Christ into discipleship and conformity to his sufferings. This way of taking into consideration the cross and resurrection of Christ does not mean that the 'kingdom of God' is spiritualized and made into a thing of the beyond, but it becomes this-worldly and becomes the antithesis and contradiction of a godless and god-forsaken world.

2. The experience of the cross and resurrection of Jesus brings not only a christological understanding of the 'kingdom of God', but also in a new sense an eschatological understanding of it. Because of their experiences of the cross and of Easter, the oldest churches did not live in a 'time of fulfilment', but in earnest looking forward to the future. To be sure, it was possible for the experiences of Easter and of the Spirit to give occasion for an eschatology of fulfilment in the Spirit, as a result of which the experiences of the cross and of the contradiction of reality appeared to be overcome in the Spirit. Only, the realism of the earthly cross of Jesus and of the contradiction everywhere perceptible in an unredeemed world in the course of the Christian mission showed this religious or cultic docetism to be an error. Thus (particularly in Paul) an eschatological view of the still outstanding kingdom of God asserted itself over against all eschatological and cultic enthusiasm. If the raising of Jesus from the dead provides the ground for a new kind of hope in the kingdom, then the promised future cannot lie simply in the very fact of the giving of the Spirit, but the 'Spirit' himself becomes the 'earnest' of the still outstanding future and therefore 'strives' against the 'works of the flesh'. If the kingdom of God implies the raising of the dead, then it is a new creation, and then the 'exalted Lord' cannot be understood as one of several cultic lords or as the 'true cultic Lord', but only as the *Cosmocrator*. The lordship of the risen and exalted Christ, as it was understood in the Hellenistic church's Christology of exaltation, is from the eschatological standpoint itself provisional and serves the final goal of the sole lordship of God, in which all

things become new. Then, however, the christological understanding of the message of the kingdom does not distort Jesus'
message of the kingdom, but makes it universal, opens it to
embrace a totality of new being. The Easter appearances are then
made the occasion for expecting the lordship of God over death
and the righteousness of God in all transient things. If the
kingdom of God begins as it were with a new act of creation,
then the Reconciler is ultimately the Creator, and thus the
eschatological prospect of reconciliation must mean the reconciliation of the whole creation, and must develop an eschatology
of all things. In the cross we can recognize the god-forsakenness
of all things, and with the cross we can recognize the real
absence of the kingdom of God in which all things attain to
righteousness, life and peace. Hence the kingdom of God can
mean no less than resurrection and new creation, and hope in
the kingdom can be satisfied with no less than this. Because of
this universality, the new hope of the kingdom leads us to
suffer under the forsakenness and unredeemedness of all things
and their subjection to vanity. It leads us to a solidarity with
the anxious expectation of the whole creation that waits for
the liberty of the children of God (Rom. 8.22), and thus it perceives in all things the longing, the travail, and the unfulfilled
openness for God's future. Thus the kingdom of God is present
here as promise and hope for the future horizon of all things,
which are then seen in their historic character because they do
not yet contain their truth in themselves. If it is present as
promise and hope, then this its presence is determined by the
contradiction in which the future, the possible and the promised
stands to a corrupt reality. In the Reformers it was said that
the kingdom of God is *tectum sub cruce et sub contrario*. This was
intended to mean that the kingdom of God is here hidden
beneath its opposite: its freedom is hidden under trial, its happiness under suffering, its right under rightlessness, its omnipotence under weakness, its glory under unrecognizability. Here
the kingdom of God was seen in the form of the lordship of the
crucified one. This is a true insight, and one that cannot be
relinquished. Only, the kingdom of God does not end in the
paradoxical form of a presence of this kind. Its paradoxical
hiddenness 'under the contrary' is not its eternal form. For
indeed it is only the resurrection hope and the mission of Christ,

the hunger for righteousness in all things and the thirst for true life, that first lead to the suffering, the weakness, the rightlessness and the unrecognizability. The contradiction does not result automatically from man's experiences with history, with sin and death, but it results from the promise and the hope which contradict these experiences and make it no longer possible to put up with them. If the promise of the kingdom of God shows us a universal eschatological future horizon spanning all things – 'that God may be all in all' – then it is impossible for the man of hope to adopt an attitude of religious and cultic resignation from the world. On the contrary, he is compelled to accept the world in all meekness, subject as it is to death and the powers of annihilation, and to guide all things towards their new being. He becomes homeless with the homeless, for the sake of the home of reconciliation. He becomes restless with the restless, for the sake of the peace of God. He becomes rightless with the rightless, for the sake of the divine right that is coming.

The promise of the kingdom of God in which all things attain to right, to life, to peace, to freedom, and to truth, is not exclusive but inclusive. And so, too, its love, its neighbourliness and its sympathy are inclusive, excluding nothing, but embracing in hope everything wherein God will be all in all. The *pro-missio* of the kingdom is the ground of the *missio* of love to the world.

It is the ground of the outgoing of the spirit in bodily obedience, because and in order that the 'inward' may become the 'outward', reality become rational and reason real – as Hegel put it, and as it can be theologically understood if by reason we understand the Spirit of God as the 'earnest' which causes the longing for a reality filled with the Spirit and brought about by the Spirit (Rom. 8.23 and I Cor. 15.42ff.).

14. SUMMARY AND REVIEW

We now proceed to sum up by attempting a review of the method we have here followed.

1. Christian eschatology speaks of 'Christ and his future'. Its language is the language of promises. It understands history as the reality instituted by promise. In the light of the present

promise and hope, the as yet unrealized future of the promise stands in contradiction to given reality. The historic character of reality is experienced in this contradiction, in the front line between the present and the promised future. History in all its ultimate possibilities and dangers is revealed in the event of promise constituted by the resurrection and cross of Christ. We took the promise contained in this event, in the sense of that which is latent, hidden, prepared and intended in this event, and expounded it against the background of the Old Testament history of promise, perceiving at the same time the tendencies of the Spirit which arise from these insights. The *promissio* of the universal future leads of necessity to the universal *missio* of the Church to all nations. The promise of divine righteousness in the event of the justification of the godless leads immediately to the hunger for divine right in the godless world, and thus to the struggle for public, bodily obedience. The promise of the resurrection of the dead leads at once to love for the true life of the whole imperilled and impaired creation. In expounding the promises in the Christ event in terms of latency and tendency, we discovered a historic process of mediation between subject and object, which allows us neither to assign the future of Christ to a place within some system of world history and of the history of salvation, and thereby make this event relative to something that is foreign to it, acquired from other experiences and imposed upon it from without, nor yet to reflect the future of Christ into the existentialistic futurity of man. The history of the future of Christ and the historic character of the witnesses and missionaries condition each other and stand in a correlation of *promissio* and *missio*. The Christian consciousness of history is a consciousness of mission, and only to that extent is it also a consciousness of world history and of the historic character of existence.

2. We have employed in various ways the concept of 'progressive revelation'. It derives from Richard Rothe and Ernst Troeltsch, and means in both writers that the impulse of the Christian spirit in the history of the West links up again and again with the spirit of the modern age and produces progressively better views of the world and of life. The progressive development of the kingdom of the Redeemer is the constantly progressing revelation of that kingdom's absolute truth and

perfection. 'Progressive revelation' here means that the revelation becomes progressive in the progress of the human spirit, or that the progress of the human spirit can be interpreted as the self-movement of absolute Spirit. Similar conclusions can be reached when it is thought possible to deduce the direction and future of the Christ event from a comprehensive chain of historic events before and after this event. The Christ event is then given its place in a historic chain that results from fate, or providence, and from the course of the facts of world history. If, however, the promise of the future of Christ arises from the resurrection of the one who was crucified, then the promise enters into such a contradiction to reality that this contradiction cannot be classified within a general dialectic of history such as can be deduced from other processes. It can be classified within the sphere of world history and history of salvation only by diminishing the contradiction in question. Only then can it be resolved in a dialectic of world history. If, however, the event of the raising of the one who was crucified is recognized to be *creatio ex nihilo*, then it is not a case here of possible changes in existing things, but of all or nothing. Then it becomes clear that this world 'cannot bear' the resurrection and the new world created by resurrection. The dialectic which would seek to bear this contradiction must be of an apocalyptic kind. The reconciling synthesis of cross and resurrection can be expected and hoped for solely in a totality of new being. The theology of saving history does indeed perceive the process of promises and events, but not the contradiction in which the promise stands to reality, and hence not the unmasking of the godless world in the cross of Christ. Only when we see the progressive, eschatological driving forces in the contradictory event of the cross and resurrection itself, do the true problems arise. The revelation – i.e. the appearances of the risen Lord – does not acquire its character of progressiveness from a reality foreign to it, from the mysteriously continuing history after Easter, but itself creates the progress in its process of contradiction to the godless reality of sin and death. It does not become progressive by 'entering into' human history; but by dint of promise, hope and criticism it makes the reality of man historic and progressive. It is the revelation of the potentiality and power of God in the raising of the one who was crucified, and the tendency and intention of

God recognizable therein, that constitute the horizon of what is to be called history and to be expected as history. The revelation of God in the cross and resurrection thus sets the stage for history, on which there emerges the possibility of the engulfing of all things in nothingness and of the new creation. The mission on which the man of hope is sent into this advance area of universal possibilities pursues the direction of the tendency of God's own action in omnipotently pursuing his faithfulness and his promise. The man of hope who leaves behind the corrupt reality and launches out on to the sea of divine possibilities, thereby radically sets this reality of his at stake – staking it on the hope that the promise of God will win the day.

3. When we speak of the 'future of Jesus Christ', then we mean that which is described elsewhere as the 'parousia of Christ' or the 'return of Christ'. Parousia actually does not mean the return of someone who has departed, but *'imminent* arrival'.[1] Parousia can also mean presence, yet not a presence which is past tomorrow, but a presence which must be awaited today and tomorrow. It is the 'presence of what is coming towards us, so to speak an arriving future'.[2] The parousia of Christ is a different thing from a reality that is experienced now and given now. As compared with what can now be experienced, it brings something new. Yet it is not for that reason totally separate from the reality which we can now experience and have now to live in, but, as the future that is really outstanding, it works upon the present by awaking hopes and establishing resistance. The *eschaton* of the parousia of Christ, as a result of its eschatological promise, causes the present that can be experienced at any given moment to become historic by breaking away from the past and breaking out towards the things that are to come.

Now this parousia of Christ is also described as *revelation of Christ*, as ἀποκάλυψις τοῦ κυρίου. But how have we then to understand the future of Christ? Can his expected future then still be conceived in the expectational category *'novum'*? Does his future then bring something new, or merely a universal repetition of what has already happened in the history of Jesus Christ? Is the future of Christ then merely an *unveiling*

---

[1] Thus A. Oepke in *TWNT* V, p. 863.
[2] Paul Schütz, *Parusie – Hoffnung und Prophetie*, 1960, p. 78.

of what has already happened in Jesus once and for all? Or does
it contain something which has not yet happened?

According to Karl Barth the future of Christ is mainly only
a matter of *unveiling*: 'Christ's coming again . . . is described in
the New Testament as *the* revelation. He will be revealed, not
only to the Church but to everyone, as the Person He is. . . . In
full clarity and publicity the "it is finished" will come to light. . . .
What is the future bringing? Not once more a turning-point
in history, but the revelation of that which *is*. It is the future,
but the future of that which the Church *remembers*, of that which
has already taken place once and for all. The Alpha and the
Omega are the same thing.'[1]

Similarly, Walter Kreck declares: '[What is expected is]
precisely the coming of *the* Lord who is proclaimed and believed
to have come. The fulfilment, to be sure, can at bottom be
nothing else but the unveiling of that which is already reality
in Jesus Christ, but this very unveiling is nevertheless now looked
forward to and awaited as future.'[2] Here it is somewhat clearer
than in Barth that revelation is understood as promise, and that
the revelation of Christ is also conceived as the fulfilment of the
promise of Christ. But if this is followed up consistently, then
the expression 'unveiling' for revelation must be dropped,
and in its stead revelation must be conceived as an event that
takes place in promise and fulfilment. The revelation of Christ
cannot then merely consist in what has already happened in
hidden ways being unveiled for us to see, but it must be expected in events which fulfil the promise that is given with the
Christ event. This Christ event cannot then itself be understood as fulfilling all promises, so that after this event there
remains only the sequel of its being unveiled for all to see. 'In
Christ all the promises of God are yea and Amen' (II Cor. 1.20),
i.e., in him they are confirmed and validated, but not yet fulfilled.
Therefore the Christian hope expects from the future of Christ
not only unveiling, but also final fulfilment. The latter is to
bring the redeeming of the promise which the cross and
resurrection of Christ contains for his own and for the world.
What, then, does the future of Christ bring? Not a mere repeti-

---

[1] K. Barth, *Dogmatik im Grundriss*, 1947, pp. 158f. (ET: *Dogmatics in Outline*, 1949,
pp. 134f.).
[2] W. Kreck, *Die Zukunft des Gekommenen*, 1961, p. 100.

tion of his history, and not only an unveiling of it, but something which has so far not yet happened through Christ. The Christian expectation is directed to no other than the Christ who has come, but it expects something new from him, something that has not yet happened so far: it awaits the fulfilment of the promised righteousness of God in all things, the fulfilment of the resurrection of the dead that is promised in his resurrection, the fulfilment of the lordship of the crucified one over all things that is promised in his exaltation. The visible and painful experience of the unredeemed state of the world is not for Christians, as for Jews, an argument against belief in the Messiah's having come, but constitutes the burning question in their prayers for the future of the Redeemer who has come. It is not because it is doubtful whether Jesus is the Christ, but because in him our redemption is confirmed, that Christians groan along with all creation under the unredeemed state of the world and long to see the universal fulfilment of his redeeming and saving acts. But if they know the Redeemer and expect the future of redemption in his name, then neither can the unredeemed state of this world of death become for them, after the fashion of Plato, a part of the insignificant world of appearance in which it is now only a matter of the demonstrating and unveiling of redemption. To be sure, the Alpha and the Omega are the same as far as the Person is concerned: 'I am Alpha and Omega' (Rev. 1.8). But they are not the same where the reality of the event is concerned, for 'it doth not yet appear what we shall be' (I John 3.2) and 'the former things' are not yet passed away, nor are 'all things' yet become new. Thus we must expect something new from the future. But if this future is expected as the 'future of Jesus Christ', then it is not expected from someone new or from someone else. What the future is bringing is something which, through the Christ event of the raising of the one who was crucified, has become 'once and for all' a possible object of confident hope. Faith in Jesus as the Christ is not the end of hope, but it is the confidence in which we hope (Heb. 11.1). Faith in Christ is the prior of the two, but in this faith hope has the primacy.

IV

ESCHATOLOGY AND HISTORY[1]

I. CRITICISM AND CRISIS

THE MODERN consciousness of history is a consciousness of crisis, and all modern philosophy of history is in the last analysis a philosophy of crisis.[2] Modern man's epochal experience of history is grounded in the experience of infinitely new and overwhelming possibilities which cannot be mastered by the customary methods of his traditions. They are new possibilities for good or for evil, for progress or for irrevocable disaster. Yet these new possibilities of a new future are always experienced in the first instance as the crisis and collapse of the hitherto known and familiar possibilities with their traditional institutions and ways of life and methods of coping with it. History overflows the banks of tradition, as it were. The dams of tradition and order everywhere begin to burst. They are no longer a match for the new experiences of history and can therefore no longer present themselves as self-evident. They become antiquated, or can be conservatively maintained only with great difficulty. They no longer possess for man the old, unquestioned obviousness of institutionalized modes of conduct. Hence they become the object of reflection and criticism, and man is thrust out into a world that is unprotected, frightening and uncertain. He finds himself in a crisis in which his existence is at stake and he is under the pressure of a vital decision. Thus it is in terms of

---

[1] For this chapter cf. my essays 'Exegese und Eschatologie der Geschichte' *EvTh* 22, 1962, pp. 31ff., and 'Verkündigung als Problem der Exegese', *Monatsschrift für Pastoraltheologie* 52, 1963, pp. 24ff.

[2] G. Mann, 'Grundprobleme der Geschichtsphilosophie von Plato bis Hegel', in *Der Sinn der Geschichte*, 1961, pp. 13f.; H. Hempel, 'Geschichte und Geschichtswissenschaft', *Vierteljahrshefte für Zeitgeschichte*, 1957, vol. 1, p. 15: 'Since Herder the historical sense has meant reflection on imperilled order.' Cf. also R. Koselleck, *Kritik und Krise. Ein Beitrag zur Pathogenese der bürgerlichen Welt*, 1959; E. Rosenstock-Huessy, *Die europäischen Revolutionen*, 1931.

crisis that history becomes perceptible to him, and historical
criticism of his traditions is the offspring of this consciousness of
crisis.

All reflection on 'history' by historians, sociologists and
philosophers of history on the continent of Europe in the nineteenth century has behind it the earthquake of the French revolution and before it the incalculable consequences of that event.[1]
In this revolution the edifice of the old institutions collapsed,
and its metaphysical stabilization with it. In it the things which
were taken for granted and commonly accepted in the cultural
and spiritual realm, and which made it possible to live a protected life, were lost. With it there came an awareness of the
totally historic character of life as the total criticalness of man's
world. 'Crisis' has ever since become the theme of historical
research and the basic concept of reflection on the philosophy
of history. Hegel applied the new concept of 'crisis' together
with its new experimental content to the whole of the past. He
knew that 'thus the movement and unrest continues. This is
the conflict, the difficulty, the problem which confronts history
and which it has in future to solve.'[2] Ranke thought it possible
to achieve a conservative mastery of this revolutionary crisis by
restoring the balance between the great powers of Europe,

---

[1] I. Kant, *Der Streit der Fakultäten*, 1798 (Philosophische Bibliothek 252, p. 87):
'A phenomenon of this kind *can never again be forgotten*, because it has disclosed in
human nature a predisposition and capacity for improvement, such as no politician
could have thought up on the basis of the course of things so far.' F. Schiller, *Über
die ästhetische Erziehung des Menschen*, 1793/4: 'A question which was otherwise
answered merely by the blind right of the stronger has now, it seems, been brought
before the judgment seat of pure reason, and whoever is capable of putting himself
at the centre of the whole and projecting his individuality to become typical of the
species, may regard himself as coadjutor on this judgment-seat of reason, in that as
a man and a citizen of the world he is at the same time also a party and sees himself
more or less closely involved in the result.' G. W. F. Hegel, *Vorlesungen über die
Philosophie der Weltgeschichte*, Werke XI, p. 557: 'As long as the sun has stood in the
firmament and the planets have revolved around it, it had never been known for
man to stand on his head, that is, on his mind, and to construct reality according
to his thoughts. Anaxagoras had been the first to say that *nous* rules the world, but
only now has man reached the stage of recognizing that thought should rule the
reality of the spirit. So this was a glorious dawn.' J. G. Fichte, *Briefwechsel* I,
pp. 349f. (ed. H. Schulz, 1925): 'My system (the doctrine of science) is the first
system of freedom. As that nation (France) sets man free from his outward chains,
so my system sets him free from the fetters of things as such, from their outward
influence, and represents him as in first principle an independent being.' F.
Schlegel, *Athenäumsfragmente*, No. 222: 'The revolutionary desire to realize the
kingdom of God is the elastic point of all progressive culture and the beginning of
modern history' (quoted according to K. Löwith, *Abhandlungen*, 1960, p. 157).

[2] Werke IX, p. 563; J. Ritter, *Hegel und die französische Revolution* (AGFNRW 63),
1957, pp. 15ff.; H. Marcuse, *Vernunft und Revolution*, 1962, pp. 15ff.

and believed in reconciliation with the old traditions.[1] Jakob
Burckhardt sought amid the anxiety for the future of the West
in its continuing crises the 'standard by which to measure the
rapidity and strength of the particular movement in which we
live'.[2] Johann Gustav Droysen asked what is the 'direction
of the flowing movement' in which all things are engaged from
the viewpoint of history.[3] The 'call' of the nineteenth century
for the study of history and the absolutely vital necessity of that
call, dates from the French revolution. 'History' has ever since
been experienced as *a permanent state of crisis*, or as permanent,
irresistible and unrestrainable revolution. Historians and
philosophers of history, whether conservative or revolutionary,
have therefore concentrated on the spiritual, political and
social mastering of this continual crisis. Historical science and
the philosophy of history have been compelled to make
'history' comprehensible, in order to make it possible to control
the chaos, the catastrophes and the crises, and therewith history
as such. The place of a world-orientation in terms of cosmology
and metaphysics has since been taken by an orientation of the
present in terms of the philosophy of history. It was precisely
the collapse of historic continuity that gave rise to that apotheo-
sis of 'history' which led to the religion of history in the messianic movements of the nineteenth century.

Now the sense for history, the interest in history and the
necessity to understand history always arise in critical times of
unrest, in which new possibilities that were hitherto unknown
and unsuspected begin to dawn on the horizon. If we are to
understand the new present and to be able to live in it, then we
must concern ourselves with the past, whether to bring the new
experiences into harmony with the traditions of the past or to
rid ourselves of the burden of the past and become free for the
new present. The experience of such crises has been in the
background of the great thinkers on history ever since Augustine's *City of God*. Since the French revolution, however, history
has been understood entirely in terms of crisis. The latter can

[1] C. Hinrichs, *Ranke und die Geschichtstheologie der Goethezeit*, 1954.
[2] J. Burckhardt, *Weltgeschichtliche Betrachtungen*, ed. W. Kaegi, 1947, pp. 59, 250ff. (ET: *Reflections on History*, 1943, p. 25).
[3] J. G. Droysen, *Historik*, 4th ed. 1960, p. 358: 'Beginning and end are hidden from the finite eye. But its scrutiny can discover the direction of the flowing movement.'

no longer be restricted to the political or the social field, but
has the tendency to become total and to make every realm
of life uncertain. The crisis becomes one of universal world
history and affects the whole existence of man and his world.
That is why the interpretations of this crisis are likewise of a total
and totalitarian kind.[1] It has therefore become absolutely
necessary to consider in terms of world history all the realms
of life which are involved in this crisis of history – and this is
still necessary even when it is evident that all such interpretations in terms of universal history have so far broken down
in face of this crisis, because they have not provided a synoptic
view of the crisis, but have themselves been an immanent
part of it and have therefore only furthered it and served
to extend it. Every crisis throws up the question of the historic
future. For when the whole existing situation is in a state
of crisis, it becomes obvious that the future can no longer
arise automatically out of the past, that it can no longer be the
natural repetition and continuation of the past, but that something new must be found in it. This means that for the present
a decision has to be made which finds no precedent in the past
and for which traditional custom no longer provides any rule.
On this decision depends the form of the future, and this decision derives its form from a vision of the future which is
hoped for or feared, to be sought or to be avoided. This, however, means that the decision which is forced upon the present
must arise from our dream of the future. Criticism of the existing situation makes the existing situation a thing of the past
and frees us to face the crisis of present decision. From the
standpoint of history such criticism is always bound up with
the utopian outlook which examines the possibilities and tendencies of things to come, anticipates them, and incorporates
them in the present decision.[2] As the criticism is born of the

---

[1] J. L. Talmon, *The Origins of Totaletarian Democracy*, 1952; *Political Messianism;
The Romantic Phase*, 1960.

[2] This is shown particularly clearly by R. Koselleck, *op. cit.*, pp. 133ff., 208ff.:
The Enlightenment's criticism of the existing situation is combined with hopes of a
'belle révolution' (Voltaire), a 'révolution totale' (Mercier) and a permanent
revolution (Rousseau). 'Nous approchons de l'etat de crise et du siècle des révolu-
tions', said Voltaire. The Illuminati, the Freemasons and the Enlighteners base
this criticism, and their expectation of the great crisis, upon utopian ideas of the
harmony of the universe, the abrogation of states and classes and the disappearance
of churches in the humanist kingdom of moral religion. If, as has been rightly
observed, German Idealism is the theory of the French revolution, or at least the

crisis, so also are the utopian ideas. This connection between utopia and criticism can be seen particularly clearly in the century which paved the way for the crisis. Everywhere in the eighteenth century the criticism of absolutism, the criticism of churches and orthodoxies that have become historical institutions, the criticism of a class-ridden society, is combined with powerful utopian ideas of the nation of mankind, of the kingdom of God and of the new natural state of man, and is exercised in the service of these ideas. In its feeling for the philosophy of history the Enlightenment emphatically no longer combines its criticism, as earlier movements in history had done, with a retrospective dream, with regeneration, reform, renaissance or reformation of the corrupt present, but with the category of the new – new age, new world, *novum organon*, *scienza nuova*, progress, final age. The criticism of the present is no longer exercised in the name of the origin and in the name of the need to restore the original golden age, but in the name of a future that has never yet been. Since 1789 the land of 'utopia' no longer lies somewhere beyond the seas, but by means of the belief in history and the idea of progress it is shifted to the future which is possible and is to be expected or desired. The utopian dream has thus become a part of the philosophy of history and moved into the realm of practical philosophy. For the first time, history is subjected to the influence of an apocalyptic millenarianism and an apocalyptic enthusiasm of spirit, for which the end is other than the origin, and the goal greater than the beginning, and the future more than all the past. A criticism that has roots of this kind, however, precipitates a crisis which sets all that has been hitherto, and all that is, 'under the shadow' of collapse. The coming of this crisis can no longer mean only the collapse of the *ancien régime*, can no longer imply only the *fin de siècle*, but sets at stake everything that man's being means for him in home, state, world and nature. Thus the identification of this crisis which began with the

---

philosophical answer to the challenge of this crisis, then it is understandable that German Idealism begins as the 'theory of the present age' and is concerned to grasp in thought its age, the revolutionary crisis—and that means history. Then it is also understandable why in Herder, Schiller, Kant, Fichte, Novalis, E. M. Arndt and Hegel the criticism of the spirit of the age is combined with utopian ideas of the kingdom of God, of world citizenship and the rational state, of the invisible church, etc.

French revolution and – closely related to it – the industrial revolution, everywhere employs apocalyptic pictures. This kind of world history means the world judgment. This kind of freedom confronts mankind with the 'fury of disappearing'. For revolutionary thinkers this crisis brings the kingdom of God or the kingdom of freedom and humanity palpably near. In this sense a political messianism seizes the new possibilities. For conservative thinkers like de Bonald, de Maistre, and later de Tocqueville and Jakob Burckhardt, this crisis sounds the trumpet of the Last Judgment. Both take this crisis as the prelude to the final battle.

For Saint-Simon 'revolution' meant 'crisis'. 'L'espèce humaine', he wrote in 1813, 'se trouve engagée dans une des plus fortes *crises* qu'elle ait essuyée depuis l'origine de son existence.'¹ This concept of crisis also emerges as early as Rousseau, but in Saint-Simon and Auguste Comte it is new. 'It means revolution, but by penetrating beyond the political foreground of the latter, it opens a view of historic and social reality in its totality. In other words, when Saint-Simon speaks of crisis, he means – and is the first to mean – *history* in a completely modern sense.'² The aim of comprehending the revolution historically, politically and sociologically is for Saint-Simon and Comte: 'Terminer la révolution'. 'It is time to complete the vast intellectual operation begun by Bacon, Descartes and Galileo. . . . This is the way to put an end to the revolutionary crisis which is tormenting the civilized nations of the world.'³ Once the circumstances, laws and origins of revolution can be thoroughly understood, then it becomes calculable and also avoidable. By means of 'social physics' the revolutionary upheavals in society become calculable and their laws are understood, just as the phenomena of nature are by modern natural science. Comte's 'philosophie positive' acquires from this background a thoroughly messianic tenor. Scientific knowledge of the world and of history will supplant the now useless epoch of metaphysics and the still older epoch of theology. World phenomena are

---

¹ N. Sombart, 'St Simon und A. Comte', in A. Weber, *Einführung in die Soziologie*, 1955, p. 87. Cf. also J. L. Talmon, *Political Messianism*, pp. 35ff. on Saint-Simon.
² J. L. Talmon, *op. cit.* (cited from the German translation, *Politischer Messianismus*, 1963, p. 88).
³ *The Political Philosophy of Auguste Comte*, translated by Harriet Martineau, 1853, vol. I, p. 16.

calculable because of the laws of their interconnection. Scientific and socio-technical civilization will become the third and last world epoch. The crises become controllable, wars avoidable. The age of eternal peace is coming, in which the really sovereign knowledge is in the hands of the sociologists. In this age there will still be endless progress in the perfecting of science and technology, but there will be no more radical alternatives and no revolutionary changes. And now, if revolution is 'crisis' and crisis means 'history', then the 'ending of revolution' by means of historical science and the 'ending of crisis' by means of sociology means no less than a comprehensive 'ending of history' through scientific knowledge of it and through its technical controllability. The 'end of history' thereby acquires palpable, because creatable and attainable, nearness. The 'loss of history' (Alfred Heuss), the 'farewell to history' (Alfred Weber), the immanent 'perfectibility of history' (Hans Freyer) through scientific enlightenment and technical manipulation, become inevitable. The enigmatic chaos of history comes to an end where it is abrogated by knowledge of history and by its controllability.

The 'science' of history, too, which arises in the shadow of revolution and the permanently smouldering crisis, acquires a positivistic, apocalyptic sense. Again and again in the nineteenth century we are told that the science of history liberates us from history. 'The historical consciousness shatters the last fetters which philosophy and natural science were unable to break. Man is now completely free' (Dilthey).[1] 'A historical phenomenon, once fully and completely known and resolved into a problem of epistemology, is for the man who knows it dead. . . . History conceived as pure science, and become sovereign, would be a sort of winding up and settlement of the life of mankind' (Nietzsche).[2] 'For the historic examination of any construction of human thought always serves to liberate us from it' (W. Herrmann).[3] Historical science thus becomes an instrument for the mastering of history. It confers on man free-

[1] W. Dilthey, *Gesammelte Schriften* VIII, p. 225.
[2] F. Nietzsche, *Vom Nutzen und Nachteil der Historie für das Leben*, Kröner 37, 1924, p. 12.
[3] W. Herrmann, *Verkehr des Christen mit Gott*, 3rd ed. 1896, p. 42. Similarly A. Eichhorn, *ZTK* 18, 1908, p. 156: critical historical research is particularly concerned 'that by means of history we should become free men as far as tradition is concerned'.

dom from history. History as science thereby acquires a tendency to do away with history as remembrance. This kind of historicism as a 'science of crisis', and in that sense the remedy against crises, has thus the tendency to destroy the interest in history and the feeling for it. The result of the historicizing and rationalizing of history is then to abolish history and leave human social life bereft of all historic character. In this sense scientific historicism stands in the service of the mystico-messianic idea of the 'end of history' and is itself a factor in the 'ending of history'.

This motif of the historical probing and investigation of historic phenomena is understandable against the background of total crisis that comes into view with the French revolution. Yet it is equally understandable that in the age of historical perfection, in the second half of the nineteenth century, the question was raised as to the price of mastering the crisis in this way. Nietzsche's book *Vom Nutzen und Nachteil der Historie für das Leben*, 1874, leaves us with the question of that 'unhistorical' element of 'atmosphere' or 'horizon' within which alone life goes on. The historical outlook leaves the future without roots, because it destroys our illusions and robs things of the atmosphere in which alone they can live and in which alone they acquire potentialities. 'All living things need to have an atmosphere, a mysterious nimbus, around them; if we rob them of this covering, if we condemn a religion, an art, a genius to be like a star circling without any atmosphere, then we ought not to be surprised at its quickly drying up and becoming hard and unfruitful. This is simply true of all great things, "which never yet succeeded without a certain amount of illusion".'[1] The question now arises as to the historic character of history, which the historian obscures in his search for facts and laws. If the revolutionary crises in human society are ended by positivistic investigation of the facts, then it is a question whether that does not also mean the ending and petrifying of the liveness of human life and the movements of the world process. It is a question whether the ending of the historic crisis which is achieved in this way is not itself a highly critical undertaking. For while an 'ending of history in history' does solve the crises in the observable realm, yet the undertaking as a whole is

[1] *Op. cit.*, p. 60.

itself exposed to a much more tremendous crisis. Whatever crises may arise within the scientific, technical world, they can be rationalized. But the scientific, technical universe itself becomes an inestimable, irrational force, of which we can no longer have a comprehensive view because we are no longer able to look beyond it to a possibly different future.[1] Thus it becomes an important question whether the concept of history which identifies 'history' with 'crisis' is adequate, and whether the science of history which resolves history into knowledge does justice to the historic character of history and to the – possibly – historic character of its own knowledge.

THE 'SOLVED RIDDLE OF HISTORY'

2. THE HISTORICAL METHOD[2]

Ever since the fundamental methodical approach to man's experience of the world by Petrus Ramus and René Descartes and its success in the natural sciences, every effort has been directed towards applying a methodical treatment also to the experiences of history and to the process of acquiring knowledge of history. The question of the historical method therefore applies not only to the technical ways in which the historian works, but also, and more comprehensively, to the peculiarity of historical knowledge and the scientific character of historical research. Without 'method' no assured knowledge can be attained. Historical methodology therefore embraces principles for historical research and principles for the critical control of their results. Since the natural sciences in the nineteenth century had not been content to collect and collate experimental results but had gone on to construct an exact and verifiable system of the laws of nature, and since exact 'science' in general meant 'natural' science, it was necessary to raise the question as to the scientific character of historical research and as to the general laws of the course of history. Although the

---

[1] This inversion was perceived especially by Max Weber. The 'disenchantment' and rationalization of the world and its history by modern science presents us with a meaningless irrationality of independent, arbitrary 'conditions' which now govern human behaviour. Cf. K. Löwith, 'Max Weber und Karl Marx', in *Gesammelte Abhandlungen zur Kritik der geschichtlichen Existenz*, 1960, p. 26.

[2] *Geschichte*, Fischer-Lexikon 24, 1961, ed. W. Besson, pp. 78ff.

peculiar character of the methods of the human sciences has been emphasized since the end of the nineteenth century by W. Dilthey, yet certain minimum requirements from the concept of science associated with natural science have been introduced also into the science of history:

(*a*) The science of history is not art, fiction or legend, but the concept of truth which underlies it is that of a verifiable truth of fact. The statements of historical science must be able to prove their historical correctness by reference to sources that can be verified by anyone at any time, and thus by reference to verifiable events. History is not 'legends and acts' (Bertram) but, in so far as it seeks assured knowledge, it depends on the verifiable agreement between statement and fact.

(*b*) The historical correctness of our knowledge of history, however, presupposes that our insights are controllable. The fact that they are bound to the sources and to the criticism of the sources means that they are bound to the controllability of their statements by reference to the reality of which the historian speaks and which he seeks to know.

(*c*) This controllability, however, presupposes that historical objects can in principle be reconstructed. Historical knowledge is dependable only when it can be verified at any time by anyone who will make the methodical effort. But if it is to be verifiable, it must always be possible to reconstruct the materials and the authoritatively documented events. This reconstructability of the facts thus becomes the methodological mark of the facts as facts. This is what distinguishes the science of history from legend and lively remembrance, from statements of experience and encounter.

(*d*) Historical science, too, works with definite hypotheses, plans, approaches and outlooks, by means of which the events are illumined and perceived as events. But now, whereas the constructions of natural science use experiment to extort an answer from nature and to let us see and understand it, historical objects are always already bound up with interpretations and outlooks in which the knowledge of them is transmitted. The historian's first task must therefore be to read the witnesses of history as 'sources', and to date, localize and trace back to the 'historical facts' the objects which are mediated by manifold processes of interpretation, bias and touching up. The historical

facts thus ascertained become the starting point for subjecting
the witnesses, interpretations and traditions to the criticism of
the historical consciousness. Thus the historical method is in
the first instance applied critically to the traditions and the
historical sources. This sort of destructive criticism of the traditions of an event, however, is itself always bound up with the
historian's own power of picturing and imagining how things
may 'in fact' have been, and is thus always combined with
reconstruction. Such reconstructions of the actual course of
events, in turn, are for their part also drafts, hypotheses and
standpoints which must be verified by reference to the sources.
Hence historical criticism has always a link with historical
imagination, whether that of the sources or our own. This
means that historical criticism is always bound up with historical heuristics.

The methodical treatment of the experience of history must
'objectify' historic reality. The historical approach must regard
past history in that historical detachment in which it can be
objectively examined. It has to establish historic reality and
must therefore presuppose that this reality is established fact,
no longer subject to change. This, understandably enough, becomes more difficult the more it is a question of 'contemporary
history'. For here the object is not firmly established but is still
in a state of flux. Here the historical observer does not stand
over against history, but in the midst of the events, and exerts
an influence on these events themselves by means of his historical diagnosis. At bottom, all history is 'contemporary
history'. The historian's object is thus engaged in a twofold
movement which 'derives first from the process character of
all past life, and secondly from the continual change in the
man who contemplates history and is himself subject to historic development'.[1] For this reason the old saying is true, that
'history has constantly to be rewritten'. The historic character
of the historical observer is the point at which there constantly
takes place the decisive process of the translating of 'present'
into 'object', of historic present into historical object, of a
history that is in a state of flux and open to the influence of our
own knowledge and decision into the retrospective contemplation of a history that has come to a standstill. The historical,

---

[1] *Geschichte*, Fischer-Lexikon, p. 80.

objectifying relation to past history is therefore itself one that is highly historic and that makes history.

3. HISTORICAL HEURISTICS

The historical method does not only work with destructive criticism of past pictures of history, in order to investigate the 'bare' facts, but must itself approach the source material with its own problems and plans. While historical criticism in the name of fact does attack the interpretations of fact in the sources, yet the facts themselves cannot possibly be known and stated without other interpretations. In the science of history, the facts are not the first datum, but the last product of a process of abstraction that moves from the traditional interpretations to what is today generally and unquestioningly taken to be 'objectivity'. 'Fact' is the substratum interpretatively mediated by the sources and traditions. The natural scientist in his experiments must isolate his object, eliminate factors which do not enter into the question and disregard other problems, if he is to attain to unequivocal results. This is very difficult in the case of historical objects, because here we have always to do with highly complicated structures whose isolation destroys the fact of their being so multifariously conditioned. Thus historical science, according as it isolates a single fact from its manifold context and reduces its questions to one problem only, must take care at the same time to move on again from the isolated and individual facts to the wider context and from the one angle of approach to the complex of other problems. Thus the individual fact can be known and evaluated only along with the general, and the general only along with the individual. The positivistic separation of fact and meaning is not one which is possible in principle, and can be asserted only when our own interpretation of what we call 'fact' remains naive, uncritical and unconscious. When Max Weber asserts that rational science 'disenchants' the world, and that the full understanding of the facts ceases where the value-judgment begins, then that is true where the value-judgment is subsequently appended in

[1] Cf. E. Rothacker, *Die dogmatische Denkform in den Geisteswissenschaften und das Problem des Historismus*, Abhandlungen der geistes- und sozialwissenschaftlichen Klasse der Akademie der Wissenschaften 6, Mainz 1954, p. 55.

order to introduce values into a world that rests on other facts, but not where the value judgment is already included within the field of judgment in which the illumination of the facts itself takes place – and within that field it is always already given.

When historical science moves on from isolated, individual facts to more general statements embracing historic processes, then there arises the *problem of the forming of historical concepts*.[1] It is necessary to make use of concepts of a generalizing and typifying kind. These concepts acquire their binding force from the standpoint and perspective of the moment, and therefore cannot claim to reflect the historic processes as such, but are heuristic modes of contemplating historic processes, and means of explaining and understanding them. They require to be confirmed by the object, and are therefore constantly open to question.

One such means is the 'historical law'. An event becomes explicable when its causes can be seen. This connection between cause and effect, however, presupposes that the plane of being on which cause and effect are connected is the same. History must then be social history or political history or cultural history, i.e. the substance of the history must be determined, if we are to be able to present a chain of cause and effect of this kind. This, however, can be demonstrated only in things of uniform character and in repetitions and in definite processes in history which have a definite, automatic character. Apart from these, historic processes are so complex that, for one thing, we cannot discover all the conditions which cause them, but always only a selection of them. Single causes can be asserted in history only by discarding or disregarding other connections. And in the second place, historical causality lacks the characteristic of reversibility.[2] We can certainly argue from effects to causes, but hardly ever from causes to effects. Hence the really historic factor lies in the concept of possibility rather than in that of necessity: we never find all the possibilities turned into unequivocal necessities. Thus the concept of causality too, can have only heuristic significance.

Another conceptual means of grasping connections is the

---

[1] R. Wittram, *Das Interesse an der Geschichte*, 1958, pp. 33ff.
[2] *Geschichte*, Fischer-Lexikon, p. 83.

discovering of 'tendencies'. This concept has been familiar in
German historical writing since Ranke. But it is applied also
in the historico-dialectical materialism of Georg Lukács and
Ernst Bloch.[1] It means that the stringency of the causality of
natural science is renounced and the transition in historic
movements is described not as a transition from *causa* to *effectus*,
but from possibility to reality. What stands between possibilities
and realized realities is not a causal necessity, but tendency,
impulse, inclination, trend, specific leanings towards something, which can become real in certain historic constellations.
Ernst Topitsch thinks this expression obscures 'the tricky problem of the relationship between act, value and independent
evolution'. R. Wittram thinks this expression can be completely void of any relation to an objective teleology and can
mean only an 'impulse' within the working of a concrete
historical event.[2] For G. Lukács and E. Bloch, 'tendency' means
something that mediates between the real, objective possibilities
and the subjective decisions, and to that extent places the historical 'facts' within the stream of the historical process and
sets the subjective decisions of the historical observer within
this same process. Then, however, the intention in employing
the heuristic medium of exploring 'tendencies' is surely to discover a directional trend on the part of history which is teleological as a whole.

E. Rothacker has recommended as a means towards the
grasping of historical complexes the concept of 'style'. 'What
is called "historical thinking" in the emphatic and passionate
use of the term has indeed its primary aim not in the establishing of facts, but in grasping as congenially as may be the appearances of the immanent *logos*, the styles in which these
facts arrange themselves.'[3] This concept, to be sure, has its
roots in the history of art and is appropriate to an aesthetic
view of things. When transferred to historic complexes, however, it means the anthropological and sociological connection
of acts and events with their 'environment' in the experiences
of the moment and in the current views of life. What is meant is
the 'style of living', the *façon de vivre*, the *façon d'agir*. Just as

---

[1] G. Lukács, *Geschichte und Klassenbewusstsein*, 1923; E. Bloch, *Das Prinzip Hoffnung*, 1959.
[2] R. Wittram, *op. cit.*, p. 44.   [3] *Op. cit.*, p. 23.

Theology of Hope

[223-24

animals have their specific kind of 'environment' of vitally
necessary openness towards the world, so also men live in a
cultural 'environment' consisting of modes of experience,
customs of living, institutions and expectations of life, in which
they perceive history and act historically. In his search for facts
the historian shatters this horizon of interpretation and experience that belongs to the history of any given moment, whereas the
truth is, that the facts and acts became 'historic' only in their particular contemporary 'environment' in the world of language,
law, *Weltanschauung*, views of life, religious ideas and economic
forms.

In much the same way the concept of 'structure' attempts to
grasp the social institutions in which history was accepted and
mastered at a given moment, by seeing them as the world of the
orders and expressions of life that exercised their influence on
history.[1] This framework of ideas leads on to the history of
'forms'. Form-critical historiography is likewise sociologically
oriented in enquiring into the institutional grounding of statements in the life of historic groups and societies, and in examining not so much the individual statement as once made, but
rather the '*Sitz im Leben*' provided for the statements by religion
law, culture, politics and art.

Lastly, the concept of the '*understanding of existence*' is also a
heuristic medium of this kind.[2] Here the phenomena of past
history are interpreted and brought to consciousness on the
basis of the possibilities of man's understandings of existence.
The heuristic model consists in 'situation' and 'decision', in
challenge and response, and past history shows how history
was experienced and responsibility received by the human
subject and how possibilities of existence were thereby discovered, grasped or destroyed. The historian is then not so much
interested in the events themselves and their causal or tenden-
tious connections with other events, but rather in the historic
character of the several existences that have been, and in the
possibilities of human existence.

Thus the range of historical concepts extends from the 'facts'
to the possibilities of existence, from 'objectivity' – in the sense

---

[1] F. Braudel, as quoted by Wittram, *op. cit.*, p. 44.
[2] M. Heidegger, *Sein und Zeit*, 8th ed. 1957, pp. 382ff. (ET by J. Macquarrie and
E. Robinson: *Being and Time*, 1962, pp. 434ff.).

of the exact natural sciences – to the unmistakable uniqueness
of human subjectivity and spontaneity. We have here selected
only a few typical examples. 'All general historical concepts
have a certain fluidity,' as R. Wittram rightly observes.[1] They
are heuristic concepts whose applicability has repeatedly to be
checked in detail. The flexibility, however, in which they resist
fixed metaphysical systematizing and logical unequivocalness,
has its ground not only in the limited historic perspective of the
observer who uses them in order to shed light on an enigmatic
reality. It has its ground also in the fact that unequivocal and
eternally established reality is not yet there to be conceived.
The concept of 'nation', or 'class', or 'culture' etc., is not a
standing category in which we can ascertain the history of the
nation, the history of the class struggle, or the history of culture,
but the real meaning of 'nation', 'class', 'church' etc., is itself
in a state of historic flux, historically disputed and therefore
engaged in historic transformation. If the basic idea of historicism is that the essence of a thing is to be grasped from its
historic development, and that the result of the historical process is decided only within the historical process itself, then the
'land of the realized, absolute concept' is not to be reached by
way of abstraction from the particular to the general, nor yet
by way of a comprehensive review of the past, but then this
land is the as yet undiscovered fore-land of history, which can
be reached from within history only in the form of fragmentary
anticipations. It is not due merely to the defective range of the
human mind that history remains dark to it, but this is due to
history itself, which has not yet reached its end and therefore
cannot yet be resolved into historical knowledge, or only in a
proleptic, fragmentary way.

4. HISTORIOLOGY

The question of historical heuristics leads of itself to the problem of the philosophy of history. 'In criticism, history of itself
becomes philosophy of history' (F. C. Baur).[2] But how can a
philosophy of history be possible in the Greek sense of knowledge and of science? If 'the essence of history is change' (J.

---

[1] R. Wittram, *op. cit.*, p. 43.
[2] F. C. Baur, as quoted by Koselleck, *op. cit.*, p. 6.

Burckhardt),¹ yet 'change' is the direct opposite of 'essence'. 'Philosophy of history' therefore appeared to J. Burckhardt to be a centaur, a contradiction in terms, 'for history co-ordinates, and hence is unphilosophical, while philosophy subordinates, and hence is unhistorical.'² Nevertheless all the general historical concepts by means of which we endeavour to understand historic complexes are bound up with definite approaches to the illuminating of reality and are therefore part and parcel of a philosophical knowledge of the world as history. If the general endeavour of human reason is towards the abolition of chance, as Wilhelm von Humboldt has said, then this endeavour is intensified in that philosophy of history which sees the experience of history as the experience of crisis and of permanent revolution. The 'nightmare of history' loses its nightmare character where it is comprehended. It is comprehended, however, where sense, an immanent *logos*, can be found in the chaotic movements of history, where necessity and dependence can be discovered in the contingent. Then history is 'comprehended', and where history is 'comprehended' in this way, there it ceases to be 'history'.

Let us take a look at this – often unconscious – transition from historical heuristics to philosophy of history in one or two specific historians.

(*a*) Even Ranke was constantly in search of a 'general bond' of history. Ranke as a historian is usually commended for turning his back on the *a priori* constructions in the speculations of German Idealism on world history, in order to address himself to the objects of history themselves in their vast abundance as these are empirically accessible to historical science. Nevertheless Ranke, too, is bound to definite speculative presuppositions in his historiography.³ Thus in his *Deutsche Geschichte im Zeitalter der Reformation* he observes: 'We may perhaps say that the ages succeed each other precisely in order that what is not

¹ *Weltgeschichtliche Betrachtungen*, ed. W. Kaegi, 1947, p. 72.
² *Ibid.*, p. 43 (ET p. 15). Nevertheless, . . . the *logos*: 'We, however, shall start out from the one point accessible to us, the one eternal centre of all things – man, suffering, striving, doing, as he is and was and ever shall be. Hence our study will, in a certain sense, be pathological in kind. The philosophers of history regard the past as a contrast to and preliminary stage of our own time as the full development. We shall study the *recurrent, constant* and *typical* as echoing in us and intelligible through us (p. 45, ET p. 17).
³ C. Hinrichs, *Ranke und die Geschichtstheologie der Goethezeit*, 1954, pp. 161ff.

possible to any of them individually may happen in all, in order
that the whole fulness of the spiritual life breathed into the
human race by the deity should come to light in the course of
the centuries.'[1] According to this, spiritual life has been
'breathed into' mankind by the deity, and that too in its 'whole
fulness' as the deity itself is infinite, and can therefore come 'to
light' in the ages of history only in successive stages. It is true
that the laws according to which it gradually emerges are obscure to us, greater and more mysterious than we think,[2] yet
it is nevertheless possible to have an inkling of the divine order
of things, for this 'divine order' is *identical with the succession of
the ages*'.[3] Hence Ranke describes it by the use of historical
concepts like 'tendencies' and 'forces'. 'Here are forces, and
spiritual forces at that, life-producing, creative forces, themselves
life, here are moral energies which we see developing. . . .
They flourish, take possession of the world, assume outward
expression in the greatest variety of forms, attack, restrict and
overpower each other: in their interrelation and succession, in
their life, their passing away or their reanimation, which then
embraces ever greater fulness, deeper significance, wider com-
pass, lies the mystery of world history.'[4] The basic philosophical
picture underlying this interpretation of the 'mystery of world
history' is manifestly the neoplatonic, panentheistic picture of
the age of Goethe. The 'idea', 'God', the 'sun' or the 'source',
does not contain within it for Ranke any dialectical principle
that is immanent to it, as for Hegel, but it emanates, while
itself always remaining extra-worldly in its unchanging, unchangeable being. Its emanations become manifest in the
stream of historic phenomena and movements, in the interplay
and succession of forces and tendencies, of moral energies and
epochs. Each of these stands in an immediate relationship to
the highest idea. Hence every epoch is *immediately* related to
God, and its value does not at all depend on what emerges
from it, but lies in its own existence, in its own self', as it is
put in the *Berchtesgadener Vorträge*.[5] 'The ideas which form the
ground of human conditions never contain perfectly within

[1] Quoted *ibid.*, p. 162.
[2] *Ibid.*, p. 164.   [3] *Ibid.*, p. 168.
[4] *Ibid.*, p. 174. The quotations are from *Die grossen Mächte*.
[5] *Ibid.*, p. 165.

them the divine and eternal source from which they spring.'[1]
And yet according to Ranke the 'inner necessity of the succession' must not by any means be overlooked. To be sure, no
final goal can be stipulated for world history. 'To stipulate a
definite goal for it (world history) would be to darken the
future and fail to recognize the limitless sweep of the movement
of world history.'[2] Nevertheless there does exist for Ranke a
goal. The goal of the developments and entanglements of
history is, that the 'whole fulness' of the spirit breathed into
mankind, the infinite multiplicity which is provided for in the
one divine idea, should come to light in the succession of the
epochs. It is not that the idea will at last stand realized and
revealed, but the totality of world history, of which there can
here be no comprehensive view, will reveal, as a sum of the
partial manifestations of the idea, the fulness of the divine
being. 'For Ranke, development consists in the succession of a
series of forms of manifestation of the one idea, all of equal
standing, which have their value in themselves and whose infinite fulness, taken all together, would supply the revelation
of the whole.' This is world history in terms of 'teleology without a *telos*', as G. Masur has called Ranke's view of history and
historiography. Thus for Ranke history is a process, but its
meaning is not contained in the end result. God appears in
history, but does not resolve himself into it. The historian's
task is to reconstruct the life of the past – and indeed to reconstruct it in that harmony which is already given in the facts of
history as a whole.

Thus Ranke had a 'vision of the whole', a basic view belonging to the philosophy of history and a faith belonging to
the theology of history. He shares this with the age of Goethe.
Yet he was modest and discreet enough not to construct history
according to this conception and not to dismiss the inexplicable
with the remark that it is really not good for the facts (Hegel).
He brings his 'idea' on the scene only at particular turning

---

[1] Quoted in C. Hinrichs, *Ranke und die Geschichtstheologie der Goethezeit*, p. 165.
Cf. also *Die grossen Mächte*, 1955, pp. 3f. and 43: 'There is no doubt that for
the historian inestimable value attaches also to the contemplation of the single
moment in its truth, of the particular development in and for itself; the particular
contains the general within it.' . . . But it contains the general within it in such a
way that 'from isolation and pure elucidation there (will) emerge true harmony'.
[2] F. Meinecke, 'Deutung eines Rankewortes', in *Zur Theorie und Philosophie der
Geschichte*, 1959, pp. 117ff.

points in history and – though this indeed is decisive – in the constructing of his historical concepts.

(*b*) In a similar way Ferdinand Christian Baur, thanks to whom historical criticism and historical thinking have become imperative for Protestant theology, attempted to comprehend history as a universal whole.[1] For him, historical criticism leads of necessity to the question of the 'real truth of history'. 'What higher task can history have at all than the ever more profound examination of the historic complex of all the phenomena that form its given object? . . . But for that reason its endeavours are very naturally also directed towards one end: by every means at its command, both by the examination of individual phenomena, and also by the classifying of individual phenomena under the higher viewpoints from which they first receive their firm place in the whole, it seeks also to penetrate what still confronts it as a solid, closed mass, in order to resolve it and make it fluid, and to draw it into the general stream of historic development in which, in the infinite concatenation of causes and effects, one thing is always the presupposition of the other, everything together upholds and maintains itself, and the only thing that would have to remain for ever uncomprehended is that which could claim in advance to stand in the midst of history outside the context of history.'[2] If, however, the 'context of history' is understood in this way, then on grounds of the philosophy of history – not of historiography – 'miracle' or 'overspringing' must be eliminated. For 'in the end the only view which can be maintained is the one which brings unity, coherence and rational consistency into our *Weltanschauung*, into our view of the gospel history, into our consciousness as a whole'. 'It is always in the context of the whole, in which it can be ascribed its specific place, that a historical truth first receives its firmness and stability.'[3] Thus for F. C. Baur, historical criticism inevitably leads on to historical speculation,[4] for

[1] Cf. E. Käsemann's introduction to the new edition of *Historisch-kritische Untersuchungen zum Neuen Testament*: F. C. Baur, *Ausgewählte Werke*, ed. K. Scholder, vol. I, 1963; and E. Wolf's introduction to F. C. Baur, *Ausgewählte Werke*, ed. K. Scholder, vol. II, 1963.
[2] *Epochen der kirchlichen Geschichtsschreibung*, quoted according to E. Wolf, *op. cit.*, p. IX.
[3] *An Dr K. Hase. Beantwortung des Sendschreibens der Tübinger Schule*, 1855, quoted according to E. Wolf, *op. cit.*, p. XI.
[4] E. Käsemann, *op. cit.*, p. XIX.

historical criticism cannot and must not lead to atomizing the facts, as in the Enlightenment, but for Baur it must in effect mean an understanding of the individual in the whole. ' "Critical historical" means that no single feature is made absolute or negated, but each is understood as a transitional link in the chain of immanent historic progress and thus of the total self-realization of the revelation of the spirit or the idea.'[1] This historical criticism is only the reverse side of historical speculation. But what becomes of 'history' when historical speculation subjects it to a total vision of this kind?

1. History becomes a 'given object confronting us'.

2. The individual 'events' of history are understood as historic 'appearances' of a comprehensive whole.

3. Historic 'moments' are taken as 'elements' in the movements of a total complex of history.

4. The complex of history is given 'rational consistency' as 'an infinite concatenation of causes and effects'.

5. 'History' becomes a summary term for reality in its totality – for the self-contained movement of a universal whole in which 'everything together upholds and maintains itself'.

6. History thus becomes the field of the manifestation of a spiritual whole. It becomes the 'eternally clear mirror in which the spirit regards itself, contemplates its own image'. In history the spirit realizes and manifests itself. In the science of history it is received back again. Thus the speculative view of history as the world of the manifestation of the spirit is in complete accord with the principle of the subjectivity of the spirit that becomes conscious of itself in historical reflection. The critical historical method, historical speculation on history as a whole, and the re-subjectifying of the spirit in the knowledge of history go together and mutually condition each other.

Here, however, there arises the question whether a critical historical method and a historical speculation of this kind still understands 'history' as being 'historic' at all, or whether in this process of knowing and comprehending history the historic character of history is not resolved into a non-historic Greek *logos*. History is turned into a self-supporting cosmos. The riddle of history is solved by means of Platonic philosophy, Hegelian dialectic and pantheistic ideas. History becomes the

[1] E. Käsemann, *op. cit.*, p. XIX.

totality of the changing, self-transforming epiphanies of the eternal present. It is not possible to see how this can be a way of 'using the ruthless application of historical criticism to repeat in a changed situation the Reformers' decision for "*sola fide*" '.[1]

(c) For Johann Gustav Droysen, the 'realm of the historical method' is 'the cosmos of the moral world'.[2] To see this moral world in its development and growth, in its successive movements, is to see it as history. This already shows at the start what Droysen takes to be the substance whose historic manifestations are to be historically examined. His 'cosmos of the moral world' is expounded in a world history of moral teleology. The place of the principle of causality is taken by the principle of moral entelechy. The mystery of the movements of history is illumined in the light of their goals. 'From observing the progress in the movement of the moral world, from recognizing its direction, from seeing goal after goal fulfilled and revealed, the contemplation of history argues to a goal of goals, in which the movement is perfected, in which all that moves and motivates this world of men and makes it hasten restlessly on becomes rest, perfection, eternal present.'[3] 'All development and growth is movement towards a goal which seeks to attain its fulfilment in the movement.'[4] 'The highest goal, which unconditionally conditions all others', motivates them all, embraces them all, explains them all, the goal of goals is not to be empirically discovered.'[5] 'Beginning and end are hidden from the finite eye. But its scrutiny can discover the direction in which the movement flows. Bound though it is to the narrow limits of here and now, it beholds the whence and the whither.'[6] Thus 'the self-certainty of our personal being, the pressure of our moral obligations and desires, the longing for perfection, unity, eternity' adds 'to the other "proofs" of the existence of God the one that for us proves most'.[7] The certainty thus acquired of a highest goal of goals that gives meaning to things, is what

---

[1] Against G. Ebeling, 'Die Bedeutung der historisch-kritischen Methode', in *Wort und Glaube*, 1960, p. 45 (ET 'The Significance of the Critical Historical Method', in *Word and Faith*, 1963, p. 56) and F. Gogarten, *Verhängnis und Hoffnung der Neuzeit*, 1958, p. 154, whose theses K. Scholder, in the preface to the above mentioned new edition of F. C. Baur's works, quotes as putting significant questions to the work of F. C. Baur.
[2] J. G. Droysen, *Historik*, 4th ed. 1960, p. 345.		[3] *Ibid.*, p. 345.
[4] *Ibid.*, p. 356.		[5] *Ibid.*, p. 356.		[6] *Ibid.*, p. 358.		[7] *Ibid.*, p. 356.

Droysen calls a 'theodicy of history', without which history
would lapse into the meaninglessness of a cyclic movement that
merely repeats itself. Thus for 'history' Droysen holds fast to the
belief in God's wise ordering of the world, which embraces the
whole human race; and 'in taking this faith, "that is an un-
doubting confidence of things not seen", and striving to spell
it out in terms of knowledge . . . therein and therein alone does
it know itself to be a science'.[1]

In Droysen the relation between history and philosophy of
history is especially interesting. The movements of history are
movements within the framework of the 'cosmos' of the moral
world. The place of the causal cosmos of the natural sciences,
however, is taken by a teleological cosmos which has its culminating point of metaphysical unity in the highest final goal,
the goal of all goals. This is manifestly the entelechy-cosmos of
Aristotelian metaphysics. The latter is combined with the
postulates of Kant's practical reason, with the need to presuppose belief in 'God and a future world'. The eschatology of
Christian hope is transposed into the teleology of the moral
reason. The *eschaton* is turned into the *telos* of all *tele* – rest, perfection, one flock and one shepherd, one nation of mankind,
one full royal freedom of moral man, a new heaven and a new
earth, return of the whole creation to God.[2] Neoplatonic *logos*
speculation and the Hegelian dialectic of the coming to itself of
absolute Spirit supply the further description of this *eschaton/telos*.

Here, too, the riddle of history is resolved. The man who is
engaged in moral action knows himself on the way to the final
solution. Our last quotation, however, shows plainly that the
question as to the meaning or meaninglessness of history is
decided in a 'pre-scientific' way, as R. Wittram observes, yet
not in an unscientific pre-scientificness but, as Droysen says, in
the foundations and motive causes of the science of history –
namely, in that believing hope in the as yet unseen future which
presses for knowledge and which calls for the historical science
that 'strives after' knowledge. This would mean that the range
of the historic consciousness, of historic remembrance and historic knowledge is always as wide as the extent to which the
historic consciousness of mission, in hope for the future and
assurance of faith, anticipates an *eschaton* of ultimate goals and

[1] *Ibid.*, p. 373.   [2] *Ibid.*, p. 357 n. 11.

aims. The historical consciousness of history has the possibilities
and limitations of its perception prescribed by a historic consciousness of mission which accepts the future in responsibly
embracing its aims and goals. If this missionary consciousness
is formulated in moral terms, as in Droysen, then the realm of
the historical method becomes the cosmos of the moral world.
It is significant that for this moral teleology Droysen can, to be
sure, take over the biblical promises of the new humanity, the
liberty of the children of God, the perfection of all historic,
finite movements in the 'eternal present', but not the cardinal
point of Christian eschatology – the resurrection of the dead.

(d) For Wilhelm Dilthey, history is a human science and the
human sciences rest on the relationship between life, expression and understanding. 'The summary expression for all that
meets us in experience and understanding is life as a complex
embracing the human race.'[1] Everywhere in history we find
expressions of life, conditions of life, objectifications of the one,
unfathomable life. 'Each *individual expression of life represents* in
this realm of objective spirit (*viz.*, in the sense of the objectification of life) something *common* to all.'[2] All expressions of life
stand in a sphere of community, and are understandable only
in such a sphere. The 'basic fact' of man's world is 'life', and
the 'essence of history' is therefore to be seen in the idea of the
'objectification of life'.[3] 'It is life of all kinds in the most varied
relationships that constitutes history. History is merely life,
seen from the standpoint of the whole of mankind as forming one
complex.'[4] Over against Hegel's starting point in the 'absolute
Spirit' Dilthey sets the 'reality of life': 'In life the totality of the
psychic complex is at work.' Hence he understands 'objective
spirit' not from the standpoint of 'reason', but as a live unity
of expressions of life and objectifications of life. The historic
'chain of effects' accordingly does not consist for him in the
causal chain of nature, but in the structure of the life of the

---

[1] *Gesammelte Schriften*, 1921ff., vol. VII, p. 131. On Dilthey's work cf. G. Misch,
Lebensphilosophie und Phänomenologie, 2nd ed. 1931; E. Rothacker, *Einleitung in die
Geisteswissenschaften*, 1920; H. Plessner, *Zwischen Philosophie und Gesellschaft*, 1953,
pp. 262ff.; O. F. Bollnow, *Dilthey*, 2nd ed. 1955, and *Die Lebensphilosophie*, 1958.
[2] *Gesammelte Schriften*, VII, p. 146.
[3] VII, p. 147: 'It is through the idea of the objectification of life that we first
acquire an insight into the essence of history. . . . Whatever aspect of its character
the spirit puts into its expressions of life today, stands there tomorrow as history.'
[4] VII, p. 276.

soul which produces values and realizes aims. The life that springs from unfathomable sources becomes intelligible to us in the endless historic objectifications of that life, so far as we ourselves have part in it. The understanding of historic expressions of life presupposes the grounding of our own life in the unfathomable stream of life, and stands in mutual interaction therewith. We understand what we experience, and can experience what we understand. 'We are first of all historic beings, before we are observers of history, and only because we are the former do we become the latter.'[1] Thus mental science or the science of life, as it grows in understanding, broadens the horizon of the things that are common to all life, and draws near to the unfathomable, infinite whole that is history. The recognition of the finitude and relativity of all historic manifestations of life does not then lead us to relativism, but sets us free for the unfathomably creative activity of life itself. 'This tangle of torturing, enrapturing questions, of intellectual delights and the pains of insufficiency and contradiction – this is the enigma that is life, the unique, dark frightening object of all philosophy . . . the face of life itself, . . . this sphinx with the body of an animal and the face of a man.'[2] True as it is that history is here taken up into the sphere of a philosophy of life and regarded as the fulness of the finite objectifications and manifestations of infinite life, yet it is equally true that for Dilthey this can also be combined with a goal: 'Man's capacity for development, the expectation of future, higher forms of human life – that is the mighty wind that drives us on.'[3]

Here, too, historic 'events' are interpreted in terms of a primary substance that is the inexhaustible source of history – in this case 'life' – and in the light of the unfathomable life process they become 'objectifications' of something. All events, ideas and movements in history have at bottom something in common, which manifests itself in them all and makes it pos-

[1] VII, p. 278.

[2] VIII, p. 140. Cf. M. Landmann, *Der Mensch als Schöpfer und Geschöpf der Kultur*, 1961. The 'anarchy of thought' and the 'relativity of values' which are so much feared in historism are changed by Landmann into the positive form of the inexhaustible fulness of creative power: 'Multiplicity of Knowledge as a Source of Creative Power', pp. 72ff.

[3] H. Nohl, postscript to W. Dilthey's *Die Philosophie des Lebens*, Philosophische Texte, ed. H. G. Gadamer, 1946, p. 98.

sible to understand them and accept them as an enrichment of
our own life. The 'riddle of history' is not rationally solved.
History is not subjected to a general formula of mathematics.
But the riddle of history is identified as the riddle of life, whose
solutions are manifested in fragmentary, finite, supersedable
form in the relations and objectifications of life. Life, unfathomable as it is, is perennial. The relations and objectifications of
life change. History becomes intelligible when it is related to an
underlying foundation, to some eternally springing, eternally
driving source, to the *hypokeimenon* of 'life'. Then 'history' is the
history of life, and in so far as 'life' is mind, the science of history
is a human science. Its knowledge and understanding of past
history is a knowledge and self-understanding of the similar in
the different. Here, too, history becomes a totality and, in the
immensurable whole of this totality, 'life' becomes epiphanous.

(e) Martin Heidegger sets out from the view of history contained in Dilthey's philosophy of life.[1] Yet for him the 'basic
weakness' of thus seeing history in terms of the philosophy of
life lies in the fact that 'life' itself has not been taken as an
ontological problem. For him, 'life' is 'essentially accessible
only in Dasein'. By 'Dasein' is meant exclusively the being of
man or – later – that in which man finds and has being. This
means that for him the place of 'unfathomable life' is taken by
Dasein as disclosed to a phenomenological analysis. History
has its roots no longer in the creative unfathomability of life,
but in the historic character, or 'historicality', of Dasein.
'Historicality, as a determining character, is prior to what is
called "history" (events of world history). Historicality stands
for the state of Being that is constitutive for Dasein's "happening" as such; and only on the basis of such "happening" is
anything like "world history" possible or can anything belong
historically to world history.'[2] This means that the origin and
the essence of history are to be sought in the finitude, temporality and historical character of the existence of man. Dasein
is finite, for it extends between birth and death. To the temporal extension of Dasein belongs death. *'Authentic Being-
towards-death – that is to say, the finitude of temporality* – is the hidden

[1] Cf. W. Müller-Lauter, 'Konsequenzen des Historismus in der Philosophie der Gegenwart', *ZTK* 59, 1962, pp. 226ff.
[2] M. Heidegger, *Sein und Zeit*, pp. 19f. (ET p. 41).

basis of Dasein's historicality.'¹ Human Dasein is 'Being-towards-death' as the inevitable possibility of existence. 'Only Being-free *for* death gives Dasein its goal outright and pushes existence into its finitude. Once one has grasped the finitude of one's existence, it snatches one back from the endless multiplicity of possibilities which offer themselves as closest to one . . . and brings Dasein into the simplicity of its *fate*.'²

If the essence of history is seen in the 'historicality' of Dasein as such in terms of this analysis, then that means turning our backs on the multiplicity of things and events, and no longer examining the course of history and its reality as such, but asking what essentially makes it possible. 'In the existential analysis we cannot, in principle, discuss what Dasein *factically* resolves in any particular case.'³ The analysis supplies only a formal structural context which provides the conditions for the various several events.

What is the view of history that comes of thus grounding history in the fundamental 'historicality' of Dasein? Like Dilthey, when in terms of the philosophy of life he interpreted history as a mental science and a science of life, so also Heidegger's existentialist interpretation of history as a science is aimed at demonstrating its ontological derivation from the historic character of Dasein itself, and seeks to construct the idea of history from the 'historicality' of Dasein. This, however, is to lay down not only the historic character of the historical subject, but also a new description of the historical object. Heidegger makes a very precise distinction between what is 'primarily historic' and what is 'secondarily historic'.⁴

The historian's primary and authentic object lies not in the individual occurrence, or in 'laws' which govern the sequence of events, but in 'the possibility which has been factically existent. . . . The central theme of historiology is the *possibility* of existence which has-been-there.'⁵ Thus in the science of history, 'historicality' in the authentic sense of the term 'understands

¹ M. Heidegger, *Sein und Zeit*, p. 386 (ET p. 438).
² *Ibid.*, p. 384 (ET p. 435).   ³ *Ibid.*, p. 383 (ET p. 434).
⁴ *Ibid.*, p. 381 (ET p. 433): 'We contend that what is *primarily* historic is Dasein. That which is secondarily historic, however, is what we encounter within-the-world – not only the things ready-to-hand, in the widest sense, but also the environing Nature as "the very soil of history". Entities other than Dasein which are historic by reason of belonging to the world are what we call "world-historic".'
⁵ *Ibid.*, p. 395 (ET p. 447).

history as the "recurrence" of the possible, and knows that a possibility will recur only if existence is open for it fatefully, in a moment of vision, in resolute repetition'.[1] This means that historical science becomes a return to the possibility (that was), a repetition of the possibility and a re-echoing of the possibility. Historical science 'will disclose the quiet force of the possible with all the greater penetration the more simply and the more concretely having-been-in-the-world is understood in terms of its possibility, and "only" presented as such'.[2] *'Repeating is handing down explicitly* – that is to say, going back into the possibilities of the Dasein that has-been-there. The authentic repetition of a possibility of existence that has been – the possibility that Dasein may choose its hero – is grounded existentialistically in anticipatory resoluteness.'[3] Thus the historian will examine past history in search of its underlying understandings of existence, and from the understandings of existence he will extract the possibilities of Dasein and present them as possibilities for today's ability to exist – in order that Dasein may choose its hero. Thus historical science once more becomes 'tradition' – viz., handing down of possibilities of existence that have been.

The secondarily historic, on the other hand, has its roots in the inauthentic historicality of Dasein. In its flight from death it loses itself in general terms of 'they' and of world history, and is dissipated in the multiplicity of all that occurs from day to day. It understands Being without further differentiation in the sense of mere presence-at-hand and becomes historically blind to the possibilities. It therefore retains and receives only the 'actual' that is left over from the world history that has been, 'the leavings, and the information about them that is present-at-hand'. It 'evades choice'. 'Loaded down with the legacy of a "past" which has become unrecognizable, it seeks the modern.'[4] To that extent historical study of this kind seeks to estrange Dasein from its authentic historicality.

It was Heidegger's distinction between authentic and inauthentic study of history which first gave rise to that dualism that splits man's relation to history into objectifying contemplation and immediate encounter, into factual positivism and

[1] *Ibid.*, pp. 391f. (ET p. 444).   [2] *Ibid.*, p. 394 (ET p. 446).
[3] *Ibid.*, p. 385 (ET p. 437).   [4] *Ibid.*, p. 391 (ET pp. 443f.).

existentialist interpretation of the past possibilities of existence, in order then 'to interpret the movements of history as possible ways of understanding human existence, thus demonstrating their relevance today'.[1]

But now, it transpires that when real history is grounded in the formal structure of the historicality of Dasein, this tends to obscure the fact that the movements, individualities and complexes of history have really happened.[2] Historical relativism, to be sure, is surmounted when the possibility of history is ontologically grounded in the historicality of Dasein. This historicality is itself not subject to history, but comes of Dasein's eternally being given thematic and problematical character by death. But this also means losing sight of history as such. 'The intended surmounting of historism becomes an unintended surmounting of history.'[3] What happens here in the name of 'historicality' and in the work of existentialist interpretation of history is again the annihilation of history. The riddle of history is the historicality of Dasein, and man knows himself in his historicality to be the solution. In his 'resoluteness' he cuts the Gordian knot. But to surmount historicism in this way is to lose history itself.

(*f*) To sum up the results of this brief review of the philosophy of history that emerges from historical heuristics, we find that the definition, comprehension and understanding of history inevitably brings about at the same time an abrogation, a negation and annihilation of history. When the primary question is that of the origin, substance and essence of history, then the concrete movements, changes, crises and revolutions which constitute history are related to some factor that does not change, always exists and has equal validity at all times. The science and philosophy of history are here striving to combine the Greek *logos* with our modern experiences of reality, and our modern experiences of crisis with the Greek *logos*.

---

[1] R. Bultmann, *Das Urchristentum*, 2nd ed. 1954, p. 8 (ET p. 12). On this dualism cf. H. Ott, *Geschichte und Heilsgeschichte in der Theologie R. Bultmanns*, 1955; J. Moltmann, 'Exegese und Eschatologie der Geschichte', *EvTh* 22, 1962, pp. 38ff. This contrasting of critical historical examination and kerygmatic interpretation, especially where it is sharpened by means of the antithesis of law and gospel, is not in harmony with the primarily and secondarily historic in Heidegger, but represents a subjectivistic exposition of the history of existence.

[2] W. Müller-Lauter, *op. cit.*, p. 254 n. 1. Similarly also C. von Krockow, *Die Entscheidung*, 1958, pp. 131f.

[3] W. Müller-Lauter, *op. cit.*, p. 253.

It has often been rightly emphasized that 'history' was
fundamentally foreign to Greek thought. Greek thought was
primarily in search of the ever existent, the unchanging, ever
true, ever good and ever beautiful. 'History', however, is that
which rises and passes, unstable and transient, and as such shows
no signs of anything that is perpetual and abiding. For that
reason it was not possible to discover in the accidental *prag-
mata* of history any *logos* of eternal, true Being. It was not
possible to 'know' history, and at bottom there was in history
nothing worth knowing either. This idea of *logos* and knowledge,
of truth and essence, plainly has its ground in the religion of
ancient Greek belief in the gods and the cosmos. Thucydides,
the historian of the Peloponnesian war, shows profound insights
into the nature of men and forces and their typical features, but
he, too, searches for what is abiding and unchanging in this
war. 'He is a man void of hope, and therefore void of wide
perspectives.'¹ He portrays a self-contained picture of 'a
history', but does not ask about 'history'. He lacks the sense
for change and newness, because there can be no divine sense in
the changing and the suddenly new. What makes divine sense
would require to have the dignity of being constant and abiding.

On the other hand it has been emphasized that the concept
of history is a creation of Hebrew prophecy. 'For the Greek
mind, historical science is synonymous with knowledge as
such. Thus for the Greeks history is and remains related merely
to the past. The prophet on the other hand is a seer. His seer's
eye fashioned the concept of history as the being of the future.
... Time becomes future ..., and the future is the primary
content of this reflection on history. In place of a golden age
in the mythological past, the eschatological future puts a true
historical existence on earth.'² This has its ground in the fact
that for Jews and Christians history means history of salvation
and history of the divine promise. The 'divine' is not seen as
that which is ever existent in constant and abiding orders and
self-repeating structures, but is expected in the future from the
God of the promises. The changes of history are not 'the changing', as measured in terms of the abiding, but they contain the

¹ G. Mann, *Der Sinn der Geschichte*, 1961, p. 15. Cf. also K. Lowith, *Meaning
in History*, 1949; E. Auerbach, *Mimesis*, 1946.
² H. Cohen, *Religion der Vernunft aus den Quellen des Judentums*, 1919, p. 302.

possible, as measured in terms of the promise of God. 'History'
is not a chaos into which the observer must bring divine order
and eternal *logos*, but history is here perceived and sought
in the categories of the new and the promised. The place
of dispassionate observation and contemplation or review is
therefore taken by passionate expectation and by participation
in forward-moving mission. The place of the question as to the
abiding essence and eternal origin of times past is taken by the
historic question of the future and of the preparations for it
and intimations of it in the past. The real category of history is
no longer the past and the transient, but the future. The perception and interpretation of past history is then no longer
archaeological, but futuristic and eschatological. Accounts of
history then belong to the genus of prophecy – prophecy that
looks back, but intends the future. If the meaning of history is
expected from the future and conceived in terms of the mission
of the present, then history is neither a tangle of necessities and
laws nor a tumbling-ground for meaningless caprice. Future
as mission shows the relation of today's tasks and decisions to
what is really possible, points to open possibilities in the real
and to tendencies that have to be grasped in the possible.

If, as we said at the beginning, modern historical study and
the modern philosophy of history is 'philosophy of crisis', the
very designation of 'history' as 'crisis' really already implies
the use of the Greek *logos* for a 'philosophy' of history. For the
word 'crisis' measures the uncomprehended new event by the
standard of the traditional order of human life, which now
finds itself in a crisis, is threatened by it, and must therefore be
rescued, preserved or renewed. The expression 'crisis' is always
related to 'order'. The 'crisis' calls the order in question and
can therefore be mastered only by means of a new order. It
then remains unnoticed that this event, which is perceived as a
'crisis', contains on the other hand also the 'new'. Philosophy
of history as a philosophy of crisis has therefore constantly
a conservative character. Historical science as an anti-crisis
science therefore fell back on the Greek *logos* with all its cosmological implications, and on the Roman concept of *ordo* with
all its political and juridical implications. If, however, the new
factor is perceived in the crisis, and history is not regarded as
a crisis of the existing order but is expected in the category

of the future, then the horizon of illumination and expectation
will have to be totally different. Philosophy of history as a
philosophy of crisis has the aim of annihilating history. An
eschatology of history, however, which revolves around the
concepts of the new and the future, of mission and the front
line of the present, would be in a position to take history as
history, to remember and expect it as history, and thus not to
annihilate history but to keep it open.

5. ESCHATOLOGY OF HISTORY – PHILOSOPHIC MILLENARIANISM

It was the theological evaluation of 'time' resulting from the
expectation of the arrival of the promised future of God in
terms of Jewish and Christian messianic thought, that first
opened the Greek mind for the problem of history and for the
philosophic idea of a purposeful, irreversible and unrepeatable
process of history. 'Just as space with its closed bounds and its
fulness of forms is the sphere of truth for the Greeks, so that of
Israel is the open, formless stream of time. In the former case
we have the circle of the cosmos returning upon itself, in the
latter the straight line of creation pressing on to infinity; in the
former the world of seeing and contemplating, in the latter
that of hearing and learning; in the former image and resem-
blance, in the latter decision and action. . . . In space is
presence and remembrance, in time danger and hope. . . . Over
against the spatial goal of perfection stands the goal of redemption to be attained in time.'[1] The combining of both spheres of
truth and both ways of thinking in the manifold encounters
between Jewish and Christian messianic ideas and Greek
thought in the course of the history of Christianity brought
about the decisive transition in Greek thinking from the static
to the dynamic, from substance to function, from the eternal
present of Being to the open possibilities of the future, from the
metaphysical glorification of the cosmos to the sense of mission
that transforms the world. The transition which arose from
such encounters can be particularly clearly seen in the philosophy of history in the nineteenth century. If in the last chapter

---

[1] M. Susman, *Das Buch Hiob und das Schicksal des jüdischen Volkes*, 2nd ed. 1948,
pp. 16f.

we saw modern historiography and modern philosophy of
history in the light of the Greek *logos* and noticed in them a
subliminal annihilation of history, yet they can also be read
from the standpoint of historic eschatology.

Since the time of Herder's *Ideen zur Philosophie der Geschichte
der Menschheit* ('Ideas on the Philosophy of the History of Mankind'), Kant's *Ideen zu einer allgemeinen Geschichte in weltbürgerlicher Absicht* ('Ideas on a Universal History, with a Cosmopolitan Intent'), Schiller's *Was heisst und zu welchem Ende
studiert man Universalgeschichte?* ('What is Universal History and
to what End is it studied?'), and finally Hegel's *Philosophy of
History,* all historians and thinkers on history have possessed a
sense of mission, a belief in a history that is meaningful and a faith
in the great task of mankind. Whether this goal is governed by
the 'vision of eternal peace' in the cosmopolitan state or, as in
national histories, by the 'mission of Prussia' (Treitschke), the
'mission of France' (Jules Michelet) or the mission of Pan-
slavism, everywhere a secular messianism becomes the dominating philosophical and political idea in the view of history.
Historiography and philosophy of history become necessary
where the foreground is occupied by the mission of a nation, or
by world redemption or the doctrine of a revolution that is now
due or the doctrine of a vitally necessary restoration. The messianic outlook becomes political and motivates men's thoughts
on history. This in itself has already brought a fundamentally
new element into the view of history in modern times as compared with Greek historiography.

It also means, further, that modern views of history can no
longer renounce the governing idea of a *universal history or world
history.* Speculations on world history and discussions about
history as a whole, and about the whole as history, first became possible as a result of Christianity's sense of mission, and
have therefore not ceased to be possible even where Christianity is no longer the centre of this mission.

Finally, it can be said that only where a knowledge of mission supplies the sense of a future and a purpose, and only so
long as that is so, and only where this knowledge finds its goal
in a universal horizon that embraces the whole world, and only
so long as that is so, is there room for the concept of growth in
time, of the uniqueness of events and of a meaningful future

that is to be expected and sought – in a word, for a historic concept of history. That is why the Dutch historian Jan Huizinga can say that the future is the real category of historic thinking.[1] And that is why Ernst Bloch is right when he insists that 'the nerve of the true historical concept is and remains the new'.[2]

The concept of history that is marked by future expectations, a sense of mission and the category of the new can, of course, also make history obscure. It depends on the nature of the future that is expected in each particular case, and on the source from which the mission emerges and the object at which it aims. Yet 'history' here remains the epitome of possible danger and possible salvation. 'History' does not become, in the sense of the Greek *logos*, the epitome of reality in its totality or of the universe. To understand and embrace history in the front-line of the present in terms of hope and forward-moving mission can therefore be dangerous as well as salutary in its effects. For where this way of perceiving history is concerned, Hölderlin's saying is true: 'Where there is danger, the salutary also grows' – as is also its reverse: where the salutary grows, there danger grows also (E. Bloch).[3] The would-be rescue for the sake of which everything else is abandoned, and which then fails, plunges everything into infinite danger of forsakenness and meaninglessness. To expect and seek a deliverance which does not embrace all that is and all that is not yet, has disastrous results when everything is staked upon it. To abandon ourselves and all existing reality to the unstable seas of history always has point only when there is a prospect of new land. If these prospects prove to be illusions, then our loss is doubled. If there are no prospects at all, then history, too, becomes pointless. But if the experience of reality as history has once arisen and the breakthrough to history has once taken place, then there can be no return to non-historic faith in the ever existing and eternally abiding cosmos. The understanding of history, of its possibilities for good and evil, of its direction and its meaning, lies in the field of hope and can be acquired only there.

---

[1] Cf. A. A. van Ruler, *Die christliche Kirche und das Alte Testament*, 1955, p. 36 n. 11.
[2] E. Bloch, *Das Prinzip Hoffnung* II, 1959, p. 1626.
[3] E. Bloch, *Verfremdungen* I, 1962, p. 219.

If from this standpoint we take another look at modern historiography and modern philosophy of history, then we shall notice that the real problem in their concepts of history is not the problem of the particular and the general, not the problem of the idea and its appearances, and so on, but the question of the relation of history to the 'end of history'. Kant remarked in his philosophy of history that philosophy, too, can have its 'millenarianism'.[1] His remark draws our attention to the fact that every understanding of history on the basis of an already existing and ascertained totality of the idea or of the primary substance or of life, and every resolution of history into knowledge, is in search of the 'end of history', and that the aporia of the philosophy of history is to be seen in its having to seek this 'end of history' *in* history. Modern philosophy of history has in fact the character of a philosophic, enlightened millenarianism: the 'ending of history in history' is, as in the old religious millenarianism, its goal. It has, further, the character of eschatological spirit mysticism. Joachim di Fiore's historico-theological idea of a third empire of the spirit has haunted and inspired the nineteenth-century view of history since Lessing. History is the 'developing God', as it was said in the age of Goethe from Herder on. Knowledge of history therefore imparts a share in the God who is becoming spirit. The idea that a third age of the – scientific – spirit will clear up the crises of history and in this way resolve enigmatic history into understood history, constituted for Lessing and Kant, for Comte and Hegel and their followers, the hidden basis for a new orientation of the world, and one that was fundamentally no longer 'metaphysical', but 'historical'. Thus wherever the philosophy of history lays down an 'essence of history', its statements, although formulated in the sense of Greek cosmology, have an eschatological character involving the 'end of history'. All the 'general bonds' or trends which historiography finds in history have therefore an eschatological tenor.

But if 'history' becomes a new concept for the 'universe' or for 'reality in its totality', then this is to coin a new concept of the cosmos and no longer take a 'historic' view of history. If reality is engaged in history, then that means precisely that it

---

[1] I. Kant, *Ideen zu einer allgemeinen Geschichte in weltbürgerlicher Absicht*, as in the edition, *Zur Geschichtsphilosophie (1784–1798)*, ed. A. Buchenau, Berlin, 1947, p. 24.

has not yet become a rounded whole. The 'whole world' would
be the sound world, the perfect world, which bears its truth
within itself and can demonstrate it of itself. Only as long as the
world is not yet sound and whole, only as long as it is open towards its truth and does not yet possess it, can we speak of
'history'. Only as long as reality itself is involved in the difference between existence and essence, only as long as human
nature is experienced in terms of the difference between consciousness and being, is there such a thing as history and is
there any need for knowledge of the future, for a sense of mission and for present decision.

But what does knowledge of history mean in that case, and
what is then the point of historiography?

6. DEATH AND GUILT AS DRIVING FORCES OF THE HISTORICAL OUTLOOK

Efforts towards a knowledge of history which take seriously
this historic character of history will begin with Friedrich
Nietzsche's protest against historism in the name of life. 'All
living things can be healthy, strong and fruitful only within a
surrounding horizon.'[1] Historism, an excess of which stifles
life, has its ground according to Nietzsche in the mediaeval
memento mori and in the 'hopelessness which Christianity
cherishes in its heart towards all coming ages of earthly existence'.[2] The historical outlook, 'when it reigns unrestrainedly
and draws all its conclusions, leaves the future without roots,
because it destroys our illusions and robs existing things of the
atmosphere in which alone they can live'.[3] For 'life' means
having a horizon, and to have a horizon means to be borne
by hope into the realm of the future and the possible. This is the
'plastic power of life' which is undermined by the historical
outlook and an excess of the historical outlook. If, however,
it is really in the name of Nietzsche's *'memento vivere'* that we
would take up and consider past history, then this 'life' would
have to be a match for the 'death' which has made past history
irretrievably past. The understanding of 'life' on the basis of
which Nietzsche enquires into the 'historical outlook's advantages

[1] *Vom Nutzen und Nachteil der Historie für das Leben*, Kröner 37, 1924, p. 5.
[2] *Ibid.*, pp. 68f.   [3] *Ibid.*, pp. 56f.

and disadvantages for life' cannot assert itself against the death that makes all things historic, or can do so only by dint of forgetting and of appealing to 'life's youth'. For this reason his protest against historism is no match for the latter and its consequences. The historian's impression is correct: 'To me the great historic events of the past always seem like frozen cataracts – pictures that have stiffened in the cold of vanished life and keep us at a distance. . . . We shiver with cold as we contemplate the greatness of – fallen empires, perished cultures, burnt-out passions, dead minds. . . . When we take these things seriously, then we can have a feeling that we historians are engaged in a curious business: we dwell in the cities of the dead, encompass shadows, censure the departed.'[1] Only the question remains, why we do it and why we do not rather flee the shadowy realm of the past. Underlying all history, in the sense of an attempt at scientific knowledge, is what has been called 'history as memory'.[2] It is true that our faculty of remembering matters of history is always selective. Remembering and forgetting are interwoven in each other. It is true that our faculty of remembering matters of history is conditioned by the imagination. The thing we remember changes its colours in the image of memory. Where these memories of history are concerned, 'history as a science' has a twofold consequence: history as a science may well turn the 'memory' into a known, historic fact by destroying it, but from its own standpoint it cannot possibly reverse the process and by its own means create new memories, unless it were to cancel itself (A. Heuss).[3] In regard to 'history as memory', however, and to the extent that it is present as such, historical science has a task of criticism and purification. It has the 'task of combatting innocent forgetfulness and guilty legend' (H. Heimpel).[4] In this sense R. Wittram has called *guilt* the 'secret motor which keeps the movement going, mostly hidden, always at work, the real *perpetuum mobile* of world history'.[5] Memories of the kind that are experienced as 'guilt' 'force themselves upon us'. They compel the present to define its position towards them, for in everything that is

[1] R. Wittram, *Das Interesse an der Geschichte*, 1958, pp. 15f.
[2] A. Heuss, *Der Verlust der Geschichte*, 1959, pp. 13ff.
[3] *Ibid.*, p. 53.
[4] H. Heimpel, *Der Mensch in seiner Gegenwart*, 1954, pp. 163f.
[5] R. Wittram, *op. cit.*, p. 17.

remembered as guilt there lurks something which is not yet over and done with, whose implications are not yet grasped, whose significance is not yet plain. When what has been, or has happened, is seen as 'guilt', then the present enters into proceedings which have not yet found their end and their solution. The past becomes determinative for the burdens and tasks of the present. To such proceedings Hegel's remark does not apply: 'As the idea of the world it (philosophy) appears only after reality has finished the process of its formation and completed itself. . . . When philosophy paints one of life's figures as grey as grey can be, then that figure has grown old and the greyness cannot be a means of rejuvenating it but only of recognizing it.'[1] Once processes in history and particular figures in life have become old, then a detached historical consideration of them is *possible* – only, then it is no longer *necessary*. Processes of this kind that are complete in themselves completely lack anything to stimulate the onset of memory. If, on the other hand, history is not yet at an end and the individual figures in its life are not yet completed, then to behold it with the eyes of Minerva's owl is not *possible*, but then, on the contrary, to perceive the open possibilities, the tendencies and directions in this process of things is *necessary*. For then it is not a case of frozen cataracts of dead facts, but of an open *fieri*, of something that is in process of becoming, in an open process of decisions and hopes. Then the science of history will not be able merely to present historical 'findings', but will have to be conscious of the fact that in all its presentations it also 'finds' and in all its ascertainings it also 'as-certains'. To this extent the science of history stands in the service of life and of the – as yet unfounded – righteousness of life in the past.

This is true not only in regard to 'history as memory' of guilt, but also in regard to death, which is always the hardest, and therefore also the most certain fact of past history. It is not merely guilt, but ultimately *death* that makes the past irretrievably past. What was, does not return. What is dead, is dead. Now if history were the history of death, then historical science would be the history of death as grasped by man, and as such would be death to all living memory. Then, however, it

[1] *Grundlinien der Philosophie des Rechts*, 4th edition, ed. Hoffmeister, 1955, Vorrede 17.

would again remain an open question what is the real motive of
the interest in history, if all history were history of death, if
history did, to be sure, include much that is in flux and in process of development, and yet the dead remained dead. Then
there would at this point be no *fieri*, but only a fact – and a bare,
uninterpretable fact at that. It would be the end of the interest
in history and of its usefulness for life, for death would here be
found to constitute a perpetual and eternal factor in the shape
of an annihilating nothingness. But now, the peculiar thing is,
that the historian can and must deal with the dead. 'The dead
are dead; but we awake them, we have dealings with them –
"eye to eye", as Ranke put it; they demand the truth from
us.'[1] This business of dealing with the history of the dead must
therefore be motivated by something that reaches beyond death
and makes death, too, a passing thing – otherwise historical
science would have no motive and would fall to pieces in face
of death. Walter Benjamin in his 'Theses on the Philosophy of
History' has declared: 'The gift of fanning the spark of hope
in the past belongs only to the historian who is convinced that
even the dead are not secure against the enemy if he wins. . . .
The Messiah comes not only as Redeemer; he comes also as
the Conqueror of Antichrist.'[2] This, however, would mean that
hope of the resurrection of the dead, and fear of Antichrist or
annihilating nothingness, is alone able to awake hopes in the
field of past history, and so to keep history in remembrance and
thus, finally, to make history as a science a live possibility. In
this sense Otto Weber, too, rightly declares: ' "History" as an
intended object of research, or as the realm in which the present
situation originated, is always a process that represents in a
manner of speaking a re-awakening of the dead. Those who
study history (*wer Geschichte "treibt"*) "make" of the "history
of death" a "history of life".'[3] The historian's re-awakening of
the dead, even if, and precisely because, it takes place only 'in
a manner of speaking', means anticipating eschatology and

[1] R. Wittram, *op. cit.*, p. 32.
[2] W. Benjamin, *Illuminationen*, ed. T. W. Adorno, 1961, p. 270.
[3] O. Weber, *Grundlagen der Dogmatik* II, 1962, p. 108. [*Geschichte treiben* ('to study
history') could also literally mean 'to drive history', and is therefore here held to
suggest that the historian himself is the driving-force that brings dead history to
life. We have attempted to reproduce the wordplay by transferring it to the prin-
cipal clause, where 'make of' is of course used in the sense of understanding, but
could also mean literally making. – *Translator*.]

projecting upon history the last act of history. The 'reason in history' has a messianic light and shows things with all their flaws laid bare and ready for redemption – or else it has no light that historically illuminates history.

How, in this light, can history be experienced and known?

It will no longer be possible to regard the past only archae-ologically and take it merely as the origin of the particular present. The past will have to be examined in regard to its own future. All history is full of possibilities – possibilities that have been profited by and not profited by, seized and blocked. In this perspective it appears full of interrupted possibilities, lost beginnings, arrested onsets upon the future. Past ages will thus have to be understood from the standpoint of their hopes. They were not the background of the now existing present, but were themselves the present and the front-line towards the future. It is the open future that gives us a common front with earlier ages and a certain contemporaneity, which makes it possible to enter into discussion with them, to criticize and ac-cept them. That is why past positions in history and the traces of vanished hopes can be taken up once more and awakened to new life. The dialectic of past happening and present under-standing is always motivated by anticipations of the future and by the question of what makes the future possible. Future is then found in the past and possibilities in what has been. The unfinished and promising character of past ages is borne in mind. The dualism of which we have spoken, in which the positivist historian strives to discover the facts of the past while the existentialist interpreter endeavours to find the existential possibilities in past existence, fails to recognize how closely fact and possibility are interwoven in history, how much new possibilities of existence depend on historic events and how full historic events are of possibilities. Only in the process of recon-ciliation between originally undivided subject-object constella-tions, when men's decisions are a response to really given possi-bilities and new real possibilities give rise to new decisions, do future prospects and ordered ends emerge. This is a thing historical positivism cannot see, because its own horizon is taken to be final and therefore cannot be subjected to question-ing in recognition of other horizons. It is a thing an existen-tialist interpretation can bring out only in the realm of man's

existence as in quest of itself, but not in the universal realm of
all being as open to the future.

7. THE PECULIARITY OF THE HISTORIAN'S UNIVERSAL CONCEPTS

What happens in this context to the historian's universal
concepts, as employed by the historical method which must
always also generalize? The philosophical presupposition for a
knowledge of history cannot then lie in a metaphysic of being,
of the idea, of unfathomable life, or of God. As long as our
reality has not yet 'completed' itself and not yet become a
rounded whole, a metaphysic of the historical universe in the
sense of the Greek *logos* is impossible. All the historian's universal concepts therefore prove to be elastic concepts which
themselves belong to history and make history. But the fact
that they are not inherently absolute does not mean that they are
adequately designated by the term 'relative'. The place of a
universal metaphysic of history is taken by a mission aimed at
the universal which is future and not yet present. The universal
concepts, themselves belonging to history, which are used by
historians in an effort to grasp what man is, what the world is,
and so on, arise only supposedly and only wrongly from abstraction. In actual fact they contain the note of prophecy and
of mission towards the future land of the 'realized generic concept'. They always contain a futuristically anticipated eschatology. In their abstractness the truth which the general concepts seek to grasp is manifested in a manner which is – literally
– *pro*-visional in view of the openness of reality. The universals
in the metaphysic of history are neither real nor merely verbal,
but constitute tendencies in the potential. They mark pro-
visionalities in the fore-land of the mission in history. They are
therefore not relative in the sense of historical relativism, but
they are surpassable in the sense that the process of history itself is open. What 'world' history is, is decided by what is desired, hoped for and re-pre-sented as the one, future world.
What the history of 'mankind' is, is decided by what mankind
one day should be and will be. Both are directly related to
present mission. Thus there exist only histories on the way to
world history, but there is not yet a world history. The lines on

which these histories are on their way *towards* world history are
all maintained by the consciousness of having a mission towards
world history.

Jakob Burckhardt has said of the historian's business:
'Actually, we should have to live in a constant intuition of the
world as a whole. Only, this would require a superhuman in-
telligence, superior to the temporally successive and spatially
limited and yet at the same time engaged in constant contemplation of it and complete sympathy with it.'[1] He was not thereby declaring the contemplation of world history to be senseless,
but rather indicating the dialectical position of man towards
history. Man neither stands *above* history, so that he could survey the world as a whole, nor does he stand wholly *within*
history, so that he would have no need to ask about the totality
and goal of history and this very question would be pointless.
Always he stands both *within* history and also *above* history.
He experiences history in the modus of being and in the modus
of having. He *is* historic and he *has* history. He must be able
to detach himself from history as an investigator and spectator,
in order to experience it in the modus of having. He must
identify himself with it as a hearer and actor, in order to experience it in the modus of being. He can neither abrogate
himself in his survey of history and turn into nothing but an
enormous eyeglass, nor can he enter into history without thought
and reflection and turn into nothing but a minute decision. He
stands both in history and above it and must conduct his life
and his thinking in this dialectical and ex-centric position. He
is like a swimmer moving in the stream of history – or it may be,
against the stream – but with his head out of the water in order
to get his bearings and above all to acquire a goal and a future.
The concepts and ideas which he can form about historic
complexes are therefore historic in a twofold sense: they are
acquired in the process of history, and they reach ahead towards future, possible land, to that extent keeping the movement
of history on the move. They are concepts which are conditioned
by history, but which also condition history. They are moved
and mobile concepts of movement. They seek not to bear the
train of history, but to carry the torch before it. For that reason
they have necessarily the character of pre-supposition, of

[1] J. Burckhardt, *op. cit.*, p. 372.

postulate, of draft and of anticipation. And for that reason they are not so much generic concepts for the subsuming of known reality as rather dynamic functional concepts whose aim is the future transformation of reality.

8. THE HERMENEUTICS OF CHRISTIAN MISSION

1. The Proofs of God and Hermeneutics

Among the presuppositions of a rational Christian theology, hermeneutic reflections on the principles of the understanding of biblical texts have today replaced the old proofs of God which once, as *theologia naturalis*, constituted the prolegomena for what Christianity says of God. This, however, is not by any means the end of these proofs of God which demonstrated the existence and nature of God, as well as the universal necessity of raising the question of God, from a reality known or accessible to all men. On the contrary, they recur in all their conceivable forms in the hermeneutic reflections in which the anterior understanding and the terms of reference for the exposition and preaching of the biblical witness to God and his actions are formulated today. G. Ebeling rightly observes: '*The understanding of what the word "God" means has its place within the sphere of radical questionableness.*'[1] It is therefore the business of a comprehensive analysis of reality to take account of that radical questionableness of reality which provides the general presupposition for the special, Christian questions and statements in theology. In the radical questionableness of reality there appears the problem of transcendence, or simply the *question* of of God, in face of which the Christian affirmation of God must prove and authenticate itself. This has much in common with the enterprise of the classical proofs of God, even if it is here no longer the existence and nature of God that is demonstrated, but the necessity of raising the question of God. What the name 'God' means, can be intelligibly shown only when it is related to a radical, and therefore necessary, questionableness of reality. 'God' is what we are asking about in and with this questionableness of reality.

The traditional proofs of God can be divided into three major groups: 1. the *proofs of God from the world*, from the cos-

[1] G. Ebeling, *Wort und Glaube*, 1960, pp. 364f. (ET p. 347).

mos or the history of reality, 2. the *proofs of God from human existence*, from the soul or from the self-consciousness of man's necessary ability and obligation to be a self, 3. the *proofs of God from 'God'*, the proofs of the existence of God, or of the quest of God, from the concept or name of God. 'God' can be sought and understood as what we are asking about in the questionableness of reality as a whole, or in the question of the unity, the origin and the wholeness of reality. 'God' can be understood as what we are asking about in what every man can himself experience as the questionableness of human existence as distinct from the things of the world. 'God' can be understood as what is to be sought and asked about in addressing ourselves to the concept, the name or the self-revelation of God. Rational Christian theology can be cosmo-theology or historico-theology, can be ethico-theology or existential theology and can be onto-theology. These are to begin with the three possibilities in terms of which it can make itself and its business intelligible. These three possibilities have their corresponding results in the principles of hermeneutics, of exegesis, and of the scientific treatment which that involves in our dealings with history and with the historic witness of the Bible. These three possibilities present themselves also for the formulating of the universal theological concepts by means of which the God of the Bible can be understood, proved and proclaimed as the God of all men.

(*a*) We begin with the *proof of God from existence*, since it is so generally employed in hermeneutics today that it is hardly consciously recognized any more as a 'proof of God'. When G. Ebeling says that the radical questionableness 'seems to arise at a totally different point from where the usual so-called proofs of God placed it', namely, 'not with the question of the *primum movens* or such like, but with the problems relating to personal being',[1] then this alternative merely shows how strong the tendency is today to understand by the 'proofs of God' only the theoretic reason's cosmological proofs of God, and then to confine oneself to the proof of God from existence – an extended and deepened form of Kant's moral proof of God. The proof of God from the existence proper to every man is to the effect that 'God' is what is asked about in the questionableness of human

[1] *Ibid.*, p. 367 (ET p. 349).

existence, limited as it is by death and therefore finite, resting
on decisions and therefore historic. The affirmation of the
existence of God accordingly cannot be understood as a universal, theoretical and objective truth, but only as an 'expression of our existence itself'.[1] For it is obviously not feasible
'to think of God as a principle of the world in the light of which
the world and with it also our existence would become intelligible'.[2] God can be grasped only when men grasp their
own existence. The existence of man, however, is historic, i.e.
the historic character of man's being is what makes him able to
be. Thus God can be grasped only where man chooses himself
as his own possibility. Both things happen together in the one
act of faith. The question which causes man to ask about God
and causes him in asking to know very well who God is, is the
question which in his historic existence he himself is. 'If his
existence were not motivated (whether consciously or unconsciously) by the enquiry about God in the sense of the Augustinian "*Tu nos fecisti ad Te, et cor nostrum inquietum est, donec
requiescat in Te*" ("Thou hast made us for thyself, and our
heart is restless until it rests in thee"), then neither would
he know God as God in any manifestation of him.'[3] This
phenomenon is revelation's point of reference. In it lies the
anterior understanding, the universal *theologia naturalis* with
which every man has to do and by reference to which alone
God's revelation can show itself to be the revelation of God.

The basic principles of hermeneutics automatically result
from this. 'In the light of this insight we shall in each instance
interpret the historical source as a genuine historic phenomenon, i.e. in the light of the presupposition that in each
instance a possibility of human existence is grasped and expressed in it.'[4] The sense of historical science, or exegesis as
the case may be, can then no longer lie in reconstructing a piece
of the past and assigning it a place in the great complex of
relationships that is called history (= world history).[5] The sense
of historical science or exegesis then lies in an existentialist
interpretation which examines the texts in search of their understanding of existence and interprets the biblical texts in the

[1] R. Bultmann, *Glauben und Verstehen* I, p. 32.   [2] *Ibid.*
[3] *Ibid.* II, p. 232 (ET p. 257); *Kerygma und Mythos* II, p. 192 (ET p. 192).
[4] *Glauben und Verstehen* I, p. 119.   [5] *Ibid.*, p. 123.

light of the dominating question of God, of God's revelation, and that means of the truth of human existence as a present possibility of existence. The principles of an understanding exposition result from the presupposed hermeneutic structure of human existence itself. If the motivating question about God is identical with man's question as to the authenticity of his own existence, then the existentialist interpretation can present itself as a true historic and true theological interpretation of the biblical texts. It finds the point of its enquiry in the question as to the understanding of human existence expressed in scripture, because the ground for this question has been supplied to it by the proof of God from existence.

To this the critic must object that man's self-knowledge cannot by any means be arrived at today in antithesis to knowledge of the world, that the historic character of human existence cannot by any means be arrived at without an understanding of the situation in world history, but invariably both can only be arrived at together.[1] Instead of the antithesis between world and self there is in reality always a correlation. For this reason the historic character of a past understanding of existence can be understood only in the context of the 'great complex of relationships' that is called history or world history. The questionability of human existence always stands in a context in which it is conditioned by the questionability of historic reality as a whole. The proof of God from existence has always an eye to the proof of God from the world. An understanding of God can therefore be acquired only in the correlation between understanding of self and understanding of the world, between understanding of history and of 'historicality' – otherwise the intended divinity of God would not be universal.

The historic character of believing existence does not by any means already constitute the authenticity of human existence itself, but it is the way to, the witness of, and the mission towards, that authenticity and truth of human nature which lies in the future, is accordingly still outstanding, and is at stake in the mission of Christian faith. The interpretation of all history

---

[1] I agree here with W. Pannenberg's criticism, *ZTK* 60, 1963, pp. 101ff., except that in place of the primacy of the world-God relationship I set the correlation of the world-God relationship and the world-existence relationship. It is neither possible to explain human nature as a piece of world, nor is the world synonymous with man's 'being-in-the-world'.

in the light of the perpetual historic character of human existence does, to be sure, surmount a specific form of positivist
historism, but like the latter it also brings the disappearance of
the real movements, differences and prospects in history.

Augustine's 'restless heart' is not a universal human presupposition for the Christian understanding of God, but is a
mark of the pilgrim people of God and a goal of the Christian
mission to all men. It is only in the light of the biblical understanding of God that human existence experiences itself as
being moved by the question of God.

(b) The *proof of God from the world* has had no further influence
on theology since Kant's critique. Yet, if the reality of the world
as a whole is understood in a new way no longer as a cosmos but
as universal history, it can be classed alongside the proof of
God from existence and can likewise become a source for the
stating of hermeneutic principles. 'God' is here experienced on
the basis of the world.[1] 'God' is here what is asked about in the
question of the one origin, the unity and wholeness of all
reality. With the question of the unity and wholeness of reality,
the question of God is also given. If, on the other hand, there
is no support for the idea of God, then there is no support for
the question of the wholeness of reality either. Thus God can
be spoken of only in the context of the perception of the unity
of all reality. But now, this unity of reality can no longer be
understood as a cosmos in the sense of Greek monotheism, since
in Greek cosmic faith the accidental events of history were
meaningless and therefore remained of no account. But if
reality in its totality of continuity and contingency is understood as history, then the structures of the biblical idea of God
become visible. The idea of God in the witnesses of the divine
history in Israel and Christianity makes it necessary to understand reality as a whole as history. This means, first, that
'world history' becomes the most comprehensive horizon for
what Christianity says of God. It means, secondly, that such a
comprehensive understanding of reality in its totality, since it
is itself historic, can only be formulated in each several instance
in the context of the present experience of reality as a whole.
It is therefore itself historically open and provisional in view of

[1] W. Pannenberg, *op. cit.*, p. 101 n. 18; *Dogma und Denkstruktur*, 1963, pp. 108f.
and n. 28.

that end of history in which the wholeness of reality will come to light.

For hermeneutics, this results in the principle that the texts which come to us from history are not to be examined merely in regard to the possibilities of existence in the several existences that have been, but have to be read in terms of their historical place and their historical time, in terms of their own historical connections before and after. The connection between then and now does not result from the perpetual finitude and historicality of human existence, but from the context of universal history which links the past with the present. The temporal, historical difference between then and now is not bridged by tracing past and present possibilities back to human existence as such, but is preserved, and yet at the same time also bridged, by the context of events that joins them both together. 'That is to say, the text can be understood only in the context of the comprehensive history which joins the past with the present – and indeed not merely with the present that today exists, but with the future horizon of present possibilities, because the meaning of the present becomes clear only in the light of the future.'[1] 'Only a conception of the course of history which does in fact join the past situation with the present and with its future horizon can provide the comprehensive horizon in which the limited present horizon of the expositor and the historical horizon of the text blend together.[2] 'Then' and 'now' are united while still preserving their peculiarity and their difference, when they 'become elements in the unity of a context of history which embraces them both'.[3] Since this comprehensive context of history can be expressed in the midst of history only in terms of a finite, provisional and therefore revisable perspective, it remains fragmentary in view of the open future.

Here it is considered necessary to give expression to 'God' in the totality of reality, and yet at the same time it is admitted to be impossible to comprehend an as yet unfinished and therefore historic reality as a 'totality'. It would therefore be better to abandon the intentions of the cosmological proof of God. As long as the reality of the world and of man in it is not yet 'whole', but its totality is historically at stake, there can be no

[1] W. Pannenberg, 'Hermeneutik und Universalgeschichte', *ZTK* 60, 1963, p. 116.   [2] *Ibid.*   [3] *Ibid.*

proof of God from it. The 'comprehensive context of history' which joins 'then' and 'now', the historical horizon and the present future horizon, is not the context of an interelated chain of events, but is a context of the history of mission and promise. The horizons do not already 'blend together' in the question as to the connection between the events of then and now, but only in the question of the intended future then and now. It is because the inadequate present raises the question of the future that past intentions, hopes and visions of the future are called to mind. In reformations and revolutions past positions towards the future are taken up. It is not only a case of the future of the present but, if this future is to be universal and eschatological, always a case also of the future of the past and the future of the dead. It is not that a 'context of history' merely 'unveils' the truth of all reality,[1] but the compiling of history 'leads', and intends to lead, to the truth of reality. The future horizon about which the present asks cannot be understood as a horizon within which to interpret the hitherto existing reality of the world in world history hitherto, but only as a horizon of promise and mission towards a new, future reality, in which everything attains to truth, to rest and to authenticity. The 'sense of the present', which is disclosed only in the light of the future, does not lie in assigning the present its place in the course of history hitherto, but its 'sense' lies in its promise and its task, its break-away from the reality that has been and is, to a new reality. The wholeness and unity of reality which is sought in terms of universal history does not result from the simple course of the world process which, one day at the last, will make reality a rounded whole, but the 'wholeness' and 'unity' of reality must, as compared with all existing reality, be a new reality in which all things become new and whole. The saved world which will prove God's divinity is one our thoughts and hopes do not yet reach at the point where we have thought history to its end, but only where God 'will be all in all'. This, in biblical terms, is the ἀνακεφαλαίωσις τῶν πάντων in which even the dead are not secure but return and rise again. It is a new reality, which does not put the finishing touch to the reality of history up to then, but so to speak rolls it up. That is

---

[1] W. Pannenberg, 'Hermeneutik und Universalgeschichte', *ZTK* 60, 1963, p. 119 n. 37.

why there is sense in asking about the future of past people
and things – not merely in order to bring the light of understanding into the dark field of history, but in order to 'kindle
in the past the spark of hope'.

(*c*) The *proof of God from 'God'* is the ontological proof of God.
It derives from Anselm of Canterbury. It was not rejected by
Kant, but it was Hegel who first made it once more the foundation of the concept of God. It is no accident that Karl Barth,
in the book on Anselm (1931) which is so important for his
own theology, took it up in a new form and combined it with
his own concept of the self-revelation of God. This proof of the
existence of God from the concept of God – 'something beyond
which nothing greater can be conceived' – or from the name or
self-revelation of God, does not assert that on the ground of
what we can learn of the reality of the world, or on the ground
of what we can ourselves experience of the reality of existence,
we must necessarily conceive of God or ask about God if we
are to be able to make clear the truth about the world and about
human nature. It says merely that whoever conceives of God
must necessarily also conceive of his existence. It has its presupposition not in a specific world-picture or a specific understanding of human nature, but in the fact that man – even the
godless man – 'hears', that he makes room in his mind for the
concept of God and has God's name, or his self-revelation in
his name, proclaimed to him. It is not necessary to conceive of
God, but if we do conceive of him, then we must conceive of
him as necessary. God is known only through 'God'. Only in
his light do we see light.

According to the hermeneutic principles which this involves,
all exegesis of historical Bible texts must have its source in the
undemonstrable event of the happening of that word in which
God is known through God, in which God himself speaks and
reveals himself. This to be sure, in contrast to the possibilities
so far discussed, is a 'starting point in the indisposable',[1] but
nevertheless implies hermeneutic and historical consequences.
In the preface to the first edition of his *Romans* in 1919, Karl
Barth still expressed these consequences in Platonic terms: 'But
my whole attention was directed towards looking *through* the

[1] G. Eichholz, 'Der Ansatz Karl Barths in der Hermeneutik', in *Antwort, K.
Barth zum 70. Gerburtstag*, 1956, p. 63.

historical to the Spirit of the Bible, who is the eternal Spirit.
. . . The understanding of history is a continuing, ever more
honest and ever more urgent conversation between the wisdom
of yesterday and the wisdom of tomorrow, which is one and
the same.'¹ In the preface to the second edition in 1921 it is
said that we should conscientiously determine what stands in
the text, and reflect upon it, i.e. wrestle with it until the wall
between the first century and our own becomes transparent,
until Paul speaks there and man hears here, until the conversation between text and reader is concentrated wholly on the
substance (which cannot be any different there and here!). 'In
seeking to understand I must advance to the point where it is
wellnigh only the riddle of the *substance* that confronts me, and
really no longer the riddle of the *text* as such, where I therefore
wellnigh forget that it is not I who am the author, where I
have understood him wellnigh so perfectly that I can let him
speak in my name and can myself speak in his name.'² But what
is the 'substance' that could bring about this blending together
of text and reader, author and hearer? What was then called
'substance and text' is in Barth later 'Word and words'. Before
all our methods of appropriating what is said in the text, and
before all blending together of the horizons then and now,
there stands in Barth the great event 'that God himself speaks',
that the 'substance' of the texts is this word in which God
reveals himself and proclaims or proves himself. Only this
event – that God proves himself in the word he speaks to man,
and thus the proof of God from God takes place in God's
word – can be the ultimate goal of all historical and theological
exegesis and bring about the blending together of times and
persons. This would mean, for 'history', that the presupposition
and goal of exegesis is not to be seen in the historic character
of existence, nor in a universal historical context, but that the
problem of the biblical stories and words lies in the fact of the
history of God in Christ for men having taken place. This
history is to be grasped neither in historical or universal historical terms, nor in terms of the history of existence, but is only
to be repeated as the kerygmatic history of God for men. The
goal of exegesis is therefore neither a believing self-under-

¹ Now in *Anfänge der dialektischen Theologie* I, ed. J. Moltmann, 1962, p. 77.
² *Ibid.* I, p. 112.

standing nor an orientation in terms of universal history, but is proclamation. The 'word of God' in the words urges us on from the exegesis of the 'words' to the proclamation of the word. Thus the place of the hermeneutic key provided by the historic character of existence is here taken by the 'history of God *for* men'. The place of the word-character of existence is taken by the sovereignty of the divine word.

As with the other proofs of God, so too the ontological proof is really a piece of anticipated *eschaton*. For that 'God proves himself through God', and that 'God is God', must undeniably imply that 'God is all in all' and that he proves his divinity in all that is and all that is not. Of this omnipotent divinity of God, however, the only sign we have here in history is the foreglow of the raising of Christ from the dead. That God is God accordingly cannot be the eternal source and background of the proclamation of Christ, but must be the promised, but as yet unattained, future goal of Christian proclamation. Barth's very expressions in their originally Platonic terms of the 'eternal Spirit' and the eternally self-identical 'substance' of the Bible show a tendency towards uneschatological, and then also unhistorical, thinking which is still to be met even in the later terms of the word of God and his self-revelation. 'The Word' in 'the words' can, rightly understood, only have an apocalyptic sense and mean the 'Word' which here in history is only to be witnessed to, only to be hoped for and expected, the 'Word' which God will one day speak as he has promised. That exegesis should lead to proclamation if it rightly follows the intentions of the text, cannot be grounded in the transcendent background of the self-revelation of God, but only in the fact that the once-for-all event of the resurrection of Christ leads to an eschatological, missionary necessity of the proclamation to all peoples. This is possible only within an eschatological horizon, but not on the ground of an eternal self-revelation of God. An onto-theological argument for the proclamation can lead to levelling down the different historic tasks and horizons of Christian mission in the ages of history.

2. *Mission and Exposition*

All proofs of God are at bottom anticipations of that eschatological reality in which God is revealed in all things to all.

They assume this reality as already present and as immediately perceptible to every man. The hermeneutic principles developed from them take the presence of God which can be demonstrated, experienced or perceived from the world, from existence or from the proclaimed name of God – were it even only because of the necessity of asking about him – and make it the point of reference for the exposition and appropriation of the historic witness of the Bible.

A 'natural theology' of this kind, however, in which God is manifest and demonstrable to every man, is not the presupposition of Christian faith, but the future goal of Christian hope. This universal and immediate presence of God is not the source from which faith comes, but the end to which it is on the way. It is not the ground on which faith stands, but it is the object at which it aims. It is only on the ground of the revelation of God in the event of promise constituted by the raising of the crucified Christ that faith must seek and search for the universal and immediate revelation of God in all things and for all. The world which proves God's divinity, and the existence which is necessarily exercised by the question of God, are here sketches for the future on the part of Christian hope. They are anticipations of the as yet unattained future land in which God is all in all. They are anthropological and cosmological sketches on the part of Christian faith, in which the God of Jesus Christ is 'imputed' or given over to all men and all reality as the God of all men and of the whole of reality. This is possible, as long as reality and the people in it are on the move in history. It is necessary, in order to outline the universal future horizon of Christian mission. Without such sketches, which involve the whole of reality and shed a meaningful light on the existence and determination of all men, Christianity would become a sect and faith would become a private religion. Such interpretations of the whole of reality and of authentic human nature, however, remain 'sketches', whose goal is the universe and the human nature that are promised and will be. They are historic and subject to change, and always depend upon the movement of the Christian mission. *Theologia naturalis* is at bottom *theologia viatorum*, and *theologia viatorum* will always concern itself with the future *theologia gloriae* in the form of fragmentary sketches.

(a) The Hermeneutics of the Apostolate

The real point of reference for the exposition and appropriation of the historic Bible witness, and the one that is their motive and driving force, lies in the mission of present Christianity, and in the universal future of God for the world and for all men, towards which this mission takes place.

The key to the hermeneutics of the historic witness of the Bible is the 'future of scripture'. The question as to the correct exposition of the Old and New Testament scriptures cannot be addressed to the 'heart of scripture'. The biblical scriptures are not a closed organism with a heart, or a closed circle with a centre. On the contrary, all the biblical scriptures are open towards the future fulfilment of the divine promise whose history they relate. The centre of the New Testament scriptures is the future of the risen Christ, which they announce, point forward to and promise. Thus if we are to understand the biblical scriptures in their proclamation, their understanding of existence and their understanding of the world, then we must look in the same direction as they themselves do. The scriptures, as historic witnesses, are open towards the future, as all promises are open towards the future. In this sense R. Bultmann is right when he declares: 'It is not at all "in themselves", nor yet as links in a causal chain, that events or historical figures are historic phenomena. They are such only *in their relationship to the future,* for which they have significance and for which the present has responsibility.'[1] 'Thus it is true also of scripture that it is what it is only in relation to its history and its future.'[2] Only, this 'future of scripture' does not yet lie in the several readers' own present, but in that which gives the momentary present its orientation towards a universal, eschatological future. Hence present perception of the 'future of scripture' takes place in that mission which plays its part in history and in the possibilities of changing history. The biblical witness is witness to a historic forward-moving mission in the past, and hence in the light of the present mission it can be understood for what it really is.

The point of reference and the aim in the exposition of the biblical witness is not something universal which lies at the

---

[1] R. Bultmann, *Glauben und Verstehen* III, p. 113.   [2] *Ibid.,* p. 140.

bottom of history or at the bottom of existence and keeps everything moving, but the concrete, present mission of Christianity
towards the future of Christ for the world. One could also say
that the point of reference in true, historic and eschatological
exposition of the Bible is the reconciliation of the godless, if
the reconciliation of the godless is understood to mean also the
calling of the heathen to participation in the historic mission
of Christianity. The link between coming history and past
history is provided in the light of this forward-moving, historic
mission. The connection between then and now in the history
of tradition is a connection in the history of promise and of
mission, for tradition, as Christians understand it, means mission that moves forwards and outwards. The word-event in
which past events are brought to expression means the event of
being called to the future of salvation in Christ and to the
present labour of hope in the service of reconciliation. It is only
in mission and promise, in the charge committed and the prospect opened, in the labour of hope, that the 'meaning of history' is grasped in a historic way and one that keeps history
moving. The link between past history and coming history is
not then supplied on the ground of an abstractly ascertained
substance of history, nor yet on the ground of the perpetual
'historicality' of human existence. The missionary direction is
the only constant in history. For in the front-line of present
mission new possibilities for history are grasped and inadequate realities in history left behind. Eschatological hope and
mission thus make men's reality 'historic'. The revelation of
God in the event of promise reveals, effects and provokes that
open history which is grasped in the mission of hope. It takes
the reality in which men live together and establish themselves,
and makes it a process of history – namely, a judicial process
concerning the truth and righteousness of life.

   The human nature of man becomes historic inasmuch as the
determination of man comes to light in historic mission.

   The reality of the world becomes historic inasmuch as in this
mission it is seen to be the field of the missionary charge and is
examined in search of real possibilities for the world-transforming missionary hope.

   God is revealed in this mission as the God who calls and
promises. He proves his existence not in terms of man's already

existing question about God, not in terms of the question as to the unity of the existing world, nor yet by means of the concept of God, but he proves his existence and his divinity by making possible the historic and eschatological possibilities of mission.

Thus the questions of true human nature, of the unity of the world and of the divinity of God are removed from the sphere of an illusionary *theologia naturalis*. These questions are raised, and answered, in the midst of the movement of mission. They are questions of the *theologia viatorum*.

(b) The Humanizing of Man in the Missionary Hope

The dominant question of all anthropology – who or what is man? who am I? – does not arise in the biblical narratives from comparing man with the animals or with the things of the world. Nor does it arise simply *coram Deo*, as Augustine and the Reformers affirmed. Rather, it arises in face of a divine mission, charge and appointment which transcend the bounds of the humanly possible. Thus Moses (Ex. 3.11) asks in face of his call to lead the exodus of the Israelites from Egypt: 'Who am I, that I should go unto Pharaoh, and that I should bring forth the children of Israel out of Egypt?' Thus, too, Isaiah (Isa. 6.5) in face of his call recognizes himself to be personally guilt-laden in the midst of a guilt-laden people: 'Woe is me! for I am undone; because I am a man of unclean lips, and I dwell in the midst of a people of unclean lips.' Thus Jeremiah in face of his call recognizes what he is and what he was: 'Ah, Lord God! behold, I cannot speak: for I am a child' (Jer. 1.6). Self-knowledge here comes about in face of the mission and call of God, which demand impossibilities of man. It is knowledge of self, knowledge of men and knowledge of guilt, knowledge of the impossibility of one's own existence in face of the possibilities demanded by the divine mission. Man attains to knowledge of himself by discovering the discrepancy between the divine mission and his own being, by learning what he is, and what he is to be, yet of himself cannot be. Hence the answer received to man's question about himself and his human nature runs: 'I will be with thee.' This does not tell man what he was and what he really is, but what he will be and can be in that history and that future to which the mission leads him. In his call man is given the prospect of a new ability to be.

What he is and what he can do, is a thing he will learn in
hopeful trust in God's being with him. Man learns his human
nature not from himself, but from the future to which the
mission leads him. What man is, is told him only by history,
declared W. Dilthey. We can here accept this statement, if we
add: the history to which the missionary hope leads him. The
real mystery of his human nature is discovered by man in the
history which discloses to him his future. In this very history of
missionary possibilities which are as yet unknown and as yet
unlimited, it comes to light that man is not an 'established
being', that he is open to the future, open for new, promised
possibilities of being. The very call to the possibilities of the
future which are as yet obscure, makes it clear that man is
hidden from himself, a *homo absconditus*, and will be revealed to
himself in those prospects which are opened up to him by the
horizons of mission. The mission and call do not reveal man
simply to himself, with the result that he can then understand
himself again for what he really is. They reveal and open up to
him new possibilities, with the result that he can become what
he is not yet and never yet was. This is why according to Old
and New Testament usage men receive along with their call a
new name, and with their new name a new nature and a new
future.

Now in the Old Testament such calls and commissions are
particular and contingent. They relate to a single people and
a few prophets and kings. They contain specific historic charges.
Hence they do not yet provide any clue to the human nature of
man as such. In the New Testament, however, mission and call
are directed 'without distinction' to Jews and Gentiles. The
call to hope and to participation in the mission here becomes
universal. The gospel call contains the summons to the eschatological hope of final and universal salvation. The gospel call
is here identical with the reconciliation of the godless and with
the instituting of believing obedience among all men. If, however, the gospel summons all men to the hope and the mission
of the future of Christ, then it is possible in the light of this
particular event to reflect also on the general structures of
human nature. For indeed the believer does not understand
himself as the adherent of a religion which is one possibility
among others, but as being on the way to true humanity, to

that which is appointed for all men. That is why he cannot present his truth to others as 'his' truth, but only as 'the truth'. The concrete humanity disclosed by the Christian mission must therefore enter into debate with the universal definitions of humanity in philosophic anthropology, and for its part also outline general structures of human nature, in which the future of faith shines as a foreglow of the future of all men. The gospel call is addressed to all men and promises them a universal eschatological future. It is delivered 'in all openness' and must therefore also assume open responsibility for its hope for the future of man. A Christian anthropology will always insist that a general, philosophic anthropology understand human nature in terms of history and conceive its historic character in the light of its future. What man is in body and soul, in partnership and society, in the domination of nature, is disclosed in its reality only from the direction of the life he lives. Human nature first becomes really determinable in the light of the determination to which it is on the way. The comparison with nature and with the animals, or the comparison with other men in the present and in history, does not yet bring out what man's nature is, but only the comparison with the future possibilities which are disclosed to him from the direction of his life, from his *intentio vitalis*. Man has no subsistence in himself, but is always on the way towards something and realizes himself in the light of some expected future whole. Man's nature is not sub-sistent, but ex-sistent. It becomes intelligible not on the ground of an underlying *substantia hominis*, but only from the perspectives in which he lives and which derive from his direction in body and soul. Man is 'open towards the world' only in that he is directionally open to determination and to the future. In other words, the *natura hominis* first emerges from the *forma futurae vitae*. It is in process of developing in the light of this 'shape of the future life', and its success in attaining to it is staked on history. Hoping in the promised new creation by God, man here stands *in statu nascendi*, in the process of his being brought into being by the calling, coaxing, compelling word of God.

A missionary exposition of the biblical witness to man's history and mission will therefore agree with the existentialist interpretation in enquiring about the new possibilities which entered the world through Israel and Christianity. It, too, will have to present these past existential possibilities as possibilities of the present understanding of existence. But it will interpret these existential possibilities as new possibilities for man's future. It will not interpret the phenomena of past history on the ground of the possibilities of human existence, but on the contrary, it will interpret the new possibilities of human existence on the basis of the 'phenomenon' of God's promise and mission and of the 'phenomenon' of the resurrection and future of Christ. It will be able to open up to man today new possibilities, prospects and goals through its exposition of that event which paves the way for the eschatological future. To this end it is necessary to take man in his selfhood along with, and not in abstraction from, the present constellation of human society, in order to subject the whole of present human reality to the future of Christ and to the possibilities of the mission that moves towards his future. The whole present situation must be understood in all its historic possibilities and tasks in the light of the future of the truth.

(c) *The Historifying of the World in the Christian Mission*

It is not mere *theoria*, in its investigation of the divine nature of the world as a cosmos, but it is only missionary practice, involved in history and bent on transformation, that first renders the world questionable in a historic way. Its questions are concerned not with the unity and wholeness of the world and with the order in a chaotic reality, but with the transformability of the world. For the eschatological hope shows that which is possible and transformable in the world to be meaningful, and the practical mission embraces that which is now within the bounds of possibility in the world. The theory of world-transforming, future-seeking missionary practice does not search for eternal orders in the existing reality of the world, but for possibilities that exist in the world in the direction of the promised future. The call to obedient moulding of the world would have no object, if this world were immutable. The God who calls and promises would not be God, if he were not the God and Lord of that reality into which his mission leads, and if he could not create real, objective possibilities for his mission. Thus the transforming mission requires in practice a certain *Weltanschauung*, a confidence in the world and a hope for the world. It seeks for that which is really, objectively possible in this world, in order to grasp it and realize it in the direction of the promised future of the righteousness, the life and the kingdom of God. Hence it regards the world as an open process in which the salvation and destruction, the righteousness and annihilation of the world are at stake. To the eye of mission, not only man is open to the future, full of all kinds of possibilities, but the world, too, is a vast container full of future and of boundless possibilities for good and for evil. Thus it will continually strive to understand world reality in terms of history on the basis of the future that is in prospect. It will therefore not search, like the Greeks, for the nature of history and for the enduring in the midst of change, but on the contrary for the history of nature and for the possibilities of changing the enduring. It does not ask about the hidden wholeness by which this world, as it is, is intrinsically held together, but about the future *totum* in which everything that is here in flux and threatened by annihilation will be complete and whole. The totality of the world is not here seen as a self-dependent cosmos of nature, but as the goal of a world history which can be understood only in dynamic terms. The world thus appears as a correlate of hope. Hope alone really takes into account the 'earnest expectation of the creature' for its freedom and truth. The obedience that comes of hope and mission forms the bridge between that which is promised and hoped for and the real possibilities of the reality of the world. The call and mission of the 'God of hope' suffer man no longer to live amid surrounding nature, and no longer in the world as his home, but compel him to exist within the horizon of history. This horizon fills him with hopeful expectation, and at the same time requires of him responsibility and decision for the world of history.

The man who is summoned by the divine promise to the transforming of the world falls outside the sphere of Greek cosmic thinking. He has here 'no continuing city', for he seeks 'the coming city of God'. His thinking will therefore not subject reality to a metaphysical transfiguration in the light of the absolute. His thinking is not directed towards mediating between the multiplicity of beings and the one, eternal being.

His experience of reality as history in all its possibilities of change is not, on the other hand, conditioned by whether history can be made at the whim of the human subject. For

him, the world can be changed by the God of his hope, and to
that extent also by the obedience to which this hope moves him.
The subject of the transformation of the world is for him therefore the Spirit of the divine hope. Thus his experience and his
expectation of history is both opened up and tied down by the
future promises of the God he believes. World reality therefore
does not become for him, as in the modern age, the material for
the exercise of duty or of technique. His thinking about the
world does not adjust things to the human subject in his imagined needs or his arbitrary prescriptions. His thinking ad-
justs things to the coming messianic reconciliation. Hence both
his world-transforming obedience and also his knowledge of,
and reflection on, the world stand 'in the service of reconciliation'. He does not take being, as it is, and link it in metaphysical
transfiguration with the absolute. He does not link things, as in
technical positivism, with his own subjectivity. Rather, he ad-
justs being to the universal, rectifying future of God. Thus his
mediation serves the reconciliation of the world with God. His
understanding does not consist in contemplating things in search
of their eternal ground. His understanding does not consist in
practical reflections on the technical appropriation of things.
His understanding consists in the fact that in sympathy with
the misery of being he anticipates the redeeming future of
being and so lays the foundation of its reconciliation, justification and stability. Thus Luther declares: '. . . a strange language and a new grammar. . . . For his will is, because we are
to be new men, that we should also have other and new thoughts,
minds and understandings and not regard anything in the light
of reason, as it is for the world, but as it is before his eyes, and
take our cue from the future, invisible, new nature for which
we have to hope and which is to come after this wretched and
miserable nature. . . .'[1] In this sense it is also possible to take
up the concluding words of T. W. Adorno's *Minima Moralia,
Reflexionen aus dem beschädigten Leben*: 'Philosophy, in the only
form in which it can still be responsibly upheld in face of
despair, would be the attempt to regard all things as they present themselves from the standpoint of redemption. Knowledge has no light save that which shines upon the world from
the standpoint of redemption: all else exhausts itself in imita-

[1] *WA* 34, II, pp. 48of.

tion and remains a piece of technique. Perspectives must be created in which the world looks changed and alien and reveals its cracks and flaws in much the same way as it will one day lie destitute and disfigured in Messiah's light. To attain such perspectives without arbitrariness or force, entirely out of sensitiveness towards things – that alone is the aim of thought.'[1]

In the field of the investigation and presentation of past history this would surely mean that the historian's aim can be neither a theodicy of history nor a self-justification of past or present history. The glory and misery of past ages do not require to contain the justification of God or of reason. Nor can they abide the positivisitic dictatorship of present subjectivity. Rather, the 'earnest expectation of the creature' seeks to come to expression in them and to attain the prospect of freedom from the powers of annihilation. In the messianic light of hopeful reason the historian must make manifest something of the 'cracks and flaws' in which past ages earnestly expect their justification and redemption. Then there is solidarity between the present and the ages of the past, and a certain contemporaneousness both in the historic alienation and in the eschatological hope. This solidarity is the true core of similarity, on the ground of which an analogical understanding becomes possible over the ages. Only this solidarity in the earnest expectation which groans under the tyranny of the negative and hopes for liberating truth, takes historic account of history and performs among the dead shades of history the service of reconciliation.

(d) *The Tradition of the Eschatological Hope*

Traditions are alive and binding, current and familiar, where, and as long as, they are taken as a matter of course and as such link fathers to sons in the course of the generations and provide continuity in time. Where this unquestioned familiarity and trustworthiness becomes problematical, an essential element in the traditions is already lost. Where reflection sets in and subjects the traditions to critical questioning, with the result that the accepting or rejecting of them becomes a conscious act, the traditions lose their propitious force. It is not only when traditions are discarded, but as soon as they are made consciously problematical, that the character of tradition

[1] T. W. Adorno, *Minima Moralia*, 1962, pp. 333f.

attaching to human life is abrogated. For the traditions are then no longer the guardian and the subject of present thought and action, but become the object of a kind of thinking which in itself and in its roots is traditionless. They can then be rejected by the revolutionary, or restored by the conservative. But from the day that we speak 'conservatively' of tradition, we no longer have it.[1]

The beginning and principle of the modern break with tradition is the basing of assured knowledge upon the method of doubt since Descartes. If the Western mind even up to modern times had been fashioned by the texts of our traditions, now – beginning already in the late Middle Ages – it develops from its own experience and the methodical assimilation of its own experience. This is for Pascal the point at which the paths of theology and modern science divide: 'When we perceive this distinction clearly, then we shall lament the blindness of those who in physics allow the validity of tradition alone, instead of reason and experiment; we shall be horrified at the error of those who in theology put the arguments of reason in place of the tradition of scripture and the fathers.'[2] Theology can teach only on the ground of the word given in tradition. But in the realms in which truth is now sought in order to be the ground for human social life, traditions become the epitome of inherited prejudice – *idola*, as Francis Bacon put it. The place of the historic forms of the spirit which live in and from traditions is taken by the abstract self-assurance of the human mind: *sum cogitans*. For the human mind the *res gestae* of history are in principle no different from the *res extensae* of nature. Hence in the field of history, too, it will seek for methodically assured, critical historical experience. This non-historic concept of reason makes traditions into accidental truths of history and finds eternal truths of reason in itself. Past history, for it, is no longer called to mind in traditions, but is 'historicized' by means of scientific reflection. 'The historical relation to the past not only presupposes that the past in question is past, but has manifestly also itself the effect of confirming and sealing this non-actuality of what has been. Historical science has taken the place of

[1] G. Krüger, *Freiheit und Weltverwaltung*, 1958, p. 223.
[2] Pascal, *Œuvres* II, p. 133, quoted by J. Pieper, *Über den Begriff der Tradition*, 1957, pp. 10f.

tradition, and this means that it occupies that place and makes it . . . impossible really to follow the ancients and thus to stand in their tradition.'[1] The historical reason is then well able to abolish traditions, but not to create new traditions. 'The pressure which tradition pre-consciously exercises on our behaviour is progressively diminished in history as a result of the advancing *science* of history.'[2]

This historical relation to history undoubtedly brings in the first instance a break with tradition whose full effects are as yet immeasurable. It is in the first instance a break with quite definite traditions of the West. The question is, however, whether we have here also a break with tradition as a characteristic feature of human existence as such. But with the beginning of the modern age the emancipated reason undergoes new experiences of history, which collapse the received edifice of tradition. The voyages of discovery to America and China bring a knowledge of peoples who cannot be classified in the classical Christian genealogies of mankind. The reason that has become sure of itself in reflection makes discoveries in nature, which antiquate the old world-picture. And finally, it produces in society new economic forms and modes of civil behaviour which destroy the traditional Christian ethic. The French revolution merely executed the testament of the Enlightenment, and was in its turn continued by the industrial revolution and our scientific technical civilization. The support of traditions and authorities, and the connection with the truth as received from of old, which was so essential for the traditional consciousness, have here no longer any constitutive significance. The place of quotation is taken by successful experiment and successful technique. As producer and consumer and in the traffic of everyday, man is the same everywhere, apart from his varied origins. Sciences and techniques thus become independent and indifferent towards the distinctions in historic origin.

These prospects have always led traditionalists, from romanticism to the present day, to paint nihilistic nightmare visions. 'If tradition were really entirely destroyed, if nihilism were

---

[1] G. Krüger, *op. cit.*, p. 216.
[2] M. Scheler, *Die Stellung des Menschen im Kosmos*, 1927, p. 31. Cf. H. G. Gadamer's criticism in *Wahrheit und Methode*, 1960, p. 267.

complete, if there were nothing at all that still endures, the
self-evident, common foundations of our human nature could
no longer be appealed to at all.'[1] The self-existent world resolves itself into mere subjective views of the world, so that in the
end nothing more would exist in itself and nihilism would be
the end of the story.[2] Then we should find ourselves in an age
'which is overtaken by the loss of tradition altogether, as a
disastrous fate, as a disappearance of support and security, as a
vanishing of all that is enduring, as a suffocating emptiness and
annihilation in the realm of spiritual life.'[3] This romantico-
nihilistic argument for the necessary readmittance of traditions,
however, is not able to integrate the 'modern age' into the
traditions of history, because it does not grasp the new kind of
progressiveness in modern ways of thinking and working. It has
regard only to the loss of origin, but does not see the gain of a
possible future in the breakaway of the modern age. Hence the
realm of history, which the modern age with its visions has
opened up before us, must be restricted again by building dams
against the overflowing charms of 'historicality'. This, however,
is to make traditions a matter of form. It is not known what
traditions are adequate to master the modern age's break with
tradition, but it is recommended that thought and action
should be marked by tradition as such.

The real mainspring of the emancipation of reason and society from the guardianship and dominance of tradition, however, lies in the eschatological, messianic passion of the 'modern
age'. The 'old' was left behind, because the presence and prospect of the 'new' appeared to have come within reach. The
hopes that had been bottled up by the old, classical traditions
put forth new life and began to influence the future of history.
'Secularization' was no apostasy from the traditions and
ordinances of Christianity, but meant in the first instance that
Christian expectations were realized in the field of world history,
and then that Christian hopes were outstripped by millenarian-

---

[1] G. Krüger, *op. cit.*, p. 123, cf. also p. 94: '*It is due only to our inconsistency that we are still alive* – to the fact that we have not really silenced all tradition. But our life is becoming visibly more historic, more frail, more catastrophic. We are on the way towards the *radical impossibility of a meaningful, common life*. . . . Under these circum-stances it is vitally necessary to break with this paradoxical, restless epoch and *once more assent to tradition in principle.*'

[2] R. Geiselmann, *Die heilige Schrift und die Tradition*, 1962, p. 81.

[3] G. Ebeling, *Die Geschichtlichkeit der Kirche*, 1954, p. 36.

ism. It was not that the 'horrors of history' overflowed the dams of the old traditions and their bonds, but that the hope that had been domesticated within them broke loose. The place of the accustomed traditions was taken by a messianism of varying content which set to work upon history. Hence we cannot set out from the assumption that the 'modern age' is really only a different age, and that the modern historical consciousness is nothing radically new, but merely constitutes a new element within that which has always determined man's attitude to the past.[1] We shall discover the element of tradition in historical thinking only when we take seriously the revolutionary and indeed millenarian elements in it. Hence we must ask: *which* traditions were broken down in the upheaval of the modern age, and what was the concept of tradition against which the revolutionary *ratio* has been able to prevail? What is the tradition of the Christian proclamation, and what does it demand of man? To this end we shall have to make a very clear distinction between the ancient classical concepts of tradition and the Christian concept of tradition, both in regard to their different content and in regard to their different modes of procedure.

The anti-revolutionary, anti-rationalistic concept of tradition in romanticism everywhere shows itself to be a restoration of the ancient classical way of thinking about tradition. Here religion and participation in the divine are bound to the tradition that has existed unbrokenly from of old.

In the ancient way of thinking about tradition,[2] the passing ages are regenerated in the times of sacred festival. Each festival and each liturgical season brings once more the time of the beginning, the time of the origin, *in principio*. The profane time of the passing and flowing away of life is halted as it were in the times of festival. The world's time renews itself each year. With each new year it acquires its original holiness again. In the times of festival men periodically become contemporaries of the gods once more and live with them again as in the first beginning. History here means falling away from the origin and degenerating from the holiness of the beginning. Tradition means the bringing back of fallen life to the primaeval age and the first origin. Primaeval mythical events are here presented.

---

[1] H. G. Gadamer, *op. cit.*, p. 267.
[2] On this section cf. the studies of M. Eliade.

For this conception of tradition, 'truth' is always bound up
with 'the old'. The prerogative of tradition is expressed in the
phrase 'from of old'.

Similarly, it is held in the classical way of thinking about
tradition that the *antiqui*, the ancestors, the *majores*, οἱ παλαιοί,
οἱ ἀρχαῖοι, are 'near the beginning, prime, original'. Authority
belongs to those 'who are better than we and dwell nearer to the
gods'.[1] 'The ancients know the truth. If we discovered it, then
we should have no need to trouble ourselves about the opinions
of men.[2] 'A gift of the gods was brought down by a certain
Prometheus in the bright glow of fire, and the ancients, who are
better than we and dwell nearer to the gods, have transmitted
this account to us.'[3] In the phrase πάλαι λέγεται, 'it was said
of old', lies the proof of the truth. 'It has been handed down
from those of early and primaeval days that the divine surrounds the whole of nature.'[4] Thus, in this conception of tradition, revelation stands at the beginning. It is from this that the
ancients who were before us and lived near the beginning
acquire their authority. It is also this which gives the old its
proved excellence and which requires its preservation. ἀνάμνησις
brings to mind again the true, original nature of things. Tradition is then μνημοσύνη, keeping in memory. To this there belongs the mythical idea of the θησαυρός, the treasure of original
truth which we have to guard, and of the *depositum*, the gift
entrusted to our charge.

On the quotation from Plato's *Philebus*, Joseph Pieper observes: 'The most important thing about his remark, however,
. . . is that this remark of Plato's is largely identical with the
answer which Christian theology for its part supplies to the same
question. When we consider the elements of Plato's characteriz-
ation of the ancients . . . then we must surely ask whether there
is any essential difference between Plato's description of the
ancients on the one hand, and on the other hand the definition
which Christian theology applies to the writer who is "inspired"
in the strict sense of the word, the author of the holy book. The
decisive feature in common is manifestly that both are conceived as the first recipients of a θεῖος λόγος, of a divine

---

[1] Plato, *Philebus* 16 c 5–9.
[2] Plato, *Phaedrus* 274 c 1, quoted in J. Pieper, *op. cit.*, p. 22.
[3] *Ibid.*   [4] Aristotle, *Metaphysics* 1074 b 1.

word.'[1] Yet is this really the case? Is the content of Greek tradition 'from of old' the same as the content of Christian proclamation? Are the apostles to be equated with Plato's primaeval ancients? Can the risen Christ be proclaimed in terms of the classical concept of tradition?

What tradition is, and how it comes about, all depends on the matter to be transmitted. The matter determines the tradition even to the extent of determining the process of tradition. In Israel it was not a primaeval mythical event that was handed down and called to mind *in principio*, but a historic event, and one which determined the nature, the life, the path and the history of Israel. When Israel remembered the 'days of ancient times' and the 'years of former generations', it was thinking not of a mythical, but of a historic past – namely, of the events of the exodus and the occupation of Canaan brought about by Yahweh. The men of old are not the primaeval ancients, but are the generation which received Yahweh's promises and experienced in history his acts of faithfulness. 'God' is here not the 'primaeval one', but the God of Abraham, of Isaac and of Jacob. The content of the tradition that was constitutive for Israel was the great acts and promises of Yahweh which are unique and unrepeatable, and therefore at the same time also determine Israel's future. Because Yahweh's acts of promise in the past open up a future to Israel – and a historic future at that – therefore the Israelite conception of tradition is not only to be interpreted in terms of retrospective questions, but at the same time also looks forwards. Yahweh's faithfulness in the past is recalled and recounted to the 'children of the future' (Ps. 78.6), in order that the 'people which shall be created' may praise Yahweh and recognize his lordship for their own present and future (Ps. 71.18; 102.18). Thus it is in order to awake confidence in Yahweh's faithfulness in the future that the historic experiences of former times are recounted. Yahweh's faithfulness is not a doctrine that has been received from the ancients of an early mythical age, but a history which must be recounted and can be expected. Thus this tradition comes from history, and its goal is future history. Now this goal itself can change in the course of Israel's history. Its aim is in the first instance the confident knowledge: such is Yahweh. As he was,

[1] J. Pieper, *op. cit.*, pp. 23f.

so he will be. This implies an element of repetition, yet not of
return to a mythical beginning, but of repetition in historic
faithfulness and constancy. If the great prophets introduce the
change which G. von Rad has called the 'eschatologizing of the
way of thinking in terms of history', then we can find in them
also an *eschatologizing of the way of thinking in terms of tradition.*
Prophecy, too, proceeds to construct a tradition. Yet it is a
construction of tradition in a new form. As the herald of history,
the prophetic word rouses men to wait on history. 'I will bind
up the testimony and seal the law among my disciples. And I
will wait upon the Lord, that hideth his face from the house of
Jacob, and I will look for him' (Isa. 8.16f.). The prophetic
word is preserved and written down 'that it may be a witness
for the time to come for ever and ever' (Isa. 30.8).[1]

To sum up the development of the conception of tradition
in Israel, it may be said that as compared with the classical
concept of tradition it has a strikingly firm, non-mythological
reference to past and future history. Promises are transmitted,
events of God's faithfulness are recounted, all pointing to the
future which has not as yet come about. In this conception of
tradition the future which is announced and promised increasingly dominates the present. This tradition of promise
turns our eyes not towards some primaeval, original event, but
towards the future and finally towards an *eschaton* of fulfilment.
We do not drift through history with our backs to the future and
our gaze returning ever and again to the origin, but we stride
confidently towards the promised future. It is not the primaeval
ancients who are near the truth and dwell nearer to the gods,
but it is to future generations that the promises are given, in
order that they may see the fulfilment.

As compared with the classical conception of tradition, the
Christian tradition of Christian proclamation has in the first
instance this much in common with the Old Testament understanding of tradition, (1) that here, too, the tradition is bound
to, and binds us to, a unique, unrepeatable, historic event –
namely, the raising of the crucified Christ – and (2) that the
process of tradition is necessitated and motivated by the future
horizon projected ahead of us 'once and for all' by this event.
Neither the once-for-all event of the resurrection of Christ

[1] Cf. H. W. Wolff, *EvTh* 20, 1960, p. 220 n. 3.

nor the eschatological future horizon of the Christian mission can be grasped by the ancient or the classical concept of tradition. Hence every formulation of the Christian tradition according to the standard of classical tradition – and since the days of anti-revolutionary romanticism such formulations have often arisen in Catholicism and frequently in Protestantism – is wrong. Both the Christian *tradendum*, or object to be transmitted, and the process of tradition in the Christian proclamation break these bounds.

(*a*) Christian proclamation begins with the raising of the crucified Christ and his exaltation to be Lord of the coming world of God. 'Christian tradition has existed ever since Easter, ever since there was a confession to the risen Lord and with it a Church.'[1] It can thus be said that Christian tradition was proclamation, and was transmitted in proclamation. Here we have a highly important distinction from the understanding of tradition both in classical and in rabbinical life. What distinguishes the proclamation of the gospel from tradition as it is there understood? Christian proclamation is not a tradition of wisdom and truth in doctrinal principles. Nor is it a tradition of ways and means of living according to the law. It is the announcing, revealing and publishing of an eschatological event.[2] It reveals the risen Christ's lordship over the world, and sets men free for the coming salvation in faith and hope. As proclamation, the gospel has to do with the advent of the coming lordship of Christ, and is itself an element in this advent. It reveals the presence of the coming Lord. This is why in Paul the proclamation of the gospel and the mission to the heathen in all the world are not derived from those who were there at the start and dwelt temporally nearer the divine, in other words from the apostles, but directly from the exalted Lord (Gal. 1.2ff.; I Cor. 9.1; I Cor. 15.8), in whose service he therefore knows himself to stand. His gospel accordingly does not seek to transmit doctrinal statements by or about Jesus, but to disclose the presence of the exalted and coming Lord. The process of the proclamation of the gospel, or of the revelation of this mystery, is therefore not described in the terminology of

[1] E. Dinkler, *RGG*[3] VI, col. 971.
[2] K. Wegenast, *Das Verständnis der Tradition bei Paulus und den Deuteropaulinen*, 1961, p. 44.

rabbinical tradition, but by new words like κηρύσσειν and
εὐαγγελίζεσθαι. 'Paul is no Christian rabbi who differs from
the teachers of late Judaism merely in regard to the content of
his tradition. Nor does his understanding of tradition result
from a mere spiritual refraction of the Jewish principle of tradition, but it is something specifically new among the conceptions
of tradition in the first century of our era.'¹ It is in understanding his gospel as the eschatological revelation of the exalted Lord that he gains the freedom which, as has often been
observed, he exercises over against the primitive Christian
tradition in doctrinal, confessional and parenetic statements.
This freedom does not, however, mean indifference on the
ground of personal inspiration. On the contrary, the gospel
which reveals the presence of the coming Lord requires a continuity with the earthly Jesus which has constantly to be discovered anew – for otherwise a myth about some new heavenly
being threatens to take the place of Jesus of Nazareth and the
gospel turns into gnostic talk of revelation. Historical knowledge
of Jesus must therefore be constitutive for the faith which awaits
the presence and future of God in the name of Jesus. It is this
identity of the exalted Christ with the earthly Jesus which in
the gospel and in the process of its proclamation links the eschatological with the historical, the apocalypse of the future with
the memory of the past. Hence for his gospel, which, as he
says, he received not from men but from the Lord, Paul requires the confirmation, and indeed the identification, of the
Jerusalem tradition of Jesus and Easter (cf. I Cor. 15.3ff.).
Not even this acceptance of historic tradition by Paul justifies
the assumption that he understood his gospel one way or another
in a traditional sense as tradition, but it plainly has christological grounds and thus means something new as compared with
his inherited conceptions of tradition or with those existing
elsewhere. The continuity of the risen Christ with the earthly,
crucified Jesus necessitates the acceptance of the historic witness about him and about what happened to him. The Easter
experiences of the raising of Jesus and his exaltation to be the
coming Lord, however, shatter any straightforward continuity
in the transmitting of the past. The fundamental process for

¹ K. Wegenast, *Das Verständnis der Tradition bei Paulus und den Deuteropaulinen*, 1961,
p. 164.

the gospel is not a continuity which has to be created in the history of transience and which results in endurance through the course of time, but it is the raising of the crucified and dead Christ to eschatological life. The fundamental process is not the surmounting of transience by something that is abiding, but it is the anticipation of the goal of history in the raising of the dead, it is the advent of the coming salvation, life, freedom and righteousness in the resurrection of Christ. It is understandable that this process which the gospel reveals must have a formative and determinative influence extending even to the process of the proclamation. The process of Christian proclamation thus implies a Christology. It cannot be deduced from the general problem of history and continuance. The gospel would be put to the service of foreign gods and ideologies if in the sense of modern romanticism it were expected to provide anti-revolutionary, Western continuity and a rescue for decaying civilizations.

(*b*) If the Christ event affects the process of proclamation even to the extent of determining the way it takes place, what is then the nature of this process? Christian proclamation shares with the Old Testament tradition its orientation towards the future. Tradition is forward-moving mission, into the new situation of the promised future. The new aspect in the Christian proclamation, however, lies in its universal mission to all peoples. Christian 'tradition' is mission that moves forwards and outwards. It does not ride the line of the generations from father to son, but spreads outwards to all men. It is not through birth, but through rebirth, that faith is propagated. And once again this is brought out with special clarity in the apostolate of Paul. Ever since his 'conversion' he has known that he is sent to the Gentile mission (Gal. 1.15f.; Rom. 1.5). Proclaiming the gospel and going to the heathen coincide for him.[1] Both have their ground in his understanding of Christ. The God who has raised Jesus from the dead is the God who justifies the godless. Just as all men are subject to sin, so Christ is the reconciliation of the whole world with God. In raising him from the dead, God has appointed Jesus to be Lord and Reconciler of the whole world. In the light of his understanding of the lordship of Christ as being universal and coming without any preconditions, we

[1] F. Hahn, *Das Verständnis der Mission im Neuen Testament*, 1964, pp. 80ff. (ET by F. Clarke: *Mission in the New Testament*, 1965, pp. 95ff.).

can understand both the universally inclusive character of his proclamation and also its peculiar, eschatologically anticipatory orientation. There is a certain Old Testament framework here: in the establishment of the obedience of faith among the heathen there already begins to happen what according to the Old Testament promise is to happen only after Israel has received salvation. There begins the eschatological glorification of God in the world. The fact that the order of the Israelite hope is thus changed, however, has its ground in the work and message of Jesus himself: the divine sovereignty which has drawn near becomes a live issue in his gracious communion with publicans and sinners, it arrives in the raising of the crucified one and becomes effectual in the justification of the godless. What is the result of this for the process of Christian proclamation, for its 'tradition'? Christian tradition is then not to be understood as a handing on of something that has to be preserved, but as an event which summons the dead and the godless to life. The process and procedure of the Christian proclamation is the calling of the heathen, the justification of the godless, the rebirth to a living hope. This is a creative event happening to what is vain, forsaken, lost, godless and dead. It can therefore be designated as a *nova creatio ex nihilo*, whose continuity lies solely in the guaranteed faithfulness of God. This continuity is to be seen not so much in the unbroken succession of bishops, but rather in the '*homuncio quispiam e pulvere emersus*', the 'little man of some kind fashioned from dust', as Calvin calls the presbyter.[1] The goal towards which Christian proclamation pro-ceeds in the process of the justification and calling of the godless, provides another clear indication of this: it is not the finally perfect triumph of that which has been approved and preserved unbroken from of old, but the 'raising of the dead', and the triumph of the resurrection life over death to the glory of the all-embracing lordship of God.

Christian tradition is proclamation of the gospel in justification of the godless. It is made possible and necessary by the raising of the crucified Christ, inasmuch as the hope of the universal future of salvation for the world is therein guaranteed. It is thus identical with eschatological mission.

---

[1] O. Noordmans, *Das Evangelium des Geistes*, 1960, p. 162, with a quotation from Calvin, *Institutio* IV.3.1.

278-79]   *Eschatology and History*   303

What significance does the above mentioned 'break with tradition' on the part of the modern age have for this tradition of Christian proclamation? What breaks down as a result of the emancipation of reason and society is the ancient and classical tradition in which the tradition of Christian proclamation was also embedded until modern times. Hence the tradition of Christian proclamation either collapses along with these traditions of the religious age, and is understood along with them as being now only a romanticist glorification of the past, or else it radically frees itself from this understanding of tradition. The Christian mission has no cause to enter into an alliance with romanticist nihilism against the revolutionary progressiveness of the modern age and to present its own tradition as a haven of traditionalism for a contemporary world now grown uncertain and weary of hoping. The emancipation of reason and society from their historic past is upheld in modern times by a millenarian enthusiasm. To this present world Christian proclamation must give an answer concerning its hope in the future of the crucified one (I Peter 3.15) by conveying to the godless justification and hope of resurrection. We cannot turn our backs on the open horizons of modern history and return to perpetual orders and everlasting traditions, but we must take these horizons up into the eschatological horizon of the resurrection and thereby disclose to modern history its true historic character.

V

EXODUS CHURCH

Observations on the Eschatological Understanding
of Christianity[1] in Modern Society

I. MODERN SOCIETY AND THE CULT OF THE ABSOLUTE

WE NOW RAISE in a concluding chapter the question of the concrete form assumed by a live eschatological hope in modern society. Here the title 'Exodus Church' is meant to focus attention on the reality of Christianity as that of the 'pilgrim people of God', as described in the Epistle to the Hebrews: 'Let us go forth therefore unto him without the camp, bearing his reproach. For here we have no continuing city, but we seek one to come' (Heb. 13.13f.). What does this mean for the social shape of Christianity in 'modern society' and for the task it has there to fulfil in the field of social ethics?

In this context we cannot speak simply of the 'Church' and mean by this the organized institution with all its public functions. Nor can we speak merely of the 'congregation' and thereby mean the company that gathers around the word and sacrament in divine service. We must follow the Reformation, and especially Luther, in speaking of 'Christianity' as represented in 'church' and 'congregation' and in Christians at their worldly callings. According to the Schmalkald Articles of 1537 'by the grace of God alone our churches are thus illumined and nurtured by the pure word and the right use of the sacrament and the knowledge of all kinds of stations and right works (*cognitione vocationum et verorum operum*)'.[2] This means, however, that Christianity must also continually present itself, and does *de facto* always present itself, in the weekday obedience

---

[1] 'Christianity' in this chapter is used not in the usual English sense of 'the Christian faith', but means the whole body of believers in every aspect of their life. – *Translator.*

[2] *Die Bekenntnisschriften der evangelisch-lutherischen Kirche*, 2nd ed. 1952, p. 411.

and the worldly callings of Christians and in their social roles. This third insight on the part of the Reformation has receded unduly into the background in the movements of the modern evangelical church towards reform. From the standpoint of sociology this is understandable, for modern, emancipated society seems to offer no chance for peculiarly Christian obedience. But from the standpoint of theology it is unintelligible, for it is precisely at this point, at which it is a question of the Christian's call in our social callings, that the decision falls as to whether Christians can become an accommodating group, or whether their existence within the horizon of eschatological hope makes them resist accommodation and their presence has something peculiar to say to the world.

When in this context we speak of *modern society*, we mean the society that has established itself with the rise of the modern industrial system. We mean, in negative terms, not the state and not the family, but that sphere of public life which is governed by the conduct of business, by production, consumption and commerce – the realm in which the relations between man and man are determined by the things of the business world and by the businesslike approach. Naturally, this social intercourse in terms of things and functions extends far into the spheres of political and family life, yet the reduction of all relationships to terms of things and facts does not have its origin in these spheres, but in the advancing possibilities of scientific, technical civilization. The society which is dominated by the modernity and progressiveness of this civilization has the peculiar characteristic of considering itself to be neutral towards matters of religion and questions of value and consequently emancipating itself from the control of history and tradition, whereby it also withdraws itself from the influence of religions and religious bodies. What are the social roles in which this modern society places faith, the congregation, the Church and finally Christianity?

Ever since classical times our Western societies had always had a definite, clearly outlined concept of religion. Since the rise of 'bourgeois society' and the 'system of needs' in industrial society, however, modern society has emancipated itself from the classical concept of religion. The Christian Church can consequently no longer present itself to this society as the religion of society.

From the days of the Emperor Constantine until far into the nineteenth century the Christian Church, despite many reformations and despite many changes in society, had possessed a clearly defined character in public social life. The place and function of the Church were firmly established. Everyone knew what was to be expected of it. It was the rise of industrial society that first destroyed the old harmony between *ecclesia* and *societas*. From the standpoint of the history of religion, the former public claims of the Christian Church had their source in the public claims of the Roman state religion.[1] Beginning with Constantine, and then consolidated in the legislation of the Emperors Theodosius and Justinian, the Christian religion took over the social place of the old Roman state religion. The Christian religion became the *cultus publicus*. It became the protector and preserver of the *sacra publica*. According to the classical view of society, it is the supreme duty (*finis principalis*) of human *societas* to see that the gods are given their due veneration. Peace and prosperity depend on the favour of the national gods. The public wellbeing and enduring stability of the state depend on the blessing of the gods of the state. 'Religion' here has the sense of pious veneration for the powers in which the divine eternity of Rome is represented, and without which there can be no such thing as 'Rome' in the fullest sense.[2] When the Christian faith took the place of the Roman state religion, then of course the public state sacrifices ceased, yet their place was taken by the Christian prayers of intercession for the state and the emperor. Thus the Christian faith became the 'religion of society'. It fulfilled the supreme end of state and society. Hence titles of the Roman emperor-priest were transferred to the pope. State and society understood the Christian faith as their religion.

In the Protestant humanism of Melanchthon, too, without which the Reformation would presumably not have got moving, princes and magistrates were appealed to in the interests of society's religious duty as understood in the classical sense.[3] The highest goal of society is the true veneration of God – so it is affirmed here also, though here to be sure in

---

[1] Cf. K. G. Steck, *Kirche und Öffentlichkeit* (Theologische Existenz heute, NF 76), 1960.

[2] W. Kamlah, *Christentum und Geschichtlichkeit*, 2nd ed. 1951, p. 134.

[3] R. Nürnberger, *Kirche und weltliche Obrigkeit bei Ph. Melanchthon*, 1937.

expounding the First Commandment in terms of the *usus politicus*. What is 'true veneration of God'? The answer was: the carrying out of the Reformation as a restoration of the true religion of the one God. A government which seeks to be religiously neutral and to restrict itself to the cultivation of peace and worldly wellbeing, was here, too, with the help of arguments from the classical view of society, represented as lunacy.

Thus the understanding of society in classical and pre-modern times always in itself implies a religious goal of society. Here we have the source of the images which are still employed today to describe the role of the Church in society: 'crown of society', 'healing centre of society', 'inner principle of the life of society'.[1] In its worship and its moral precepts, the human and material is raised to the plane of the divine, and the Eternal and Absolute stoops to the plane of earthly society. When today the 'loss of a centre' is lamented in a disintegrating society, then that is an expression of the longing for such a pre-modern, religious integration of men combined to form a society.

Modern society, however, acquired its nature and its power precisely through its emancipation from this religious centre. Hegel was one of the first to perceive the rise of the modern, emancipated society which destroys all the forces of tradition, and to analyse it, following the British national economy, as a 'system of needs'.[2] It is the society which emancipates itself in principle from all presuppositions in regard to the orders of human life as laid down by historic tradition, and finds its content solely in the constant and consistent nature of man's needs as an individual and their satisfaction by means of collective and divided labour. According to its own principles, it contains nothing but what is demanded by 'the ascertaining of *needs* and the satisfying of the *individual* by means of his labour and by means of the labour and satisfaction of the needs of *all the rest*'.[3] That means that this society, in contradistinction to all previous societies, restricts itself to such social relationships as

[1] Thus Pius XII: 'As the life principle of human society the Church, drawing upon the deep sources of her inner riches, must extend her influence to every realm of human existence' ('Grundsätze der sozialen Neuordnung', originally broadcast in German, published in *Acta Apostolicae Sedis* 41, 1949, p. 462).

[2] *Rechtsphilosophie*, § § 188ff. Cf. J. Ritter, *Hegel und die französische Revolution*, 1957, pp. 36ff.

[3] *Rechtsphilosophie*, § 188.

bind individuals together in the satisfying of their needs by means of their divided labour. Men here associate themselves with each other necessarily only as the bearers of needs, as producers and consumers. Everything else that makes up a man's life – culture, religion, tradition, nationality, morals, etc. – is excluded from the necessary social relationships and left to each man's individual freedom. Social intercourse thus becomes abstract. It emancipates itself from the particular historic conditions from which we have come, and becomes irresistibly universal. 'The non-historic nature of society is its historic essence.'[1] The future and the progressiveness of this society bear no relation to its origin. This, however, makes social intercourse totalitarian. 'Need and labour, when exalted to such universality, thus form in themselves a tremendous system of community and mutual interdependence, a self-propelled system of dead creatures.'[2] 'Civil society . . . is the tremendous power which seizes hold of man and demands from him that he work for it and make it the medium of all he is and does.'[3] Hegel sees in this the approach of the age of universal conformity, of mediocrity and the mass. But he differs from modern critics of culture in seeing also the other side of the dialectic. The general objectification of social intercourse in the modern world, and its reduction to a question of things and facts and functions, bring at the same time also a tremendous disburdening of the individual. Beyond the system of needs and of division of labour in civil society, the 'private person whose aim is his own interest'[4] necessarily becomes the citizen (*citoyen*) and subject of this society. The individual becomes the 'son of civil society'.[5] Thus the revolutionary idea of the freedom of all men which goes back to the French revolution comes to its own with the birth of modern working society from the industrial revolution. The latter is its necessary presupposition and the condition on which it becomes possible. 'It is precisely through its abstract, non-historic character that society gives free rein to subjectivity's right to particularity.'[6] In its emancipation from history, society finds its ground in the satisfying of needs through labour, and thus gives man free

---

[1] J. Ritter, *op. cit.*, p. 41.
[2] *Jenenser Realphilosophie*, ed. J. Hoffmeister, 1931, p. 239.
[3] *Rechtsphilosophie*, § 238 Zus. [4] *Rechtsphilosophie*, § 187.
[5] *Rechtsphilosophie*, § 238. [6] J. Ritter, *op. cit.*, p. 43.

rein in all his other life relationships. All other life relationships are relieved of social necessity. It is only from the standpoint of need that we can speak of 'the concrete conception
that is called man'.[1] In civil society man counts because he is
man, and not because he is a Jew, Catholic, Protestant, German or Italian.[2] The modern subjectivity in which we today
experience ourselves as individual and personal human beings,
is a result of the disburdening of social intercourse by reducing
it to terms of practical affairs.

Hegel's analyses thus make it clear that the age of increasing
mass organization is at the same time dialectically also the age
of individuality, and that the age of socialization at the same
time became the age of free associations. Any critic of culture
who attacks the age of mass movement, of objectification, of
materialism, etc., and sees the salvation of culture in the re-
gaining of personal humanity, accordingly fails to recognize
the nature of modern society, and is himself moving within that
dualism of subjectivity and objectification which is the basic
principle of this very society.

'The society of conformity and mediocrity supplies the individual with a tremendous diversity of individual variations in
matters of taste, evaluation and opinion, so that the most motley
assortment of informal groupings weaves its way across the
constant bureaucratic uniformity of the major organizations,
and the age of a new uniformity of conduct is yet at the same
time also the age of a peculiar unfolding of the things of the
soul and the intellect.'[3] 'Conformity and individualization both
have their roots in the fact that the social ties and relationships
are becoming slacker and less binding, that . . . while the
mobility of industrial society facilitates accommodation to the
model of uniform social behaviour, it is equally favourable towards the opportunity of reserving the private and personal
sphere from social conventions and constraints.'[4] Hence the
dilemma does not by any means consist in the fact that man, who
is conditioned and claimed by modern social intercourse only in
functions which only partially involve him, now encounters his
fellow man only as a 'representative' of socially predetermined

[1] *Rechtsphilosophie*, § 190.   [2] *Rechtsphilosophie*, § 209.
[3] A. Gehlen, 'Mensch trotz Masse. Der Einzelne in der Umwälzung der Gesellschaft', in *Wort und Wahrheit* 7/1952, pp. 579ff.
[4] H. Schelsky, *Die skeptische Generation* (1957), 1963, p. 297.

roles. Rather, it lies in the question how man can endure, and even live in, the state of being torn between the rational objectification of his social life on the one hand and the free and infinitely variable subjectivity conferred on him on the other.

There arises also the further question whether everything that is thus dismissed from modern society's abstract bond of association, and left to the freedom of the subject, does not become functionless and necessarily fall to pieces, when it can no longer acquire any social relevance. This applies especially to religion and culture. Once bereft of social necessity, they threaten to become the playthings of inclination and the tumbling ground for varieties of unreal and ineffective beliefs and opinions.

Hegel, however, was able to recognize the movement of the spirit as acting precisely *in* this torn and divided state of objectification and subjectivity. It is not the romanticist's self-preservation from this tornness and his way of shutting himself off from it, but only self-emptying surrender to it that proves the power of the spirit.

What became of the Christian Church in its social significance as a result of this development in society? The result of this development was, that it lost the character of *cultus publicus* to which it had been accustomed for more than a thousand years. It became something which in its religious form it never was and which, moreover, from the theological standpoint of the New Testament it can never seek to be – namely, a *cultus privatus*. The cult of the Absolute is no longer necessary for the integration of this society. The Absolute is now sought and experienced only in our liberated, socially disburdened subjectivity. 'Religion' ceases to be a public, social duty and becomes a voluntary, private activity. 'Religion' in the course of the nineteenth century becomes the religiosity of the individual, private, inward, edifying. By giving free rein to religion and leaving it to the free unfolding of the personality in complete freedom of religious choice, modern society as a modern 'society of needs' emancipates itself from religious needs. This process was furthered by many revivalist and pietist movements within Christianity. There prevailed within it a pious individualism, which for its own part was romanticist in form and withdrew itself from the material entanglements of society. The Church thus slipped over into the modern *cultus privatus* and produced in theology and pastoral care a corresponding self-consciousness as a haven of intimacy and guardian of personality for a race that had developed a materialist society and felt itself not at home there. This certainly means that the Christian religion is dismissed from the integrating centre of modern society and relieved of its duty of having to represent the highest goal of society, but that is not by any means the end of it. On the contrary, society can assign to it other roles in which it is expected to be effective. While it is true that in these roles it has nothing more to do with the *finis principalis* of modern society, yet it can exercise dialectical functions of disburdening for the men who have to live in this society. This allows it infinite possibilities of variation, but they are the possibilities of self-propulsion and self-development within the bounds of the general social stagnation imposed on the Christian faith as being a matter of religion.

2. RELIGION AS THE CULT OF THE NEW SUBJECTIVITY

The first and most important role in which industrial society expects religion as the cult of the absolute to be effective, is undoubtedly that of providing the transcendental determination of the new, liberated subjectivity. The primary conception of religion in modern society assigns to religion the saving and preserving of personal, individual and private humanity. It is expected that the materialist industrial system must be supplied from 'somewhere or other' with a human foundation which is a match for this world of things that has swollen to such incalculable dimensions.[1] It is expected that 'the man of our day may once again become a vessel to receive the influx of transcendent forces'.[2] 'Islands of meaning' are sought in a world which, while it is certainly not meaningless, is nevertheless non-human. 'If it were possible . . . to establish a humanity which was a match for the secondary system, then this secondary system would have restored to it the foundation which it has itself destroyed'.[3] Now as a result of the fact that all things and conditions can be manufactured by dint of technique and

---

[1] H. Freyer, *Theorie des gegenwärtigen Zeitalters*, 1958, p. 243.
[2] G. Mackenrodt, *Sinn und Ausdruck der sozialen Formenwelt*, 1952, p. 200.
[3] H. Freyer, *op. cit.*, p. 244.

organization, the divine in the sense of the transcendent has disappeared from the world of nature, of history and of society. The world has become the material for technical reshaping by man. The gods of cosmological metaphysics are dead. The world no longer offers man a home and an abiding shelter.

Its place has been taken, however, by a 'metaphysic of sub-jecthood',¹ in which the world of objects is submitted to plan-ning by the human subject. To be sure, the gods of cosmological metaphysics are dead. Rationalization has 'disenchanted' the world (Max Weber), and secularization has stripped it of gods. Yet this was possible only on the basis of the modern metaphysic of 'subjecthood'. The latter has disclosed to man his freedom over against the world as the possible work of his hands. In so doing it demands of man at the same time also responsibility for the world. The world is surrendered to the reason of man.

The saving of man's humanity in the midst of industrial culture is therefore seen in the cultivation and development of this metaphysic of 'subjecthood'. H. Schelsky advises us to re-flect once more on an 'inwardness', on a 'spirituality' beyond the relationships that have been reduced to materialist terms. He sees this possibility of metaphysics in our technical scientific civilization as consisting in the mental attitude of 'constant metaphysical reflection'. 'This is the form in which the thinking subject constantly seeks to hasten ahead of his own objectifica-tion, and thus assures himself of his superiority to his own world process.'² 'However much of his reflection the subject may surrender to the mechanical process, he becomes only the richer thereby, because ever new powers of reflection flow to him from an inexhaustible and boundless inwardness.'³ By means of this mental attitude of constant metaphysical reflection the subject manifestly reflects itself out of all its objectifications,

¹ M. Heidegger, *Holzwege*, 1957, p. 237.
² H. Schelsky, *Der Mensch in der wissenschaftlichen Zivilisation*, 1961, p. 45. Much the same already in 'Ist Dauerreflexion institutionalisierbar?', *Zeitschrift für evan-gelische Ethik* 1, 1957, pp. 135ff. and *Ortsbestimmung der deutschen Soziologie*, 1959, p. 105: 'It could be asked, what is the universal standpoint of man in our society, at which he stands beyond social constraint and thus over against society? The answer would be: the reflecting subjectivity which does not conclusively expand itself in any social fulfilment or does not suffer itself to be conclusively determined by any social force, the moral conscience which does not find in social reality any conclusive criterion for confirming or rejecting it, the religious faith which does not feel itself ultimately bound to any social reality, not even its own.'
³ G. Günther, 'Seele und Maschine', *Augenblick*, vol. 3/1, p. 16, quoted according to H. Schelsky, *Der Mensch in der wissenschaftlichen Zivilisation*, p. 45.

takes them back again into itself and its freedom, and
gains from its own self an endless influx of new possibilities. All
social realities are traced back again in the detachment of reflection and irony to the possibilities arising in the subject. It is
plain that behind this advice for the saving of humanity there
stands the concept of transcendental subjectivity found in early
idealism and developed by Fichte. It is a question, however,
whether this 'reflective philosophy of transcendental subjectivity', as it was already called by Hegel, does not separate the
human subject in a romanticist way from relationships that
have become petrified, abandon these latter to themselves in
their meaningless, inhuman petrification, and seek to save the
individual in himself.

In harmony with this romanticist metaphysic of subjecthood
and this mental attitude of constant metaphysical reflection
there then appears also the theology which takes the cult of the
absolute that has become of no significance in our social relationships and cultivates it as the transcendent background of
modern existence. This is the theology which presents itself
as 'doctrine of the faith' and finds the place of faith in the
transcendental subjectivity of man. It is a theology of existence,
for which 'existence' is the relation of man to himself as this
emerges in the 'total reflection of man on himself'. This theology
assigns faith its home in that subjectivity and spontaneity of
man which is non-objectifiable, incalculable and cannot be
grasped in his social roles. It localizes faith in that ethical
reality which is determined by man's decisions and encounters,
but not by the pattern of social behaviour and the self-contained
rational laws of the economic circumstances in which he lives.
In 'total reflection' on himself man becomes aware of a selfhood
that is unmistakably his own, and in so doing he distinguishes
himself from the modern world and sees it as a secularized
world which is nothing but world. The self which here emerges,
however, becomes the 'pure receiving' of the transcendent
and divine.[1] The modern metaphysic of subjecthood with its
consequences in the secularization of the world must then be
represented as a consequence of Christian faith, and Christian

[1] F. Gogarten, *Der Mensch zwischen Gott und Welt*, 1952, pp. 181ff. ('Die Perso-
nalität. Christlicher Glaube als Reflexion'), esp. pp. 187ff. Here the distinction
must not be overlooked which Gogarten makes between idealist subjectivity and
the personal character of faith.

faith must be represented as the truth behind this metaphysic of subjecthood. Faith as the 'total reflection of man on himself' (F. Gogarten) then presents itself as the truth and radicalization of the mental attitude of 'constant metaphysical reflection' (H. Schelsky). In this theology, Christian faith is transcendent as compared with everything meaningful that can be socially communicated. It is not provable – but its unprovability, so it is said, is its very strength – and consequently it is also irrefutable. Unbelief alone, as being the contrary decision, is its enemy. As constant reflection it cannot be given institutional form,[1] but is itself transcendence as compared with social institutions. It has primarily to do with the 'self-understanding' of the human subject in the technical world. It sees 'God' not as a God of the world or of history or of society, but rather as the unconditioned in the conditional, the beyond in the things of this world, the transcendent in the present.[2] The adjectives which are used to describe the peculiarity of this religious experience are all contrapuntally related to the objectified, material, non-human relationships of industrial society. It is a 'thing that happens or comes about again and again from instance to instance', an 'unexpectable event', 'openness for God's encounters' and readiness for self-transformation in God's encounters. Faith is the receiving of one's self from God. This places it in a position of radical loneliness, makes it 'individual', de-secularizes it in the midst of an organized society. This gives man the freedom 'to stride confidently through darkness and perplexity, and to venture and bear the responsibility for action in the loneliness of his own decision.'[3]

In the 'inability to make anything of the world of objects',[4] which is typical of existentialism, the Christian ethic is then reduced to the 'ethical demand'[5] to accept one's self and take

---

[1] H. Schelsky, 'Ist Dauerreflexion institutionalisierbar?', *op. cit.*

[2] R. Bultmann, 'Der Gottesgedanke und der moderne Mensch', *ZTK* 60, 1963, pp. 335ff. (ET by R. W. Funk in *World Come of Age*, ed. R. Gregor Smith, 1967, pp. 256ff.). Pp. 346f. (cf ET p. 271): 'The concept of God which can find, can seek and find as a possibility of encounter, *the unconditioned in the conditional*, the beyond in the things of this world, the transcendent in the present, is the only one that is possible for modern man.'

R. Bultmann, *Glauben und Verstehen* III, 1960, p. 196.

[4] E. Topitsch, 'Zur Soziologie des Existentialismus', in *Sozialphilosophie zwischen Ideologie und Wissenschaft*, 1962, p. 86.

[5] K. Løgstrup, *Die ethische Forderung*, 1959, p. 232: 'There are no absolute, revealed demands, but only the one radical demand.' Cf. W. D. Marsch, 'Glauben und Handeln in der "technisch-organisatorischen Daseinsverfassung"', *Monatsschrift für Pastoraltheologie* 52, 1963, pp. 269ff.

responsibility for the world in general. But it is no longer able
to give any pertinent ethical instructions for the ordering of
social and political life. Christian love accordingly quits the
realm of justice and of the social order. It is a thing that comes
about in each several event of spontaneous co-humanity, in
the I-thou relationship which is immediate and not objectively
mediated. Justice, social order and political righteousness, once
they have been rendered so void, must then be understood
positivistically as pure organization, as matters of power and
law. The 'neighbour' who is the object of Christian love is then
the man who encounters us at any given moment, our fellow
man in his selfhood, but he can no longer be known, respected
and loved in his juridical person and his social role. Our
'neighbour' comes on the scene only in personal encounter, but
not in his social reality. It is the man within arm's length or
at our door who is our neighbour, but not man as he appears
in the social and juridical order, in questions of aid to under-
developed countries and race relationships, in social callings,
roles and claims.

If, however, we now examine the dialectic of modern, dualistic society, it transpires that the metaphysic of subjecthood and
the cult of the absolute in transcendental subjectivity are due
to specific, modern social conditions. The 'category of individuality' is itself a product of society.[1] 'A personality is an
institution in the form of a *single* instance.'[2] It is not as if modern,
scientific technical civilization were only an objectification of
the infinitely creative subjectivity of man. The modern subjectivity of man for its part also owes its freedom, its spontaneity and its infinite inward resources to the ways in which
modern, materialist society relieves it of its burdens. A cultural
saving of humanity by means of the cultivating and deepening
of our subjectivity in constant metaphysical reflection, in art
and religion, is romanticist escapism as long as social conditions
are not changed. Where conditions are left as they are, this
cultural saving of humanity automatically acquires the function of stabilizing these social conditions in their non-humanity,
by providing the inner life of the heart with the things which it
has to do without in the outside world.

[1] T. W. Adorno, *Sociologica* II, 1962, p. 100.
[2] A. Gehlen, *Die Seele im technischen Zeitalter*, 1957, p. 118.

A theology which settles faith in the 'existence' of the individual, in the sphere of his personal, immediate encounters and decisions, is a theology which from the viewpoint of sociological science stands at the very place to which society has banished the *cultus privatus* in order to emancipate itself from it. This faith is in the literal sense socially irrelevant, because it stands in the social no-man's-land of the unburdening of the individual – that is, in a realm which materialist society has already left free to human individuality in any case. The existential decision of faith consequently hardly provokes the counter-decision of unbelief any longer, and is consequently not really engaged in a struggle with unbelief at all. What it actually does constantly provoke is its own non-committal character – namely, the now notorious attitude of refusing to take sides in disputes of faith that have long become socially irrelevant, the well known 'religion void of decision'.[1] The battle of faith is socially no longer necessary, since for social life it has no longer any binding character. The transcendent point of reference which is constituted by man's free subjectivity, and in view of which this proclamation addresses him, has already been socially neutralized before it can be made use of in the decision of faith. Hence this theology threatens to become a religious ideology of romanticist subjectivity, a religion within the sphere of the individuality that has been relieved of all social obligations. Nor does the appeal of its existential radicality prevent the Christian faith, as thus understood, being brought to social stagnation.

3. RELIGION AS THE CULT OF CO-HUMANITY

The second role in which modern society expects religion to be effectual consists in the transcendent determination of co-humanity as community.

Since the beginning of the industrial revolution the roman-

---

[1] Cf. H. O. Wölber's essay in sociographical evaluation, *Religion ohne Entscheidung*, 1959; also E. Stammler, *Protestanten ohne Kirche*, 1960. H. J. Iwand had as early as 1929 pointed to the self-abrogation of decision in the appeal for decision (*Deutsche Literaturzeitung*, 1929, col. 1228): 'The very act of confronting man with the decision also frees him from it, since thanks to this theoretical manipulation the decision for or against God stands like two possibilities before man, and in the end we have once more to resort after all to the urge of imperatives and the enticement of value-judgments, in order to prise man out of the neutrality in which we have artificially placed him.'

ticist reaction to the conditions that seem to rob man of his humanity has clung again and again and in ever new forms to the idea of '<u>community</u>'. 'True human community is . . . that between man and man; i.e. the community in which man finds himself by surrendering himself to the other.'[1] This form of complete disclosure of personal co-humanity in 'community' is then always set in a polemical relation to its antithesis in the concept of 'society': society is an artificial, arbitrary, organized arrangement between men for practical and businesslike purposes. The dominant factor in it is not the will to be a self, but rational purposefulness, convention, and a businesslike approach. It is pseudo-community and brings man merely to a semblance of existence. This kind of society is seen above all in the 'large industrial cities',[2] whereas community apparently means the idyllically conceived village conditions of pre-modern times.

This idea of community, which is held to promise the saving of culture from technical civilization, has its origins in the age of romanticism. It is found in the *Communist Manifesto* as the revolution's goal in a 'free association of free individuals', in that community of the future in which division of labour is abolished, in which man is the highest being in man's eyes, in which each can exchange 'love only for love, trust only for trust', which accordingly produces 'man with his all-embracing and profound mind' as its constant reality, in which the total loss of man in capitalist society is followed by the total recovery of man. This idea of community is found in detail in Ferdinand Tönnies,[3] and through him inspired the youth movement and a vast array of community movements at the beginning of the twentieth century. It is found again in the sociologically critical and nationalistically revolutionary idea of the *community of nations*. Hans Freyer canvassed it in 1931 in his 'revolution

---

[1] So the very apt definition by R. Bultmann, 'Formen menschlicher Gemeinschaft', in *Glauben und Verstehen* II, p. 263 (ET: 'Forms of Human Community', *Essays Philosophical and Theological*, p. 292). In this essay Bultmann is apparently taking up the ideas of community advanced by F. Tönnies.
[2] Cf. Rilke's poem quoted by R. Bultmann, *op. cit.*, p. 266 (ET p. 295):
> The cities play us false . . .
> Nought of that broader real activity
> That is your prize as further you mature
> Occurs in them. . . .
For a criticism of the romanticist criticism of large cities, cf. H. P. Bahrdt, *Die moderne Grosstadt* (Rowohlts deutsche Enzyklopädie 127), 1961.
[3] F. Tönnies, *Gemeinschaft und Gesellschaft*, 8th ed., 1935 (reprinted 1963).

from the right': industrial society, which rests on nothing but the calculation of matter and forces, has no solid foundation but hangs in the air. It has no vitality to give it a peculiar rationality of its own. It is a *perpetuum mobile* of material values, work quotas, commercial media and mass needs. The revolution from the left has come to a dead end in the trade unions and has already been merged into this industrial world. But where can man assert himself as man over against this system? 'The people is the antagonist of industrial society. The principle of the people against the principle of industrial society.' This story has not been played out, but the tide is rising in the village against the industrial city. Primaeval forces of history, decrees of the Absolute, flow to man once more from the people. In the life of the people, in the man of the people and in the people's state the 'earth' rises up as it were against the abstract, non-committed, inhuman system of industrial society. Man and earth find each other again. The principle of industrial society has become invalid, because there are men who are no longer defined by their social interest. The 'human emancipation of man', which Marx expected from the revolution of the proletariat, is here expected from the life of the people. 'Man is free when he is free amid his people, and this too in his *Lebensraum*. Man is free when he stands within a common will which carries on its history on its own reponsibility.'

The idea of community, however, is found with socially critical and socially therapeutic intent also in Roman Catholic social teaching. According to *Mater et Magistra*, it is essential 'that the above mentioned groups present the form and substance of a true community, that is, that the individual members be considered and treated as persons and encouraged to take an active part in the ordering of their lives'. It follows that 'whether the enterprise is private or public . . . every effort should be made that the enterprise should be a community of persons'. 'In such a way, a precious contribution to the formation of a world community can be made, a community in which all members are . . . conscious of their own duties and rights, working on a basis of equality for the bringing about of the universal common good.'[1]

---

[1] *Mater et Magistra*: ET as Appendix to E. Guerry, *The Social Teaching of the Church*, 1961, pp. 185, 190, 208.

Yet in the course of the progress of industrial society this ideal of community has also lost its revolutionary power and been integrated into the industrial system. It has often been shown by sociologists and critics of culture that modern society is not by any means on the way to becoming a totalitarian ant-hill in which any and every activity is governed by rules and regulations, but that this age of conformity and indiscrimination, of vast organizations and economic combines, is at the same time also the age of small, specialist groups and of confidential relationships within narrow circles. The super-organizations and macro-structures in the economic world are answered by the micro-structures of informal groups, bodies, societies, clubs, etc. 'Here the isolation of man is checked, and these informal, unofficial institutions are manifestly acquiring increasing significance.'[1] Alexis de Tocqueville had already observed this in the American democracy of last century: 'The first thing that strikes the observation is an innumerable multitude of men, all equal and alike, incessantly endeavouring to procure the petty and paltry pleasures with which they glut their lives. Each of them, living apart, is a stranger to the fate of all the rest; his children and his private friends constitute to him the whole of mankind. As for the rest of his fellow citizens, he is close to them, but he does not see them; he touches them, but he does not feel them; he exists only in himself and for himself alone.'[2]

In the circle of his friends, his intimate colleagues, neighbours and children, at home, in the choral society and the local community, it is as if man's businesslike and inhuman outlook were suddenly blown away. Here he is 'man', and is permitted to be man. Perhaps, as A. Gehlen thinks,[1] all these small ties provided by the intimate groups combine to form a sort of cement for the total structure of society: 'the vast utility organizations and the individuals pitch-forked into them do not by any means constitute the whole of the truth.'

Amongst and between these small groups the church, too, as a congregation can have its place and carry out its function. Here it can become a refuge of the inner life, away from the

[1] A. Gehlen, *op. cit.*, p. 74.
[2] *Democracy in America* II, Book IV, ch. 6; ET by Henry Reeve, rev. ed., 1948, vol. II, p. 318 (World's Classics ed., 1946, p. 579).

supposedly 'soulless' world of affairs. Conditions in the vast industrial complexes transcend our intellectual range and can no longer be mastered morally. Responsibility for the 'modern world' as such can no longer be expected of anyone. The objectifications of our scientific technical civilization have reached such vast and independent proportions that they can no longer be re-subjectified. In return, they leave free a small-scale world, in which responsibilities can be assumed in limited communities. Here Christian congregations can offer human warmth and nearness, neighbourliness and homeliness, 'community' which is not utilitarian but nevertheless meaningful, and therefore also readily called 'genuine'. The 'authentic' living relationship between man and man is here not channelled and prescribed in patterns of behaviour appropriate to rational ends. Here life can still be carried on in freedom, it evades formal fashioning and cannot be subjected to constraint and control. Here, instead of complying with the technically necessary rules of conduct in society, it is possible in human spontaneity to produce ever new solutions in ever new combinations of circumstances. In this non-preformed, unorganized, unofficial realm which is left free by industrial society, clubs, sects and communities of every kind thrive. Here Christian communities and groups, too, can become a kind of Noah's ark for men in their social estrangement. They become islands of genuine co-humanity and of authentic life in the rough sea of circumstances which the ordinary man can after all do nothing to alter. Here the Christian churches can become rallying points for integration, and would thereby no doubt have fulfilled a social aim. For the subliminal existence of free communities of this kind is for modern society a most salutary thing, because in the domestic economy of the human soul it can provide a certain compensation for the economic and technical forces of destruction. This, however, does nothing to alter the stern reality of the loss of the human in 'society'. It provides only a dialectical compensation and a disburdening of the soul, so that in the alternating rhythm of the private and the public, of community and society, man can endure his official existence today.

It is entirely in harmony with the social significance of 'community' in this sense when Christian theology of various persuasions sets over against the officially and legally constituted

Church the 'true Church' as a 'genuine community', as a 'spiritual church' (R. Sohm), as a 'spiritual community of persons' (E. Brunner), as a 'community of faith' and a 'community in the transcendent' (R. Bultmann), and sees its existence as 'pure happening' and 'unexpectable event' in spontaneous encounters and decisions. The Church is then an absolutely non-worldly phenomenon, which in contrast to the planned society of rational ends is described in the categories of 'community'. It is then still possible to speak of the Christian Church's responsibility for 'the world', but hardly any longer of Christian callings in the world. Yet it must surely be plainly recognized that such a church, as 'community' and as 'pure event', cannot disturb the official doings of this society and certainly cannot alter them – indeed, it is hardly any longer even a real partner for the social institutions. True, the man who feels estranged and longs for authentic life and genuine community, for the spontaneity of experience, of making his own decisions and of transforming himself, is here met halfway and has his longing fulfilled. But it is fulfilled only in the personal esoteric realm in which he is relieved of social demands. Nor does the emphasis on the genuineness and authenticity of life in this personal community prevent Christian neighbourliness being brought to a social standstill.

4. RELIGION AS THE CULT OF THE INSTITUTION

A third role in which modern society expects the Christian religion to be effectual is, surprisingly enough, once more to be found today in the institution with all it involves in the way of officialdom and official claims. Modern, post-Enlightenment culture is again more ready to play into the hands of religion than was the pre-industrial age of the eighteenth century.[1] After the hectic decades of the founding of industrialism, in which vast social dislocations made men uncertain in their behaviour and therefore also susceptible to ideologies, industrial society in the highly industrialized countries is today again consolidating itself in new institutions. These new institutions, however, in turn relieve man of the permanent pressure of decision to which he is subjected in times of uncertainty.

[1] A. Gehlen, *op. cit.*, p. 43.

Stereotyped patterns of conduct give them an enduring, stable and communal character. Thus there emerges a new store of unvarying customs and axioms in work, consumption and intercourse. A 'beneficial unquestioningness' (A. Gehlen) spreads over life. This kind of institutionalizing of official, social life certainly springs from the permanent need of security on the part of man, who experiences himself in history as a 'creature at risk' and therefore also endeavours to resolve the historic character of his history into a cosmos of institutions. This institutionalizing, however, brings about at the same time by an inner logic the suspension of the question of meaning. 'The conduct which they have made habitual has the purely factual result of suspending the question of meaning. To raise the question of meaning is either to have taken a wrong turning, or else to express consciously or unconsciously a need for something other than the existing institutions.'[1] For the latter are of course relationships and modes of conduct which must be axiomatic and unquestioning. The institutionalizing of public life is today producing in the highly industrialized countries an everywhere perceptible disappearance of ideologies. Ideologies as a means of giving purpose and meaning to life are becoming increasingly superfluous. This makes them optional and private. To be sure, it can be said even in the midst of institutionalized life: 'In the world of machines and "cultural values", of great alleviations, life slips away like water between the fingers that would hold it because it is the highest of goods. From out of unfathomable depths it is called in question.'[2] Yet this questionableness is experienced only in the free realm of subjectivity, and no longer in terms of the uncertainty and the historic character of the outside world.

This tendency towards the institutionalization of public life, together with the fact that the arts and sciences have become so abstract that only caricatures of them can now find ideological application, has had the result that the Christian religion is left alone and unopposed on the field of ideologies and world views in the highly industrialized countries. Darwinism in its day was bitterly contested by the Christian confessions. Modern genetics, however, whose technical consequences are beyond our range of

[1] A. Gehlen, *Urmensch und Spätkultur*, 1956, p. 69.
[2] *Ibid.*, p. 289.

vision, does not disturb them, because this is a science of boundless complexity and cannot turn into a speculative opponent. Christian theology accordingly finds itself in a position of being able to assert a neo-dogmatism and say things which can neither be proved nor contested on the ground of real experience, and which can therefore acquire for modern man a binding character which he hardly even disputes any more. On the contrary, he is prepared to delegate to the Church as an institution the problems regarding his own believing decision, and to leave the detailed questions to theological specialists. If, however, the vital decisions are delegated to the Church as an institution, which is then regarded as an institute for relieving us of them, then the result is the religious attitude of an institutionalized non-committal outlook. 'Christianity' becomes a social axiom and is relegated to one's environment. Matters of theological dispute are regarded as 'confessional witch-hunting' and banished from public life. On the other hand, the ecclesiastical institution of religious modes of conduct acquires a new social significance. For indeed even the modern, institutionalized consciousness retains somewhere on the margin an inkling of the horrors of history. It does not find articulate expression in normal times. Yet this subliminal consciousness of crisis results in a general, if also non-committal, recognition of the religious institutions as the guarantors of life's security in general. The institution of the churches then has the effect of being an ultimate institution overshadowing the institutional security of life, and one from which security is expected against the ultimate fears of existence. In this respect, too, Christianity has a certain social significance for modern society. Yet it is the significance of an institutionalized non-committal outlook. This, too, is religious movement within the limits of a social standstill. It is Christianity as prescribed by the social *milieu*.[1]

This brief sketch of the new social roles of religion, of the Church and of the Christian faith has made it plain that these roles – 'religion as the cult of subjectivity', 'religion as the cult of co-humanity' and 'religion as the cult of the institution' – are

[1] C. Amery, *Die Kapitulation oder der deutsche Katholizismus heute*, 1963, p. 117, demands an 'exodus from the environment': '*Sentire cum Ecclesia* is a thing which *can require us to break with existing Catholicism.*'

not the result of the goodwill or illwill of individual men, nor can they be laid to the charge of theologies determined by the history of ideas, but arise from that which, difficult as it is to grasp, must be called the socially 'axiomatic'. The theological 'self-understanding' (*Selbstverständnis*) of the Christian faith always stands in a relation to the socially 'axiomatic' (*Selbstverständliche*). Only where we become critically aware of this connection can the symbiosis be resolved and the peculiar character of the Christian faith come to expression in conflict with the things that are socially axiomatic. If Christianity, according to the will of him in whom it believes and in whom it hopes, is to be different and to serve a different purpose, then it must address itself to no less a task than that of breaking out of these its socially fixed roles. It must then display a kind of conduct which is not in accordance with these. That is the conflict which is imposed on every Christian and every Christian minister. If the God who called them to life should expect of them something other than what modern industrial society expects and requires of them, then Christians must venture an exodus and regard their social roles as a new Babylonian exile. Only where they appear in society as a group which is not wholly adaptable and in the case of which the modern integration of everything with everything else fails to succeed, do they enter into a conflict-laden, but fruitful partnership with this society. Only where their resistance shows them to be a group that is incapable of being assimilated or of 'making the grade', can they communicate their own hope to this society. They will then be led in this society to a constant unrest which nothing can allay or bring to accommodation and rest. Here the task of Christianity today is not so much to oppose the ideological glorification of things, but rather to resist the institutional stabilizing of things, and by 'raising the question of meaning' to make things uncertain and keep them moving and elastic in the process of history. This aim – here formulated to begin with in very general terms – is not achieved simply by stirring up 'historicality', vitality and mobility in the realms which are socially unburdened but have been brought socially to general stagnation. It is achieved precisely by breaking through this social stagnation. Hope alone keeps life – including public, social life – flowing and free.

5. CHRISTIANITY WITHIN THE HORIZON OF THE EXPECTATION OF THE KINGDOM OF GOD

'Christianity' has its essence and its goal not in itself and not in its own existence, but lives from something and exists for something which reaches far beyond itself. If we would grasp the secret of its existence and its modes of behaviour, we must enquire into its *mission*. If we would fathom its essence, then we must enquire into that *future* on which it sets its *hopes* and expectations. If Christianity in the new social conditions has itself lost its bearings and become uncertain, then it must once again consider why it exists and what is its aim.

It is generally recognized today that the New Testament regards the Church as the 'community of eschatological salvation', and accordingly speaks of the gathering in and sending out of the community in terms of a horizon of eschatological expectation.[1] The risen Christ calls, sends, justifies and sanctifies men, and in so doing gathers, calls and sends them into his eschatological future for the world. The risen Lord is always the Lord expected by the Church – the Lord, moreover, expected by the Church for the world and not merely for itself. Hence the Christian community does not live from itself and for itself, but from the sovereignty of the risen Lord and for the coming sovereignty of him who has conquered death and is bringing life, righteousness and the kingdom of God.

This eschatological orientation is seen in everything from which and for which the Church lives. The Church lives by the word of God, the word that is proclaimed, that pronounces and sends. This word has no magical quality in itself. 'The proclaimed word is directed towards that which in every respect *lies ahead of it*. It is open for the "future" which comes to pass *in* it, yet which in its *coming to pass* is recognized to be still *outstanding*.'[2] The word which creates life and calls to faith is *pro*-clamation and *pro*-nouncement. It provides no final revelation, but calls us to a path whose goal it shows in terms of promise, and whose goal can be attained only by obediently following the promise. As the promise of an eschatological and

---

[1] On what follows cf. O. Weber, *Grundlagen der Dogmatik* II, 1962, pp. 564ff.
[2] O. Weber, *op. cit.*, p. 570.

universal future, the word points beyond itself, forwards to coming events and outwards into the breadth of the world to which the promised coming events are coming. This is why all proclamation stands in the eschatological tension of which we have spoken. It is valid to the extent that it is *made* valid. It is true to the extent that it announces the future of the truth. It communicates this truth in such a way that we can *have* it only by confidently *waiting* for it and wholeheartedly *seeking* it. Thus the word has an inner transcendence in regard to its future. The word of God is itself an eschatological gift. In it the hidden future of God for the world is already present. But it is present in the form of promise and of awakened hope. The word is not itself the eschatological salvation, but acquires its eschatological relevance from the coming salvation. What is true of the Spirit of God is true also of the word of God: it is an earnest of things to come, and binds us to itself in order to point and direct us to greater things.

The same is true of Baptism and the Lord's Supper. Baptism, too, is 'ahead of itself'. In baptizing men into the past death of Christ, it seals men for the future of the kingdom that is being brought by the risen Christ. It is only as an eschatological Church that the baptizing Church has the right to perform the act of baptism, i.e. its title to this judicial and creative act derives from its openness towards that which is as yet only on the way towards it. Likewise, the Lord's Supper, is not to be regarded in terms of mystery and cult, but eschatologically. The congregation at the Table is not in possession of the sacral presence of the Absolute, but is a waiting, expectant congregation seeking communion with the coming Lord. Thus Christianity is to be understood as the community of those who on the ground of the resurrection of Christ wait for the kingdom of God and whose life is determined by this expectation.

If, however, the Christian Church is thus oriented towards the future of the Lord, and receives itself and its own nature always only in expectation and hope from the coming of the Lord who is ahead of it, then its life and suffering, its work and action in the world and upon the world, must also be determined by the open foreland of its hopes for the world.[1] Meaning-

[1] Similarly also H. D. Wendland, 'Ontologie und Eschatologie in der christlichen Soziallehre', in *Botschaft an die soziale Welt*, 1959, pp. 141ff.

ful action is always possible only within a horizon of expectation, otherwise all decisions and actions would be desperate thrusts into a void and would hang unintelligibly and meaninglessly in the air. Only when a meaningful horizon of expectation can be given articulate expression does man acquire the possibility and the freedom to expend himself, to objectify himself and to expose himself to the pain of the negative, without bewailing the accompanying risk and surrender of his free subjectivity. Only when the realization of life is, so to speak, caught up and held by a horizon of expectation, is realization (*Verwirklichung*) no longer – as for romanticist subjectivity – the forfeiting (*Verwirkung*) of possibilities and surrender of freedom, but the gaining of life.

The Christian Church which follows Christ's mission to the world is engaged also in following Christ's service of the world. It has its nature as the body of the crucified and risen Christ only where in specific acts of service it is obedient to its mission to the world. Its existence is completely bound to the fulfilling of its service. For this reason it is nothing in itself, but all that it is, it is in existing for others. It is the Church of God where it is a Church for the world. Now this modern phrase 'Church for the world' is very vague. It could of course be understood to the effect that personal faith, or the fellowship of the congregation, or the Church as an institution loyally fulfils the social roles in which modern society expects it to be useful. 'Church for the world', however, does not mean a solidarity that is bereft of ideas and a co-humanity that is void of hopes, but service of the world and work in the world as and where God wishes it and expects it. The will and expectation of God are voiced in the mission of Christ and in the apostolate. The Church lays claim to the whole of humanity in mission. This mission is not carried out within the horizon of expectation provided by the social roles which society concedes to the Church, but it takes place within its own peculiar horizon of the eschatological expectation of the coming kingdom of God, of the coming righteousness and the coming peace, of the coming freedom and dignity of man. The Christian Church has not to serve mankind in order that this world may remain what it is, or may be preserved in the state in which it is, but in order that it may transform itself and become what it is promised to be.

For this reason 'Church for the world' can mean nothing else
but 'Church for the kingdom of God' and the renewing of
the world.¹ This means in practice that Christianity takes up
mankind – or to put it concretely, the Church takes up the
society with which it lives – into its own horizon of expectation
of the eschatological fulfilment of justice, life, humanity and
sociability, and communicates in its own decisions in history
its openness and readiness for this future and its elasticity towards it.

One of the first senses in which this happens is in the missionary proclamation of the gospel, that no corner of this world
should remain without God's promise of new creation through
the power of the resurrection. This has nothing whatever to
do with an extension of the claim to sovereignty on the part of
the Church and its officials, or with an attempt to regain the
old privileges accruing from the cult of the Absolute. 'Missions
perform their service today only when they infect men with
hope.'² This kindling of live hopes that are braced for action
and prepared to suffer, hopes of the kingdom of God that is
coming to earth in order to transform it, is the purpose of
mission. It is the task of the whole body of Christians, not
merely the task of particular officials. The whole body of Christians is engaged in the apostolate of hope for the world and
finds therein its essence – namely that which makes it the
Church of God. It is not in itself the salvation of the world, so
that the 'churchifying' of the world would mean the latter's
salvation, but it serves the coming salvation of the world and is
like an arrow sent out into the world to point to the future.

What missionary proclamation of the promises of God means,
becomes clear from the Old Testament background of the
Christian mission. In the Christian mission of hope there begins to happen already what according to Old Testament
prophecies, especially in Isaiah and Deutero-Isaiah, is to
happen only after Israel has received salvation and Zion is
established. With the resurrection of Christ the divine lordship that has drawn near enters into the process of realization,
in that Jews and Gentiles, Greeks and barbarians, bond and

---

¹ This is made specially clear in the Dutch Reformed Church's *Fundamenten en
Perspektiven van Belijden* of 1949 in Art. 8 and Art. 13, as also in the corresponding
Kerkorde Art. VIII, 'Van het apostolaat der Kerk'.
² J. C. Hoekendijk, *Mission – heute*, 1954, p. 12.

free, come to the obedience of faith and thereby attain to eschatological freedom and human dignity. If we take seriously this eschatological background in the prophets, against which the proclamation of the gospel by Christianity takes place, then the goal of the Christian mission must also become plain. It aims at reconciliation with God (II Cor. 5.18ff.), at forgiveness of sins and abolition of godlessness. But salvation, σωτηρία, must also be understood as *shalōm* in the Old Testament sense. This does not mean merely salvation of the soul, individual rescue from the evil world, comfort for the troubled conscience, but also the realization of the eschatological *hope of justice*, the *humanizing of man*, the *socializing* of humanity, *peace* for all creation. This 'other side'[1] of reconciliation with God has always been given too little consideration in the history of Christianity, because Christians no longer understood themselves eschatologically and left earthly eschatological anticipations to the fanatics and the sects. Yet it is only in the light of this 'other side' of reconciliation that Christians can get beyond the religious relief functions which they are expected to perform for a society left to itself, and can gain new impulses for the shaping of man's public, social and political life. If the Christian mission which brings to all men righteousness by faith arises against the background of the Yahwist promise to Abraham (Gen. 12.3) and of the prophetic eschatology of Isaiah (Isa. 2.1–4; 25.6–8; 45.18–25; 60.1–22), by turning these expectations into present activity, then its horizon must embrace not only the establishment of the obedience of faith among the Gentiles (Rom. 15.18), but also that which the Old Testament hopes for in terms of blessing, peace, righteousness and fulness of life (cf. Rom. 15.8–13). This is anticipated in the power of that love which unites strong and weak, bond and free, Jews and Gentiles, Greeks and barbarians in a new community.

6. THE CALLING OF CHRISTIANS IN SOCIETY

The coming lordship of the risen Christ cannot be merely hoped for and awaited. This hope and expectation also sets its

---

[1] W. Dirks, *Frankfurter Hefte*, 1963, p. 92. Cf. W. D. Marsch, 'Glauben und Handeln', *Monatsschrift für Pastoraltheologie* 52, 1963, pp. 281f.

stamp on life, action and suffering in the history of society. Hence mission means not merely propagation of faith and hope, but also historic transformation of life. The life of the body, including also social and public life, is expected as a sacrifice in day-to-day obedience (Rom. 12.1ff.). Not to be conformed to this world does not mean merely to be transformed in oneself, but to transform in opposition and creative expectation the face of the world in the midst of which one believes, hopes and loves. The hope of the gospel has a polemic and liberating relation not only to the religions and ideologies of men, but still more to the factual, practical life of men and to the relationships in which this life is lived. It is not enough to say that the kingdom of God has to do only with persons;[1] for one thing, the righteousness and peace of the promised kingdom are terms of relationship and accordingly have to do also with the relationships of men to each other and to things, and secondly, the idea of an a-social human personality is an abstraction. The reason why Christian hope raises the 'question of meaning' in an institutionalized life is, that in fact it cannot put up with these relationships and sees the 'beneficial unquestioning-ness of life' in them only as a new form of vanity and death. It is in fact in search of 'other institutions', because it must expect true, eternal life, the true and eternal dignity of man, true and just relationships, from the coming kingdom of God. It will therefore endeavour to lead our modern institutions away from their own immanent tendency towards stabilization, will make them uncertain, historify them and open them to that elasticity which is demanded by openness towards the future for which it hopes. In practical opposition to things as they are, and in creative reshaping of them, Christian hope calls them in question and thus serves the things that are to come. With its face towards the expected new situation, it leaves the existing situation behind and seeks for opportunities of bringing history into ever better correspondence to the promised future.

The Reformers' rediscovery of the 'universal priesthood of all believers' made it plain that the call of the gospel is issued to every man. Everyone who believes and hopes is *vocatus* and has to offer his life in the service of God, in the work of his kingdom and the freedom of faith. For the Reformers, this call in our

---

[1] P. Althaus, *Evangelisches Kirchenlexikon* III, col. 1931.

earthly life took concrete shape in our 'callings'. The mission
and call of the Christian Church fan out, so to speak, into the
world in our earthly callings in services, commissions and
charismata towards the earth and human society. In our worldly
callings, the lordship of Christ and the freedom of faith penetrate into the world as *'politia Christi regnum suum ostendentis
coram hoc mundo. In his enim sanctificat corda et reprimit diabolum,
et ut retineat evangelium inter homines, foris opponit regno diaboli
confessionem sanctorum et in nostra imbecillitate declarat potentiam
suam'* ('the city of Christ in which he displays his kingdom in
face of this world. For in these he sanctifies our hearts and re-
strains the devil, and in order to maintain the gospel among
men he openly opposes the confession of the saints to the kingdom of the devil and declares his power in our weakness.')[1] Our
earthly doings, as a result of the fact that since the Reformation they have been designated 'calling', i.e. *vocatio, klēsis,* have
acquired a new theological significance. The *vita christiana,*
the Christian life, no longer consists in fleeing the world and in
spiritual resignation from it, but is engaged in an attack upon
the world and a calling in the world.[2] Only, as the Reformation
progressed, it became obscure who actually appoints these
earthly callings. The revolutionary social movements of the
fanatics caused the Reformers more and more to neglect the
call to discipleship in the freedom of faith and to concentrate
on the concern for order and its preservation. The new idea of
calling was transformed into a doctrine of the two kingdoms,
in which it was more and more a matter of adjusting questions
of competence as between the divine institutions of church,
state, business and home.[3] Thus the Confession of Augsburg XVI
declares that the gospel brings no new laws and ordinances into
the world, and does not dissolve the political and economic
orders, *'sed maxime postulat conservare tamquam ordinationes Dei
et in talibus ordinationibus exercere charitatem'* ('but chiefly demands both the preservation of the ordinances of God and the
exercise of charity in all such ordinances'). Our callings do

[1] Melanchthon, *Apologie* IV, 189. The significance and consequences of this statement have been emphasized by E. Wolf in many of his writings. Cf. H. Weber,
'Der sozialethische Ansatz bei Ernst Wolf', *EvTh* 22, 1962, pp. 58off.
[2] D. Bonhoeffer, *Ethik,* 1949, p. 198 (ET by N. Horton Smith: *Ethics,* 1955,
p. 223).
[3] E. Wolf, 'Schöpferische Nachfolge', in *Spannungsfelder der evangelischen Soziallehre,* 1960, p. 36.

remain the several places of love's orderly service to the world
for God, only it remains an open question whence this 'several-
ness' derives. The vocational ethics of Protestantism has usually
had recourse at this point to the postulate of a second source
of revelation. The 'call' which leads to specific callings was
derived by Karl Holl from the coinciding of two voices – the
'inner call' heard in the gospel, and the voice which comes to
us from things themselves and their necessity. Like Bismarck,
he would hear in each given historic situation itself 'the footsteps of the God who strides through history'.[1] Thus the call to
our calling comes from both voices together – from the call
of God in the gospel of Christ, and from the call of the God of
history. At this point Emil Brunner put 'providence': 'The
"place" of the action, the here and now . . . is the place
given by God.'[2] Others have sought amid the multiplicity of
possibilities in society and history certain ever-existing, abiding
basic orders such as marriage and family, church and state, on
the basis of which the many possibilities are to be elucidated as
variations. They have called these basic orders God's 'created
orders', his 'preserving orders', his 'mandates', his 'fundamental ordinances', or institutions given along with human
nature. This means, however, that the place of call is always
seen as something given or predetermined, so that the call and
the obedience of faith can then bring about only inner modifica-
tions in the *exercitium caritatis* at this place and in the predetermined vocational role. Typical of this are the lines in Johann
Heermann's hymn: 'Grant me with diligence to do thy will,
thy statutes in my station to fulfil.' But the 'station' or the vocational role in society had then in terms of a theology of creation or of history to be accepted as fate and seen as God-given.
The '*conservare*' of the Confession of Augsburg XVI has always
set a highly conservative stamp on the vocational ethics of
Protestantism. And since, once left to themselves, forces of a
totally different kind took over the determination of the place
and role of men's 'callings', the call and mission of the believer
was able to work itself out only in the inward fulfilment of his
calling. The determining of the concrete historic form of the

[1] K. Holl, 'Die Geschichte des Wortes Beruf', *Gesammelte Aufsätze* III, 1928,
p. 219.
[2] E. Brunner, *Das Gebot und die Ordnungen*, 1932, p. 184 (ET by O. Wyon: *The
Divine Imperative*, 1937, p. 200).

above-mentioned 'orders' was left to what happened to be the prevailing powers.

In actual fact, however, the call to discipleship of Christ is not aimed at faithful and loving fulfilment of our calling under the prescribed conditions – whatever the God or the forces prescribing them. On the contrary, this call has its own goal. It is the call to join in working for the kingdom of God that is to come. The Reformers' identification of call and 'calling' was never intended to dissolve the call in the calling, but *vice versa* to integrate and transform the 'callings' in the call. The *call* according to the New Testament is once for all, irrevocable and immutable, and has its eschatological goal in the hope to which God calls us.[1]

Our *callings*, however, are historic, changing, changeable, temporally limited, and are therefore to be shaped in the process of being accepted in terms of call, of hope and of love. The call always appears only in the singular. The callings, roles, functions and relationships which make a social claim on man, always appear in an open multiplicity. Always man stands in a multi-layered network of social dependences and claims. Our modern society is conspicuously no longer a society of stations, but is rather to be described as a society of mobile jobs. It lays open to man a multitude of chances and demands of him elasticity, adaptability and imaginativeness.

Amid this fulness and wealth of conditions and possibilities, the decisive question for Christian existence is not whether and how man in the fluctuating variety of his social commitments, or at the point of intersection of all these roles in which he is always only partially involved, can be 'himself' and can maintain his own identity and continuity with himself.[2] The point of reference of his expressions and renunciations, his activities and sufferings, is not a transcendental Ego upon which he could and must repeatedly reflect in the midst of all his distractions. But the point of reference is his call. It is to this, and not to himself, that he seeks to live. It is this that gives him identity

[1] Rom. 8.29; 11.29; I Cor. 1.9, 26; Phil. 3.14; Eph. 4.11f.; Heb. 6.4ff. and frequently.
[2] This humanistic question is not one that theology can take over by identifying man's personal being with his being as God's creature, so that then not only his personal being, but also his creaturely being along with it, falls outside the framework of modern functionalized society and a theology of creation endeavours to rescue man's personality from being turned into a thing.

and continuity – even, and indeed precisely, where he expends himself in non-identity. He does not require to preserve himself by himself, in constant unity with himself, but in surrendering himself to the work of mission he is preserved by the hope inherent in that mission. The callings, roles, conditions and claims which society lays upon him are therefore not to be examined in regard to whether and how they fully occupy his own self or estrange him from himself, but in regard to whether and how far they afford possibilities for the incarnation of faith, for the concretion of hope, and for earthly, historic correspondence with the hoped-for and promised kingdom of God and of freedom. The criterion for the choice of a calling, for changing our calling, for spare-time activities, as well as for the acceptance and shaping of the process of socialization, is constituted solely by the mission of Christian hope.

The horizon of expectation within which a Christian doctrine of conduct must be developed is the eschatological horizon of expectation of the kingdom of God, of his righteousness and his peace with a new creation, of his freedom and his humanity for all men. This horizon alone, with its formative effect on the present, leads a man in missionary hope to oppose and suffer under the inadequacies of the present, brings him into conflict with the present form of society and causes him to discover the 'cross of the present' (Hegel). The place and situation in which the call to the hope of the gospel reaches men is, to be sure, the concrete *terminus a quo* of their calling, but not its *terminus ad quem*. Only Christians who no longer understand their eschatological mission as a mission for the future of the world and of man can identify their call with the existing circumstances in the social roles of their callings and be content to fit in with these. But where the call is seen within the horizon of expectation proper to it, there our believing obedience, our discipleship and our love must be understood as 'creative discipleship'[1] and 'creative love'.[2]

'Creative discipleship' cannot consist in adaptation to, or preservation of, the existing social and judicial orders, still less can it supply religious backgrounds for a given or manufactured

---

[1] A phrase of Ernst Wolf's, *op. cit.*
[2] Cf. W. Pannenberg's essay, 'Zur Theologie des Rechtes', *Zeitschrift für evangelische Ethik* 7, 1963, pp. 1ff., esp. 20ff.

situation. It must consist in the theoretical and practical recognition of the structure of historic process and development inherent in the situation requiring to be ordered, and thus of the
potentialities and the future of that situation. Luther, too, could
claim this creative freedom for Christian faith: '*Habito enim
Christo facile condemus leges, et omnia recte judicabimus, imo novos
Decalogos faciemus, sicut Paulus facit per omnes Epistolas, et Petrus,
maxime Christus in Euangelio.*' ('For when we have Christ we
shall easily issue laws, and judge all things aright, and even
make new decalogues, as Paul does in all his epistles, and Peter,
and above all Christ in the Gospel.'[1]) 'Creative discipleship' of
this kind in a love which institutes community, sets things right
and puts them in order, becomes eschatologically possible
through the Christian hope's prospects of the future of God's
kingdom and of man. It alone constitutes here in our open-
ended history the appropriate counterpart to that which is
promised and is to come. 'Presentative eschatology' means
nothing else but simply 'creative expectation',[2] hope which sets
about criticizing and transforming the present because it is
open towards the universal future of the kingdom.

From this standpoint the nowadays increasingly difficult
problem of 'man and society' or 'freedom and estrangement',
or man and work, must find a different answer from that which
is possible on the ground of a humanism of transcendental
subjectivity. German Idealism and the European Romanticism which followed it were the first reactions to the new conditions created by the industrial revolution. From that age and
that way of thinking comes the idea that man must become
identical with himself because primarily and originally he was
and is so. But in order to become identical with himself and
live 'in constant unity with himself' (Fichte), he must again and
again collect himself from his outgoings, recall himself from
the lostness of surrender, turn from his distractions to reflect
upon himself and his true, eternal Ego. All acts which man allows to issue from himself acquire an independent existence
according to laws of their own, and thus rob him of his freedom.
His products grow too much for him, so that the creator has to
bow to the things he has created. His personal relationships

[1] *WA* 39, I, 47, quoted according to E. Wolf, *op. cit.*, p. 35.
[2] E. Bloch, *Tübinger Einleitung in die Philosophie* II, 1964, p. 176.

change into factual relationships which develop a logic of their own and stand on their own feet. In so doing they estrange man from his true nature, and he can no longer rediscover himself in them. Consequently, the individual must be able to take these factualized, independent forces which have turned into complexes of constraint and subject them once more to himself, to appropriate them again and take them back into himself, to see through them and be conscious of them.¹ This return from estrangement is apparently possible in two ways – the way of *utopia*, and the way of *irony*. Karl Marx in his early days thought it possible on the ground of his social pathology of early industrial conditions to realize the classical German educational ideal of the 'profound and thoroughly versatile man' by means of the revolutionary abolition of capitalist exploitation, class society and division of labour in a future 'association of free individuals'. In Western social philosophy today, on the other hand, we repeatedly find attempts to retain the idea of estrangement and regain the human nature of man by means of transcendental reflection. 'I no longer coincide with my social "I", even if at every moment I am together with it. I can now in my social existence be conscious of the *role*, so to speak, which I take upon me or put up with. I see myself and my roles falling apart.'² By means of such reflections, the self-consciousness of man withdraws itself from the compromising, confusing, social reality. In constant reflection, in irony and in criticism of the corruptness of conditions, it regains that detachment in which it thinks to find its infinite possibilities, its freedom and superiority. Yet this subjectivity reflecting upon itself, which does not expend itself in any social task, but soars above a reality that has been degraded into an 'interplay of roles' – this faith that feels itself bound to no reality, not even its own –

¹ On the significance of Fichte's idea of identity for Marx's theory of estrangement and Freud's theory of the complex, cf. A. Gehlen, *Über die Geburt der Freiheit aus der Entfremdung*, Archiv für Rechts- und Sozialphilosophie, 1952, p. 350. For this paragraph cf. also H. Plessner, *Das Problem der Öffentlichkeit und die Idee der Entfremdung*, 1960, and T. Litt, *Das Bildungsideal der deutschen Klassik und die moderne Arbeitswelt*, 1955.
² K. Jaspers, *Philosophie* II, 1932, p. 30. Similar conclusions are reached also by R. Dahrendorf, *Homo Sociologicus. Ein Versuch zur Geschichte, Bedeutung und Kritik der Kategorie der sozialen Rolle*, 1960, and 'Soziologie: 1. Der Mensch als Rollenspieler', in *Wege zur pädagogischen Anthropologie*, 1963, where Dahrendorf endeavours to come to grips with the (to my mind justified) objections of Tenbruck, Plessner, H. P. Bahrdt, A. Gehlen and Janoska-Bendl.

turn man into a 'man without attributes' in a 'world of attributes without man' (R. Musil). They rescue the humanity of man in an inner emigration in which man now only 'accompanies' his outward life, and in so doing they abandon conditions to final corruption.

When, by means of reflection, subjectivity is withdrawn from its social reality, then it loses contact with the real conditions of society and robs these conditions of the very forces which it requires in order to give them human shape and vindicate them to the future.[1] 'Whoever attempts to get rid of the antinomy by proscribing the world of organized labour as being the result of a mistake, and by recommending a withdrawal into the inward life as being the only possible way of salvation from the consequences of this mistake, abandons that world to a disorder that will sooner or later also lay hold of his artificially defined spiritual world.'[2]

A thing is alive only when it contains contradiction in itself and is indeed the power of holding the contradiction within itself and enduring it.[3] It is not reflection, recalling man's own subjectivity from its social realization, that brings him back his possibilities and therewith his freedom, but this is done only by the hope which leads him to expend himself and at the same time makes him grasp continually new possibilities from the expected future. Human life must be risked if it would be won. It must expend itself if it would gain firmness and future. If, however, we are thus to risk expending ourselves, then we need a horizon of expectation which makes the expending meaningful – and moreover, a horizon of expectation which embraces the realms and areas in which and for which the work we do in our self-expending is to take place. The expectation of the promised future of the kingdom of God which is coming to man and the world to set them right and create life, makes us ready to expend ourselves unrestrainedly and unreservedly in love and in the work of the reconciliation of the world with God and his future. The social institutions, roles and functions are means on the way to this self-expending. They have therefore to be shaped creatively by love, in order that men may live together in them more justly, more humanely, more peacefully,

[1] H. Plessner, *op. cit.*, p. 20.	[2] T. Litt, *op. cit.*, p. 123.
[3] G. W. F. Hegel, *Werke* IV, p. 67.

and in mutual recognition of their human dignity and freedom. They have therefore not to be taken as 'reliefs' (A. Gehlen), and not as a lapse into estrangement or as a benumbing of life, but as ways and historic forms of self-expending, and hence also as events and processes which are open towards the future of God. Creative hope historifies these conditions, and thus opposes their immanent tendencies towards stabilization – and still more the 'beneficial unquestioningness' of life in them. Faith can expend itself in the pain of love, it can make itself 'into a thing' and assume the form of a servant, because it is upheld by the assurance of hope in the resurrection of the dead. For love, we always require hope and assurance of the future, for love looks to the as yet unrealized possibilities of the other, and thus grants him freedom and allows him a future in recognition of his possibilities. In the recognition and ascription of that human dignity of which man is deemed worthy in the resurrection of the dead, creative love finds the comprehensive future in view of which it loves.

As a result of this hope in God's future, this present world becomes free in believing eyes from all attempts at self-redemption or self-production through labour, and it becomes open for loving, ministering self-expenditure in the interests of a humanizing of conditions and in the interests of the realization of justice in the light of the coming justice of God. This means, however, that the hope of resurrection must bring about a new understanding of the world. This world is not the heaven of self-realization, as it was said to be in Idealism. This world is not the hell of self-estrangement, as it is said to be in romanticist and existentialist writing. The world is not yet finished, but is understood as engaged in a history. It is therefore the world of possibilities, the world in which we can serve the future, promised truth and righteousness and peace. This is an age of diaspora, of sowing in hope, of self-surrender and sacrifice, for it is an age which stands within the horizon of a new future. Thus self-expenditure in this world, day-to-day love in hope, becomes possible and becomes human within that horizon of expectation which transcends this world. The glory of self-realization and the misery of self-estrangement alike arise from hopelessness in a world of lost horizons. To disclose to it the horizon of the future of the crucified Christ is the task of the Christian Church.

INDEX OF NAMES